DATE DUE

BRODART, CO. Cat. No. 23-221

Media Depictions of Brides, Wives, and Mothers

Media Depictions of Brides, Wives, and Mothers

Edited by Alena Amato Ruggerio, PhD

Published by Lexington Books
A wholly owned subsidiary of The Rowman & Littlefield Publishing Group, Inc.
4501 Forbes Boulevard, Suite 200, Lanham, Maryland 20706
www.rowman.com

10 Thornbury Road, Plymouth PL6 7PP, United Kingdom

"Christian Patriarchy Lite: TLC's 19 Kids and Counting." *The Journal of Religion and Popular Culture*, Vol. 22 (3), available online. Reprinted courtesy of *The Journal of Religion and Popular Culture*.

British Library Cataloguing in Publication Information Available

Library of Congress Cataloging-in-Publication Data

Ruggerio, Alena Amato, 1975–
Media depictions of brides, wives, and mothers / Alena Amato Ruggerio.
p. cm.
Includes bibliographical references and index.
ISBN 978-0-7391-7708-2 (cloth : alk. paper) — ISBN 978-0-7391-7709-9 (electronic)
1. Women in mass media. 2. Sex role in mass media. 3. Brides. 4. Wives. 5. Mothers. I. Title.
P94.5.W65R84 2012
306.874'3—dc23

2012028525

™ The paper used in this publication meets the minimum requirements of American National Standard for Information Sciences—Permanence of Paper for Printed Library Materials, ANSI/NISO Z39.48-1992.

Printed in the United States of America

To Letha Dawson Scanzoni

with much love

Contents

Acknowledgments ix

Introduction 1

Part I Television

1 Domesticating Matrimonial Monstrosity: *Bridezillas* and Narratives of Feminine Containment 11
Alyssa Ann Samek

2 The Reality of Televised Motherhood: The Personal Quest and Feminine Test of Kate Gosselin 27
Mary Frances Casper and Deneen Gilmour

3 Marriage, Friendship, and Scandal: Constructing a Typology of Media Representation of Women in *Desperate Housewives* 39
Paula Hopeck and Rebecca K. Ivic

4 Ancient Archetypes in Modern Media 49
Deborah A. Macey

5 Christian Patriarchy Lite: TLC's *19 Kids and Counting* 63
Christy Ellen Mesaros-Winckles

Part II Film

6 Punishing Unfaithful Wives and Working Mothers: Messages of Postfeminism in Contemporary Film 77
Erika M. Thomas

7 Love and Lack: Media, Witches, and Normative Gender Roles 91
Victoria L. Godwin

8 Head Above *Water*: Applying Nussbaum's "Capabilities Approach" to Deepa Mehta's 2005 Film 103
Lauren J. DeCarvalho

Part III News Coverage

9 Feminine Style and Militant Motherhood in Antiwar Discourse: Cindy Sheehan as Grieving Mother and/or Left-Leaning Radical 115
Heidi E. Hamilton

10 Grisly Mama: Carnivorous Media Coverage of Sarah Palin 129
Alena Amato Ruggerio

11 "Stand by Your Man" Revisited: Political Wives and Scandal 143
Hinda Mandell

12 "Taking Care of the Children and the Country": Nancy Pelosi and the Trope of Motherhood in Partisan and Mainstream Media 155
Sheryl L. Cunningham

13 Local Media Madness: How One City's Media Helped Perpetuate the Myth of the "Perfect" Coach's Wife 169
Diana L. Tucker

14 Who's Framing Whom? Michele Bachmann and the (Primary) Politics of Motherhood 181
Ann E. Burnette

Part IV Internet

15 Momtinis, Not Martyrs: Examining 'Anti-Mom' Blogs, Muted Groups, Standpoints, and the Struggle over Motherhood 197
Rita L. Rahoi-Gilchrest

16 Love Thy Mother? Traitorous Constructions of Motherhood in "Outsmart Mother Nature with Tampax" Campaign 209
Dacia Charlesworth

17 Taking the Audience Perspective: Online Fan Commentary about the Brides of *Mad Men* and Their Weddings 223
Lynne M. Webb, Marceline Thompson Hayes, Hao-Chieh Chang, and Marcia M. Smith

Index 237

Contributors 243

About the Editor 247

Acknowledgments

I extend deep gratitude to . . .

All the contributing authors, A. Lenore Lautigar, Johnny Simpson, Lindsey Frederick, Robert Westfall, Daniel White, Melissa L. Michaels, Melody Love, Alissa Arp, Kim Olson, Jody Waters and the Department of Communication at Southern Oregon University, Erika Leppmann and the SOU Faculty Development Committee, Penny Thorpe, Diana Maltz, Warren Hedges, Bobby Arellano, Chazlyn Lovely, Emily Miller-Francisco, Mark-Shawn Moore, Vassia Vassiliou, Robert Ivie, Roger Aden, Raymie McKerrow, Deborah and Gerald Amato, Letha Dawson Scanzoni, Linda Bieze, and the rest of my families of origin and choice, including Tifa, Yuffie, and Aeris, who deserve feline editorial credits.

And most of all, Bradley. Τα μάτια σου λάμπουν σαν αρκουδάκι στη βροχή.

Introduction

Alena Amato Ruggerio

The astounding image commissioned for the cover of this book is a digital photo manipulation by British artist Daniel White.[1] I find it equal parts gorgeous and disturbing. On the one hand, we see the visual markers of the normative performance of bridal beauty: the model's slender body is clothed in a strapless creation of pearls, lace, and sequins; her wedding rings display enough bling to prove her wealth; even her spikes curve with delicate femininity over her forearms. Yet, of course, she is not the idealized bride because of those spikes and scales and claws. She symbolizes something monstrous underlying the mythos of the bride—and eventually the wife and mother. What would a marriage be like with that kind of beast? And if she had children, how long would it be before she ate them?

Bring Me My Tiara

Perhaps I feel discomfited because the image hits too close to home. While the term "bridezilla" was not in common parlance when I got married, I dragged my fiancé to five different cities shopping for a wedding dress, exchanged my ring set at the jeweler three times, made detailed to-do lists for each of the fifteen (yes, fifteen) members of our wedding party, and tried to sue the photographers. Although no one factor completely explains my mania, I lay part of the blame at the feet of Princess Leia. My vision of the perfect bride was imprinted when I first saw *Star Wars: A New Hope* and thought the final scene was a wedding, not a medal ceremony. It was a reasonable mistake for a media-consuming five-year-old to make. After all, I had just watched Princess Leia prove herself a worthy romance object for the space pirate hero, and there she was at the end of the film standing in front of a crowd in a luminous white gown. In that universe, instead of exchanging rings, the bride must have to slip victory medals over the heads of her groom and his Best Wookiee, right? At five years old, film and television were already socializing my expectations of what it meant to perform femininity in romantic and family roles.

Fast-forward a few decades to my own wedding, and although in my bespectacled rotundity I would have been classified by the culture as closer to the scaly monster than the slim and creamy-skinned Princess Leia (actor Carrie Fisher famously wrote that she was instructed to drop to ninety-five pounds for the film),[2] at least I could still have her joyful trumpet music and fairy tale ending. That's an example of one key feature of the topic of brides, wives, and mothers: we are constantly comparing media imagery to our own or our loved ones' experiences of inhabiting those roles, and inevitably falling short.

The chapters that follow come from deeply personal places, but then move from there to the academic deconstruction of social norms. In *Where the Girls Are: Growing up Female with the Mass Media*, Susan J. Douglas points out that feminists—caricatured since the 1970s as man-hating, child-eating harpies—have often been juxtaposed against the docile images of white-wedding brides, subservient wives, and happy mothers on our television screens.[3] Yet most of the feminist scholars I know—including the ones featured in this book—are also in domestic relationships of one kind or another. We all have to find a way to live in the middle space between those two caricatured extremes, both critiquing and inhabiting the same reality.

Complex Media Depictions

I wanted to create this volume not just to exorcize that inner five-year-old who once pined for the Princess Leia wedding but also for my current college students, who, in their Communication Research Strategies course, often formulate research questions about women's depictions in the media. They are hungry for resources to help them make sense of the popular culture and political communication artifacts they encounter in their daily lives. It's a nice entry point for Digital Native[4] undergraduates—some of whom would still repudiate the label of feminist and eschew the protest methods of earlier generations—to begin their critique of gender injustice with the messages sent from the multiple electronic screens in whose glow they bathe each day. To the students in courses on gender, race, and media; sociology of mass media; feminist rhetorical theories; rhetorical criticism; popular culture; television studies; gender, sexuality, and women's studies; and communication and gender, I say welcome to the conversation. Come for the *Kate Plus 8* and "momtini" blogs, and stay for the metaphor criticism and Audience Reception Theory.

The media depictions of women as brides, wives, and mothers explored in this book are complex. The collection of authors featured here is diverse; they bring a variety of feminist rhetorical and media criticism approaches from across the communication discipline as they analyze how the media (including television, film, news coverage, and the Internet) shape and are shaped by our social expectations of the performance of women's identities. Each contributor shares a focus on the most recent research from feminist communication scholars as we productively complicate and critique media portrayals of women's domestic relationships.

This book is the most recent in a long history of feminist media criticisms, but it is one of the few to use a communication perspective to focus exclusively on representations of women in their specific identities as brides, wives, and mothers.[5] That category of brides, wives, and mothers provides an interesting confluence of the biological and the social. Although the neural cascade of chemicals that is romantic love and the physical act of birth are grounded in the corporeal, we cannot experience them except through the filter of the rhetorical. Kenneth Burke defines rhetoric not as empty or flowery words but as the process of humans making meanings, "forming attitudes," and "inducing actions" through the exchange of symbols.[6] The implication is that there is always a frame of interpretation situated between reality and our understanding of it. Pair bonding and reproduction are lizard-brain primal, but we learn how to interpret our experiences as brides, wives, and mothers through our interactions with other people—a process cemented by media messages telling us what is popular, what is normal, and what it's all supposed to mean.

Kenneth Burke and Feminist Media Criticism

The bad news, according to Burke, is that there's never going to be a world where messages that divide us from each other don't exist. Part of the human condition is that we cannot inhabit each other's molecules or directly download thoughts into each others' heads, so we fail to recognize our oneness and must resort to interacting via discursive and visual symbols.[7] That's why communication—including the output of our televisions, cameras, radios, computers, and the iGadget du jour—matters so much that it should be central to feminism: we can't get to economics, religion, sexuality, or politics except through rhetoric.

The good news is we have a choice as to how to communicate given the inevitability of division. Our rhetorical choices can either draw us together with our common humanity or alienate us from one another by emphasizing our differences. So the first step is to become more conscious of those options, which Burke terms the comic and the tragic, the latter being so often perpetuated unthinkingly. The second step is to expose misogyny, homophobia, and every -ism for what they are: tragic-frame rhetorics that foreground our differences to the point that others become animals, objects, or diseases (Othering) and are thus easier to literally or symbolically slaughter (victimage).[8] Such tragic practices are often unintentional; I don't believe writers, directors, producers, political journalists, and bloggers are a psychotic bunch of woman-haters (well, maybe a few); they're just trying to hawk their products. But songs sell downloads and television shows sell ads by repeating sexist stories that work because the tragic frame *seems* so natural, something we take for granted as the only possible reality. Part of our job in the academy, then, is to reveal as rhetorically constructed the symbolic acts of domination that feel like the unvarnished truth. Even if they are not working from an explicitly Burkeian perspective, many of the chapter authors point out the mechanisms of the tragic process of Othering embedded in mass media production and the content of the messages.

The next step is to highlight the comic frame of rhetoric when we see it and to equip message-makers to forge further identification across differences. Burke does not intend the comic as "funny ha-ha." Instead, he is referencing a metaphor of the ancient Greek stage, where comedies were characterized by the audience laughing at the flaws of the protagonist because they recognized those fallibilities within themselves. Just as the Greeks saw themselves reflected in the actors' eyes, so too must we search with humility to find where we are consubstantial with others when enacting the comic frame of rhetoric.[9] It is unwise, therefore, to demonize the producers of media as towering evil even when we passionately disagree with their output. The more constructive mindset is to consider them foolish and misguided and to then search for the substance we have in common. You will read in this book that media representations are not always failures when it comes to feminism; sometimes, they create new forms of expression that honor women's self-determination in all its variety and women's struggles for systemic change. We need to celebrate those media portrayals that present women as fully human, making it harder for women to be symbolically, and sometimes literally, annihilated. Women are not merely objects, passive victims of the patriarchal gaze; we are active creators of the comic.

Although protesting misogyny has never been as easy as just turning off the television, boycotting a product, or avoiding the movie theatre, it becomes increasingly difficult to turn away as the tyranny of electronic devices and the ubiquity of social media grow. Yet neither turning away nor attempting to censor the distasteful speech that creates sexist, unhealthy, unobtainable images of women is the solution—better to replace it with more constructive speech that reconfigures the relationships women inhabit in the media and spurs activism in our own lives. You would think that would be easier in an era in which smart phones and laptops make us mass message producers and distributors, but our imaginations are still constrained by what we've been told is possible and worthy of depiction. Even successful alternative messages eventually get sucked back into the hegemonic machine.[10] Yet we still have the choice not to mindlessly swallow what they feed us, and challenging and then remaking the pablum for oppositional purposes is easier when we have the skills of media critique. As Lorraine Gamman and Margaret Marshment write in *The Female Gaze: Women as Viewers of Popular Culture*, "If the language of popular media changes in our direction, then maybe we can re-appropriate it for our own purposes."[11] Once equipped with rhetorical savvy and media literacy, we can use our screens as tools for creativity, resistance, and the popularization of feminist sensibilities that can in turn affect the material reality of economics, religion, sexuality, and politics.

The final step is to turn the critical lens upon ourselves. Every time we create an "us," we are simultaneously creating a "them." Apropos of the theme of the book, enacting comic rhetoric is not a one-time event like a wedding; it's more like an ongoing marriage. Just as every day I have to wake up and decide whether I'm going to keep my marriage vows, with every communication message I send, I have to recommit to choosing identification. That's why Burke calls it the "comic corrective" instead of the "comic cure": our responsibility for external critique and internal reflection is constant.

An Overview of *Media Depictions of Brides, Wives, and Mothers*

There is no single way for women to perform romantic and domestic roles, any more than there is a single way to perform the identity of "woman" itself. Each chapter presents a different perspective on the question, How do media oppress and liberate brides, wives, and mothers? This volume comes at a time in the United States when the wedding industry has its own genre of reality television shows; when the push for full equality for gay couples forces state referenda, court rulings, and military policy to grapple with what the institution of marriage should mean; and when parents caught in a recession with global repercussions that left more fathers out of work than mothers can no longer assume their children will exceed their standard of living. Out of these contexts arises a multiplicity of scholarly voices commenting on what it means to women when our practices of marrying, mating, and mothering are represented and misrepresented on media screens.

The volume opens with Alyssa Ann Samek's assertion that as unrelenting pressure is asserted over today's brides to consume for their weddings to the point of monstrosity, so too are the viewers of WE tv's *Bridezillas* pressured to hyperconsume, subverting the ostensible message of female empowerment in the show. In chapter two, Mary Frances Casper and Deneen Gilmour examine the TLC series *Jon & Kate Plus 8* (after the divorce, *Kate Plus 8*) to determine what happens to reality star Kate Gosselin when the cameras and editing machines shape her "struggle with parenthood and personhood." ABC's *Desperate Housewives* illustrates how the primary theme of social relationships can be a mixed blessing for the protagonists in their roles of wives and mothers. Paula Hopeck and Rebecca K. Ivic conclude that although the characters enjoy each other's support, their relationships are also the source of scandal. Deborah A. Macey takes on other famous television quartets from *Golden Girls*, *Living Single*, and *Sex and the City*, connecting the characters in each foursome to the archetypes of the iron maiden, sex object, child, and mother. In the final chapter of the television section, TLC's *19 Kids and Counting* becomes the site of the uncharacteristically comfortable relationship between evangelical Christianity, the Quiverfull movement, and the camera. Author Christy Ellen Mesaros-Winckles argues that the patriarchal gender roles enacted by Jim Bob and Michelle Duggar normalize a previously marginalized theology for their primarily female viewers.

At the start of Part II on brides, wives, and mothers in film, Erika M. Thomas's chapter examines how the "bad" women of *Fatal Attraction*, *Unfaithful*, and *The Devil Wears Prada* are punished for their ambitions and passions. Witches in film and television are the focus of chapter seven, in which Victoria L. Godwin asserts that *The Craft*, *Practical Magic*, and similar productions rob female Wiccan practitioners of their own agency, replace it with a reliance on external male forces, and discipline the women into standard patriarchal positions. Lauren J. DeCarvalho compares the experiences of the women in the final film, Deepa Mehta's *Water*, with feminist philosopher Martha Nussbaum's list of the ten functional capabilities every human being should have in their lives, showing how the Hindu widows of 1938 rural India are robbed of each of these basic rights.

Part III, dedicated to news coverage, begins with Heidi E. Hamilton's findings on antiwar protestor Cindy Sheehan. Sheehan's choice to ground her opposition to President George W. Bush in militant mother rhetoric, according to Hamilton, contains both persuasive strengths and limitations. The double-edged sword of rhetorical appeals is echoed in my own chapter, in which I argue that Sarah Palin's ostensibly powerful language of attack dogs, caribou hunting, mama grizzlies, and partisan red meat triggered the dark side of the carnivore metaphor. Hinda Mandell addresses the phenomenon of the stony-faced wives at the press conferences of their politician husbands caught in sexual indiscretions. Mandell reminds us that the public impression of the wives in these scandals "standing by their men" to affirm hegemonic expectations of traditional matrimony fails to include the possible private negotiations occurring in those marriages. The photograph of Nancy Pelosi taking office as Speaker of the House surrounded by children is the focus of Sheryl L. Cunningham's work, in which she illustrates how Democratic Party women come under fire because they "articulate motherhood in a way that violates partisan turf." Politicians are not the only women in the news; Diana L. Tucker's chapter presents the media construction of the so-called "lovely wives" of prestigious head coaches of sports teams, specifically the Ohio State Buckeyes. In the last chapter of this unit, Ann E. Burnette explores the interplay between the newspaper media's framing of conservative Republican presidential candidate Michele Bachmann and Bachmann's own strategic invocation of political motherhood.

Rita L. Rahoi-Gilchrest kicks off Part IV with her examination of "anti-mom blogs" that protest both patriarchal expectations and the genre of mommy blogging to present an alternative view of motherhood online. The "Outsmart Mother Nature with Tampax" advertisements span multiple forms of media, but Dacia Charlesworth draws special attention to the web clips of "Mother Nature" aggressively pursuing unsuspecting women and trying to hand them their "monthly gift," a campaign Charlesworth identifies as further stigmatizing the reproductive function of women's bodies. Lynne M. Webb, Marceline Thompson Hayes, Hao-Chieh Chang, and Marcia M. Smith conclude this collection with their analysis of online discussions of the weddings in AMC's *Mad Men* across eleven fansites. They share fans' interpretations of the weddings depicted in the first season as they debate topics ranging from child brides to cultural standards for a "big" wedding.

There is a rich multiplicity at the crossroads where media literacy, feminist criticism, nuptial rituals, marital relationships, and parental identities converge. Long after these artifacts of analysis become passé and hipster comedians on VH1 mock what we used to watch in the early decades of the twenty-first century, what will remain are the insights about how the meanings we make by exchanging discursive and visual symbols with one another across mass channels affect us individually and systemically.

Of French Protestants and Future Scholarship

In graduate school, I shared with a friend a recurring joke we called "What about the Huguenots?" It originated after a particularly frustrating religious studies seminar in which our fellow grad students relentlessly skewered a journal article author for what she failed to address ("But what about the Huguenots?!") to the exclusion of any attempt to take the work on its own merits and acknowledge what she did say. It is so much easier to tear apart what has already been created than to do the creating. I am keenly aware of what has been omitted from this current collection. I wish there were chapters featuring lesbian marriages, grandmothers, female politicians from an array of other countries across the globe, books and magazines and other print media, childfree wives, transwomen and genderqueers, children's music, historical artifacts, more international films, polyamorous weddings, more authors of color, comparative explorations of men as grooms, husbands, and fathers . . . the list of what is not here has no end. But rather than decrying the absence of these Huguenots, be the one who writes or edits the next book that will address some of those lacunae and move the conversation ever forward on a topic that continues to expand and change.

In the meantime, you are invited to apply the insights from each chapter that did make it into this collection to your own set of myths, stereotypes, and assumptions about gendered expectations of women's domestic identities. Discover how your views of these roles have been influenced by the media, replace them with images of equality and justice, and extend that advocacy to influence our material world.

Television, film, news coverage, the Internet, and other media have become avenues for both the perpetuation of gender stereotypes and the expression of empowerment for brides, wives, and mothers. Today, the love-hate relationship I began at age five with the *Star Wars* saga continues with the novels that tell the rest of Princess Leia's story. Leia becomes an ass-kicking Knight of the New Republic in her own right, but not without openly worrying about being separated at length from her husband, Han Solo, and possibly failing as a parent to her three children, one of whom eventually turns to the Dark Side of the Force and is slain by his sibling. Leia ends up becoming a more powerful Jedi than her brother Luke Skywalker, yet she'll be forever known as the chick in the metal bikini. She represents both the hegemonic domination and the resistance of those brides, wives, and mothers in the media whose depictions we explore in the following pages.

Notes

1. Cover photo "With This Claw, I Thee Wed," adapted from ThinkStock by Daniel White, http://danwhitephotography.co.uk. Used with permission.

2. Carrie Fisher, *Shockaholic* (New York: Simon and Schuster, 2011).

3. Susan J. Douglas, *Where the Girls Are: Growing up Female with the Mass Media* (New York: Times Books, 1994), 8.

4. Marc Prensky, *Teaching Digital Natives: Partnering for Real Learning* (Thousand Oaks, CA: Corwin, 2010).

5. See Mary-Lou Galician and Debra L. Merskin, *Critical Thinking About Sex, Love, and Romance in the Mass Media* (Mahwah, NJ: Lawrence Erlbaum, 2007); Mary-Lou Galician, *Sex, Love, and Romance in the Mass Media: Analysis and Criticism of Unrealistic Portrayals and Their Influence* (Mahwah, NJ: Lawrence Erlbaum, 2004).

6. Kenneth Burke, *A Rhetoric of Motives* (Berkeley: University of California Press, 1950), 41.

7. Burke, *Motives*, 130.

8. Kenneth Burke, *Philosophy of Literary Form* (Berkeley: University of California Press, 1973), 39–40, 202–203.

9. Kenneth Burke, *Attitudes Toward History* (Berkeley: University of California Press, 1961), 41–42.

10. Antonio Gramsci, *Selections from the Prison Notebooks* (New York: International Publishers, 1971).

11. Lorraine Gamman and Margaret Marshment, *The Female Gaze: Women as Viewers of Popular Culture* (Seattle: Real Comet Press, 1989), 4.

Bibliography

Burke, Kenneth. *A Rhetoric of Motives*. Berkeley: University of California Press, 1950.

———. *Attitudes Toward History*. Berkeley: University of California Press, 1961.

———. *Philosophy of Literary Form*. Berkeley: University of California Press, 1973.

Douglas, Susan J. *Where the Girls Are: Growing up Female with the Mass Media*. New York: Times Books, 1994.

Fisher, Carrie. *Shockaholic*. New York: Simon and Schuster, 2011.

Galician, Mary-Lou, and Debra L. Merskin. *Critical Thinking About Sex, Love, and Romance in the Mass Media*. Mahwah, NJ: Lawrence Erlbaum, 2007.

Galician, Mary-Lou. *Sex, Love, and Romance in the Mass Media: Analysis and Criticism of Unrealistic Portrayals and Their Influence*. Mahwah, NJ: Lawrence Erlbaum, 2004.

Gamman, Lorraine, and Margaret Marshment. *The Female Gaze: Women as Viewers of Popular Culture*. Seattle: Real Comet Press, 1989.

Gramsci, Antonio. *Selections from the Prison Notebooks*. New York: International Publishers, 1971.

Prensky, Marc. *Teaching Digital Natives: Partnering for Real Learning*. Thousand Oaks, CA: Corwin, 2010.

PART I

Television

Chapter 1

Domesticating Matrimonial Monstrosity: *Bridezillas* and Narratives of Feminine Containment

by Alyssa Ann Samek

"Tune in to watch what can happen to a woman somewhere between 'Will you marry me?' and 'I do.'"[1] The Women's Entertainment cable network (WE tv) promises "more meltdowns [and] confrontations" as the protagonist morphs into a bridezilla—a frightening caricature of emotion and irrationality when things do not go her way. And yet, according to one wedding marketing website of the same name, a bridezilla is no longer "the passé image of a screaming, out of control, psychopathic bride raging through her wedding with bulging veins and gritted teeth." Rather, the marketers argue, "She is continually redefining herself as a confident woman who knows what she wants and goes after it. . . . Bridezillas of today are strong, intelligent women who are not only well-versed in the arts of fashion, beauty and pop culture, but they also have a clear image of who they are and how their wedding will reflect themselves and their brand new husband."[2] For the thousands of businesses interested in sharing in the eight billion dollar global wedding industry, harnessing the power of the bridezilla helps them "get [her] what she wants" when it comes to creating the perfect day. These contradictory characterizations raise the question, Should we fear or seek to emulate the bridezilla?

Bridezilla is part of what Chrys Ingraham calls the "wedding ideological complex" that supports the transnational wedding industry, or the "wedding-industrial complex."[3] I seek to amplify Ingraham's extensive analysis of cultural obsession and mediated representations of "*white* weddings as distillations of class, gender, and racial hierarchies" by focusing on the prevalence of the monstrous bridezilla figure.[4] I argue that the bridezilla upholds binary gender constructs to discipline women while thinly disguising the hegemonic hetero-patriarchal structures undergirding the American wedding culture through postfeminist narratives of empowerment and choice. Grounding my analysis in Gothic literary conventions, feminist media studies, and postfeminist scholarship, I maintain that the bridezilla concept ties together cultural notions of feminine perfection, consumption, and competition in the shape of the monstrous. Within the wedding-themed reality show *Bridezillas*, narratives of consumption and domestication ultimately resolve the "problem" of uncontrollable femininity and contain the "beast." This example of popular mediated representations of femininity reveals the power and persistence of "enlightened sexist" narratives that index hegemonic gender ideologies in a seemingly innocuous entertainment form.

This chapter will first discuss the rising popularity of wedding-themed reality television shows, then turn to critical and feminist media scholarship that attends to the ideological dynamics that permeate mediated culture and support hegemonic representations of gender, race, class, and sexuality. I locate the bridezilla figure in Gothic literary traditions of the "monstrous-feminine," and consider what current iterations of such female monsters indicate about the cultural perspectives on feminism and threats to patriarchal power.

Weddings and Gender in (Reality) Television

Weddings have long provided an easily recognizable and relatable formula for television shows of all genres. Chrys Ingraham argues that scripted television programs have long incorporated marriage or wedding-themed storylines to drive ratings and conquer network sweeps weeks season after season.[5] While this trend continues, the last several years have also witnessed the burgeoning of wedding-themed reality television shows. From a broad perspective, these shows fall into loosely defined types. Some narrate a couple's journey to the altar, like The Learning Channel's *A Wedding Story*. Others, like *The Bachelor* and *The Bachelorette*, feature a dating competition among women and men respectively, whittling down the competitive field after several dates to culminate with a choice by the Bachelor/Bachelorette, a proposal, and a highly stylized wedding. Some shows—including *Say Yes to the Dress*, *Platinum Weddings*, and *My Fair Wedding*—chronicle the intensive wedding planning process. More recently, shows have added a wedding twist to the concept of bodily transformation or weight-loss reality shows. For example, one CW network offering, *Shedding for the Wedding*, spins the weight-loss competition concept popularized by NBC's *The Biggest Loser* by taking engaged couples through the process of extreme weight loss and emotional transformations as they concurrently plan the wedding of their dreams.[6] In the end, the couple who loses the most weight over the three-month competition wins the prized wedding. One television blogger notes that *Shedding* offers a "less offensive" alternative to shows like *Bridalplasty* that take the pressure for matrimonial perfection to the extreme. *Bridalplasty* pitted women against each other in an episodic, series-length competition for a prize of multiple plastic surgery procedures before their wedding day.[7] The popularity and prevalence of wedding-themed reality shows and their subsequent websites offer increased interactivity among brides, brides-to-be, and the various victims of bridal rage, demonstrating the power of the representations offered within the shows.

The large majority of wedding-themed reality shows appear on cable networks that explicitly target a female demographic, although shows like *The Bachelor*, *The Bachelorette*, *Shedding for the Wedding*, and *Bridalplasty* appear on network television. Brides, wedding dresses, and the perfect wedding are central concerns for several cable networks such as WE tv and The Learning Channel (TLC). Both offer a series of original reality television programming including TLC's *Say Yes to the Dress* and *A Wedding Story*, and WE tv's *Bridezillas*, *Rich Bride Poor Bride*, *My Fair Wedding*, and *Platinum Weddings*. Scholars have analyzed the ways in which programming on cable networks like TLC, Lifetime, and WE tv specifically targets women. Jennifer Maher analyzes TLC's *A Wedding Story* and argues that it "affirm[s], naturaliz[es], and showcas[es] only the most traditionally gendered of weddings."[8] Her analysis reveals that even when presented with possibilities of resistance, the narratives are edited to reinforce the centrality of romantic love as "the pinnacle of a woman's existence."[9] These shows are part of a larger network of lifestyle programming that supports compulsory heterosexuality by feeding consumption-based American Dream narratives to their ravenous viewership. Working hand in hand with cable networks like WE tv and TLC, wedding-themed reality programs are dedicated to encouraging and normalizing heterosexual life pathways—the "femininity life cycle"—from dating to marriage to reproduction and childrearing to maintaining home life.[10] TLC's lineup of *A Dating Story*, *A Wedding Story*, and *A Baby Story* epitomizes this trajectory.[11] Maher adds that the shows' argument regarding romantic love is consistently couched in fairytale discourse, and that argument supports extravagant consumption, even to the point of staging a wedding at Sleeping Beauty's Castle in Disneyworld. According to *A Wedding Story* and other shows, only a "platinum" wedding can fulfill the wildest of fairytale dreams. This assumption crystallizes the link between media representations on reality television and the wedding industry.

Media representations of perfect, enormous, extravagant, and largely straight weddings nourish the multibillion-dollar wedding industry. More than 540,000 businesses have a vested interest in couples using their services and products to create wedding perfection.[12] Given the nature of this industry, pairing with reality television is an unsurprising match made in heaven. Susan Murray and Laurie Ouellette actually define reality television as "an unabashedly commercial genre united . . . [by] a professed ability to more fully provide viewers an unmediated, voyeuristic, view of the 'entertaining real.'"[13]

Bridezillas differs from other wedding-themed shows in its focus on brides' devolution into hysteria and monstrosity as they plan their wedding. In some respects, it is the only wedding-themed reality television show that echoes the freak show, presenting the odd or freakish for audience amusement and profit.[14] It removes both the competition element and fully-developed relationship narratives, focusing viewers instead on witnessing the transformation and subsequent domestication of the bride. The show and corresponding website create and recreate the figure of bridezilla, combining the sexist stereotypes of the hysterical and the monstrous to maintain what Suzanne Leonard calls the "web of fantasy, consumption, competition, and false promise that inflect popular definitions of [marriage]," which undercut the power women exert in planning and executing their weddings.[15] Documenting ordinary women as they transform into the monstrous bridezilla, the show emphasizes the grotesque while implying that *any woman* could morph in this way. *Bridezillas* aims to "celebrate the real as a selling point," with each episode revolving around a recurring narrative.[16] In this story, the regular woman-turned-monster in the midst of wedding planning undergoes trials and tribulations over a set course of time, ending with a beautiful wedding to her (male) fiancé. *Bridezillas* uses the monstrous to teach audiences about the boundaries of gender propriety, power, and the threats associated with feminism.

Reality television narratives, like other popular cultural texts, comprise unique sites of ideology where "power is produced, reproduced, and maintained in culture."[17] Rhetorical and critical cultural scholars argue that power is deeply rooted within media texts. Critical media scholars like Shugart, Dow, Gitlin, and Fiske have demonstrated the importance of studying television and film as indexes of cultural ideologies.[18] Todd Gitlin argues much of entertainment television's power resides in how it "relays and reproduces and processes and packages and focuses ideology."[19] Helene Shugart adds, "cultural texts that are not marked overtly as 'political' ought to, nonetheless, be apprehended as embodiments of power relations with a significant impact on social order."[20] Feminist scholars have analyzed how gender, feminism, feminists, and power are represented in popular media, concerned with how media texts tell stories about what it means to be and live as a woman in a contemporary U.S. context. Though wedding-themed reality television shows are not political, their content—narrative and visual—index powerful ideologies of gender, sexuality, class, and race.

Postfeminism or Enlightened Sexism?

Known variously as postfeminism, third-wave feminism, or enlightened sexism, feminist critiques of television and popular culture over the last several decades have specifically attended to how feminist discourses have been appropriated for masculinist or patriarchal purposes.[21] Feminists have long lamented the turn toward increasingly antifeminist (sometimes conflated with postfeminist) discourses, particularly in the media. Though definitions vary slightly, scholars have broadly rejected the notion that the "post" implies a time "after feminism." Instead, they have developed a definition of postfeminism, particularly in the context of media, as "texts that appear to advance the tenets of feminism while actually supporting oppressive social structures," thus "undoing" the advancements of feminist activism.[22] This move depends most centrally on an assumption of what Susan Douglas calls "embedded feminism,"[23] in which aspects of feminism have become part of the "cultural landscape" and "transformed into a Gramscian common sense."[24] Because it has risen to this level of "common sense," Douglas argues, new fantasies of female power can be created, largely focusing on sexual and consumption power. For Bonnie Dow, this reimagining of power dismisses as "irrelevant or threatening . . . the most radical aspects of feminism, those centered in sexual politics and a profound awareness of power differences between the sexes at all levels and in all arenas."[25] Mary Douglas Vavrus adds that the "more provocative challenges, such as those grounded in critiques of capitalism and class privilege" are rejected by a postfeminist move.[26] To be sure, "power through products" is antithetical to earlier generations of feminism and yet proves central to postfeminism as a "revision of feminism that encourages women's private consumer lifestyles."[27] Douglas adds that the mass media perpetuate notions of female empowerment by emphasizing the importance of achieving perfection (bodily and consumer) and exercising sexual power.[28] Douglas, Dow, Vavrus and others analyze mediated texts as sites of what Angela McRobbie calls "machinations" working to "undo feminism while simultaneously appearing to be engaging in a well-informed and even well-intentioned response to feminism."[29]

The bridezilla figure reinforces these notions of postfeminism, although I support Douglas's call to shift the term to "enlightened sexism." Douglas defines enlightened sexism as a discourse that "insists that women have made plenty of progress because of feminism," even achieving full equality, so it is acceptable to "resurrect sexist stereotypes of girls and women."[30] She proffers her linguistic shift to eliminate confusion surrounding the term "postfeminism," re-centering sexism as the problem rather than feminism. *Bridezillas* unabashedly emphasizes the exaggerated consumption associated with the wedding industry, offering similar "fantasies of power" that serve patriarchal power structures while cloaking those very structures in narratives of choice, power, and control.[31] By reconceptualing and reclaiming the bridezilla persona, the wedding industry and its marketing teams have refashioned this persistent sexist image to fulfill similarly limited performances of femininity in the wedding ritual. Part of the power of the bridezilla figure comes from its intelligibility and symbolic potentiality within the lengthy Gothic literary and film traditions.

Gothic Monstrosity in a White Dress

Bridezilla, as a figure, conforms to the conventions of Gothic literature and the horror film genre: she is the hideous monster who crystallizes the fears associated with feminine sexual, economic, and political power. Judith Halberstam explains, "Gothic fiction is a technology of subjectivity, one which produces the deviant subjectivities opposite which the normal, the healthy, and the pure can be known. Gothic . . . may be loosely defined as the rhetorical style and narrative structure designed to produce fear and desire within the reader."[32] Production of fear and desire rely on an excess of symbolic meaning, captured in the shorthand of the monster figure. When experienced by a viewer, Halberstam continues, the "fear of and desire for the other" can translate into "fear of and desire for the possibly latent perversity lurking within the [viewer] herself." This process, she argues, is disciplinary, as she points to moralistic narratives embedded in Victorian Gothic fiction.[33] The standards of normalcy are stabilized, George Haggerty adds, through the use of imbalance.[34]

As the bride transforms into the monstrous 'zilla, the hyperbolic figure emerges in direct response to cultural pressures for perfection. She is what Barbara Creed calls "the monstrous-feminine," a term that "emphasizes the importance of gender in the construction of her monstrosity."[35] Countering the prevalence of victimized women in horror films, Creed's feminist study of the monstrous-feminine draws on Freudian psychoanalytic frameworks to analyze the female monster. Appearing variously as the vampire, witch, monstrous womb or mother, non-human animal, beautiful killer, or psychopath,[36] the monstrous-feminine reveals more about "male fears than about female desire or feminine subjectivity," writes Creed. Similarly, the bridezilla figure simultaneously defies and reinforces sexist notions of femininity. In line with Creed's use of Julia Kristeva's notion of the abject, the bridezilla becomes monstrous by crossing or threatening to cross boundaries between human and nonhuman, normal and supernatural, properly gendered and gender-deviant.[37] Merged with historical and contemporary practices and representations of the wedding ritual, the bridezilla figure is rooted in sexist characterizations of women as hysterical, irrational, overly emotional, and always poised to "lose it."[38] These performances thus represent the fears and problems associated with the specter of uncontrolled femininity. The necessary response—containment and domestication—conforms not only to the practices used to uphold dominant gender ideologies, but also to the response to Godzilla in popular film, a symbolically freighted monster that animates the metaphoric leap into the world of gender ideologies.[39]

"Can't Talk to Her, Can't Kill Her. Here Comes Bridezilla!"[40]

Adopting the monster of Gothic literature and popular film as its central concept, *Bridezillas* evolved over time into an increasingly grotesque, exaggerated demonstration of these narratives of enlightened sexism. *Bridezillas* started airing on the Women's Entertainment network in 2003 and ran consecutively for seven seasons through 2010. While later episodes are consistent in form and content, the first two seasons differed in both production quality and gendered perspective. Early episodes follow several Manhattan couples through the wedding planning process, creating a low-budget documentary feel as the camera crew clumsily interviews vendors, wedding planners, family members, and friends in addition to the brides and grooms.

The show hit its production stride by the second season, sticking to the established formula of featuring multiple brides per episode, but consistently ending each with closure to one of the stories: a wedding to end the reign of terror for one bridezilla. While *Bridezillas* shows brides (and, for that matter, couples) of various ethnicities, body types, socio-economic statuses, family statuses, and relationship maturity levels, it does not deviate from the narrative of heterosexual, romantic love or its focus on consumption.

The other significant change after the first season involved replacing a hegemonically masculine voiceover with a female narrator. This change shifted the audience's perspective and the source of judgment regarding the monstrous. Whereas the masculine voice is appropriate for the earlier documentary-style aesthetic, it feels out of place when depicting a bride's experience in a dress or floral shop. In other words, the judgment came from a different gendered location. Aurally and symbolically shifting the narration to a woman's voice captures the enlightened sexist message of feminine competition and recurring judgment among women.

The smoother production qualities of later episodes changed the pacing to emphasize more meltdowns and more monstrous exhibitions presented for audience judgment along a traditionally feminine yardstick of propriety. The shift toward outrageous televised spectacle clearly sought to match viewer and reality-genre expectations. One commenter reviewing the first season asks, "Who knew there were boring Bridezillas?" Noting that "Season [Six] had become a bit too overly dramatic, even unrealistic," the reviewer emphasizes the differences between the earlier and later aesthetic, stating that "Season [One's] quiet, tasteful conservative [brides] . . . make for dull tv."[41] Dull television is the last thing producers want to create. Confirming the shift from the documentary-like "reality" to the increasingly hyperbolic pace and editing style, the review reveals the pressure to out-produce other wedding-themed reality programs. In this way, *Bridezillas* stands out by weaving together multiple narratives of wedding planning and centralizing monstrous transformations in each episodic frame.

Narratives of Fierce Consumption: "It's MY Day."

Bridezilla episodes show many ways in which women might transform into the monstrous. Each episode begins by introducing viewers to the brides, their grooms, and perhaps family and friends before declaring she is a potential bridezilla. When this declaration is made, the visual action halts as "Bridezilla" is digitally stamped across a still image of the bride. Each episode introduces the brides in similar fashion, describing her in two or three ways, noting her bridezilla status, and then offering a smattering of edited clips as evidence of the transformation. For instance, in one episode, Thuy is described as a "churchgoer, dog-lover, and potential bridezilla," followed by clips of her berating her fiancé and telling a seamstress, "You have to service me; I'm the bride."[42] The same episode introduces the story of young bride Adrianna. With three weeks to plan her wedding, the stress has "unleashed Adrianna's dark side," the narrator reports.[43] Adrianna then appears on the screen to declare, "I'm gonna plow you over if you get in my way." The narrator confirms, "Adrianna: loving fiancée, hopeless romantic, potential bridezilla!"[44] Introducing Jada and Julius, the narrator explains, "Already a perfectionist, making her own wedding flawless has turned Jada into a creature even she wouldn't recognize. Jada: devoted fiancée, level-headed professional, potential bridezilla!"[45] These examples demonstrate how the narrator sets up the impending monstrous transformations and frames each narrative arc. Many brides even welcome the label "bridezilla," wearing it as a badge of empowerment and wielding it as license for "going bridal" or "playing the bride card."[46] This is another way in which the narratives of choice and control collide with contradictions of sexist representations of feminine power.

There are several "triggers" that catalyze the transformation process. Creating the perfect wedding at all costs is one catalyst that fuels the monstrous transformation for some brides. Though all the narratives focus on this desire, Jada's story is especially driven by her perfectionist goals. A middle- to upper-class Black professional, Jada's drive for perfection terrorizes her fiancé, Julius; her half-dozen bridesmaids; and all of the wedding professionals helping to create her vision. Over the course of her four-episode narrative arc, Jada is consumed with visual symmetry, even demanding that Julius demote one of his groomsmen to ensure balance in the photos. She resembles a drill sergeant at the dress shop, lining her bridesmaids up as she barks out orders about their nails and hair and meticulously inspects the lengths of their dresses for absolute uniformity. These scenes are repeated in subsequent episodes and teasers to consistently reframe Jada's story through her quest for perfection. Although Jada references her professional background as the source of her high expectations, this power is undermined as the show uses it to portray her as a bridezilla. Viewers *could* interpret Jada as a model of feminist success, financially independent and financing her own wedding after achieving professional success and economic power. Yet because her economic power fuels consumption and her monstrous transformation, Jada's narrative continually devolves into a sexist representation, focusing on the victims of her perfectionist rage.

Jada is not the only bride consumed with perfection. Most bridezillas completely lose it when it comes to their dress. For bridezillas Jada, Thuy, Karen, Antonella, and others, the white wedding dress—one of the central stressors associated with wedding planning in many shows—catalyzes the transformation into the monstrous within the *Bridezillas* format. As viewers follow these brides into dress shops, they can visually consume the central element of a white wedding—the dress—while witnessing the various meltdowns that can occur in regard to the dress and, frequently, the veil. These scenes invite viewers to share the joy associated with imagining the big day—in effect, to vicariously experience the pleasure of consumption through the "reality" of the show. All the typical trappings associated with planning a white wedding, from meticulous hairstyling to throwing a reception, all receive extensive treatment by the show as contexts for bridezilla sightings.

The show leaves no question that the transformation has occurred; the clips are edited to string together pieces of evidence. Many individuals testify on screen to the presence of the bridezilla. Thuy's fiancé John confirms her transformation, noting that "on a scale from one to ten," Thuy's level of "bitchiness" registers at an eight. Bridezilla Adrianna's mother Brenda assumes the bulk of her daughter's wedding planning and the "brunt of [her] temper tantrums." Doing so, she confirms, "She is a bridezilla. Yes, she can be a bitch sometimes, let me tell you. She's stubborn. She's just like me—I'm the mother-zilla!"[47] In general, *Bridezillas* depicts women as unable to manage the stress associated with planning the wedding of their dreams and equates bitchiness with monstrosity. By framing it as such, the show blames the women for desiring the ideal wedding, which is what transforms them into the bridezilla. To emphasize the monstrous even further, the show frequently features brides dissolving into tears, getting into screaming matches, and walking out on their families, grooms, and wedding professionals.

Carnage of Bridezilla's Wrath

The bridezilla is not alone on her day; many other people take the brunt of her destructive and emotional wrath. *Bridezillas* shows the wide variety of people held to the mercy of the monster including the groom, bridesmaids, mother-of-the-bride, and future mother-in-law. In one scene, bridezilla Bessa clashes with a land manager over the rehearsal dinner location. The manager denies her entry without payment and refuses to budge, noting that she would not let Bessa in "with that attitude." Bessa explains to her fiancé that she will not say sorry to the manager. Upon meeting the groom, the manager says, "Good luck. . . . You've got a mouthy bride."[48] *Bridezillas* make their grooms cry, even threatening to call off the wedding "because they are stressed out."[49] When bridezilla Levitriss's fiancé hesitates at her suggestion of a three-karat, $30,000 diamond ring, she storms out of the jewelry store exclaiming, "This is MY day and he is getting in my way."[50] Planning the reception is also dramatic for bridezilla Courtney, who argues with her fiancé over the seating arrangement. The episode depicts his futile efforts to negotiate with her while she screams, storms in and out of rooms, and throws things.

Wedding industry professionals frequently shoulder the brunt of the bridezilla's wrath. Bridezilla Valerie, for instance, insists she wants a chocolate cake instead of vanilla a mere eighteen hours before her wedding. She berates her helpless baker, repeatedly yelling, "I want my chocolate cake!" As the voiceover explains, Valerie eventually "erupts like a volcano," smashing her hand into a defenseless frosted tasting cake for emphasis.[51] In another scene, Valerie receives a relaxing facial, though the voiceover says she cannot handle "even one hour without drama." Soon, she "freaks out on her faultless facialist," dramatically grabs a handheld mirror, pulls it to her face and exclaims, "Oh my God, I'm going to look like shit on my wedding day."[52] These videos are edited to hyperbolize the stress of putting on a large event in such a way that, according to Amanda Marcotte, provides an "opportunity to have your friends, relatives, and neighbors pass judgment on your taste and find it wanting." She argues that the pressure to be perfect also comes from external sources, who question one's degree of love for a partner if perfection is not relentlessly sought.[53] By extending the potential competitive and judgmental audience to the network viewership, *Bridezillas* capitalizes on the knowing and judging viewer who ultimately reinforces the sexist portrayals of the women/brides in these shows.

Domesticating the Beast

While *Bridezillas* focuses almost exclusively on the beastly transformation, extreme consumption, and raging wrath of the bridezilla, each episode neatly closes one narrative arc with scenes of the wedding ceremony, and occasionally the wedding reception. By providing narrative closure, the show supports the notion of bridezilla as a temporary phenomenon, resolved and domesticated through the wedding ritual. Indeed, regardless of how "alternative" the couple seems to be, the wedding ceremonies often feature traditional formats including fathers giving away their daughters to the groom, traditional wedding vows with versions of "to obey," and announcements of the couple as "Mr. and Mrs. His-First-Name His-Last-Name." In these ways, the narrative is predictably consistent with hetero-patriarchal norms associated with white weddings.[54] Thus, the out-of-control beast that emerges is instantly tamed as her expectations are met. The producers even feature the newlyweds commenting on the bride's successful transformation back to the non-beastly. This narrative closure is unsurprising, especially given the genre of wedding-themed reality shows. Even though *Bridezillas* lacks literal competition between women, couples, or singles for the ultimate wedding, the wedding is clearly framed as the prize that fulfills the dreams of the bridezilla and saves her victims from continued pain and destruction. Indeed, the traditional patriarchal staging of the wedding clearly instantiates the groom as the one in charge of the relationship by the end of the narrative.

Conclusion

As *Bridezillas* moves the viewer through the stresses associated with the planning process, it "mobiliz[es] the consumer . . . to create an ethos of unlimited consumption" and cultivates an environment of competition among women in the process.[55] This consumption works on two levels: within the monstrous figure and within the audience. Halberstam, in her discussion of Gothic novels, elaborates on this connection to capitalist consumption, noting that monsters *sell*. The tried-and-true formula of showing increasingly grotesque scenes of bridezilla debauchery over multiple seasons demonstrates the profitability and sustainability of such content. Moreover, Halberstam explains that Gothic fictions "thematize the monstrous aspects of both production and consumption" and create "a public who consumes [that] monstrosity, who revels in it, and who then surveys its individual members for signs of deviance or monstrosity, excess or violence."[56] Even though viewers may be horrified with the monstrosity on the screen, the show invites them to consume both the monstrous *and* to position themselves to visually (and perhaps literally) consume the products on display.

Such consumption on the show cultivates what Douglas calls "the ironic, knowing viewer" whereby "the people on the screen may be rich, spoiled, or [monstrous], but you, O superior viewer, get to judge and mock them, and thus are above them."[57] By illustrating how the monstrous emerges within the bride in the midst of wedding-planning, the show teaches viewers how to detect the monster within themselves or in their community of soon-to-be-married friends. Moreover, inserting the audience member into this presentation of "the real," the show replicates a competitive environment within which women are pitted against one another in terms of sexual and/or consumption power, in addition to the power to survey each other (and themselves) for signs of deviance.

The postfeminist-grotesque is a profitable construct within the reality genre, in which the prominence of wedding-themed reality shows reveal their lasting power as part of the wedding-ideological complex in service of the wedding-industrial complex. The show *Bridezillas* exemplifies how the monstrous-feminine undermines contemporary narratives of empowerment. In so doing, it distills the most extreme fears and anxieties about gender, namely femininity. Analysis of the bridezilla figure through this reality television show reveals the ease and persistence of sexist representations of women that undermine efforts to show their fierce power and clear capability to get what they want.

The show relies on hyperbolized gender differences to highlight the monstrosity of women violating expectations surrounding femininity. The voiceover and video editing show the brides' frustration with their fiancés' inability to make significant decisions and the expectation that the men go above and beyond to please their betrotheds' every whim. Depicted as competitive, controlling perfectionists, bridezillas are even worse in the presence of their grooms. In service of "her day," she wrests power from her husband-to-be (who is assumed to make decisions in non-wedding contexts). Working from the assumption that brides make the decisions for the wedding, bridezilla narratives frequently show grooms yielding to even the most extreme bridal demands. These narratives thus create a caricature of feminine power run amok, drawing on antifeminist fears of male emasculation. Yet the bridezilla construct allows a space for exerting this power only as long as viewers presume she will assume an "appropriate" role in marriage. As such, the bridezilla is depicted as a temporal figure, a transformation resolved once the wedding ceremony completes the narrative.

The subsequent domestication of the monster shuts down alternative interpretations of her empowerment. Meanwhile, though brides can eschew the wedding-industrial complex through online options—including websites like Offbeat Bride, Bucking the Wedding Industry, and a multitude of same-sex wedding sites—the expectations for brides and the specter of bridezilla tacitly remain intact. For instance, bloggers at Bucking the Wedding Industry call for brides to consciously avoid the wedding-industrial complex because maintaining "your sanity and ability to remain human may well rest on avoiding the evil wedding industry."[58] Thus, even within a pep talk for brides in search of alternatives, the blog dually critiques the industry and calls for brides to maintain sanity and avoid turning into the monstrous bridezilla.

Critiquing wedding-themed cultural texts is not new.[59] Feminist and queer activists have challenged the institution of marriage, the wedding ritual, and the wedding industrial complex for decades. In *Passionate Politics*, lesbian feminist activist Charlotte Bunch recalls radical feminist actions at bridal fairs and other bridal industry events during the 1960s and 1970s.[60] By centering narratives of gender and how they reproduce narratives of sexuality, this analysis interrogates heteronormativity and the way rituals like weddings maintain patriarchal norms.[61] Specifically, bridezilla narratives function within a matrix of heteronormative power, utilizing the monstrous (or queer) to stabilize the "normal."[62] As such, this analysis seeks to illuminate another aspect of what Yep calls the "violence of heternormativity" as it functions within wedding-themed texts like *Bridezillas*.[63] Transgressing gender boundaries in the wedding planning process (queering that boundary) is presented as a usurpation of male power rather than a collaborative enterprise. As such, the narrative echoes fearful antifeminist claims that feminism is solely an effort to take power away from men. This demonstrates the power of postfeminist/enlightened sexist representations as they blame feminism for the problems of unruly women in need of control. Thus, while the groom remains silent or silenced throughout the episodes as his bridezilla fiancée runs amok, he symbolically regains his position of power at the narrative's closing wedding ritual.

Notes

1. *Bridezillas*, Women's Entertainment TV Networks, accessed January 13, 2011, http://www.wetv.com/bridezillas/index.html.

2. "Bridezilla Defined," Bridezilla.com, accessed January 13, 2011, http://www.bridezilla.com/bridezilla-defined.

3. Chrys Ingraham, *White Weddings: Romancing Heterosexuality in Popular Culture*, 2nd ed. (New York: Routledge, 2008), 38.

4. Ingraham, *White Weddings*, 111.

5. Ingraham, *White Weddings*, 177.

6. "About," *Shedding for the Wedding* show website, accessed March 10, 2011, http://www.cwtv.com/shows/shedding-for-the-wedding/about. The show has the same producers as *The Biggest Loser*.

7. Angel Cohn, "*Shedding for the Wedding*: Less Offensive Than *Bridalplasty*, But Far Tackier," *The Telefile Blog* (blog), accessed March 10, 2011, http://www.televisionwithoutpity.com/telefile/2011/02/shedding-for-the-wedding-less.php.

8. Jennifer Maher, "What Do Women Watch? Tuning into the Compulsory Heterosexuality Channel," in *Reality TV: Remaking Television Culture*, eds. Susan Murray and Laurie Ouellette (New York: New York University Press, 2004), 202.

9. Maher, "What Do Women Watch?" 203.

10. Michael Warner, *The Trouble with Normal: Sex, Politics, and the Ethics of Queer Life* (New York: The Free Press, 1999), 47.

11. Maher, "What Do Women Watch?" 197–99.

12. "The Wedding Business Report 2010," WE tv Networks, accessed February 1, 2011, http://www.theweddingreport.com/wmdb/index.cfm?action=reports.index&rpt=wedbiz2010; Ingraham, *White Weddings*, 39.

13. Susan Murray and Laurie Ouellette, *Reality TV: Remaking Television Culture*, 2nd ed. (New York: New York University Press, 2009): 3, 6.

14. See Robert Bogdan, *Freak Show: Presenting Human Oddities for Amusement and Profit* (Chicago: University of Chicago Press, 1988).

15. Suzanne Leonard, "Marriage Envy," *Women's Studies Quarterly* 34 (2006), 45.

16. Murray and Ouellette, *Reality TV*, 4.

17. Helene A. Shugart, "Ruling Class: Disciplining Class, Race, and Ethnicity in Television Reality Court Shows," *Howard Journal of Communications* 17 (2006), 80.

18. Shugart, "Ruling Class," 79–100. See also John Fiske, *Television Culture* (New York: Methuen, 1987) and Todd Gitlin, "Looking Through the Screen," in *Watching Television*, ed. Todd Gitlin (New York: Pantheon, 1986): 3–8.

19. Todd Gitlin, "Prime Time Ideology: The Hegemonic Process in Television Entertainment," *Social Problems* 26 (1979): 253.

20. Shugart, "Ruling Class," 80.

21. Anderson and Stewart, "Politics and the Single Woman," 598; Michelle L. Hammers, "Cautionary Tales of Liberation and Female Professionalism: The Case Against *Ally McBeal*," *Western Journal of Communication* 69 (2005): 167–182; and Helene A. Shugart, Catherine Egley Waggoner, and D. Lynn O'Brien Hallstein, "Mediating Third-Wave Feminism: Appropriation as Postmodern Media Practice," *Critical Studies in Media Communication* 18 (2001): 194–210.

22. Senda-Cook, "Postfeminist Double Binds," 20.

23. Susan J. Douglas, *Enlightened Sexism: The Seductive Message That Feminism's Work Is Done* (New York: Henry Holt & Co., 2010), 9.

24. Angela McRobbie, *The Aftermath of Feminism: Gender, Culture, and Social Change* (Los Angeles: Sage, 2009), 6.

25. Bonnie J. Dow, *Primetime Feminism: Television, Media Culture and the Women's Movement Since 1970* (Philadelphia: University of Pennsylvania Press, 1996), 88.

26. Mary Douglas Vavrus, *Postfeminist News: Political Women in Media Culture* (Albany: State University of New York Press, 2002), 22.

27. Senda-Cook, "Post-Feminist Double Binds," 20; Vavrus, *Postfeminist News*, 2.

28. Douglas, *Enlightened Sexism*, 10.

29. Angela McRobbie, "Post-Feminism and Popular Culture," *Feminist Media Studies* 4 (2004): 255.

30. Douglas, *Enlightened Sexism*, 9.

31. Douglas, *Enlightened Sexism*, 5.

32. Judith Halberstam, *Skin Shows: Gothic Horror and the Technology of Monsters* (Durham, NC: Duke University Press, 1995), 2.

33. Halberstam, *Skin Shows*, 13.

34. George E. Haggerty, *Gothic Fiction/Gothic Form* (Philadelphia: University of Pennsylvania Press, 1989), 2.

35. Barbara Creed, *The Monstrous Feminine: Film, Feminism, and Psychoanalysis* (London: Routledge, 1993), 3.

36. Creed, *Monstrous Feminine*, 1.

37. Creed, *Monstrous Feminine*, 11.

38. *Bridezillas*, accessed January 14, 2011, http://www.youtube.com/watch?v=Au5o1heu0CA &feature=channel.

39. Yomata Inuhiko, "The Menace from the South Seas: Honda Ishiro's *Godzilla* (1954)," in *Japanese Cinema: Texts and Contexts*, eds. Alastair Phillips and Julian Stringer, 102–111 (London: Routledge, 2007). Yomata Inuhiko argues that over time, the iconic monster has assumed multilayered meanings; it has symbolically captured and conveyed nationalist, anti-nuclear, and war-time ideological tensions, demonstrating its long-tested ability to shift meanings depending on international and national contexts.

40. This line comes from the theme song used for the series during the second season in 2004.

41. K. Heard, "Who Knew There Were Boring Bridezillas?" Amazon Online Marketplace, accessed January 14, 2011, http://www.amazon.com/Bridezillas-Complete-Season-Mindy-Burbano/product-reviews/B000FEBWH6/ref=cm_cr_dp_synop?ie=UTF8&showViewpoints=0&sortBy=bySubmissionDateDescending#R3GJJONU8KI5V0.

42. "Episode One," 2004 episode of *Bridezillas* (We tv, 2003–2010, DVD).

43. "Episode One," 4:39.

44. "Episode One," 4:53.

45. "Episode One," 8:15.

46. "Going Bridal," *Bridezillas*, accessed February 3, 2011, http://www.youtube.com/watch?v=x7Z4uXV4AzM.

47. "Episode One," 6:39.

48. "The Groom Is Doomed," *Bridezillas*, accessed January 14, 2011, http://www.youtube.com/watch?v=OgqjjxSXuQ4&feature=relmfu.

49. "Bride Makes Groom Cry," *Bridezillas*, accessed January 14, 2011, http://www.youtube.com/watch?v=mqJbNACxmlk&feature=relmfu.

50. "Bridezillas Go Crazy!" *Bridezillas*, accessed January 14, 2011, http://www.youtube.com/watch?v=uQ8PL9f3g6s&feature=channel.

51. "Bridezilla Cake Smash!" *Bridezillas*, accessed January 14, 2011, http://www.youtube.com/watch?v=iserIaPGwuo.

52. "Bridezilla Facial Freakout!" *Bridezillas*, accessed January 14, 2011, http://www.youtube.com/watch?v=_nyDaLg_co0&feature=channel.

53. Amanda Marcotte, "The Wedding-Industrial Complex: Don't Get Recruited, Since No One Makes Officer," in *It's a Jungle out There: The Feminist Survival Guide to Politically Inhospitable Environments* (Berkeley: Seal Press, 2007), 35.

54. Ingraham, *White Weddings*, 38.

55. Angela McRobbie, "Young Women and Consumer Culture: An Intervention," *Cultural Studies* 22 (2008): 541.

56. Halberstam, *Skin Shows*, 12.

57. Douglas, *Enlightened Sexism*, 14.

58. "On Avoiding the Wedding Industrial Complex—A Pep Talk," Bucking the Wedding Industry, accessed February 1, 2011, http://www.buckingtheweddingindustry.com/2010/02/10/first-a-pep-talk.

59. For instance, see Bonnie J. Dow, "Hegemony, Feminist Criticism, and *The Mary Tyler Moore Show*," *Critical Studies in Mass Communication* 7 (1990): 261–274; Karrin Vasby Anderson and Jessie Stewart, "Politics and the Single Woman: The '*Sex and the City* Voter' in Campaign 2004," *Rhetoric & Public Affairs* 8 (2005): 595–616; and Samantha Senda-Cook, "Postfeminist Double Binds: How Six Contemporary Films Perpetuate the Myth of the Incomplete Woman," *Rocky Mountain Communication Review* 6 (2009): 18–28.

60. Charlotte Bunch, *Passionate Politics: Feminist Theory in Action* (New York: St. Martin's Press, 1987), 31.

61. Diane Raymond, "Popular Culture and Queer Representation," in *Gender, Race, and Class in Media*, eds. Gail Dines and Jean M. Humez 98–99 (Thousand Oaks, CA: Sage, 2003). See also Theresa de Lauretis, "Queer Theory: Gay and Lesbian Sexualities, An Introduction," *differences: A Journal of Feminist Cultural Studies* 3 (1991), iv.

62. Haggerty, *Gothic Fiction/Gothic Form*, 2; Bogdan, *Freak Show*.

63. Gust A. Yep, "The Violence of Heteronormativity in Communication Studies: Notes on Injury, Healing, and Queer World-Making," *Journal of Homosexuality* 45 (2003), 13.

Bibliography

Anderson, Karrin Vasby, and Jessie Stewart. "Politics and the Single Woman: The '*Sex and the City* Voter' in Campaign 2004." *Rhetoric & Public Affairs* 8 (2005): 595–616.

Bogdan, Robert. *Freak Show: Presenting Human Oddities for Amusement and Profit*. Chicago: University of Chicago Press, 1988.

Bridezilla. "Bridezilla Defined." Accessed January 13, 2011. http://www.bridezilla.com/bridezilla-defined.

Bridezillas. "Bride Makes Groom Cry." Accessed January 14, 2011. http://www.youtube.com/watch?v=mqJbNACxmlk&feature=relmfu.

———. "Bridezilla Cake Smash!" Accessed January 14, 2011. http://www.youtube.com/watch?v=iserIaPGwuo.

———. "Bridezilla Facial Freakout!" Accessed January 14, 2011. http://www.youtube.com/watch?v=_nyDaLg_co0&feature=channel.

———. "Bridezillas Go Crazy!" Accessed January 14, 2011. http://www.youtube.com/watch?v=uQ8PL9f3g6s&feature=channel.

———. *Bridezillas*. Accessed January 14, 2011. http://www.youtube.com/watch?v=Au5o1heu0CA&feature=channel.

———. "Going Bridal." Accessed February 3, 2011. http://www.youtube.com/watch?v=x7Z4uXV4AzM.

———. "The Groom Is Doomed," Accessed January 14, 2011. http://www.youtube.com/watch?v=OgqjjxSXuQ4&feature=relmfu.

Bucking the Wedding Industry. "On Avoiding the Wedding Industrial Complex—A Pep Talk." Accessed February 1, 2011. http://www.buckingtheweddingindustry.com/2010/02/10/first-a-pep-talk.

Bunch, Charlotte. *Passionate Politics: Feminist Theory in Action*. New York: St. Martin's Press, 1987.

Cohn, Angel. *The Telefile Blog* (blog). "*Shedding for the Wedding*: Less Offensive Than *Bridalplasty*, but Far Tackier." Accessed March 10, 2011. http://www.televisionwithoutpity.com/telefile/2011/02/shedding-for-the-wedding-less.php.

Creed, Barbara. *The Monstrous Feminine: Film, Feminism, and Psychoanalysis*. London: Routledge, 1993.

de Lauretis, Theresa. "Queer Theory: Gay and Lesbian Sexualities, An Introduction." *differences: A Journal of Feminist Cultural Studies* 3 (1991): iii-xviii.

Douglas, Susan J. *Enlightened Sexism: The Seductive Message That Feminism's Work Is Done*. New York: Henry Holt & Co., 2010.

Dow, Bonnie J. "Hegemony, Feminist Criticism, and *The Mary Tyler Moor Show*." *Critical Studies in Mass Communication* 7 (1990): 261–274.

———. *Primetime Feminism: Television, Media Culture and the Women's Movement Since 1970*. Philadelphia: University of Pennsylvania Press, 1996.

"Episode One," 2004 episode of *Bridezillas*. WE tv, 2003–2010. DVD.

Fiske, John. *Television Culture*. New York: Methuen, 1987.

Gitlin, Todd. "Looking Through the Screen." In *Watching Television*, edited by Todd Gitlin 3–8. New York: Pantheon, 1986.

———. "Prime Time Ideology: The Hegemonic Process in Television Entertainment." *Social Problems* 26 (1979): 251–266.

Haggerty, George E. *Gothic Fiction/Gothic Form*. Philadelphia: University of Pennsylvania Press, 1989.

Halberstam, Judith. *Skin Shows: Gothic Horror and the Technology of Monsters*. Durham, NC: Duke University Press, 1995.

Hammers, Michelle L. "Cautionary Tales of Liberation and Female Professionalism: The Case against *Ally McBeal*." *Western Journal of Communication* 69 (2005): 167–82.

Heard, K. Amazon Online Marketplace. "Who Knew There Were Boring Bridezillas?" Accessed January 14, 2011. http://www.amazon.com/Bridezillas-Complete-Season-Mindy-Burbano/product-reviews/B000FEBWH6/ref=cm_cr_dp_synop?ie=UTF8&showViewpoints=0&sortBy=bySubmissionDateDescending#R3GJJONU8KI5V0.

Ingraham, Chrys. *White Weddings: Romancing Heterosexuality in Popular Culture*, 2nd ed. New York: Routledge, 2008.

Inuhiko, Yomata. "The Menace from the South Seas: Honda Ishiro's *Godzilla* (1954)." In *Japanese Cinema: Texts and Contexts*, edited by Alastair Phillips and Julian Stringer, 102–111. London: Routledge, 2007.

Leonard, Suzanne. "Marriage Envy," *Women's Studies Quarterly* 34 (2006), 43–64.

Maher, Jennifer. "What Do Women Watch? Tuning into the Compulsory Heterosexuality Channel." In *Reality TV: Remaking Television Culture*, edited by Susan Murray and Laurie Ouellette. New York: New York University Press, 2004.

Marcotte, Amanda. "The Wedding-Industrial Complex: Don't Get Recruited, Since No One Makes Officer." In *It's a Jungle out There: The Feminist Survival Guide to Politically Inhospitable Environments*. Berkeley: Seal Press, 2007.

McRobbie, Angela. "Post-Feminism and Popular Culture." *Feminist Media Studies* 4 (2004): 255–64.

———. *The Aftermath of Feminism: Gender, Culture, and Social Change*. Los Angeles: Sage, 2009.

———. "Young Women and Consumer Culture: An Intervention," *Cultural Studies* 22 (2008): 531–50.

Murray, Susan, and Laurie Ouellette. *Reality TV: Remaking Television Culture*, 2nd ed. New York: New York University Press, 2009.

Raymond, Diane. "Popular Culture and Queer Representation." In *Gender, Race, and Class in Media*, edited by Gail Dines and Jean M. Humez, 98–99. Thousand Oaks: Sage, 2003.

Senda-Cook, Samantha. "Postfeminist Double Binds: How Six Contemporary Films Perpetuate the Myth of the Incomplete Woman." *Rocky Mountain Communication Review* 6 (2009): 18–28.

Shedding for the Wedding. "About." Accessed March 10, 2011. http://www.cwtv.com/shows/shedding-for-the-wedding/about.

Shugart, Helene A. "Ruling Class: Disciplining Class, Race, and Ethnicity in Television Reality Court Shows." *Howard Journal of Communications* 17 (2006): 79–100.

Shugart, Helene A., Catherine Egley Waggoner, and D. Lynn O'Brien Hallstein. "Mediating Third-Wave Feminism: Appropriation as Postmodern Media Practice." *Critical Studies in Media Communication* 18 (2001): 194–210.

Vavrus, Mary Douglas. *Postfeminist News: Political Women in Media Culture.* Albany: State University of New York Press, 2002.

Warner, Michael. *The Trouble with Normal: Sex, Politics, and the Ethics of Queer Life.* New York: The Free Press, 1999.

WE tv Networks. "The Wedding Business Report 2010." Accessed February 1, 2011. http://www.theweddingreport.com/wmdb/index.cfm?action=reports.index&rpt=wedbiz2010.

Women's Entertainment TV Networks. *Bridezillas.* Accessed January 13, 2011. http://www.wetv.com/bridezillas/index.html.

Yep, Gust A. "The Violence of Heteronormativity in Communication Studies: Notes on Injury, Healing, and Queer World-Making." *Journal of Homosexuality* 45 (2003): 11–59.

Chapter 2

The Reality of Televised Motherhood: The Personal Quest and Feminine Test of Kate Gosselin

by Mary Frances Casper and Deneen Gilmour

The recent surge in reality television programming has provided a window into the worlds of women struggling with parenthood and personhood. Motherhood has undergone the same blurring and fracturing in the media as other gender-based identity categories.[1] It is depicted as a quest for personal completion, and female behavior is regulated and normalized through examples of appropriate mothering. These women serve as both role models and warnings, allowing viewers a fly-on-the-wall perspective of family functions and dysfunctions.

The reality television process effectively splits the lives of participants. While they cannot help but be impacted by the surrounding cameras and production crews, the subjects are expected to continue living as "normal" people. The families we see in reality programming are not normal—it is the unique nature of their makeup or activities that evokes curiosity and drives viewership. The more unusual the family, the greater the potential for high ratings. The growing celebrity status of reality television mothers is itself a double-edged sword: the "reality" in reality television creates the expectation that the people we see on television are the same off camera and indeed in every aspect of their lives. While their children are expected to grow and change, reality television mothers are expected to fit a narrowly defined television trope: the mom.

This chapter examines motherhood in the media as portrayed by Kate Gosselin (*Kate Plus 8*) in TLC reality programming. We argue that appropriate motherhood, which equates to morality,[2] is paralleled with the Freudian Madonna/whore dichotomy through television tropes. Motherhood then becomes a test of both personhood and character. Women are legitimized by moral motherhood and delegitimized by immoral motherhood. Reality programs thus become mythic in nature, serving as modern fables to teach women proper behavior by providing "real" evidence of consequences for compliance or noncompliance.

Motherhood, Morality, and Media

As female professional status has grown, so has the inherent conflict between the traditional role of nurturer and contemporary role of professional. Burnett found that most women describe their current lives and their children's lives as much busier than those of their parents or their younger selves a generation ago.[3] Social science scholars posit that the frenzied pace is due to several factors. In a pattern that's been growing for decades, more women are in the labor force in full-time jobs.[4] Women's roles in the professional world have increased, but, conversely, their cleaning and child-rearing duties have not decreased proportionally at home, causing stress and strain as they seek to balance work and family responsibilities.[5] Gender role strain—partners' disagreements about who should do what and who is doing more—can contribute to perceptions of unfairness[6] and cause marital strain.[7] Burnett believes other factors, including the quickening pace of life due to technology, contribute to a lifestyle that is causing some women to feel greater pressure and stress.[8]

Some contemporary women harbor a love-hate relationship with their roles. The duality of their lives—two all-consuming sets of responsibilities often in conflict with each other—is a never-ending frustration.[9] Acculturated to postmodern America's drive to earn and spend, most women face the economic reality that without their paychecks, the family could not pay its bills. Traditionally, the woman was a homemaker—literally the one who made a home for the husband and children. A good homemaker—a good mother—was expected to enable her husband's and children's dreams, nurturing the young while often ignoring or postponing her personal aspirations to instead make real the dreams of her children.[10]

Workplace demands—indeed, the demand of earning money—combined with an ever-quickening pace of life make it difficult for an individual to maintain a coherent, stable identity. Dally states that the traditional role of homemaker was inextricably tied to caring for children and home. Dally goes on to say that economic changes in Western society during the 1970s and 1980s caused a "crisis in motherhood."[11] Women received warnings that any separation between a mother and her children could cause psychological damage to both. Often, women were told pursuing a career was bad for their children and working outside the home relegated them to the category of "abnormal mothers."[12] The idealization of motherhood led to a crisis for mothers and children, Dally concludes, because few women have discovered a way to reconcile the oppositional demands of motherhood and professionalism. On top of oppositional demands, living in overdrive can create dialectical tensions, defined as opposing needs or tendencies as they relate to the fragmentation of female roles.[13]

Green finds the media use a double link of iconography to moral character and moral character to social destiny.[14] Using this translation, women as homemakers can be seen as a symbol of achieving the ideal American family. Women who embrace this image yet are unable to sustain the media construct of the "ideal" family may judge themselves as failing, as behaving inappropriately or in a shameful manner. Appeals for public and policy support of family values carry the implication that "virtually every aspect of society can be reduced to questions of individual moral character and behavior."[15] The ideology of family in the media has become a "coercive ideological symbol" equating morality and conventional sexuality,[16] just as the term "family values" has been broadly used to invoke support for idealized, nostalgic visions of America and American family life. While such images no longer represent most American families, they are invoked often enough in the media to remain an accepted social ideal.[17]

The media perpetuate social ideals while presenting unrealistic versions of American life. Weimann found there are fewer women than men on television. Women are seen indoors more often than outdoors, and they appear more frequently in sitcoms and soap operas than action films and dramas.[18] Specific female "types" are created repeatedly: the imp, the goodwife, the harpy, the bitch, and the ever-present victim.[19] Reality television perpetuates the goodwife, a woman who strictly adheres to the feminine sphere of family and home by providing both the icon and the contrasting spectacle of women violating feminine ideals.

As women juggle career and children, home and husband while trying to find a comfortable balance, some have begun to draw on nostalgia-driven collective memory,[20] calling on the saner, simpler past mythologized by television, films, and advertisements. Despite our yearning for a kinder, simpler time, we understand media life is not real life, and our favorite characters are created fictions. Even so, Richins found exposure to idealized images leads media consumers to compare, often unconsciously, their own lives with those represented in media. Repeated exposure to idealized images raises media consumers' expectations and influences their perceptions of how their lives ought to be.[21] It is no wonder then that we turn to the real people of reality programs for affirmation of our lives and lifestyle choices.

Price found reality television creates an "illusory everyday" that both supplements and subsumes existing understandings of the world through the perpetuation of social tropes and the incarnation of mythic ideals. The familiarity of family life and traditional American ideologies "invite a link with the viewers' own possible experiences for cultural identification and reinforcement."[22] In essence, reality programming validates viewers' own lives by reinforcing understandings of how people "should" live. Family life becomes both familiar and exotic, something to watch because we know it, but we don't know it quite like this. The mothers in reality programming represent mythic ideals of True Womanhood: the spiritual core of the family, content at home and fulfilled in the role of mother and wife.[23] While the mythic mother may run counter to the lived reality of viewers' own fragmented lives, mythic True Womanhood still serves as the measuring stick that reality mothers are held to.

TLC: The Reality of Reality Television

TLC is a cable network owned by Discovery Communications, LLC, which promotes itself as "the leading global real-world media and entertainment company."[24] TLC began as The Learning Channel, with programming focused on lifelong learning, "bringing viewers life's lessons that they cannot learn in books."[25] Scarborough Research reports that from September 2010 to August 2011, the bulk of TLC viewers fit a key demographic: educated (college or higher) female (57.4 percent) professionals (32.5 percent) with discretionary income (median household income $84,690) who both own their own homes (65.3 percent) and are at an age (25–54) when they are focused on family and working to create a stable environment.[26] The network reports availability "in more than 97 million homes in the U.S., nearly 8 million homes in Canada and through the website at www.tlc.com."[27]

Over time, TLC programming has shifted from documentary-style, somewhat academic content to personal stories that focus on women and family life.[28] Programs can be broken into three broad categories, each of which showcases traditions and traditional ideologies: self, marriage, and motherhood (*A Baby Story*, *Four Weddings*, *My Big Fat Gypsy Wedding*, *Say Yes to the Dress*, *The Little Couple*); family life and unique families

(*19 Kids and Counting, Cake Boss, Kate Plus 8, Little People, Big World*); and homemaking and cooking (*DC Cupcakes, Home Made Simple, Kitchen Boss, Next Great Baker*). In contrast, a fourth category offers deviant versions of American life and traditions (*Extreme Couponing, Freaky Eaters, Hoarding: Buried Alive, I Didn't Know I Was Pregnant, LA Ink, My Strange Addiction, Police Women of Broward County, Sister Wives, Strange Sex, Toddlers & Tiaras, What Not to Wear*). Such programming dichotomizes lifestyles and behaviors, normalizing traditional, heterosexual, paternalistic relationships through comparison with those existing outside the boundaries of narrowly defined social standards. Mothers exploiting children, families rummaging through piles of trash, women in nontraditional careers or exhibiting strange behaviors—all become the sideshow viewed by visitors safely ensconced in normalcy.

Jon & Kate Plus 8

The Gosselins married in June 1999. Then known by her maiden name Kreider, Kate worked as a registered nurse while Jon was a network engineer.[29] Unable to conceive because of Kate's polycystic ovary syndrome, the couple began fertility treatments shortly after marriage. Their intrauterine insemination (IUI) resulted in the birth of twin daughters, Cara and Madelyn, on October 8, 2000.[30] By 2003, the couple again sought to expand their family with the help of a fertility specialist. "We figured we would have twins again," Kate told *People* magazine.[31] But she became pregnant with sextuplets. On May 10, 2004, at thirty weeks gestation, Kate gave birth to six babies: Alexis, Hannah, Aaden, Collin, Leah, and Joel. "I've fought through a pregnancy where every minute was a battle," Kate told the magazine. "I will not fail my kids."[32]

The Gosselin family made national news and quickly became part of the TLC network's cadre of family reality programs. *Kate Plus 8* (originally *Jon & Kate Plus 8*) was one of the highest-rated programs on the network. TVGuide.com calls *Jon & Kate Plus 8* "a breakout hit chronicling life with a Pennsylvania family with two sets of multiples (twins and sextuplets)."[33] Interest in the family developed when the Gosselins were featured in two hourlong specials on Discovery Health—"Surviving Sextuplets and Twins" and "Sextuplets and Twins: One Year Later"—before moving to TLC as a reality series.

Jon & Kate Plus 8 ran for five seasons from 2007 to 2011. The first four seasons "offer a mostly endearing look at life in a large family, but the series took a more serious turn in Season 5 when Jon and Kate announced they were separating."[34] Viewers literally watched the sextuplets grow from infants to schoolchildren while simultaneously witnessing the Gosselin's marriage go from traditional and united to strained, combative, and, finally, broken. The Gosselins separated in 2009 under heavy media scrutiny, which revealed that Jon had engaged in multiple extramarital affairs. For a brief time, Kate was portrayed as the wronged wife—until she agreed to continue filming the show under the title *Kate Plus 8* and was accused of exploiting her children for fame and money. Jon filed an unsuccessful lawsuit attempting to stop filming, and while filming continued for a time, the program was canceled in 2011.

Kate Gosselin

Kate Gosselin personifies the tension between traditional motherhood and the drive for personal success—the kind of personal success that can provide for a family's needs—as well as the conflicting reactions women receive when they make these choices. Over a five-year period, mother and wife Kate Gosselin went from overwhelmed housewife to celebrity single mom. Originally promoted as a traditional family with unique challenges brought on by the birth of sextuplets, the early seasons focused on family milestones and traditions, Kate's cleanliness standards, family road trips, household organizing, thrifty shopping tips, potty training, and birthday parties.[35]

But it was Jon and Kate's relationship that drove the story. Reducing thirty to forty hours of filming into a one-hour episode allowed producers to tailor viewer perceptions of the couple. Kate, a self-described perfectionist, was shown as a critical, demanding taskmaster who ruled her home with a will of iron. Jon, on the other hand, appeared inept, indecisive, unfocused, and sometimes surly. Storylines focused on the parents emphasize both these differences and stereotypical gender roles as Jon cancels "his weekend trip to the country with the guys" and takes "the boys to the golf course for a day of sporty fun" as well as to a baseball game and the gym.[36] When Kate goes out of town, "Jon finds himself challenged by things he never considered before such as how to get eight kids to school on time." Kate's dominance is recognized when "Jon gets to do things his way," and viewers are asked, "Will he be able to survive without Kate's help" or gain "a newfound appreciation for his wife?"[37]

Kate is both the powerhouse behind the family and the focus of most episodes. True to the goodwife persona, she keeps house, organizes, shops, clips coupons, transports kids to school, plans educational trips, and tries to meet the needs of her growing children. While Jon squires his sons to manly pursuits, she takes the girls to the grocery store and to a pottery painting studio. Kate's life is typically described in terms of the children. "Now that the twins have started first grade, Kate is home alone all day with just the sextuplets," and she "begins looking for a well-qualified nanny . . . to find the perfect and much-deserved help she needs" as she "struggles to find room in the house for the kids to play."[38] Even her appearance is a reflection of family needs as Kate gets a "wardrobe makeover" because "Jon really doesn't care for the way Kate dresses."[39]

After the third season, several episodes acknowledge the impact being on camera has had on the family and address viewer responses and questions. For the first time, we see the family treated as celebrities rather than as subjects. Jon and Kate face the camera and respond to viewers, share anecdotes, and reminisce about their lives in a mediated version of chatting over coffee. A photo shoot for the cover of *Good Housekeeping* and visits with professional baker Duff Goldman, chef Emeril Lagasse, and the cast of *Orange County Choppers* remind viewers that the Gosselins are more than "just folks."

While the fourth season ends with Jon and Kate renewing their wedding vows on a beach in Hawaii, the Season Five premiere of *Jon & Kate Plus 8* was preceded by tabloid and mainstream news about the Gosselins' crumbling marriage. Airing in late May 2009, the episode shows the couple—clearly at odds—planning their sextuplets' fifth birthday party. In the show's interview segments, Jon and Kate make it clear their commitment to each other is over but insist they are both committed to the children and the show. By this time, the show had become the couple's sole income for providing for their large family.

After the episode aired, viewers sounded off on *TV Guide*'s online comment board about the sickening feeling of watching a marriage—indeed, a family—fall apart on television. One example:

> Last night's premiere made me sick to my stomach. I have nothing to say against either Jon or Kate about the drama surrounding their marriage, because I imagine that there is a lot more to it than any of us know. Marriages and divorces are such sticky and incredibly private things that it feels wrong even postulating. I can understand why they may have started the show in the first place—overwhelmed by the sudden increase in their family and unsure of how they would handle it financially—this show seemed like a great solution. But I think the heart of the show has always been the kids, and when it becomes drama about the marriage—I think it's time to turn the cameras off once and for all. There's nothing appealing to me about watching a real family fall apart on tv. Though I will say, that Kate's sort of hardened edge that has often annoyed me in the past—I think it's making her come off as incredibly well held together and strong right now.[40]

With the end of the marriage and Jon moving out of the house, the show was renamed *Kate Plus 8* for the 2010 and 2011 seasons. The show was canceled at season's end in 2011 after 150 episodes.[41] In the divorce decree, Kate retained ownership of their rural Pennsylvania home and primary custody of the children.

During the series run, Kate was raised from typical house frau to symbolic supermom. While she was lauded by right-to-life supporters for choosing to move forward with a multiple-child pregnancy, she was also criticized for being demanding and controlling as well as for dominating her husband. As the show's popularity grew, hating Kate Gosselin became sport among some. When the show's cancellation was announced in 2011, TVGuide.com reported: "Everyone who hates Kate can feel great. TLC has canceled *Kate Plus 8*, which continued the adventures of mother Kate Gosselin and her brood of eight kids minus ex-husband Jon."[42] Conversely, Kate Gosselin's fans admired her parenting pluck, aplomb, and ability to face raising eight small children without their father. Other fans simply liked to watch her hairstyle change or comment on her wardrobe and looks.

Kate's appearance, particularly her hair, was a hot topic on gossip shows and social media alike. TLC still maintains a "Kate's Hairstyles Slideshow" featuring the evolution of Kate's hair from "classic mommy look" to "hot pixie" to "the classic Kate Gosselin look established in 2007" to "total Hollywood glam."[43] Once Jon and Kate separated, she visually moved from goodwife to vixen with hair extensions and expert highlights, the TLC website noting "as we leave behind her rocky personal life, Kate smoothes out her look."[44] Her hair changes from brunette to platinum, becoming "an extension of her confident personality" as she "leaves her old life squarely behind her." She had a long, highlighted "choppy manageable mom-on-the-go look" when *Kate Plus 8* drew to a close.[45]

These images also demonstrate the way Kate was framed within the program. The first image of the hairstyle slideshow begins with Kate obviously posed for a typical family photo in a traditional cable-knit sweater and khakis with a lapful of babies. Her skin is pale, her hair is dark, and her teeth are slightly yellowed. The next image shows her on the floor in front of baby cribs wearing sweatpants and a T-shirt in what appears to be a casual snapshot, again covered in babies and holding a box of wipes. She wears little makeup and no jewelry. In the following image, her hair is cut, colored, and styled, she wears subtle makeup and pearl earrings, and her shirt is color-coordinated with that of her daughter, who is reaching out to her. Both are smiling, and the changing table and surrounding room appear immaculate. It looks like a typical commercial for household products or child's cough syrup. The next is another snapshot, this time with Kate carefully made up and playing with her children outside. The 2008 shot shows a much different Kate. She wears designer clothes, strings of pearls, and expertly applied makeup, and she seems much more formal and put together. Her appearance reeks of personal stylist. By 2009, she is comfortable in her designer duds and superstar sunglasses, her teeth are a blinding white, and her skin is a sun-kissed bronze. As her hair gets longer, her clothes become increasingly revealing, her tan darkens, and her teeth continue to lighten. She is slim, fashionable, and sexy. Over the course of seven years, we see a woman transition from mother to celebrity, from parent to manager. What began as a couple struggling to care for their brood ends with an appearance-obsessed prima donna and her posse of nannies, bodyguards, assistants, and children.

The topic of Kate and her beauty naturally leads to discussion of cosmetic surgery, including one she had during the show's early years. After Kate's abdomen stretched to carry six babies at one time—and eight babies within three years—plastic surgeon Lawrence Glassman offered to give her a tummy tuck free of charge. Kate filmed the surgery for an episode of *Sextuplets and Twins: One Year Later* on Discovery Health, the precursor show to *Jon & Kate Plus 8*. More than six years later, gossip magazines and websites buzz with talk of Kate's supposed plastic surgeries and face "filler" injections.[46] Only she and her medical staff know the truth. She is a fitness fanatic who runs marathons, so it is possible her good looks owe to exercise and a healthy diet. Plenty of "Kate through the years" photos are available online. People may judge for themselves how and why Kate Gosselin's appearance changed from run-of-the-mill mom to perfectly coiffed and dressed celebrity by 2010 and 2011 and why she posed in an itty-bitty bikini for the cover of a magazine.

Some fans felt sorry for Kate because, at times, Jon appeared to be child number nine, always making messes and unable to make decisions or take a stance without Kate's input. He seemed to like to play as much as the kids did. Others felt Kate was too hard on her husband and that she spoke to him in ways they found degrading. Whether you believed Kate married a slug or Jon married a shrew, the couple and their adorable eight children achieved high ratings for TLC. The phrase "Jon and Kate plus eight" was practically a household word by 2009 when their divorce moves and countermoves became daily news alongside gossip column headlines about Jon's extramarital affairs.

Years earlier, Kate had to leave her nursing job and concentrate full time on taking care of her children. After a couple of years, Jon left his job, too. Being reality TV parents became their full-time careers. After all, a highly rated national cable television show was a good way to pay the bills for a family of ten, and the arrangement let both parents be home with the children most of the time—except when they were away on a press junket or out promoting one of Kate's three books. When their marriage fell apart, Jon moved from their rural Pennsylvania home to New York. Kate stayed with the children while fans and haters speculated how the couple would pay for the stylish and travel-rich lifestyle the TLC paychecks had afforded them. Some thought Kate would return to nursing. Others wondered if she'd start another television show. A rumored show called *Twist of Kate* never materialized.[47] In November 2011, she took a job as a CouponCabin.com blogger, serving as a high-profile but money-saving mom dishing out tips.[48] In early episodes of the show, Kate often clipped coupons to help cover grocery and diaper bills, and she chided Jon when he picked up groceries without using the coupons she'd carefully clipped.

In early 2012, Kate Gosselin launched a business venture called "Sail with Kate!" The online advertisement invited people to sail with Kate on a Royal Caribbean cruise ship in August 2012.[49] In a press release, cruise bookers announced business was brisk, and although they had expected family reservations, they were getting many single reservations.[50] Kate is, after all, a beautiful thirty-six-year-old woman. She does, however, come with eight small children—a challenge few men would rush to accept.

Twisted Version of Womanhood and Motherhood

Although *Twist of Kate* never materialized as a TLC show, the title describes what happened to Kate Gosselin and the public perceptions of her as the goodwife as TV cameras peered into every aspect of her home, family, and personal life for seven years.

Just as mediated motherhood has been blurred and fractured along with other gender-based identity categories, contemporary culture fragments Kate Gosselin's roles.[51] Viewers are supposed to see her as a supermom patiently and meticulously rearing her large brood, a modern-day throwback to the days when our grandmothers and great-grandmothers routinely gave birth to eight children (and family legend had it that grandma raised eight or ten kids with ease).

As she attempts to be both a mother and a woman responsible for supporting eight children, her roles fracture and her persona blurs in front of the cameras. Is she a sexy thirty-six-year-old out on the town, pausing for paparazzi? Is she a breadwinner? Is she a maternal caretaker? It is clear from public reaction that the audience struggles to see her as all three: sexually attractive; a smart, ambitious breadwinner; and a committed, caring mother.

For Kate Gosselin, motherhood was supposed to function as her sole quest for personal completion. But the very act of filming motherhood and female behavior regulates both by "normalizing" through examples of appropriate and inappropriate mothering. The camera causes Kate to struggle with parenthood and personhood. As reality television mom extraordinaire, Kate Gosselin serves as both a role model and a warning: here is what happens if a woman dares attempt to be both parent and person. Here is what happens when the goodwife transforms into a sexual being, interpreted by many in the public as a whore.

The ever-present cameras in the Gosselin home split Kate's persona and personal life. To viewers, she morphed from "normal" to "abnormal" simply because they saw what happened on *Jon & Kate Plus 8* (the normal) and found out what really happened with their faltering marriage (the abnormal) via mainstream and gossip-oriented media. Ultimately, Kate Gosselin couldn't fit within the trope of changeless television mother for two reasons. First, the trope is unrealistic and even mythic. Second, as a divorced mother of eight small children and the more focused, ambitious, and responsible of the two parents, Kate was forced by financial circumstances to step out of the mom trope and into the earner role.

Somewhat remarkably, motherhood in today's culture still equates to morality. Motherhood, then, is easily paralleled with the Freudian Madonna/whore dichotomy, especially given the tropes of reality television. On camera and off, contemporary motherhood plays out as a test of personhood and character. Early on in *Jon & Kate Plus 8*, Kate Gosselin is legitimized by moral motherhood. Later, she is delegitimized by immoral motherhood as she steps outside the home, both as a woman and earner.

Ultimately, Kate Gosselin's fall from "moral motherhood" functions as a modern sexist fable to teach women proper behavior by providing "real" evidence of consequences for noncompliance. Via Kate Gosselin's "reality" tale, we learn that a finer line exists between Madonna and whore than most women imagined, and we see what happens when the quest for personhood—whether as earner, celebrity, or sexual being—causes a woman to step beyond strictly defined moral motherhood.

Notes

1. David Gauntlett, *Media, Gender, and Identity: An Introduction* (New York: Routledge, 2002).

2. Philip Green, *Cracks in the Pedestal: Ideology and Gender in Hollywood* (Amherst: University of Massachusetts Press, 1998).

3. Ann Burnett, "The Fast-Paced Lifestyle and Marriage: Cramming in Just One More Thing" (paper presented at the National Communication Association convention, Atlanta, GA, 2001).

4. Arlie Russell Hochschild, *The Second Shift: Working Parents and the Revolution at Home* (New York: Vining Press, 1989); Pat M. Keith and Robert B. Schafer, *Relationships and Well-Being over the Life Stages* (New York: Praeger Publishers, 1991); Barbara J. Risman, Maxine P. Atkinson, and Stephen P. Blackwelder, "Understanding the Juggling Act: Gendered Preferences and Social Structural Constraints," *Sociological Forum* 14 (2000): 319–44; Pepper Schwartz, "Quality of Life in the Coming Decades," *Society* 36 (1999): 55–60; Beth Anne Shelton, *Women, Men, and Time* (New York: Greenwood Press, 1992).

5. Scott Coltrane, *Gender and Families* (Thousand Oaks, CA: Pine Forge Press, 1998); Mary Beth Grover and Julie Androshick, "Financial Chemistry: Dual-Income Couples Share Tips for Marital and Financial Success," *Forbes*, June 14, 1999, 238; Michael Harvey and Danielle Weise, "Global Dual-Career Couple Mentoring: A Phase Model Approach," *Human Resource Planning* 21 (1998): 33–49; Ann Colin Herbst, "Married to the Job," *McCall's*, November 1996, 124, 130–33; Hochschild, *The Second Shift*; Jerry A. Jacobs and Kathleen Gerson, "Who Are the Overworked Americans?" *Review of Social Economy* 56 (1998): 442–59; Steven L. Nock, "The Problem with Marriage," *Society* 36 (1999): 20–27; "All Work and No Play," *Canada and the World Backgrounder* 62 (March 1997): 22–26.

6. PatriciaVoydanoff and Brenda W. Donnelly, "The Intersection of Time in Activities and Perceived Unfairness in Relation to Psychological Distress and Marital Quality," *Journal of Marriage and Family* 61 (1999): 739–45.

7. Keith and Schafer, *Relationships and Well-Being.*

8. Burnett, "The Fast-Paced Lifestyle."

9. Sylvia Gearing, "If I'm Such a Success, Why Do I Feel This Way?" *Executive Female* 18 (1995): 46–51.

10. Deneen Gilmour, "The 'Simple Life' for Sale: The Rhetorical Appeal of Nostalgic Homes," *American Communication Journal* 8 (2006), accessed January 25, 2012, http://www.ac-journal.org/?page_id=15; Deneen Gilmour, "Nostalgia for Sale: Extending Burke's Theory of Substance to Idealized Images of Home," *Kaleidoscope* 5 (2006): 57–72.

11. Ann Dally, *Inventing Motherhood: The Consequences of an Ideal* (New York: Schocken Books, 1982), 9.

12. Dally, *Inventing Motherhood*, 11.

13. Leslie A. Baxter, "A Dialectical Perspective on Communication Strategies in Relational Development," in *A Handbook of Personal Relationships: Theory, Research, and Interventions*, ed. Steve W. Duck (New York: John Wiley & Sons, 1998), 257–73; Leslie A. Baxter, "A Dialogic Approach to Relationship Maintenance," in *Communication and Relational Maintenance*, ed. Daniel J. Canary and Laura Stafford (San Diego: Academic Press, 1994), 233–54; Leslie A. Baxter, "Dialectical Contradictions in Relational Development," *Journal of Social and Personal Relationships* 7 (1990): 69–88.

14. Green, *Cracks in the Pedestal.*

15. Jean Hicks, "Economizing Family Values," review of *Hitting Home: Feminist Ethics, Women's Work, and the Betrayal of "Family Values,"* by Gloria H. Albrecht, *Cross Currents* 53 (2003): 122–25.

16. Green, *Cracks in the Pedestal,* 61.

17. "That catch phrase of conservative politics, 'family values,' has been discredited in the minds of many for its idealization of '*Leave it to Beaver*' culture . . . but the rhetoric of family values has proved remarkably resilient—morphing, as it did in the last election cycle, into localized 'prairie values,' 'Texas values,' and the even more curious, 'Arkansas values.'" Hicks, "Economizing Family Values," 1.

18. Gabriel Weiman, *Communicating Unreality: Modern Media and the Reconstruction of Reality* (Thousand Oaks, CA: Sage Publications, 2000), 124–125.

19. Diana M. Meehan, *Ladies of the Evening: Women Characters of Prime-Time Television* (Metuchen, NJ: Scarecrow Press, 1983).

20. Robert Harimon and John Louis Lucaites, "Public Identity and Collective Memory in U.S. Iconic Photography: The Image of 'Accidental Napalm,'" *Critical Studies in Media Communication* 20 (2003): 35–66.

21. Marsha L. Richins, "Social Comparison, Advertising, and Consumer Discontent," *American Behavioral Scientist* 38 (1995): 593–607.

22. Emma Price, "Reinforcing the Myth: Constructing Australian Identity in 'Reality TV,'" *Continuum: Journal of Media & Cultural Studies* 24 (2010): 456–57, doi: 10.1080/10304311003703157.

23. Barbara Welter, "The Cult of True Womanhood: 1820–1860," *American Quarterly* 18 (1966): 151–74.

24. "TLC," Discovery Communications, LLC, accessed January 25, 2012, http://adsales.discovery.com/networks/tlc.

25. "Cablevision Advertising Sales 2012," Cablevision Advertising Sales 2012, accessed January 25, 2012, http://www.cvadsales.com/network_tlc.html.

26. "Cablevision Advertising Sales 2012"; Erik H. Erickson, *Identity and the Life Cycle* (New York: W. W. Norton & Company, 1980).

27. "TLC."

28. "TLC TV Shows," Discovery Communications, LLC, accessed January 25, 2012, http://tlc.discovery.com/tv/tv-shows.html.

29. Vickie Bane, "The Gosselins Get Real," *People,* October 13, 2008, 70–75.

30. Bane, "Gosselins Get Real."

31. Bane, "Gosselins Get Real."

32. "Kate Gosselin," *People.com,* accessed April 8, 2012, http://www.people.com/people/kate_gosselin/0,,,00.html.

33. "*Jon & Kate Plus 8* on TLC," *TVGuide.com,* accessed April 8, 2012, http://www.tvguide.com/tvshows/jon-kate-plus-8/287169.

34. "*Jon & Kate Plus 8* on TLC."

35. "*Jon & Kate Plus 8*: Episode Guide," TLC, accessed January 28 2012, http://tlc.howstuffworks.com/tv/kate-plus-8/jon-and-kate-plus-8-season-1-episode-guide.htm.

36. "*Jon & Kate Plus 8*: Episode Guide."

37. "*Jon & Kate Plus 8*: Episode Guide."

38. "*Jon & Kate Plus 8*: Episode Guide."

39. "*Jon & Kate Plus 8*: Episode Guide."

40. laytonw5, "*Jon & Kate Plus 8* Episode Discussion: 'Turning 5 & the Future,'" *TVGuide.com,* accessed April 8, 2012, http://www.tvguide.com/tvshows/jon-and-kate-plus-8-2009/episode-1-season-5/turning-5-and-the-future/287169.

41. "*Jon & Kate Plus 8* on TLC."

42. "*Jon & Kate Plus 8* on TLC."

43. "Kate Gosselin's Changing Hairstyle Pictures," TLC, accessed April 8, 2012, http://tlc.howstuffworks.com/tv/kate-plus-8/kate-hairstyle-pictures.htm.

44. "*Jon & Kate Plus 8*: Episode Guide."

45. "*Jon & Kate Plus 8*: Episode Guide."

46. "Did Kate Gosselin Bring New Face to New Job?" *US Weekly*, accessed April 8, 2012, http://today.msnbc.msn.com/id/45401368/ns/today-entertainment/t/did-kate-gosselin-bring-new-face-new-job/#.TyJH7CPgJ.

47. Michelle Tauber, "Our Year of Change," *People*, June 7, 2010, 72–76.

48. "Kate Gosselin Gets Back to Work, Lines up New Job," Access Hollywood, accessed April 8, 2012, http://news.yahoo.com/kate-gosselin-gets-back-lines-job-203310656.html.

49. "Sail with Kate!" Alice Travel, accessed April 8, 2012, http://www.kategosselincruise.com.

50. "Join Reality Star Kate Gosselin on a Spectacular Ship," Kate Gosselin Cruise Caribbean, accessed January 26, 2012, http://www.kategosselincruise.com.

51. Gauntlett, *Media, Gender, and Identity.*

Bibliography

Access Hollywood. "Kate Gosselin Gets Back to Work, Lines up New Job." Accessed April 8, 2012. http://news.yahoo.com/kate-gosselin-gets-back-lines-job-203310656.html.

Alice Travel. "Sail with Kate!" Accessed April 8, 2012. http://www.kategosselincruise.com.

"All Work and No Play," *Canada and the World Backgrounder* 62 (March 1997): 22–26.

Bane, Vickie. "The Gosselins Get Real." *People*, October 13, 2008.

Baxter, Leslie A. "A Dialectical Perspective on Communication Strategies in Relational Development." In *A Handbook of Personal Relationships: Theory, Research, and Interventions*, edited by Steve W. Duck, 257–73. New York: John Wiley & Sons, 1998.

———. "A Dialogic Approach to Relationship Maintenance." In *Communication and Relational Maintenance*, edited by Daniel J. Canary and Laura Stafford, 233–54. San Diego: Academic Press, 1994.

———. "Dialectical Contradictions in Relational Development." *Journal of Social and Personal Relationships* 7 (1990): 69–88.

Burnett, Ann. "The Fast-Paced Lifestyle and Marriage: Cramming in Just One More Thing." Paper presented at the National Communication Association convention, Atlanta, Georgia, 2001.

Cablevision Advertising Sales 2012. "Cablevision Advertising Sales 2012." Accessed January 25, 2012. http://www.cvadsales.com/network_tlc.html.

Coltrane, Scott. *Gender and Families*. Thousand Oaks, CA. Pine Forge Press, 1998.

Dally, Ann. *Inventing Motherhood: The Consequences of an Ideal*. New York: Schocken Books, 1982.

Discovery Communications, LLC. "TLC." Accessed January 25, 2012. http://adsales.discovery.com/networks/tlc.

———. "TLC TV Shows." Accessed January 25, 2012. http://tlc.discovery.com/tv/tv-shows.html.

Erickson, Erik H. *Identity and the Life Cycle*. New York: W. W. Norton & Company, 1980.

Gauntlett, David. *Media, Gender, and Identity: An Introduction*. New York: Routledge, 2002.

Gearing, Sylvia. "If I'm Such a Success, Why Do I Feel This Way?" *Executive Female* 18 (1995): 46–51.

Gilmour, Deneen. "Nostalgia for Sale: Extending Burke's Theory of Substance to Idealized Images of Home." *Kaleidoscope* 5 (2006): 57–72.

———. "The 'Simple Life' for Sale: The Rhetorical Appeal of Nostalgic Homes." *American Communication Journal* 8 (2006). Accessed January 25, 2012. http://www.ac-journal.org/?page_id=15.

Green, Philip. *Cracks in the Pedestal: Ideology and Gender in Hollywood*. Amherst: University of Massachusetts Press, 1998.

Grover, Mary Beth, and Julie Androshick. "Financial Chemistry: Dual-Income Couples Share Tips for Marital and Financial Success." *Forbes*, June 14, 1999.

Harimon, Robert, and John Louis Lucaites. "Public Identity and Collective Memory in U.S. Iconic Photography: The Image of 'Accidental Napalm.'" *Critical Studies in Media Communication* 20 (2003): 35–66.

Harvey, Michael, and Danielle Weise. "Global Dual-Career Couple Mentoring: A Phase Model Approach." *Human Resource Planning* 21 (1998): 33–49.

Herbst, Ann Colin. "Married to the Job." *McCall's*, November 1996.

Hicks, Jean. "Economizing Family Values." *Review of Hitting Home: Feminist Ethics, Women's Work, and the Betrayal of "Family Values,"* by Gloria H. Albrecht. *Cross Currents* 53 (2003): 122–25.

Hochschild, Arlie Russell. *The Second Shift: Working Parents and the Revolution at Home*. New York: Vining Press, 1989.

Jacobs, Jerry A., and Kathleen Gerson. "Who Are the Overworked Americans?" *Review of Social Economy* 56 (1998): 442–59.

Kate Gosselin Cruise Caribbean. "Join Reality Star Kate Gosselin on a Spectacular Ship." Accessed January 26, 2012. http://www.kategosselincruise.com.

Keith, Pat M. and Robert B. Schafer. *Relationships and Well-Being over the Life Stages*. New York: Praeger Publishers, 1991.

laytonw5. "*Jon & Kate Plus 8* Episode Discussion: 'Turning 5 & the Future.'" *TVGuide.com*. Accessed April 8, 2012. http://www.tvguide.com/tvshows/jon-and-kate-plus-8-2009/episode-1-season-5/turning-5-and-the-future/287169.

Meehan, Diana M. *Ladies of the Evening: Women Characters of Prime-Time Television*. Metuchen, NJ: Scarecrow Press, 1983.

Nock, Steven L. "The Problem with Marriage." *Society* 36 (1999): 20–27.

People.com. "Kate Gosselin." Accessed April 8, 2012. http://www.people.com/people/kate_gosselin/0,,,00.html.

Price, Emma. "Reinforcing the Myth: Constructing Australian Identity in 'Reality TV.'" *Continuum: Journal of Media & Cultural Studies* 24 (2010): 451–9, doi: 10.1080/10304311003703157.

Richins, Marsha L. "Social Comparison, Advertising, and Consumer Discontent." *American Behavioral Scientist* 38 (1995): 593–607.

Risman, Barbara J., Maxine P. Atkinson, and Stephen P. Blackwelder. "Understanding the Juggling Act: Gendered Preferences and Social Structural Constraints." *Sociological Forum* 14 (2000): 319–44.

Schwartz, Pepper. "Quality of Life in the Coming Decades." *Society* 36 (1999): 55–59.

Shelton, Beth Anne. *Women, Men and Time*. New York: Greenwood Press, 1992.

Tauber, Michelle. "Our Year of Change." *People*, June 7, 2010.

TLC. "*Jon & Kate Plus 8*: Episode Guide." Accessed January 28 2012. http://tlc.howstuffworks.com/tv/kate-plus-8/jon-and-kate-plus-8-season-1-episode-guide.htm.

———. "Kate Gosselin's Changing Hairstyle Pictures." Accessed April 8, 2012. http://tlc.howstuffworks.com/tv/kate-plus-8/kate-hairstyle-pictures.htm.

TVGuide.com. "*Jon & Kate Plus 8* on TLC." Accessed April 8, 2012. http://www.tvguide.com/tvshows/jon-kate-plus-8/287169.

US Weekly. "Did Kate Gosselin Bring New Face to New Job?" Accessed April 8, 2012. http://today.msnbc.msn.com/id/45401368/ns/today-entertainment/t/did-kate-gosselin-bring-new-face-new-job/#.TyJH7CPgJ.

Voydanoff, Patricia, and Brenda W. Donnelly. "The Intersection of Time in Activities and Perceived Unfairness in Relation to Psychological Distress and Marital Quality." *Journal of Marriage and Family* 61 (1999): 739–45.

Weimann, Gabriel. *Communicating Unreality: Modern Media and the Reconstruction of Reality*. Thousand Oaks, CA: Sage Publications, 2000.

Welter, Barbara. "The Cult of True Womanhood: 1820-1860." *American Quarterly* 18 (1966): 151–74.

Chapter 3

Marriage, Friendship, and Scandal: Constructing a Typology of Media Representations of Women in *Desperate Housewives*

by Paula Hopeck and Rebecca K. Ivic

The constantly changing role of the "working woman" is represented differently across televised programming. Possibly the most famous example is the television series *Desperate Housewives*, which first aired in 2004. It began by focusing on four women's experiences with housework, marriage, divorce, children, and friendships. The show sparked newspaper articles nationwide about how the characters compare with real housewives.[1] *Desperate Housewives* focuses on four women who live seemingly blissful lives in an idyllic neighborhood—but in reality, this utopia is riddled with crime, scandal, and hardship. The all-knowing Mary Alice Young, whose narration in each episode provides the audience with much more information than the characters know about each other (and in some cases, themselves), reveals that lives in the suburbs are not as they seem.

Mass communication research has examined role representations for decades.[2] This chapter argues that role representation lends insight into themes and sensationalism derived from this popular television show. The present research examines the character portrayals in *Desperate Housewives* to better understand those role representations and uncover unique and relevant themes. More specifically, the study examines the range of themes that occurs throughout the show and how the characters consequently embody different traits. With approximately 13.1 million nightly viewers,[3] *Desperate Housewives* features a diverse set of richly developed characters, making it a compelling exemplar of the changing role of women's work.

The first season presents the problems faced by the four female protagonists (aptly described as homemakers and housewives in the first episode). Susan Mayer is a single mother of a teenage daughter. Her ex-husband, Karl, cheated on her with his secretary. Lynette Scavo is a former advertising executive who left her career to raise a family, which includes four misbehaving children all under the age of six. Bree van de Kamp is the obsessive-compulsive wife striving for suburban perfection with a husband and two children; in the first episode, this perfection is upended when Bree's husband asks for a divorce. A former model, Gabrielle Solis is married to a high-powered executive who showers her with gifts but is never home to provide her with companionship, thus prompting Gabrielle to begin an affair with her teenage gardener. None of the women appear happy in their position as housewife. Numerous burdens are explored through these four characters, including financial hardship and fragmented relationships between the wives and their children, husbands, ex-husbands, and in-laws. The problems established in the first season are themes that continue throughout subsequent seasons.

Media Representations of Working Women

In the 1970s and 1980s, substantial research was conducted on the topic of women and the workforce, from which by contrast we derive our conceptions of women who do not work outside the home.[4] Rosabeth Moss Kanter produced one of the more extensive works on women's involvement in corporations. Her ethnography centers on a company where the executives were typically men and the secretaries and receptionists were typically women. There were a few women in executive positions, although these women exhibited the "masculine"[5] traits expected in those roles. Women who sought executive positions were told the company was concerned that women would get married, spend more time with their children, or take more time off, which would indicate a lack of commitment to the company.[6] Kanter also noted the role wives played for husbands employed by the corporation. Often, the wives were also part of the representation of the company and contributed to the roles of their husbands, including hosting company events.[7] The female employees of the organization were also expected to establish good relationships with the male employees' wives; however, if wives became jealous of the female employees, they would suggest to their husbands not to promote the female employees.[8]

Television can create inaccurate perceptions of reality, especially when representing women at work and home.[9] As Atkin, Moorman, and Lin discuss, television producers have a wide-reaching impact on television portrayals.[10] At the time of their writing twenty years ago, the shows that predominantly featured working women were *Roseanne*, *Designing Women*, and *Murphy Brown*.[11] Television shows in the 1980s and 1990s often portrayed women working as secretaries, nurses, teachers, and household help.[12] During this era, women appeared more often on television, but these depictions did not represent women's real varying roles in the workplace and their homes.[13]

Television has since broadened its representations of women's roles, but highly sensationalized shows like *Desperate Housewives* challenge the idea of working women. In some instances, the show portrays women as highly sexualized, waiting for their husbands to arrive home from work. In others, the women are at an impasse, struggling between wanting to work and having to care for a household at the same time.

More than thirty years later, work-life balance issues still persist for women, and in some cases, for men as well.[14] As suggested by Jenkins, many women have to balance work, home, and possibly caring for aging parents.[15] Lyness and Judiesch conclude that promotion potential and the perception of work-life balance—two measures perceived to be in contention with each other in the 1970s—are increasingly complementary.[16] Social support, which has foundationally been defined as a communicative process,[17] is also an important factor for working individuals. Social support provides interpersonal resources that address the "strain inherent in living."[18] A transactional process, social support typically occurs in voluntary ways through relationships such as friendships.[19]

The scholarly literature indicates that the topic of working women—and the contrast created by its silence on women who do not earn a paycheck—has intrigued researchers for decades. What remains unanswered is whether *Desperate Housewives* parallels the literature, if the concerns of feminist scholars are reflected in the show, and how the role of housewife is constructed. The goal of this chapter is to determine which themes construct the role of housewife in *Desperate Housewives*.

Method

In this study, we examine the first season of *Desperate Housewives* (2004–2005) as the primary data set. We exclude the special episode "Sorting out the Dirty Laundry" because the special episodes are syntheses of the season and characters. While watching all twenty-three episodes, we noted scenes and dialogue that addressed issues of work specifically for women (in general or about a specific character). These include but are not limited to discussions about parenting, running a household, cleaning, cooking, and being a wife. Additionally, we noted when a female character referred to a career held prior to being a "housewife" and when other characters referenced a career previously held by a female character.

Once the notes were compiled, we discussed the emerging themes, which we developed based on Owen's thematic analysis of forcefulness, repetition, and recurrence.[20] Forcefulness is indicated by a change in the normal delivery of dialogue (increased volume, for example). Repetition occurs when the characters consistently use the same wording to describe work. Recurrence is indicated by a similar connotation of work, although the characters may have used different words to discuss it.

We then used Owen's thematic analysis to construct a typology while guided by the constant-comparative method[21] of using the data to develop and evolve theory. This method allowed us to code the data by generating categories based on the themes.[22] Comparing each theme and the resulting examples in the first season of *Desperate Housewives* helped us richly interpret the data and answer the present research questions while organizing a hierarchy of the overarching themes most represented in the show. This typology serves as a foundation on which further research can be developed.

We constructed the typology using Research Ware's Hyper Research 2.8 software.[23] We entered the data themes in the Code List Editor and connected the themes to create a "code map" of relationships. Although many themes emerged from the data, we looked only at those that answered our two research questions.

Following the work of Vande Berg and Streckfuss, we considered a major (or foreground) character one "whose speaking and action role served an important plot function."[24] For the purposes of this research, we paid special attention to characters described in voiceover by Mary Alice Young, the omniscient housewife who provides insight that only the audience and certain characters are privy to, thus indicating the character would serve an important function in that episode or eventually in the series. Mothers (and mothers-in-law) of characters were also given particular attention as comparisons with main characters and generational perceptions of work.

Analysis and Results

The following themes emerged as central to the role of women and work in *Desperate Housewives*: careers, scandal, and social support. Careers appear to take a back seat to scandal, but the subtlety of careers is what constructs many of the storylines in the first season. The most obvious concerns Lynette, who is introduced in the first episode as a successful businesswoman who (it is implied) stays home with her children because her husband suggests it. Lynette struggles with being a mother, particularly with controlling her three sons. Throughout the season, her apparent failure at parenting is presented in stark contrast to her success in business. She tells a former colleague whom she meets in a grocery store that being a mother "is the best job ever." A wiser Mary Alice lets the audience know this is pure sarcasm. In the second episode, Lynette is pulled over by a police officer because her children are misbehaving while she is driving. The officer tells her to control her children because "it is her job." In the next episode, Lynette's lack of help is confirmed when she and Tom are invited to a dinner party hosted by the van de Kamps. Lynette is excited about going, but Tom wants to stay in because he is tired. To a weary Lynette holding a laundry basket in a messy kitchen, Tom flippantly says, "You remember what it was to *work* a sixty-hour week." In the end, Tom agrees to stay home with the children while Lynette goes to the party. As Lynette outlines her instructions for taking care of the children, Tom says, "They're just kids." Lynette's new job is dismissed by her husband, who has no idea what she does. Even Lynette has trouble coming to terms with the fact that she is no longer as successful as she was.

Lynette, however, is also savvy at leveraging her former career to alleviate some of her responsibilities. When her children become too much for their teachers to handle, Lynette considers the possibility that she might have to home-school them. The other option is to make a donation to a private school so her children will be accepted. The only way to make the donation is for Tom to sell his boat. Tom at first resists the idea, until Lynette reminds him that she sacrificed her career—which was more successful than his—and now it is his turn to sacrifice. Lynette gives Tom a choice between selling the boat so the children can go to private school and him home-schooling the children while she goes to work. Tom agrees to sell the boat.

Gabrielle is the other housewife who had a career prior to marriage: modeling. She often refers to her modeling days and what she achieved before she moved to the suburbs. Although often portrayed as being spoiled by husband Carlos Solis, Gabrielle has earned many of the material goods in her house with her modeling money. Additionally, when Carlos is arrested for importing goods manufactured by slave labor and their bank accounts are frozen, it is Gabrielle who "comes out of retirement" to earn money. To hide their financial problems, she tells her friends she is modeling for fun, not work.

After being fired from one of her modeling assignments, Gabrielle must take a job working at a cosmetics counter, which does not appear to last for longer than the episode. From then on, Gabrielle and Carlos continue to hide their financial problems. Although Gabrielle does not work, she finds ways to save—such as stealing a portable toilet when their sewage system backs up. Although Gabrielle does not work in a traditional sense, she uses what she learned from the modeling business in her current position as housewife.

Scandal

For the women of *Desperate Housewives*, part of the job description of wife involves family scandal. Every episode features outrageous behavior in the form of mysteries, murders, and plots. For example, Gabrielle attempts to sabotage Carlos throughout the show, but as Carlos faces imprisonment and the possibility of losing their home arises, Gabrielle ensures she gets to keep the house.

In another narrative arc, Lynette tries to sabotage Tom's job out of fear he is having an affair with his coworker Annabelle. Lynette has lunch with one of her former colleagues in an attempt to find Tom another job. The colleague is hesitant about hiring Tom, so Lynette suggests Annabelle instead.

When the women gather together, they perpetuate this notion of scandal by discussing neighborhood rumors. One evening, Susan, Lynette, Gabrielle, and Bree are playing card games together and gossiping about how Maisy Gibbons's sex client list is likely going to be released. We see the shock on each of their faces.

Most troubled by this news is Bree, whose husband (Rex) is a former client of Maisy's. Bree appears to be the target of the most scandals on Wisteria Lane. Although she does not engage in acts of sabotage, she is often the object of sabotage herself. In one episode, Rex has a heart attack while in the company of Maisy Gibbons. Rex patronizes Maisy because he likes to be dominated during sex, something prim and proper Bree abhors. Yet she resigns herself to the wifely dominatrix task, striving to keep it a secret. While still appearing to love Rex, Bree begins a friendship with George Williams, the local pharmacist. George is obsessed with Bree, even going so far as to fill Rex's prescription with a potentially dangerous medication. Although he pretends to just want a friendship with Bree, George's feelings are eventually revealed. Bree feels betrayed, prompting George to break into her house, where George discovers Rex's secret. He tells Bree he learned about it by overhearing Rex's friends. Bree, now feeling betrayed by Rex, confronts a weakened Rex, who protests any deception and then has another heart attack. Rex dies in the final episode of Season One, right after leaving Bree a note that reads, "I understand and I forgive you," thinking she had intentionally poisoned him. After learning of Rex's death, the normally composed Bree genuinely sobs in her dining room.

Social Support

Evident in almost every episode of *Desperate Housewives* is some form of social support. Most episodes depict the wives getting together in the evening to play games and gossip. This demonstrates social support because the women have a common interest in connecting with each other and talking about the latest events in the neighborhood.

Social support often appears in the form of the four main characters supporting each other, although this support is nuanced. For example, Lynette's addiction to ADD medication becomes evident when she leaves her children with Susan and drives off. Prior to this meltdown, Lynette is on the phone with Tom, who is away on a business trip. Obviously getting no support from Tom, Lynette finds comfort in Susan and Bree. After finding her alone in the park and listening to how she became addicted to ADD medication, Susan and Bree reassure her. They say having four young children is difficult and she just needs to get some assistance. Lynette protests, arguing that other mothers raise their children well without any help. Susan tells Lynette she was "out of her mind every day" when Julie was younger, and Bree confesses she "used to use [Danielle and Andrew's] naptimes to cry." Lynette tearfully tells Susan and Bree that mothers need to talk to each other about these struggles. Although Lynette still needs help with her children, she no longer takes the ADD medication. In this example, the theme of social support is foregrounded as a service the housewives provide for each other.

Typology

The primary themes that emerged from the analysis (careers, scandal, social support, children as weapons, and children as gifts) are represented in the typology. To connect these themes, we examine their underlying characteristics.

The characters' social relationships are at the heart of the primary themes. Social relationships contribute to the characters' supportiveness toward each other. Social support emerges when the women advise each other in situations with difficult children, potential break-ups, and marital difficulties. These sessions typically occur during informal gatherings such as game night or seeing each other in the neighborhood.

The typology indicates how many of the experiences are centered on the social relationships among the characters. Social relationships can lead to the positive aspect of social support between friends or romantic partners. On the other hand, scandal also results from social relationships. Children can be used as weapons that lead to scandal or to avoid scandal. They may also be gifts, serving as symbols of accomplishment. Kids may be tied to successful careers or ones marred by scandal. Retirement is related to careers, but retirement may also cause scandal within a specific industry. The themes reveal a larger structure of nuances in the relationships and portrayals of characters in *Desperate Housewives.*

Discussion

The general themes in this analysis parallel the role of housewife in the media and scholarly literature. The show represents an increase in the number of women featured on television—not just the housewives but also the mothers and daughters of the protagonists. Cuddy, Fiske, and Glick's conclusion that women are either respected or liked but not both is also subtly addressed in *Desperate Housewives*, particularly in the case of Lynette, who primarily identifies as a former executive rather than a housewife.[25] Lynette also appears, however, to enact the research of Rosabeth Kanter. As the wife of an executive, Lynette is responsible for hosting dinner parties and being an important support for Tom. She sabotages Annabelle when she becomes jealous of all the time Tom spends with her, reinforcing themes from Kanter's work about wives of corporate executives. This example demonstrates that perhaps television has not advanced as much as one would hope as far as the role of women is concerned. Where it does excel, however, is in demonstrating the importance of social support,[26] particularly among women who rely on each other to get through difficult times.

Demographically, the show appears to be changing with the times, featuring a variety of types of families, including divorced, separated, married, and married with children (Susan, Bree, Gabrielle, and Lynette respectively). Additionally, the Solises occupy a prominent role in the series, whereas Latinos have typically been underrepresented on television. Regrettably, both Gabrielle and Carlos are criminals, which does nothing to counteract stereotypes.[27] Bree's conservative Christianity also parallels research on the connection between religion and the decision to become a housewife.[28] It is never clear why Bree becomes a housewife (the other characters have explicit reasons), but her religion is one possibility.

Now in its eighth and final season at the time of this writing, the characters in *Desperate Housewives* still face similar dilemmas to those introduced in the opening season. The notable difference is that at the endpoint of the show, the housewives have shifted toward careers. Susan is an art teacher's aide, Lynette returns to a job in advertising, Bree owns a business, and Gabrielle accepts modeling jobs.

Notes

1. Kellie B. Gormly, "*Desperate Housewives*? Not Today's Homemakers," *Pittsburgh Tribune-Review*, February 15, 2005; Alessandra Stanley, "Me, Myselves, and I: Disparate Housewife," *New York Times*, January 15, 2009.

2. Travis L. Dixon and Daniel Linz, "Overrepresentation and Underrepresentation of African Americans and Latinos as Lawbreakers on Television News," *Journal of Communication* 50 (2000): 136–37; Jake Harwood and Karen Anderson, "The Presence and Portrayal of Social Groups on Prime-Time Television," *Communication Reports* 15 (2002): 85; Glenn G. Sparks and Robert M. Ogles, "The Difference Between Fear of Victimization and the Probability of Being Victimized: Implications for Cultivation," *Journal of Broadcasting & Electronic Media* 34 (1990): 353–54.

3. Ronald Grover and Andy Fixmer, "'*Desperate Housewives*' Hold out for Pay Raise at ABC," *Bloomberg*, accessed January 14, 2011, http://www.bloomberg.com/news/2011-01-13/-desperate-housewives-hold-out-for-pay-raise-in-drama-at-abc.html.

4. Alan Booth, David R. Johnson, Lynn White, and John N. Edwards, "Women, Outside Employment, and Marital Instability," *American Journal of Sociology* 90 (1994): 570; Myra Marx Ferree, "Working-Class Jobs: Housework and Paid Work as Sources of Satisfaction," *Social Problems* 23 (1976): 433–34; Cecilia L. Ridgeway, "Predicting College Women's Aspirations from Evaluations of the Housewife and Work Role," *Sociological Quarterly* 19 (1978): 281–82.

5. Rosabeth Moss Kanter, *Men and Women of the Corporation* (New York: Basic Books, 1977), 22–23.

6. Kanter, *Corporation*, 66–67.

7. Kanter, *Corporation*, 105.

8. Kanter, *Corporation*, 107.

9. Michael Elasmar, Kazumi Hasegawa, and Mary Brain, "The Portrayal of Women in U.S. Prime Time Television," *Journal of Broadcasting and Electronic Media* 43 (1999): 25–26; Nancy Signorielli and Susan Kahlenberg, "Television's World of Work in the Nineties," *Journal of Broadcasting and Electronic Media* 45 (2001): 12–13.

10. David J. Atkin, Jay Moorman, and Carolyn A. Lin, "Ready for Prime Time: Network Series Devoted to Working Women in the 1980s," *Sex Roles* 25 (1991): 680.

11. Atkin, Moorman, and Lin, "Ready for Prime Time," 677.

12. Signorielli and Kahlenberg, "Television's World of Work," 20.

13. Elasmar, Hasegawa, and Brain, "The Portrayal of Women," 33; Nancy Signorielli, "Television and Conceptions About Sex Roles: Maintaining Conventionality and the Status Quo," *Sex Roles* 21 (1989): 359; Signorielli and Kahlenberg, "Television's World of Work," 12–13.

14. Karen S. Lyness and Michael K. Judiesch, "Can a Manager Have a Life and a Career? International and Multisource Perspectives on Work-Life Balance and Career Advancement Potential," *Journal of Applied Psychology* 93 (2008): 800.

15. Carol L. Jenkins, "Women, Work, and Caregiving: How Do These Roles Affect Women's Well-Being?" *Journal of Women & Aging* 9 (1997): 40.

16. Lyness and Judiesch, "Can a Manager Have a Life?" 800–801.

17. Brant R. Burleson, Terrance L. Albrecht, Daena Goldsmith, and Irwin G. Sarason, introduction to *Communication of Social Support: Messages, Interactions, Relationships, and Community*, ed. Brant R. Burleson, Terrance L. Albrecht, and Irwin G. Sarason (Thousand Oaks, CA: Sage Publications, 1994), xii.

18. Geoff Leatham and Steve Duck, "Conversations with Friends and the Dynamics of Social Support," in *Personal Relationships and Social Support*, ed. Steve W. Duck with Roxane Cohen Silver (London: Sage Publications, 1990), 2.

19. Burleson, Albrecht, Goldsmith, and Irwin, introduction, xiii; Carolyn E. Cutrona, Julie A. Suhr, and Robin MacFarlane, "Interpersonal Transactions and the Psychological Sense of Support," in *Personal Relationships and Social Support*, ed. Steve W. Duck with Roxane Cohen Silver (London: Sage Publications, 1990), 31–32.

20. William Foster Owen, "Interpretive Themes in Relational Communication," *Quarterly Journal of Speech* 70 (1984): 275.

21. Barney Glaser, *Theoretical Sensitivity: Advances in the Methodology of Grounded Theory* (N.p.: Sociology Press, 1978), quoted in Anselm L. Strauss, *Qualitative Analysis for Social Scientists* (Cambridge: Cambridge University Press, 1987), 22.

22. Juliet Corbin and Anselm Strauss, *Basics of Qualitative Research*, 3rd ed. (Thousand Oaks, CA: Sage Publications, 2008), 160.

23. Research Ware, Hyper Research (Version 2.8) [Software], 2007, http://www.researchware.com.

24. Leah R. Vande Berg and Diane Streckfuss, "Prime-Time Television's Portrayal of Women and the World of Work: A Demographic Profile," *Journal of Broadcasting and Electronic Media* 36 (1992): 197.

25. Amy J. C. Cuddy, Susan T. Fiske, and Peter Glick, "When Professionals Become Mothers, Warmth Doesn't Cut the Ice," *Journal of Social Issues* 60 (2004): 711.

26. Burleson, Albrecht, Goldsmith, and Irwin, introduction, xii; Cutrona, Suhr, and MacFarlane, "Interpersonal Transactions," 31–32.

27. Signorielli and Kahlenberg, "Television's World of Work," 142.

28. Darren E. Sherkat, "'That They Be Keepers of the Home': The Effect of Conservative Religion on Early and Late Transitions into Housewifery," *Review of Religious Research* 41 (2000): 354.

Bibliography

Atkin, David. J., Jay Moorman, and Carolyn A. Lin. "Ready for Prime Time: Network Series Devoted to Working Women in the 1980s." *Sex Roles* 25 (1991): 677–85.

Booth, Alan, David R. Johnson, Lynn White, and John N. Edwards. "Women, Outside Employment, and Marital Instability." *American Journal of Sociology* 90 (1984): 567–83.

Burleson, Brant R., Terrance L. Albrecht, Daena J. Goldsmith, and Irwin G. Sarason. Introduction to *Communication of Social Support: Messages, Interactions, Relationships, and Community*. Edited by Brant R. Burleson, Terrance L. Albrecht, and Irwin G. Sarason. Thousand Oaks, CA: Sage Publications, 1994.

Corbin, Juliet, and Anselm Strauss. *Basics of Qualitative Research: Techniques and Procedures for Developing Grounded Theory*. Thousand Oaks, CA: Sage Publications, 2008.

Cuddy, Amy J. C., Susan T. Fiske, and Peter Glick. "When Professionals Become Mothers, Warmth Doesn't Cut the Ice." *Journal of Social Issues* 60 (2004): 701–718.

Cutrona, Carolyn E., Julie A. Suhr, and Robin MacFarlane. "Interpersonal Transactions and the Psychological Sense of Support." In *Personal Relationships and Social Support*, edited by Steve W. Duck with Roxane Cohen Silver, 30–45. London: Sage Publications, 1990.

Dixon, Travis L., and Daniel Linz. "Overrepresentation and Underrepresentation of African Americans and Latinos as Lawbreakers on Television News." *Journal of Communication* 50 (2000): 131–54.

Elasmar, Michael, Kazumi Hasegawa, and Mary Brain. "The Portrayal of Women in U.S. Prime Time Television." *Journal of Broadcasting and Electronic Media* 43 (1999): 20–34.

Ferree, Myra Marx. "Working-Class Jobs: Housework and Paid Work as Sources of Satisfaction." *Social Problems* 23 (1976): 431–41.

Glaser, Barney. *Theoretical Sensitivity: Advances in the Methodology of Grounded Theory*. N.p.: Sociology Press, 1978.

Gormly, Kellie B. "*Desperate Housewives*? Not Today's Homemakers." *Pittsburgh Tribune Review*, February 15, 2005.

Grover, Ronald, and Andy Fixmer. *Bloomberg*. "'Desperate Housewives' Hold out for Pay Raise at ABC." Accessed January 14, 2011. http://www.bloomberg.com/news/2011-01-13/-desperate-housewives-hold-out-for-pay-raise-in-drama-at-abc.html.

Harwood, Jake, and Karen Anderson. "The Presence and Portrayal of Social Groups on Prime-Time Television." *Communication Reports* 15 (2002): 81–97.

Jenkins, Carol L. "Women, Work, and Caregiving: How Do These Roles Affect Women's Well-Being?" *Journal of Women & Aging* 9 (1997): 27–45.

Kanter, Rosabeth Moss. *Men and Women of the Corporation*. New York: Basic Books, 1977.

Leatham, Geoff, and Steve Duck. "Conversations with Friends and the Dynamics of Social Support." In *Personal Relationships and Social Support*, edited by Steve Duck with Roxane Cohen Silver, 1–29. London: Sage Publications, 1990.

Lyness, Karen S., and Michael K. Judiesch. "Can a Manager Have a Life and a Career? International and Multisource Perspectives on Work-Life Balance and Career Advancement Potential." *Journal of Applied Psychology* 93 (2008): 789–805.

Owen, William Foster. "Interpretive Themes in Relational Communication." *Quarterly Journal of Speech* 70 (1984): 274–87.

Research Ware. Hyper Research (Version 2.8) [Software], 2007, http://www.researchware.com.

Ridgeway, Cecilia L. "Predicting College Women's Aspirations from Evaluations of the Housewife and Work Role." *Sociological Quarterly* 19 (1978): 281–91.

Sherkat, Darren E. "'That They Be Keepers of the Home': The Effect of Conservative Religion on Early and Late Transitions into Housewifery." *Review of Religious Research* 41 (2000): 344–58.

Signorielli, Nancy. "Television and Conceptions About Sex Roles: Maintaining Conventionality and the Status Quo." *Sex Roles* 21 (1989): 341–60.

Signorielli, Nancy, and Susan Kahlenberg. "Television's World of Work in the Nineties." *Journal of Broadcasting & Electronic Media* 45 (2001): 4–22.

Sparks, Glenn G., and Robert M. Ogles. "The Difference Between Fear of Victimization and the Probability of Being Victimized: Implications for Cultivation." *Journal of Broadcasting & Electronic Media* 34 (1990): 351–58.

Stanley, Alessandra. "Me, Myselves, and I: Disparate Housewife." *New York Times*, January 16, 2009.

Strauss, Anselm L. *Qualitative Analysis for Social Scientists*. Cambridge: Cambridge University Press, 1987.

Vande Berg, Leah R., and Diane Streckfuss. "Prime-Time Television's Portrayal of Women and the World of Work: A Demographic Profile." *Journal of Broadcasting and Electronic Media* 36 (1992): 195–210.

Chapter 4

Ancient Archetypes in Modern Media

by Deborah A. Macey

In her book *Gendered Lives*, Julia T. Wood describes four stereotypes of women in the workplace: the iron maiden, sex object, child, and mother. The iron maiden is defined as independent, ambitious, competitive, and masculine. Often perceived as a bitch, she is the woman who rises through the ranks in male-dominated professions. The sex object characterizes women solely by their sexuality, conforming to heterosexist norms of beauty. The child represents women as less competent than men; her work is trivialized and undervalued. The mother provides comfort and support to coworkers. In addition to and despite her professional title, the mother-as-worker's duties involve fixing coffee, acting as secretary, and planning social events.[1]

In this chapter, I argue that the characters found in the television shows *Golden Girls*, *Living Single*, and *Sex and the City* reflect these four archetypes. Archetypal representations exist in every culture, in the West harking back at least as far as Greek mythology;[2] their articulations, however, must be culturally specific to make the characters relevant to modern audiences. It is important not only to identify these patterns but also to contextualize them by describing how meaning is created and sustained through these representations as well as how they are complicated by factors of age and race.

Recombinant Television, Stereotypes and Archetypes, and Media Representations

Recombinant Television

In our mediated world, television serves as our modern storyteller, teaching us about the world as myths of earlier oral cultures once did. It is commonplace to see the same characters reappearing in television narratives. Over the past two decades, viewers have been inundated with the White male working class buffoon and his sexy, more sophisticated, and sometimes surly wife. Examples include *King of Queens* (1998–2007), *According to Jim* (2001–2009), *Everybody Loves Raymond* (1996–2005), and *The Simpsons* (1989–present). These representations are not a new phenomenon; they have been present throughout television history in series such as *The Honeymooners* (1955–1956), *All in the Family* (1971–1979), and *The Flintstones* (1960–1966). Sociologist Todd Gitlin calls this reworking of similar characters and themes recombinant television.[3] There are many reasons formulaic characters and programs continue to appear, including cost reductions and time constraints. Networks avoid risk by incorporating formulas that have proven success.[4] More importantly, Butsch asserts that the prevalence of the working class buffoon "illustrates ideological hegemony, the dominance of values in mainstream culture that justify and help to maintain status quo."[5] The prevailing understandings in the White, working class recombinant sitcom depict working class men as incompetent and in need of supervision, thus legitimizing their lower class status.[6]

With regard to personal, heterosexual relationships, the working class buffoon is portrayed as the likeable but inept partner/father figure, incapable of cleaning or watching children, thus reinforcing gender expectations and constructing the female partner as the neurotic, nagging, domestic shrew who bullies her husband like a domineering tyrant. This maintains women's position as the natural guardian of the private sphere. Television is not simply entertainment but a powerful socializing agent that shapes and reflects contemporary culture, requiring that we not only recognize these prevalent portrayals but also investigate their meanings.

Archetype and Stereotypes

Carl Jung introduced the idea of archetypes in psychology as primordial forms in the collective *un*conscious expressed through myth and fairytale.[7] Archetypes are frameworks or structures, not specific content, that reflect latent, pre-existing patterns of behavior. In television, archetypes manifest as the broad blueprint of the recombinant characters. Unlike stereotypes that are often negative, specific, and historical, these character types are fluid and shifting. While Jung asserts that archetypes are "empty and purely formal,"[8] they are imbued with meanings that are often unconsciously assumed and rarely interrogated.

Bolen asserts that archetypes "evoke feelings and images, and touch on themes that are universal and part of our human inheritance."[9] Bolen suggests that these shared understandings are conveyed through archetypal stories. If television is a modern-day storyteller, then it makes sense that television producers would use evocative archetypes to capture audiences. In addition, the lack of interrogation allows patterns to persist and become naturalized within cultural norms, ringing true to our understanding of human nature.[10] Each culture's ideological social, economic, and political systems can be projected onto an archetype. These archetypes placed within a hegemonic system can then become stereotypes.

Stereotypes are overly simplistic, one-dimensional, and generally negative types that are used to define an entire group. While stereotypes can change over time, they usually become concretized within specific cultural contexts. Ramírez Berg asserted that stereotypes are the sum of "category making" (archetypes) plus ethnocentrism and prejudice used by in-groups to characterize and thus marginalize out-groups.[11] Stereotypes relate to power relations among groups. Similar archetypes are used to categorize different marginalized groups, thus creating negative stereotypes that are used to justify historic and institutionalized oppression. For example, the Asian American Fu Man Chu, African American buck, Latin American bandito, and Native American savage stereotypes are all derived from a masculine archetype. While the archetype is the general pattern or form, the stereotypical representations portray these figures and ultimately their representative groups as hyper-violent, hypersexualized, and uncivilized. These negative representations create fear among White Americans and are used to justify exclusion, exploitation, enslavement, seizure of property, and extermination.[12]

Feminine stereotypes such as the African American Jezebel, Native American princess, Latin American harlot, and Asian American dragon lady are derived from the sex object archetype. While Aphrodite, the Greek mythological embodiment of the sex object archetype, has both good and bad qualities, the racialized stereotypes focus on the negative and are used to oppress these marginalized groups.[13] While the media often employ stereotypes, particularly for its villains, they also tap into these easily recognizable archetypal patterns and reflect them back to audiences.

While Jung discusses archetypes in terms of a collective unconscious and Bolen maintains that real women embody goddess characteristics, this chapter understands archetypes as part of a collective media consciousness and the archetypal portrayals as an ideological vehicle for reflecting contemporary women's experiences. The term "archetype" represents the broad patterns of typical characters commonplace in the media. These character types are not stereotypes in the way stereotypes are often negative and concretized but instead are malleable. Carrying cultural ideology in their mediated representations, they have been updated to reflect current cultural values and norms.

Media Representations

Recurring characters and formulas are not only typical of male-lead programs as discussed with the White male working class buffoon, but they are also present in series with female leads. After discovering Wood's stereotypical workplace roles for women,[14] I began to see the iron maiden, sex object, child, and mother everywhere, re-presented in ways that seem normal and natural to audiences. They are found in music lyrics such as Meredith Brooks's "Bitch," films such as *Mona Lisa Smile* and *The Sisterhood of the Traveling Pants*, and literature such as the American classic *Little Women*. This quartet also appears in the three television shows included in this study: *Golden Girls*, *Living Single*, and *Sex and the City*. At first glance, these shows appear to be about different people: older White women in suburban Miami, Florida; twenty-something African American women in Brooklyn, New York; and thirty-something White professional women in Manhattan. Each series was seen as groundbreaking: *Golden Girls* for its prominence of older women in primetime, *Living Single* for its focus on Black actors and producers, and *Sex and the City* for its frank discussions of sex. This essay, however, reveals striking similarities among them.

Textual Analysis

This textual analysis expands Dow's analysis of five prime-time television series, specifically *Designing Women*'s use of the archetypal quartet.[15] Dow argues that television serves a "distinctive rhetorical function in defining feminism."[16] This chapter uses the rhetorical function of television to explore not only the discourse of feminism in popular culture but also the discourses of gender, age, race, and sexuality. The selection of these series offers a sample of U.S. women of different ages and races across a twenty-year timeframe. *Golden Girls* ran from 1985 to 1992 on NBC and is still in syndication on the Hallmark Channel. *Living Single* was a part of FOX's narrowcasting programs from 1993 to 1998 and remains in syndication on Oxygen. *Sex and the City* arose from HBO's original programming in 1998. HBO produced new shows for six seasons and sold edited versions for syndication on TBS. The characters in *Golden Girls*, *Living Single*, and *Sex and the*

City are reincarnations of similar archetypes, reflecting Gitlin's notion of recombinant television.[17] While each series is lauded as original, these recombinant characters indicate otherwise.

Golden Girls

In *Golden Girls*, Rose (Betty White) embodies the child. While Rose was occasionally sexual or demonstrated nurturance, her overwhelming characteristics conform to the child archetype. Blanche (Rue McClanahan) embodies the experienced sex object. Comments made by and about her often reference her many sexual exploits. Dorothy (Bea Arthur) dominantly represents the iron maiden archetype. While Sophia (Estelle Getty) has a smaller role in the first season, she at times embodies the iron maiden but more dominantly represents the mother archetype. The characters are established immediately. In the opening scene of the first episode, Dorothy enters complaining about a new generation of students where she teaches. Her grumblings reflect the cynical, self-righteous tone of the iron maiden. Rose is upset because there are too many sad people where she works. Dorothy reminds her that she works in grief counseling. Rose's lack of common sense marks her as the child. Blanche's entrance signifies her as the sex object. She is wearing fur, representing her upper class status, and has cucumbers on her eyes to maintain her youthful appearance. Blanche states provocatively that she doesn't "need them on her thighs," implying that her thighs are as lovely as ever.[18]

Markers of age pervade this series. For example, in the first episode, Dorothy says, "I would kill to be 40 again." She continues talking about how, when with a group of 20-something teachers, she had forgotten that she was older than them and when she looked in the mirror, she didn't recognize the person staring back at her. Rose responds, "Who was it?"[19]

When Sophia first appears in the scene, she is met by Dorothy, who shouts curiously, "Ma?" marking Sophia as the mother archetype.[20] While Sophia's representation does not always fall neatly into the mother archetype, she embodies the ethnic mother stereotype from the old country, complete with stories from Sicily, her pocketbook secured tightly to her arm, a slap on the back of the head if you have done something wrong, and enough Italian cooking to feed an army. When it is suspected that Sophia might be having a heart attack, she continues to offer the doctor food she spent the day cooking. Sophia not only wants the doctor to eat, but she also wants to see his delighted expression about the good taste.[21] When Sophia does not fit into the mother archetype, she generally becomes the iron maiden with her quick-witted, sarcastic remarks about herself and others. For example, Sophia says Blanche "looks like a prostitute," calls Blanche's boyfriend a "scuzzball," and tells Rose to "get a poodle" to cure her loneliness.[22]

Sophia's dialogue marks her as old. In response to Dorothy suggesting she should see a doctor because she looks pale, Sophia states, "I'm an old White woman. You want color, talk to Lena Horne."[23] In another episode, Sophia informs Rose that the man in her bed is dead. Rose questions Sophia in disbelief. Sophia responds, "You don't think I'd recognize death? I lived in a retirement home. Death visited more often than children."[24] Sophia moves beyond the mother archetype because her age allows her the freedom to step out of rigid mothering roles set for women. She can be flippant and funny instead of nurturing. Because age and aging are such prominent features in this series, a distortion of archetypes occurs. Even so, Dorothy, Blanche, Rose, and Sophia represent the archetypal patterns of iron maiden, sex object, child, and mother respectively. While *Golden Girls* offers viewers portrayals of women beyond their thirties, the repetitive nature of these archetypal mediations provides a limited and sometimes caricatured representation of women.

Living Single

As in *Golden Girls*, the characters on *Living Single* immediately fall into the four archetypes. With her hopeful outlook and wide-eyed expressions, Synclaire (Kim Coles) represents the child. Regine (Kim Fields) embodies the sex object. Although she has fewer sexual encounters than the other characters, her sex object status stems mostly from her superficial focus on appearance, need to be desired by men, and belief in the magnetism of her own beauty. Max (Erika Alexander) symbolizes the iron maiden. Max's career as a lawyer and her antagonism toward men reflect this status. As the lead of this series, Khadijah (Queen Latifah, née Dana Owens) represents the mother archetype.

In the first scene of episode one, Synclaire sits at her desk wearing an oversized newsboy cap. As she answers the phone in a strange accent, Khadijah questions her. Synclaire responds, "I'm making them think we're international."[25] Khadijah's questioning resembles that of a mother with a teenage daughter who has recently acquired the style and persona du jour of her peers. This first scene establishes the dynamic between the child and mother archetypes. Khadijah supports Synclaire by employing her at the office of *Flavor*, a magazine about urban African American culture. This contributes to Khadijah's standing as the mother by giving her a venue to provide advice and solace to the Black community. Regine, who works at an upscale boutique, enters the scene wearing a short skirt, low-cut blouse, and high heels. She brags about her new man, "Good news . . . couldn't wait for you to get home to rub your noses in it . . . the stretch limo outside belongs to my new boyfriend." She continues talking about how they went out for lunch but "never made it out of the limo . . . he ate caviar from my cleavage, and we drank champagne from my shoes . . . he could be the one . . . he is fine, educated, wealthy, and has a butt with dents on the side with the promise of power." Khadijah admonishes Regine, "You need to start looking beyond the man's wallet."[26] This exchange explicitly portrays Regine as the sex object and Khadijah as the mother. In her first appearance, Max embodies the iron maiden when she swaggers into the apartment and boasts, "My look and my law were fierce . . . don't touch me unless you want to get burned." She has short, angular braids and often wears suits. In addition to her shortened masculine name, Max carries a briefcase to signify her powerful position as a successful lawyer. When discussing her divorce case, Max declares, "Someone's got to protect women's rights,"[27] reflecting the iron maiden archetype as the carrier of a feminist agenda.

Later in this same episode, Synclaire discovers that Regine's boyfriend is married. Like a child, Synclaire cannot contain herself, blurting this news out to Regine. To comfort Regine, Khadijah puts her arm around her and says, "Look . . . listen, as much as I love to be right—and you know mother does love to be right—I wish I was wrong this time, but girl, the man is married."[28] "Look" and "girl" are linguistic indicators of their racial identity as Black women. In this particular case, "girl" marks solidarity among the women, whereas "Look" acknowledges the position Khadijah is taking with Regine might cause strife.[29] Khadijah calls herself a mother while also providing consolation, which is representative of the mother archetype. Khadijah further advises, "You have to start taking care of yourself." Regine says, "You're right, Khadijah." Khadijah responds to the camera, "Mother always is."[30] Khadijah refers to herself as "Mother," but she also exemplifies the iron maiden as she is often the voice of reason among the group. This representation of the strong, independent but nurturing mother reflects the Black mother's need to be self-reliant and stoic to prepare herself and her children for the harsh realities of racial oppression. bell hooks says this "strong black woman is practically deified in black life" and "makes care for material well-being synonymous with the practice of loving."[31] Khadijah's representations of the mother archetype, intersected by race, allow her to simultaneously embody mother and iron maiden archetypes.

When the iron maiden is intersected by race as in the case of Max, the archetype becomes hypersexualized. Max's suits, while representative of her high-powered position in the masculine domain of law, are often so short her power seems derived from sexuality. This is an example of Max's embodiment of the iron maiden and sex object archetypes. Another example of the iron maiden archetype acting in a sexualized way occurs when Max, consumed by her sexual needs, leaves her friends to have sex.[32] While she dominates men in her relationships, Max sexually objectifies herself. These disruptions to the archetypes in *Living Single* reflect notions of race, specifically the strong, independent mother and the hypersexualized black body. hooks connects this idea of the hypersexual woman of color to the colonization of the Black body. This body is seen as a site for exotic, otherworldly, and primitive pleasure.[33] Sexualizing Max, who portrays the iron maiden, diminishes the power, strength, and independence this archetype typically characterizes. This sexualization turns Max from a feminist iron maiden to a sex-crazed buffoon.

Sex and the City

Since this show revolves around sex, all of the characters are sexualized even though they fall distinctly into the archetypal patterns. Charlotte's (Kristin Davis) prescribed romantic ideals of love and marriage, prim and proper demeanor, and ultrafeminine style place her neatly in the child archetype. Samantha (Kim Cattrall) portrays the sex object archetype with a zeal never before seen on television. She loves her body and indulges its every desire. Miranda (Cynthia Nixon) personifies the iron maiden archetype. As a lawyer, she is in a highly masculine profession. She dominates the men she dates and is cynical of their affections.

As the voice-over narrator, Carrie (Sarah Jessica Parker) serves as the primary storyteller and connecting character: the mother archetype. The narratives revolve around social and sexual relationship mores, which Carrie grapples with while doing "research" for her columns. Carrie ponders whether women can have "sex like men"—that is, without feeling.[34] The other characters seek Carrie's motherly counsel, particularly Charlotte the child. Charlotte contemplates having a threesome with her boyfriend, Jack, and confides in Carrie about a dream she had. Carrie advocates, "Dreams are a good way to experiment." When Charlotte asks, "Do you think it means I should do it?" Carrie responds, "It's your call, but don't do it just to make Jack happy." Charlotte suggests, "But maybe it will bring us closer." Carrie responds, "Sweetie, don't you think it's weird you are thinking about sleeping with someone you don't know to get closer to Jack?" Charlotte queries,

"How well do we ever know the people we sleep with?" In a voiceover, Carrie describes Charlotte, "That was the thing about Charlotte, just when you were about to write her off as a Park Avenue Pollyanna, she'd say something so right on you'd think she was the Dali Lama." Charlotte interrupts this narration, "Do you think my hair is too shiny today?" Carrie continues, "And then she'd say something else."[35] This exchange establishes the characters of Carrie and Charlotte as mother and child archetypes respectively. While Carrie offers comfort and advice, Charlotte asks silly, childlike questions.

Charlotte embodies the child archetype in other ways, specifically through her controlled sexuality. Even though she considers having a threesome with her boyfriend, sexual experimentation is out of character for Charlotte. This is confirmed in the same episode when Carrie asks in a voice-over, "If Charlotte was actually considering a threesome, who wasn't?"[36] If the sweet, proper, naïve Charlotte would contemplate a threesome, it must be conventional. Charlotte finds herself in other uncomfortable sexual situations as she tries to negotiate the narrow boundaries between the good girl who "plays by the rules" and the adult single woman dating in Manhattan. In one episode, Charlotte's boyfriend wants to have anal sex with her. Again, she confides in Carrie for advice. In a hilarious cab scene, each archetype weighs in on the subject. Carrie arranges to pick up the other women because Charlotte "needs all the girl support" she can get. For Carrie, the mother, this issue is about demonstrating support. For the iron maiden, Miranda, the issue is power: "It's all about control. . . . If he goes up there, either he'll have the upper hand, or you will. . . . The question is if he goes up your butt, will he respect you more or less? . . . That's the issue." Samantha, the sex object, chimes in, "Front, back, who cares? A hole is a hole. . . . This is a physical expression that the body was designed to experience and P.S., it's fabulous." For Samantha, everything is about sexual pleasure. Charlotte ends this exchange still confused, "What are you talking about? I went to Smith," implying this is not proper talk for her genteel upbringing. Ultimately, Charlotte decides she cannot be "the up-the-butt girl" because "men don't marry the up-the-butt girl . . . whoever heard of Mrs. Up-the-Butt . . . no, no, no . . . I can't. I want children and nice bedding."[37] While Charlotte's embodiment of the child positions her as uptight, her decision not to compromise for the man's desire demonstrates real strength in understanding what is right for her, even if her reasoning is lacking.

In opposition to Charlotte's prudishness, Samantha embodies the sex object archetype with fervor, constantly and explicitly describing her sexual exploits. For example, Samantha sleeps with the young chef of a new restaurant her public relations firm is promoting. The morning after, Samantha calls Carrie, "I am so fucked . . . I mean literally . . . I have been fucked every way you can be fucked." Carrie stops her, chiding, "If you keep talking like that I'm going to have to charge you by the minute." Samantha continues, "Him on top, me on top, me on my side . . . on his side, on his face . . . have you ever done that? . . . Do it immediately."[38] Samantha's sexuality is essentialized.

Miranda Hobbs is the sarcastic cynic of the group, especially when it comes to love. She is the epitome of the ambitious liberal feminist career woman, pointing out the double standards between the sexes and offering legal assistance when necessary. She believes in equality but not in romantic fairy tales. Miranda is seen as sexually unappealing for a threesome when the other women exclude her from their choice of sexual third.[39] This notion of the sexually unappealing iron maiden is significant because it reflects the real-life backlash suggesting unattractive women believe in feminism because they are unable to get a man. Miranda wears big, masculine business suits and wears her stark red hair in a blunt cut. In one scene, her suit comes with a masculine tie. In this same scene, Miranda says in response to Carrie's concern about her new relationship, "It's not like we're throwing out our schedules."[40] For the iron maiden, career trumps matters of the heart.

Discussion

The archetypes of the iron maiden, sex object, child, and mother appear in all three series and function ideologically to produce different discourses of women. Depending on how the characters are represented, their discourse can be privileged or trivialized.

The Iron Maiden Archetype

At best, the ideological function of the iron maiden is to carry a feminist perspective. At worst, this character is simply perceived as bitchy. If the iron maiden is portrayed as the buffoon as in the case in *Murphy Brown*, Dow asserts that feminist perspective is depicted as a cautionary tale rather than a progressive agenda.[41]

Both Miranda from *Sex and the City* and Max from *Living Single* are lawyers working at big firms; their vocation upholds rather than challenges patriarchal systems. Serving as the feminist archetype, these characters are progressive only in the sense that they depict women as highly paid professionals who can compete with men in the public sphere. Dorothy's job as a high school teacher might seem like feminized work; however, she is the only character in *Golden Girls* with a career. As a divorcée, Dorothy knows the importance of being independent, and she has experienced the struggles a woman faces when a marriage dissolves. She lives in a culture where, after a divorce, men's standard of living rises while women's drops significantly.[42] Men tend to remarry within a year after a divorce—generally to younger women.[43] Dorothy's circumstances reflect these inequities as she shares rent with and cares for her mother while her ex-husband remarries younger women. Although Max and Miranda point out some gender inequities, they do not experience the consequences, whereas Dorothy lives them.

Of the three iron maidens, Dorothy's perspective is the most privileged, Max's stance is the most ridiculed, and Miranda develops the fullest throughout the series. While sometimes portrayed as masculine and unattractive, Dorothy is always depicted as smart. Her perspective is privileged because she is the voice of reason in the group. Dorothy's appearance might be ridiculed, but her progressive ideas rarely are, thus privileging a feminist perspective. Of the three series, *Golden Girls* is the most feminist, in part because of Dorothy's privileging and in part because the series tackles many social issues, specifically addressing the impact on older women. I would assert that because of the age of the women in this series, adhering to gender norms is less compulsory.

Max is the most ridiculed and therefore least feminist character of the three iron maidens, although more feminist than the child and sex object archetypes within *Living Single*. While Max has a powerful career, dominates the men in her life, and spouts comments about the women's movement, her buffoon-like and hypersexualized performances discount her feminist import. Her histrionics are humorous, but her superficial feminist stance lacks Dorothy's depth and privilege. Khadijah, the mother archetype, assumes this more feminist perspective in *Living Single*.

Miranda's viewpoint is less privileged, often neutralized or ridiculed. Unlike her iron maiden cohort, Miranda's character develops over the course of the series. Her masculine façade and unattractiveness soften, she wears fewer business suits and more dresses, and her hair color lightens from a sharp red to a strawberry blonde.

Without an iron maiden archetype, a feminist message cannot be maintained within a series. Hubert argues that after Ellen DeGeneres came out on her sitcom, the series was unable to maintain a gay rights political agenda. While Hubert attributes this apathy to network fears and DeGeneres's own aversion to this kind of platform,[44] I argue that *Ellen* lacked the iron maiden archetype character to carry a progressive agenda. This series consists of Ellen Morgan (Ellen DeGeneres), a caregiving and connecting character reflective of the mother archetype; Paige Clark (Joley Fisher), the sex object archetype; and Audrey Penney (Clea Lewis), who becomes the chipper optimist, a child archetype with a squeaky voice. Without the iron maiden, *Ellen* simply did not have a character to voice feminist politics.

The Sex Object Archetype

Samantha, Regine, and Blanche embody the sex object archetype in *Sex and the City*, *Living Single*, and *Golden Girls* respectively. Although each of these characters owns her sexuality, this archetype has little substance beyond sex. While these characters are reduced to their sexual exploits, they can still be powerful characters in that they unabashedly own their sexuality, desire sex for their own pleasure, and genuinely love their bodies. Lorde describes the erotic as powerful: "Our most profoundly creative source . . . when I speak of the erotic, I speak of it as an assertion of the life force of women: of that creative energy empowered, the knowledge and use of which we are now reclaiming in our language, our history, our dancing, our loving, our work, our lives."[45] Since women's sexuality has historically been a source of constraint and vulnerability,[46] seeing these sex objects celebrate their sexualities sends a powerful message. Because they are so often ridiculed, the celebration of self is displaced with self-absorption.

Blanche's most progressive aspect is that she revels in her own beauty and makes it known how much and how often she enjoys sex. While this same statement can be made about the other women, it is more significant for Blanche because of her age. Older women are commonly portrayed in the media as sexless;[47] Blanche shatters these narrow views with her many "sexcapades." While Blanche is progressive in some ways, she pits herself against the other women, often putting down the others' appearance to praise her own, presenting her as a less feminist character.

While Blanche's sexual drive might have been considered outrageous in the eighties, *Sex and the City*'s Samantha raises the sex object archetype to a new art form. Samantha's sexual encounters are unapologetically about pleasure, not commitment. As with Blanche, her sexuality is often so over the top, one might miss the significance of this character and reduce her to debauchery. Although Samantha grows somewhat toward the end of the series when she commits to a partner, she, like Blanche, develops very little and is often reduced to a sexual joke. It is interesting that a series touted for its sexual progressiveness depicts a stagnant and regressive sex object archetype. This reductive focus on one aspect of a person's character reflects experiences gay men and lesbian women encounter as their identities are oftentimes reduced solely to their sexuality.

Unlike her sex object cohort, Regine uses sex as a tool to get what she wants. She finds pleasure in sex but seeks to "get a man" to support her in the pretentious lifestyle she has fashioned for herself. Regine's performance of gender, race, and class parallels Helen Gurly Brown's "Cosmo Girl," a malleable identity with a beautiful and moneyed aura to capture a man from a higher class. Regine epitomizes this "beautiful phony" as she focuses on snaring a man dishonestly.[48] Regine's performance is disempowering for women. As she develops beyond this archetype, Regine's role in the series diminishes, and she leaves before the series finale. The series is not left without a sex object archetype as Max's hypersexualized performance fulfills this role.

The Child Archetype

The characters Rose (*Golden Girls*), Synclaire (*Living Single*), and Charlotte (*Sex and the City*) portray the child archetype. This child archetype carries traditional values, harking back to a simpler time. Charlotte, Synclaire, and Rose's portrayals of the child archetype reduce women to little girls. Each child archetype is optimistic about life and love. The child archetype portrays a naiveté that seems ridiculous in adult women. She is dismissed and disparaged even when her discourse is important. This is typical of Rose and Synclaire. Charlotte, while still naïve, is not portrayed as dimwitted, and therefore her discourse has import. Even though their circumstances change, Rose and Synclaire do not develop throughout the series. They are as simple and optimistic in the first season as they are in the last. Charlotte's character, on the other hand, develops throughout the series, and this provides some privileging of the discourse surrounding her. This privileging reflects tenets of third-wave feminism's desire for the feminine as well as some modern feminist backlash.

Charlotte is complex and contradictory. She lives by antiquated rules in a modern urbane setting. While her character is not one-dimensional, her focus on marriage is problematic. Charlotte challenges the virgin/whore dichotomy while trying to maintain a "good girl" image. Media messages that portray girls in this virgin/whore dichotomy are ubiquitous. Girls are told to be virtuous yet alluring and sexual.[49] This is not only a dangerous image for girls, but it is impossible. The three child archetypes embody the virgin/whore dichotomy when depicted as sexual prudes, but once in a sanctioned relationship they exhibit an uninhibited sexual prowess, thus legitimizing this impossible virgin/whore mediated expectation.

The Mother Archetype

Sophia of *Golden Girls*, Khadijah of *Living Single*, and Carrie of *Sex and the City* represent the mother archetype. These archetypes contain the most variance, although there are some similarities. The most defining mother characteristic is storytelling.

Sophia typifies the ethnic mother stereotype. She tells stories about the "old country." This stereotypical embodiment of the mother archetype and her age contribute to her static role. While there are some beautiful mother/daughter moments in *Golden Girls*, Sophia is reduced to an eccentric old woman. Compared to the other women in the series, she has a smaller role packed with punchlines. Sophia does not serve as the connecting character to the others in the series as Khadijah and Carrie do. This minor role may reflect our societal devaluation of seniors, particularly senior women, or the reduced role mothers play in their adult daughters' lives. It might also illustrate the role reversal that sometimes occurs when adult children care for their aging parents. While Sophia provides some nurturing, she basically serves as the tactless voice pointing out the flaws in the other characters. Age gives Sophia permission to act in such ways as she feels less bound by feminine social norms.

Khadijah and Carrie each serve as the star vehicle and connecting character in their respective series, privileging their discourse. Each plays a motherly character the others seek out for counsel. Both are advice-giving journalists: Khadijah owns her own magazine and Carrie writes her own column. Khadijah, as the owner of a Black urban magazine, also serves as the conveyor of culture for her community. Her role is much more feminist than the other two mother archetypes and even Max, the iron maiden in *Living Single*. Khadijah is the voice of reason. She provides physical and monetary support to her younger cousin Synclaire, the child archetype. Khadijah is feminist in her independence, both in the workplace and in relationships. This portrayal of the strong, independent Black "mother" is typical in Black communities.[50]

As the *Sex and the City* narrator, Carrie has a privileged omnipresence. Her role is much less feminist than Khadijah's as she tries to remain the neutral observer. Carrie's most empowering impact on social norms involves her interrogation of dating mores, although she often quells the feminist discussion in the series through her neutrality. She is wrought with insecurities. As much as these insecurities drive the narratives of the series, they also reduce Carrie's feminist import.

Conclusion

Golden Girls, *Living Single*, and *Sex and the City* all contain representations of the iron maiden, sex object, child, and mother archetypal patterns. While each series is praised as groundbreaking, the archetypal representations indicate otherwise. *Golden Girls* highlights older women; *Living Single* breaks many racial barriers in television; and *Sex and the City* portrays the intimate lives and friendships of women, but their archetypal representations limit the diversity of women's roles in television. In addition, these archetypes function in specific ways. If the series contains a feminist perspective, the iron maiden generally voices it, whereas the child archetype represents more traditional values. In general, the sex object archetypes portray an individualized notion of sexual freedom for women, and the mother archetype serves as a connecting character. Since television serves as our modern storyteller, reflecting hegemonic norms and values, these limited representations in television's most popular series contribute to society's understanding of women's roles and thus hinder further advancements toward diversity and equality.

Notes

1. Julia T. Wood, *Gendered Lives: Communication, Gender, and Culture* (Belmont, CA: Wadsworth Publishing Company, 1997).

2. The iron maiden, sex object, child, and mother archetypes are represented by the goddesses Artemis, Aphrodite, Persephone, and Demeter respectively. See Jean Shinoda Bolen, *Goddess in Everywoman: A New Psychology of Women* (New York: Harper & Row Publishers, 1984) and Christine Downing, *The Goddess: Mythological Images of the Feminine* (New York: Continuum Publishing Company, 1981).

3. Todd Gitlin, *Inside Primetime* (New York: Pantheon Books, 1983).

4. Gitlin, *Inside Primetime*; Richard Butsch, "Ralph, Fred, Archie, and Homer: Why Television Keeps Re-Creating the White Male Working Class Buffoon," in *Gender, Race, and Class in Media: A Text-Reader*, ed. Gail Dines and Jean McMahon Humez (Thousand Oaks, CA: Sage Publications, 2003), 575–85.

5. Butsch, "Ralph, Fred, Archie, and Homer," 576.

6. Butsch, "Ralph, Fred, Archie, and Homer."

7. Carl Gustav Jung, *Archetypes and the Collective Unconscious* (New York: Bollingen Foundation, 1959).

8. Jung, *Archetypes*, 79.

9. Bolen, *Goddess in Everywoman*, 6.

10. Bolen, *Goddess in Everywoman*; Stuart Hall, "The Work of Representation," in *Representation: Cultural Representations and Signifying Practices*, ed. Stuart Hall (Thousand Oaks, CA: Sage Publications, 2003), 13–74.

11. Charles Ramírez Berg, *Latino Images in Film: Stereotypes, Subversion, and Resistance* (Austin: University of Texas Press, 2002), 15.

12. Donald Bogle, *Toms, Coons, Mulattoes, Mammies, and Bucks: An Interpretive History of Blacks in American Films* (New York: Continuum International Publishing Group, 2004); Peter X. Feng, *Identities in Motion: Asian American Film and Video* (Durham, NC: Duke University Press, 2002); Chyng Feng Sun, "Ling Woo in Historical Context: The New Face of Asian American Stereotypes on Television," in *Gender, Race, and Class in Media: A Text-Reader*, ed. Gail Dines and Jean McMahon Humez (Thousand Oaks, CA: Sage Publications, 2003), 656–64; Jacquelyn Kilpatrick, *Celluloid Indians: Native Americans and Film* (Lincoln, NE: University of Nebraska Press, 1999); Ramírez Berg, *Latino Images in Film*; Ronald Takaki, *A Different Mirror: A Historical Multicultural America* (Boston: Back Bay Books, 1993).

13. Bogle, *Toms*; Feng, *Identities in Motion*; Feng Sun, "Ling Woo"; Kilpatrick, *Celluloid Indians*; Ramírez Berg, *Latino Images in Film*; Takaki, *A Different Mirror*.

14. Wood, *Gendered Lives*.

15. Bonnie J. Dow, *Prime-Time Feminism: Television, Media Culture, and the Women's Movement Since 1970* (Philadelphia: University of Pennsylvania Press, 1996).

16. Dow, *Prime-Time Feminism*, 6.

17. Gitlin, *Inside Primetime*.

18. "The Engagement," *Golden Girls*, performed by Bea Arthur, Betty White, Rue McClanahan, and Estelle Getty (September 14, 1985, Witt/Thomas/Harris Productions, NBC).

19. "The Engagement."

20. "The Engagement."

21. "The Heart Attack," *Golden Girls*, performed by Bea Arthur, Betty White, Rue McClanahan, and Estelle Getty (November 23, 1985, Witt/Thomas/Harris Productions, NBC).

22. "The Engagement."

23. "The Triangle," *Golden Girls*, performed by Bea Arthur, Betty White, Rue McClanahan, and Estelle Getty (October 19, 1985, Witt/Thomas/Harris Productions, NBC).

24. "In a Bed of Rose's," *Golden Girls*, performed by Bea Arthur, Betty White, Rue McClanahan, and Estelle Getty (January 11, 1986, Witt/Thomas/Harris Productions, NBC).

25. "Judging by the Cover," *Living Single*, performed by Queen Latifah, Kim Coles, Kim Fields, and Erika Alexander (August 29, 1993, SisterLee Productions, FOX).

26. "Judging by the Cover."

27. "Judging by the Cover."

28. "Judging by the Cover."

29. Karla Danette Scott, "'When I'm with My Girls': Identity and Ideology in Black Women's Talk About Language and Cultural Borders" (PhD diss., University of Illinois, Urbana-Champaign, 1995).

30. "Judging by the Cover."

31. bell hooks, "Living to Love," in *Women's Lives: Multicultural Perspectives*, ed. Gwyn Kirk and Margo Okazawa-Rey (Boston: McGraw Hill, 1993), 233.

32. "Living Kringle," *Living Single*, performed by Queen Latifah, Kim Coles, Kim Fields, and Erika Alexander (December 19, 1993, SisterLee Productions, FOX).

33. bell hooks, "Eating the Other," in *Black Looks: Race and Representation*, ed. bell hooks (Boston: South End Press, 1992), 21–39.

34. "Sex and the City," *Sex and the City*, performed by Sarah Jessica Parker, Kristin Davis, Kim Cattrall, and Cynthia Nixon (June 6, 1998, HBO Productions, HBO).

35. "Three's a Crowd," *Sex and the City*, performed by Sarah Jessica Parker, Kristin Davis, Kim Cattrall, and Cynthia Nixon (July 26, 1998, HBO Productions, HBO).

36. "Three's a Crowd."

37. "Valley of the Twenty-Something Guys," *Sex and the City*, performed by Sarah Jessica Parker, Kristin Davis, Kim Cattrall, and Cynthia Nixon (June 28, 1998, HBO Productions, HBO).

38. "Valley of the Twenty-Something Guys."

39. "Three's a Crowd."

40. "Valley of the Twenty-Something Guys."

41. Dow, *Prime-Time Feminism*.

42. Richard R. Peterson, "Re-Evaluation of the Economic Consequences of Divorce," *American Sociological Review* 61 (1996): 528–53.

43. Gwyn Kirk and Margo Okazawa-Rey, *Women's Lives: Multicultural Perspectives* (Boston: McGraw Hill, 2007).

44. Susan J. Hubert, "What's Wrong with This Picture? The Politics of Ellen's Coming out Party," in *Gender, Race, and Class in Media: A Text-Reader*, ed. Gail Dines and Jean McMahon Humez (Thousand Oaks, CA: Sage Publications, 1999), 608–12.

45. Audre Lorde, "Uses of the Erotic: The Erotic as Power," in *Women's Lives: Multicultural Perspectives*, ed. Gwyn Kirk and Margo Okazawa-Rey (Boston: McGraw Hill, 1984), 173.

46. Kirk and Okazawa-Rey, *Women's Lives*.

47. Jean Kilbourne, *Can't Buy My Love: How Advertising Changes the Way We Think and Feel* (New York: Touchstone, 1999).

48. Laurie Ouellette, "Inventing the Cosmo Girl: Class Identity and Girl-Style American Dreams," in *Gender, Race, and Class: A Text Reader*, ed. Gail Dines and Jean McMahon Humez (Thousand Oaks, CA: Sage Publications, 1999), 120.

49. Kilbourne, *Can't Buy My Love*.

50. hooks, "Living to Love."

Bibliography

Bogle, Donald. *Toms, Coons, Mulattoes, Mammies, and Bucks: An Interpretive History of Blacks in American Films*. New York: Continuum International Publishing Group, 2004.

Bolen, Jean Shinoda. *Goddess in Everywoman: A New Psychology of Women*. New York: Harper & Row Publishers, 1984.

Butsch, Richard. "Ralph, Fred, Archie, and Homer: Why Television Keeps Re-Creating the White Male Working Class Buffoon." In *Gender, Race, and Class in Media: A Text-Reader*, edited by Gail Dines and Jean McMahon Humez, 575–85. Thousand Oaks, CA: Sage Publications, 2003.

Dow, Bonnie J. *Prime-Time Feminism: Television, Media Culture, and the Women's Movement Since 1970*. Philadelphia: University of Pennsylvania Press, 1996.

Downing, Christine. *The Goddess: Mythological Images of the Feminine*. New York: Continuum Publishing Company, 1981.

Feng, Peter X. *Identities in Motion: Asian American Film and Video*. Durham, NC: Duke University Press, 2002.

Feng Sun, Chyng. "Ling Woo in Historical Context: The New Face of Asian American Stereotypes on Television." In *Gender, Race, and Class in Media: A Text-Reader*, edited by Gail Dines and Jean McMahon Humez, 656–64. Thousand Oaks, CA: Sage Publications, 2003.

Gitlin, Todd. *Inside Primetime*. New York: Pantheon Books, 1983.

Hall, Stuart. "The Work of Representation." In *Representation: Cultural Representations and Signifying Practices*, edited by Stuart Hall, 13–74. Thousand Oaks, CA: Sage Publications, 2003.

hooks, bell. "Eating the Other." In *Black Looks: Race and Representation*, edited by bell hooks, 21–39. Boston: South End Press, 1992.

———. "Living to Love." In *Women's Lives: Multicultural Perspectives*, edited by Gwyn Kirk and Margo Okazawa-Rey, 231–36. Boston: McGraw Hill, 1993.

Hubert, Susan J. "What's Wrong with This Picture? The Politics of Ellen's Coming out Party." In *Gender, Race, and Class in Media: A Text-Reader*, edited by Gail Dines and Jean McMahon Humez, 608–12. Thousand Oaks, CA: Sage Publications, 1999.

"In a Bed of Rose's." *Golden Girls*. Performed by Bea Arthur, Betty White, Rue McClanahan, and Estelle Getty. January 11, 1986, Witt/Thomas/Harris Productions, NBC.

"Judging by the Cover." *Living Single*. Performed by Queen Latifah, Kim Coles, Kim Fields, and Erika Alexander. August 29, 1993. SisterLee Productions, FOX.

Jung, Carl Gustav. *Archetypes and the Collective Unconscious*. New York: Bollingen Foundation, 1959.

Kilbourne, Jean. *Can't Buy My Love: How Advertising Changes the Way We Think and Feel*. New York: Touchstone, 1999.

Kilpatrick, Jacquelyn. *Celluloid Indians: Native Americans and Film*. Lincoln, NE: University of Nebraska Press, 1999.

Kirk, Gwyn, and Margo Okazawa-Rey. *Women's Lives: Multicultural Perspectives*. Boston: McGraw Hill, 2007.

"Living Kringle." *Living Single*. Performed by Queen Latifah, Kim Coles, Kim Fields, and Erika Alexander. December 19, 1993. SisterLee Productions. FOX.

Lorde, Audre. "Uses of the Erotic: The Erotic as Power." In *Women's Lives: Multicultural Perspectives*, edited by Gwyn Kirk and Margo Okazawa-Rey, 198–201. Boston: McGraw Hill, 1984.

Ouellette, Laurie. "Inventing the Cosmo Girl: Class Identity and Girl-Style American Dreams." In *Gender, Race, and Class: A Text Reader*, edited by Gail Dines and Jean McMahon Humez, 116–28. Thousand Oaks, CA: Sage Publications, 1999.

Peterson, Richard R. "Re-Evaluation of the Economic Consequences of Divorce." *American Sociological Review* 61 (1996): 528–53.

Ramírez Berg, Charles. *Latino Images in Film: Stereotypes, Subversion, and Resistance*. Austin: University of Texas Press, 2002.

Scott, Karla Danette. "'When I'm with My Girls': Identity and Ideology in Black Women's Talk About Language and Cultural Borders." PhD diss., University of Illinois, Urbana-Champaign, 1995.

"Sex and the City." *Sex and the City*. Performed by Sarah Jessica Parker, Kristin Davis, Kim Cattrall, and Cynthia Nixon. June 6, 1998. HBO Productions. HBO.

Takaki, Ronald. *A Different Mirror: A Historical Multicultural America*. Boston: Back Bay Books, 1993.

"The Engagement." *Golden Girls*. Performed by Bea Arthur, Betty White, Rue McClanahan, and Estelle Getty. September 14, 1985. Witt/Thomas/Harris Productions. NBC.

"The Heart Attack." *Golden Girls*. Performed by Bea Arthur, Betty White, Rue McClanahan, and Estelle Getty. November 23, 1985. Witt/Thomas/Harris Productions, NBC.

"The Triangle." *Golden Girls*. Performed by Bea Arthur, Betty White, Rue McClanahan, and Estelle Getty. October 19, 1985. Witt/Thomas/Harris Productions, NBC.

"Three's a Crowd." *Sex and the City*. Performed by Sarah Jessica Parker, Kristin Davis, Kim Cattrall, and Cynthia Nixon. July 26, 1998. HBO Productions. HBO.

"Valley of the Twenty-Something Guys." *Sex and the City*. Performed by Sarah Jessica Parker, Kristin Davis, Kim Cattrall, and Cynthia Nixon. June 28, 1998. HBO Productions. HBO.

Wood, Julia T. *Gendered Lives: Communication, Gender, and Culture*. Belmont, CA: Wadsworth Publishing Company, 1997.

Chapter 5

Christian Patriarchy Lite: TLC's *19 Kids and Counting**

by Christy Ellen Mesaros-Winckles

"Barefoot and pregnant" lost cachet decades ago, but in the world of the conservative Christian movement Quiverfull, the adage is alive and well. Nowhere is the image of a barefoot and pregnant wife more prevalent than on The Learning Channel's (TLC) reality television show *19 Kids and Counting,*[1] which brings viewers into the home of Michelle and Jim Bob Duggar and their nineteen children. Due to the popularity of their show, the Duggars have become the unofficial spokespeople for the Quiverfull movement.

Since the show premiered in 2008, the Duggars have published two books, *The Duggars! 20 and Counting*[2] and *A Love That Multiplies.*[3] They average thirty speaking engagements a year,[4] including appearances at Focus on the Family headquarters in Colorado Springs and on the radio program *Focus on the Family Daily.* While the Duggars regularly quote Psalm 127 (the Quiverfull theme Bible verse), support the Christian patriarchy organization Vision Forum, and espouse the virtues of having mega-sized families, they still refuse to classify themselves as "Quiverfull," denying the title in their latest book, *A Love That Multiplies*[5] and in numerous *People* magazine interviews.[6] Although they refuse to claim the label, the Duggars' theology leaves little doubt that they are the nation's most popular Quiverfull family.

The Duggar family's ideology is most prevalent in the show's first season, where they introduce themselves and their beliefs to the American public. In subsequent seasons, their religious beliefs are downplayed in the opening sequence as the show shifts its focus to the daily difficulties of managing the family's large size. Little of the warlike Quiverfull rhetoric is at the forefront. On the contrary, the Duggars paint a serene picture of life, their devotion to the family unit captivating both secular and Christian audiences. Yet subtle, disturbing messages emerge that many viewers easily overlook. Conformity and a rigid male leadership hierarchy often place women associated with the Quiverfull movement in subservient roles. *19 Kids and Counting* provides a platform for the Quiverfull movement to gain legitimacy by attempting to highlight the idyllic notions of the movement while downplaying patriarchal gender roles and strict family conformity.

---

*An earlier version of this chapter was published in *The Journal of Religion and Popular Culture* 22 (Fall 2010) under the title "TLC and the Fundamentalist Family: A Televised Quiverfull of Babies." Reprinted with permission.

In this chapter, I use feminist televisual narrative analysis[7] as a rhetorical framework to evaluate the moral messages presented in a television show from both a visual and textual perspective. This method allows multiple elements of *19 Kids and Counting* to be examined, including the nonverbal communication between family members, the set, clothing, and dialogue. Televisual narrative analysis relies heavily on Walter Fisher's narrative paradigm, which maintains that all rhetoric is laden with values and that narrative probability and narrative fidelity determine the persuasiveness of these values. Probability is defined as a coherent, logical story. Fidelity is the truth behind those stories as it rings true in the lives of the storytellers and the audience.[8] *19 Kids and Counting* establishes narrative probability as Duggar family life is played out on camera. Their religious beliefs provide fidelity to the story as the Duggars attempt to convince the audience their way is best for raising healthy, godly children. I focus on episodes from the first season and then conclude with the Season Nine finale, which details the family's continued belief that a large family is a biblical mandate. The episodes "Josh Gets Engaged," "Duggar Dating Rules," and "A Very Duggar Wedding" depict the strict dating expectations, relationship guidelines, and roles of women in the Quiverfull movement. I illustrate the increasing acceptance of the Quiverfull lifestyle by mainstream evangelical culture in the episode, "Duggars: All You Wanted to Know," which closes the eighth season of the show. The chapter ends with a description of how far the Duggars are willing to go to promote their theology amidst the events surrounding the miscarriage of their twentieth child, depicted in the ninth season finale "A Duggar Loss."

Understanding the Quiverfull Theology

Because Quiverfull adherents believe God should control family size, they do not practice any form of birth control and often have enormous families. The movement is a relatively small branch of the Christian faith, with adherents in the thousands to possibly low ten thousands from different fundamentalist and conservative evangelical denominations.[9] While the movement is small, the Duggars have brought it to the forefront of American popular culture. Until the Duggar family burst onto the cable television landscape, the Quiverfull movement had flown under the media radar for almost twenty years.

The television coverage has evolved from the family's first television special in 2004—*14 Children and Pregnant Again!*[10]—which premiered on TLC and was followed with three more television specials before the Duggars' current show began in 2008.[11] In 2010, *19 Kids and Counting* ranked in the top of the TLC lineup alongside shows such as *Kate Plus 8*, averaging at least a million viewers.[12]

While there may only be several thousand adherents of the Quiverfull movement, the Duggars have given it a prominent place in popular culture, attracting more media coverage than most larger religious groups ever receive. The movement first gained traction in the late 1980s through the writings of anti-feminist Mary Pride.[13] In her work, Pride preaches that the decline of the Christian family resulted from women seeking jobs outside the home and allowing other people to have control of their children's schooling and upbringing. The term "Quiverfull" did not come into widespread use until five years later, with Rick and Jan Hess's book *A Full Quiver: Family Planning and the Lordship of Christ.*[14] *A Full Quiver* stresses the importance of the Old Testament and the lifestyle of the ancient Israelites, who had large families, as the primary justification for the movement.

Given their belief that it is God's will for Christians to produce large families, those who practice the Quiverfull ideology oppose all forms of birth control, including natural family planning. Quiverfull families are also strong advocates of traditional domestic roles that center on male headship. Followers subscribe to a literal interpretation of scripture, citing both Old and New Testament passages about a woman's homemaker role and wifely submission to her husband's authority. They view homemaking and mothering as the higher calling for women, who should devote their lives to raising godly children.[15] At the core of Quiverfull beliefs is a gender ideology that stresses male headship and compliance to the movement's dogma.

Known to trigger cases of spousal abuse,[16] conservative views on male headship originate in literal readings of passages like Ephesians 5:22–23, "Wives, be subject to your own husbands, as to the Lord. For the husband is the head of the wife, as Christ also is the head of the church, He himself being the Savior of the body."[17] Women who believe in male headship and traditional family roles see nothing wrong with a literal biblical interpretation.[18] While more mainstream evangelical families find ways to maintain the traditional Christian rhetoric of male headship in a society that increasingly requires dual-income households,[19] Quiverfull families do not compromise on the belief that a woman's role is as a mother and homemaker. Any attempt to adapt to American culture is seen as giving in to secular society.[20]

The Quiverfull ideology is deeply rooted in dispensational Christian rhetoric, which focuses on the need to populate the world with Christians so that when Christ returns to earth, the children of these families will be "like arrows in the hand of a warrior." Bible passages such as Psalm 127:3–5 have become the foundation for Quiverfull dispensational dogma: "Behold, children are a gift of the Lord: the fruit of the womb is the reward. Like arrows in the hand of a warrior, so are the children of one's youth. How blessed is the man whose quiver is full of them; they shall not be ashamed when they speak with their enemies in the gate."[21] The movement's emphasis on creating a Christian army to fight against depravity and the moral downfall of society also places importance on creating the "right" type of Christian families, which takes on a decidedly racist overtone. This image comprises middle-class Caucasian families who are trying to out-populate Muslim, African, and Latin American countries to keep "enemies from the gate."[22]

Quiverfull Dating and Marriage

The Quiverfull ideology of male headship is best illustrated in the first season of the show when the Duggars' oldest son, Josh, marries after a courtship period. Courtship has gained widespread acceptance in both evangelical and fundamentalist Christian circles due to the success of books such as Joshua Harris's *I Kissed Dating Goodbye.*[23] Quiverfull adherents also follow this courtship routine, which requires the man and woman to spend long hours with each other's families. Only after the man has declared his intention to marry is the couple allowed to go on dates chaperoned by those other than their parents. The courtship process focuses heavily on the man taking the initiative and the woman responding to his overtures. This concept of male leadership in courtship reinforces the Quiverfull ideology of male headship in the home, where women have limited control over family size and family decisions. In the Duggar family, the courtship rules are rigid, as is evidenced when Josh Duggar gets engaged to Anna Keller, whom he met at a home-schooling conference.

Anna comes from an ultra-conservative Free Will Baptist family of eight children, and she shares Josh's Quiverfull beliefs about family planning. When Josh and Anna get engaged in the episode "Josh Gets Engaged," he flies down to her family's home in Florida for her twentieth birthday and proposes to her at a local restaurant. Throughout the entire engagement planning process, it is Anna's father, Mike Keller, and Josh who provide the most input for planning Anna's future. For example, before flying to Florida, Josh calls Mike Keller to ask his permission to court his daughter, saying, "I know I've talked with your daughter quite a bit, and I really feel like the Lord would be leading me into a relationship with her, and I was, ah, wanting to ask your permission to ask for your daughter's hand in marriage."[24] While buying balloons for Anna as an engagement/birthday present, Josh notes, "Courtship for me means boy meets girl, and then that young man goes to the father of that young lady and expresses his interest in his daughter, and once the father has given the permission, then this young man can then enter into a relationship with the daughter and get to know her better, and that's what I did with Anna."[25] Josh's courtship narrative focuses on male dominance. The decision to date and marry is not left up to the woman but is instead decided by her suitor and parents. Anna is not even consulted until after the decision has been reached.

Soon after Josh proposes, the couple drives to Arkansas to see Michelle and Jim Bob. Anna's parents later arrive at the Duggar house to meet their future in-laws and share in the celebration during the "Duggar Dating Rules" episode. When asked about Anna and Josh marrying young, Mike Keller notes, "She loves children. She's excited. And, you know, it's their decision. They . . . they want to trust the Lord also like Michelle and Jim Bob. They want to have all the children that God wants to give them."[26] This ideal of submission to familial norms is further evidenced by the way the children interact with their parents and the women interact with the men. *17 Kids and Counting* uses an interview/observation format. The documentary crew interviews the Duggar children and parents to help provide a framework for the day-to-day activities portrayed on the show. In "Duggar Dating Rules," Josh shares his philosophy on dating and marriage, "My parents are very wise. I went to them. They knew what was involved in getting married. They got married young. My dad was nineteen, my mom was seventeen. So, it wasn't unusual. I don't think that the age was really important to them. I think it was more the maturity."[27]

Josh's narrative illustrates a traditional conformity approach to family communication. Like many other Quiverfull families, the Duggars stress strict adherence to family rules. Josh has been raised to ask his parents' permission before any major life decisions, and he listens to his parents first and foremost. This conformist ideology is further emphasized in the way Quiverfull women interact with their husbands/fiancés. During scenes in "Duggar Dating Rules," Michelle and Anna sit quietly beside their men, nodding their heads in agreement as their partners talk. The women initiate or respond to conversation, but only in a manner that affirms the opinions of the men. In Anna's case, she gazes adoringly at Josh, absorbing everything he says and nodding in agreement.

In many conservative Christian families, especially Quiverfull ones, male dominance of family communication is prevalent. Anna Keller, Michelle Duggar, and Anna's mother Suzette Keller demonstrate the common mindset of allowing the men to dominate the conversation and lead the family in major decisions. As the fundamentalist Christian writer Nancy Wilson notes, "What a great protection it is to have a head to submit to, rather than being swayed by our own emotions, whims, and fears. A woman must cultivate a high view of her head, both the position God has given him over her as well as the authority God has given him."[28]

Headship in the Quiverfull movement is further emphasized in "A Very Duggar Wedding." On the wedding day, Anna is left to handle last-minute details while Josh and Jim Bob go off to the junior church room to have a man-to-man chat. Jim Bob sits in a tall chair while Josh straddles a child's chair and looks up at his father, waiting for advice. Jim Bob presents his son with the book *Staying in Love for a Lifetime*,[29] makes oblique reference to marital sex, and advises Josh in how to express to Anna that she is cherished:

> To you, one of the most important things about life will be having a physical relationship, but to your wife, one of the most important things will be to talk and share her heart every day with you . . . for her to be able to express it to you and for you to respond that you care about her, that you care about the little things in her life. This will show her that you love her, and cherish her and care about her. . . . You've got a wonderful bride here, we're so thankful for Anna, and I think both of you will complement each other wonderfully and this will be a dynamic marriage.[30]

Toward the end of the scene, pictures of Anna flash across the screen as tender music plays in the background. Anna is shown working in the kitchen, preparing for their wedding, looking adoringly at Josh, saying "I love you," and helping with children. The images reinforce the marital roles Anna and Josh are about to step into—Josh as head of the house and provider and Anna as wife and mother handling domestic duties.

Both Josh and Anna have committed to following the example of their parents and conforming to the ideology under which they were raised. The pastor who marries them is explicit about their domestic roles:

> Joshua, placing yourself under the headship of Christ, faithful to lead Anna in the ways of the Lord as her priest, protector, and provider. Anna, placing yourself under the leadership of Joshua, submitting to his authority as his helpmate, being loyal, supportive, following his direction through Christ in your lives. Also, do both you commit to trust God with the size of your family? Allowing him to determine the timing of each child and as parents training them in the ways of God.[31]

In their vows, Josh and Anna clearly state their intention to follow the Quiverfull lifestyle, and within a year, they are expecting their first child.[32] In the following years, Anna experiences one miscarriage and gives birth to their second child, averaging at least one pregnancy a year.[33] Quiverfull couples such as Jim Bob and Michelle and Josh and Anna place special emphasis on Psalm 127, which says children are a blessing, as well as on Old Testament passages such as Genesis 1:28, which outlines God's command to Adam and Eve to be fruitful and multiply.[34] The literal interpretation of these verses plays a significant role in Quiverfull ideology, which considers any form of family planning a direct violation of God's command to populate the earth with Christians and a rejection of God's plan to bless that family with children. In recent interviews, the Duggars said the reason they allow the show to document their lives is to provide a platform for sharing their Christian faith and beliefs on family life.[35] They might be open about their faith, but they do not want to admit they follow the Quiverfull ideology. Nevertheless, their show has helped the movement gain widespread tolerance and is recognized by Quiverfull activists as an outreach tool to promote the Quiverfull lifestyle.

Christian Pop Culture and Gender Roles

With the close of *19 Kids and Counting*'s ninth season, it is clear the rhetoric of Quiverfull patriarchy has gradually become more acceptable to mainstream evangelicals. For example, the Duggars were invited to speak at Focus on the Family[36] and to visit the set of the popular Christian film *Courageous*.[37] In addition, a special episode titled "Duggars: All You Wanted to Know" features soft-ball questions from visitors to the Focus on the Family headquarters.[38] As rhetorician Helen Sterk emphasizes, patriarchy has controlled biblical interpretation for centuries, resulting in the vast majority of Christian cocultures seeking biblical interpretation and spiritual leadership in an almost exclusively male context.[39] Because Focus on the Family is the primary evangelical family organization, its support of the Duggars' lifestyle legitimizes not only male headship but also the framing of opposition to birth control as a "sanctity of life" issue.[40] Placing the Quiverfull lifestyle in a pro-life context helps a fringe Christian theology gain mainstream evangelical acceptance, as the rise of pro-life and anti-contraception presidential candidate Rick Santorum clearly illustrates.[41] By manipulating biblical interpretation and positioning the Quiverfull ideology as respect for the "sanctity of life," these organizations are, as Rebecca Chopp puts it, "denying access of language" to women and using language to instead promote an extreme socio-symbolic order. [42] These subtexts of *19 Kids and Counting* make a feminist narrative approach crucial, allowing us to draw out the subtle themes of male headship and the oppressive religious ideology while ultimately providing a framework for revealing the potentially harmful themes the show promotes.

Such Christian use of popular culture as a promotional platform for religious rhetoric is not a new occurrence. Naturally, a media format that has become an intrinsic part of the American experience is ideal for promoting a religious ideology. As Quentin Schultze notes, "Television programming is religious because its stories are the shared narratives of American culture."[43] The Duggar family story is a perfect example: it is relatable to anyone—regardless of religious affiliation—interested in putting family first. While the Duggar narrative appeals to a broad audience, it also reinforces a conservative Christian worldview on family hierarchy. Television programs such as *19 Kids and Counting* often contain a traditional family structure, with all other family structures portrayed as the "before conversion" example of secular society.[44] When women are depicted in religious programming, it is usually in conjunction with domestic roles and never as independent from the family structure.[45] Michelle Duggar is relegated to the role of housekeeper, teacher, and caretaker, while the husband leads the dominant family narrative. The subtle themes regarding a woman's role in the home, marriage, and society are the dominant narratives of the show. To the casual observer, however, these themes are not immediately discernible in a show that seems the picture of idyllic family life.

Consequently, themes of repression and traditional gender ideology are easily overlooked on a cable network such as TLC, where the target audience is females and the network's slate of reality shows reinforces traditional gender roles. TLC's formatting is part of a larger reality trend that focuses on traditional heterosexuality, marriage, and family life.[46] Since average TLC viewers are already prone to agree with a traditional family structure, they would find nothing unusual in the Duggar family's lifestyle. Jennifer Maher notes that the TLC shows *A Wedding Story* and *A Baby Story* "reveal the discontent of perfect love as we've been coached to feel and live it as well as the repetition of compulsion such dissatisfaction engenders. If feminists could politicize this dissatisfaction, we might go far in breaking the hold that compulsory heterosexuality has over our culture."[47] Like *A Wedding Story* and *A Baby Story*, *19 Kids and Counting* plays into normative gender roles, portraying Jim Bob and Michelle Duggar as a loving couple devoted to their family. As the show progresses, the loving nature of the family unit becomes the central theme while the religious convictions influencing their lifestyle are rarely discussed. *19 Kids and Counting* presents a subversive oppositional discourse[48] that implicitly argues for the acceptability of large families in which the women are relegated to purely domestic functions.

Until recently, the Duggars' narrative painted only a positive picture of the Quiverfull movement, but these types of idyllic depictions of Quiverfull life can mask potential danger. The premature birth of their nineteenth child due to Michelle Duggar's preeclampsia in December 2009 brought the Quiverfull lifestyle under increased scrutiny in mainstream media. Baby nineteen, Josie Duggar, was born three months premature, and the lives of both mother and baby were in danger immediately before and after the birth.[49] Even given Michelle and Josie Duggar's health complications, both Jim Bob and Michelle announced they were open to having more children if it was God's will.[50] Michelle Duggar openly draws comparisons between her life-threatening complications in delivering Josie and the suffering of Jesus Christ. In the Season Eight finale, "Duggars: All You Wanted to Know," Michelle takes John 15:13 out of context and equates her health complications to Christ's love for his disciples and willingness to sacrifice himself for their salvation. Michelle says, "Looking into the face of Josie, I'd do it again. I would do it again. I would. . . . As I thought long and hard about that (her health), I realized there was no greater love than this, that a man would be willing to lay down his life. I think as a mom and a parent, you'd be willing to do that for your child, even the child that's not here yet. I would be willing to do that."[51] Jim Bob and Michelle view Josie's health complications as another way to share their faith. They firmly believe God could have healed her instantly but chose to allow Michelle to endure a difficult pregnancy and Josie to be born early to glorify God. As Michelle noted, during the months while Josie was hospitalized, she always cited 2 Corinthians 12:9 to explain to people that "My [God's] grace is sufficient for thee; for my strength is made perfect in weakness. Most gladly therefore will I rather glory in my infirmities, that the power of Christ may rest upon me."[52] The Duggars' response to Josie's birth once again illustrates their strong belief in preordained roles. Michelle is destined to be a mother and have babies, no matter what the health risks, because that is the biblically mandated role for women.

True to their word that they wanted more children, the Duggars announced Michelle's pregnancy with baby number twenty at the end of Season Eight in November 2011. Michelle said, "If God sees fit to bless us with another little one, then He ultimately will be the one in control."[53] By December 2011, however, Michelle had miscarried and given birth to a stillborn baby girl they named Jubilee Shalom. The family invited further controversy by holding a funeral service for the baby and passing out photos of Jubilee's hand in the hand of her mother. The Now I Lay Me Down to Sleep Foundation, a nonprofit photography organization specializing in death photos of infants, took the photos for the Duggar family.[54] While the Duggars maintain the photos were for family use only, passing them out at the funeral is another indication of how far they will go to promote their beliefs that every child is a gift from God and every pregnancy is God-ordained. A few weeks after denouncing the photos of Jubilee being made public, the family made the images public on their website along with an audio letter from Michelle to Jubilee. The photo of Jubilee's tiny hand in her mother's hand is displayed as Michelle talks in voice-over: "We were so thankful to God when we found out we were expecting you. So often in society, babies are looked upon as a problem, trial, or responsibility, but God says babies are a blessing. We do not believe that babies are a bother, a headache, or a financial drainer, or a career interrupter. . . . You were only here with us such a short time. It's an awesome thought to me that you fulfilled your life's purpose in such a short time."[55] Michelle's audio letter to Jubilee makes a strong statement about the family's views on children, gender roles, and a specific predestined plan for every individual. It is one of the strongest statements the Duggars have publicly made regarding their religious beliefs and is directly in line with Quiverfull and Christian patriarchy ideology.

Despite the news coverage of Michelle Duggar's last two pregnancies, there is still a lack of public awareness about the darker aspects of the Quiverfull movement. More research is needed to fully understand the stress this lifestyle can place on a woman's physical and psychological health. For instance, Andrea Yates—the Texas mother who received national attention for drowning her five children in a bathtub in 2001—is an extreme example of this mental and emotional strain. Few people realize Yates and her husband subscribed to the movement's beliefs,[56] and this further emphasizes the need to highlight the Quiverfull ideology. While women such as Michelle Duggar and Andrea Yates seem willing to comply with the Quiverfull lifestyle, there is a difference between accepting a lifestyle because of a choice and being coerced into a lifestyle based on religious propaganda. Yates and the Duggar women often do not learn about life beyond Quiverfull, nor do they understand how the emphasis on a literal interpretation of the Bible places pressure on them to continue in the Quiverfull lifestyle to maintain their Christian faith. In the lives of many Quiverfull families, there is little separation between religious salvation and their natalist lifestyle. While the Duggars attempt to paint a peaceful picture of the Quiverfull life, the underlying narrative suggests all is not as it seems.

Notes

1. The show premiered in 2008 under the title *17 Kids and Counting*. As the Duggar family grew with each new birth, the title changed to *18 Kids and Counting* in 2009 and *19 Kids and Counting* in 2010.

2. Jim Bob Duggar and Michelle Duggar, *20 and Counting! Raising One of America's Largest Families—How They Do It* (Brentwood, TN: Howard Books, 2008).

3. Jim Bob Duggar and Michelle Duggar, *A Love That Multiplies: An Up-Close View of How They Make It Work* (Brentwood, TN: Howard Books, 2011).

4. Mentioned in "Duggars Focus on the Family," *19 Kids and Counting*, performed by Jim Bob Duggar and Michelle Duggar (June 14, 2011; Figure 8 Films), TLC.

5. Duggar and Duggar, *A Love That Multiplies*, 92.

6. Alicia Dennis, "Still Growing," *People*, August 23, 2010, 54; Alicia Dennis, "Our Hearts Haven't Changed," *People*, February 15, 2010, 80.

7. Janis Page, "Towards a Theory of Narrative Analysis: What We See on HGTV" (paper presented at the annual meeting for the International Communication Association, Dresden, Germany, June 19–23, 2006).

8. Walter Fisher, *Human Communication as Narration: Toward a Philosophy of Reason, Value, and Action* (Columbia, SC: University of South Carolina Press, 1987), 64.

9. Kathryn Joyce, "Quiverfull Conviction: Christian Mothers Breed 'Arrows for the War,'" *Nation* (November 27, 2006), 11.

10. *14 and Pregnant Again!* Directed by Kirk Streb (September 6, 2004, Figure 8 Films), Discovery Channel.

11. *Raising 16 Children*; *16 Children and Moving In*; *On the Road with 16 Children.*

12. "OWN: Oprah Winfrey Network and TLC Seal Off-Network Licensing Deal to Acquire '*Undercover Boss*' from CBS Television Distribution," CBS Television Distribution, Press Release, 2010, accessed April 12, 2012, http://www.cbstvd.com/press_release_detail.aspx?newsID=189.

13. Mary Pride, *The Way Home: Beyond Feminism and Back to Reality* (Wheaton, IL: Crossway Books, 1985).

14. Rick Hess and Jan Hess, *A Full Quiver: Family Planning and the Lordship of Christ* (Brentwood, TN: Wolgemuth & Hyatt Publishers, 1990).

15. Samuel A. Owen Jr., *Letting God Plan Your Family* (Wheaton, IL: Crossway Books, 1990), 51.

16. Nancy Nason-Clark, "Religion and Violence Against Women: Exploring the Rhetoric and Response of Evangelical Churches in Canada," *Social Compass* 43 (1996): 515–36.

17. Ephesians 5:22–3, New American Standard Version.

18. Yoav Lavee and Ruth Katz, "Division of Labor, Perceived Fairness and Marital Quality: The Effect of Gender Ideology," *Journal of Marriage and Family* 64 (February 2002): 27–39.

19. Melinda Denton, "Gender and Marital Decision Making: Negotiating Religious Ideology and Practice," *Social Forces* 82 (March 2004): 1151–80.

20. Margaret Bendroth, "Fundamentalism and the Family: Gender, Culture, and the American Pro-Family Movement," *Journal of Women's History 10* (Winter 1999): 35–54.

21. Psalm 127: 3–5, NASV.

22. Kate Dixon, "Multiply and Conquer," *Bitch* 37 (Fall 2007): 38.

23. Joshua Harris, *I Kissed Dating Goodbye* (Sisters, OR: Multnomah Books, 2003).

24. "Josh Gets Engaged," *17 Kids and Counting*, performed by Jim Bob Duggar and Michelle Duggar (October 6, 2008; Figure 8 Films), TLC.

25. "Josh Gets Engaged."

26. "Duggar Dating Rules," *17 Kids and Counting*, performed by Jim Bob Duggar and Michelle Duggar (October 6, 2008; Figure 8 Films), TLC.

27. "Duggar Dating Rules."

28. Nancy Wilson, *The Fruit of Her Hands: Respect and the Christian Woman* (Moscow, ID: Cannon Press, 1997), 17.

29. Ed Wheat with Gloria Okes Perkins, *Staying in Love for a Lifetime* (Nashville, TN: Thomas Nelson, 2001).

30. "A Very Duggar Wedding," *18 Kids and Counting*, performed by Jim Bob Duggar and Michelle Duggar (January 25, 2009; Figure 8 Films), TLC.

31. "A Very Duggar Wedding."

32. Mike Celizic, "Duggar Family: Another Baby on the Way!" TodayShow.com, accessed October 9, 2009, http://today.msnbc.msn.com/id/30156915/ns/parenting_and_family.

33. Alicia Dennis, "Another Duggar Baby on the Way," *People*, accessed October 9, 2009, http://www.people.com/people/article/0,,20441165,00.html.

34. Owen, *Letting God Plan*, 44.

35. Dena Ross, "Duggars: The Most Wholesome Family on TV: Interview with Michelle and Jim Bob Duggar," Beliefnet.com (n.d.), 1.

36. "Duggars Focus on the Family."

37. "Duggars Go Hollywood," *19 Kids and Counting*, performed by Jim Bob Duggar and Michelle Duggar (August 10, 2010; Figure 8 Films), TLC.

38. "Duggars: All You Wanted to Know," *19 Kids and Counting*, performed by Jim Bob Duggar and Michelle Duggar (November 8, 2011; Figure 8 Films), TLC.

39. Helen M. Sterk, "How Rhetoric Becomes Real: Religious Sources of Gender Identity," *Journal of Communication and Religion* 12 (1989): 30.

40. "The Blessing of Raising a Large Family (Part 1 of 2)," *Focus on the Family Daily*, July 28, 2011.

41. Jo Pizza, "The Duggar Family's Prayers for Rick Santorum Come True in Iowa," Fox News, accessed April 12, 2012, http://www.foxnews.com/entertainment/2012/01/04/duggar-familys-prayers-for-rick-santorum-come-true-in-iowa.

42. Rebecca Chopp, *The Power to Speak* (New York: Crossroad Publishing Company, 1989), 25.

43. Quentin Schultze, "Secular Television as Popular Religion," in *Religious Television: Controversies and Conclusions*, eds. Robert Abelman and Stewart M. Hoover (Norwood, NJ: Ablex Publishing, 1990), 243.

44. Julia Mitchell Corbitt, "The Family as Seen Through the Eyes of the New Religious-Political Right," in *Religious Television: Controversies and Conclusions*, eds. Robert Abelman and Stewart M. Hoover (Norwood, NJ: Ablex Publishing, 1990).

45. Robert Abelman, "The Depiction of Women in Religious Television," *Journal of Communication and Religion* (September 1991): 3–4.

46. Kirsty Fairclough, "Women's Work? *Wife Swap* and the Reality Problem," *Feminist Media Studies* 4 (November 2004): 344–47.

47. Jennifer Maher, "What Do Women Watch? Tuning in to the Compulsory Heterosexuality Channel," in *Reality TV: Remaking Television Culture*, eds. Susan Murray and Laurie Ouellette (New York: New York University Press, 2004), 212.

48. John Fiske, *Television Culture* (New York: Methuen, 1987), 47.

49. Luchina Fisher and Lauren Cox, "Michelle Duggar Has Premature Girl in Emergency C Section," ABCNews.com, accessed April 12, 2012, http://abcnews.go.com/Health/Television/michelle-duggar-birth-19th-child-emergency-section/story?id=9311401.

50. Dennis, "Our Hearts Haven't Changed," 80.

51. "Duggars: All You Wanted to Know."

52. Duggar and Duggar, *A Love That Multiplies*, 57, 66.

53. "Duggars: All You Wanted to Know."

54. Luchina Fisher, "The Duggar Family Copes with the Loss of Jubilee," ABC News, accessed April 12, 2012, http://abcnews.go.com/blogs/entertainment/2011/12/duggar-family-copes-with-loss-of-jubilee/; NILDMTS: Now I Lay Me Down to Sleep, "About Us," accessed April 12, 2012, http://www.nowilaymedowntosleep.org/about_us.

55. "Jubilee Shalom Duggar," Duggar Family Website, accessed January 7, 2012, http://www.duggarfamily.com/content/jubilee.

56. Dixon, "Multiply and Conquer," 39.

Bibliography

14 and Pregnant Again! Directed by Kirk Streb. September 6, 2004. Figure 8 Films. Discovery Channel.

"A Very Duggar Wedding." *18 Kids and Counting*. Performed by Jim Bob Duggar and Michelle Duggar. January 25, 2009. Figure 8 Films. TLC.

Abelman, Robert. "The Depiction of Women in Religious Television." *Journal of Communication and Religion* (September 1991): 1–14.

Bendroth, Margaret. "Fundamentalism and the Family: Gender, Culture, and the American Pro-Family Movement." *Journal of Women's History* 10 (Winter 1999): 35–54.

"The Blessing of Raising a Large Family (Part 1 of 2)." *Focus on the Family Daily*. July 28, 2011.

Celizic, Mike. "Duggar Family: Another Baby on the Way!" TodayShow.com. Accessed October 9, 2009. http://today.msnbc.msn.com/id/30156915/ns/parenting_and_family.

Chopp, Rebecca. *The Power to Speak*. New York: Crossroad Publishing Company, 1989.

Corbitt, Julia Mitchell. "The Family as Seen Through the Eyes of the New Religious-Political Right." In *Religious Television: Controversies and Conclusions*. Edited by Robert Abelman and Stewart M. Hoover. Norwood, NJ: Ablex Publishing, 1990.

Dennis, Alicia. "Another Duggar Baby on the Way." *People*. Accessed October 9, 2009. http://www.people.com/people/article/0,,20441165,00.html.

———. "Our Hearts Haven't Changed." *People*. February 15, 2010.

———. "Still Growing." *People*. August 23, 2010.

Denton, Melinda. "Gender and Marital Decision Making: Negotiating Religious Ideology and Practice." *Social Forces* 82 (March 2004): 1151–80.

Dixon, Kate. "Multiply and Conquer." *Bitch* 37 (Fall 2007).

"Duggar Dating Rules." *17 Kids and Counting*. Performed by Jim Bob Duggar and Michelle Duggar. October 6, 2008. Figure 8 Films. TLC.

Duggar Family Website. "Jubilee Shalom Duggar." Accessed January 7, 2012. http://www.duggarfamily.com/content/jubilee.

Duggar, Jim Bob, and Michelle Duggar. *20 and Counting! Raising One of America's Largest Families—How They Do It*. Brentwood, TN: Howard Books, 2008.

———. *A Love That Multiplies: An Up-Close View of How They Make It Work*. Brentwood, TN: Howard Books, 2011.

"Duggars: All You Wanted to Know." *19 Kids and Counting*. Performed by Jim Bob Duggar and Michelle Duggar. November 8, 2011. Figure 8 Films. TLC.

"Duggars Focus on the Family." *19 Kids and Counting*. Performed by Jim Bob Duggar and Michelle Duggar. June 14, 2011. Figure 8 Films. TLC.

"Duggars Go Hollywood." *19 Kids and Counting*. Performed by Jim Bob Duggar and Michelle Duggar. August 10, 2010. Figure 8 Films. TLC.

Fairclough, Kirsty. "Women's Work? *Wife Swap* and the Reality Problem," *Feminist Media Studies* 4 (November 2004): 344–47.

Fisher, Luchina. "The Duggar Family Copes with the Loss of Jubilee." ABC News. Accessed April 12, 2012. http://abcnews.go.com/blogs/entertainment/2011/12/duggar-family-copes-with-loss-of-jubilee.

Fisher, Luchina, and Lauren Cox. "Michelle Duggar Has Premature Girl in Emergency C Section." ABCNews.com. Accessed April 12, 2012. http://abcnews.go.com/Health/Television/michelle-duggar-birth-19th-child-emergency-section/story?id=9311401.

Fisher, Walter. *Human Communication as Narration: Toward a Philosophy of Reason, Value, and Action*. Columbia, SC: University of South Carolina Press, 1987.

Fiske, John. *Television Culture*. New York: Methuen, 1987.

Harris, Joshua. *I Kissed Dating Goodbye*. Sisters, OR: Multnomah Books, 2003.

Hess, Rick, and Jan Hess. *A Full Quiver: Family Planning and the Lordship of Christ*. Brentwood, TN: Wolgemuth & Hyatt Publishers, 1990.

"Josh Gets Engaged." *17 Kids and Counting*. Performed by Jim Bob Duggar and Michelle Duggar. October 6, 2008. Figure 8 Films. TLC.

Joyce, Kathryn. "Quiverfull Conviction: Christian Mothers Breed 'Arrows for the War.'" *Nation*. November 27, 2006.

Lavee, Yoav, and Ruth Katz. "Division of Labor, Perceived Fairness and Marital Quality: The Effect of Gender Ideology." *Journal of Marriage and Family* 64 (February 2002): 27–39.

Maher, Jennifer. "What Do Women Watch? Tuning in to the Compulsory Heterosexuality Channel." In *Reality TV: Remaking Television Culture*. Edited by Susan Murray and Laurie Ouellette. New York: New York University Press, 2004.

Nason-Clark, Nancy. "Religion and Violence Against Women: Exploring the Rhetoric and Response of Evangelical Churches in Canada," *Social Compass* 43 (1996): 515–36.

NILDMTS: Now I Lay Me Down to Sleep. "About Us." Accessed April 12, 2012. http://www.nowilaymedowntosleep.org/about_us.

Owen, Jr., Samuel A. *Letting God Plan Your Family*. Wheaton, IL: Crossway Books, 1990.

"OWN: Oprah Winfrey Network and TLC Seal Off-Network Licensing Deal to Acquire '*Undercover Boss*' from CBS Television Distribution." CBS Television Distribution. Press Release, 2010. Accessed April 12, 2012. http://www.cbstvd.com/press_release_detail.aspx?newsID=189.

Page, Janis. "Towards a Theory of Narrative Analysis: What We See on HGTV." Paper presented at the annual meeting for the International Communication Association, Dresden, Germany, June 19–23, 2006.

Pizza, Jo. "The Duggar Family's Prayers for Rick Santorum Come True in Iowa." Fox News. Accessed April 12, 2012. http://www.foxnews.com/entertainment/2012/01/04/duggar-familys-prayers-for-rick-santorum-come-true-in-iowa.

Pride, Mary. *The Way Home: Beyond Feminism and Back to Reality*. Wheaton, IL: Crossway Books, 1985.

Ross, Dena. "Duggars: The Most Wholesome Family on TV: Interview with Michelle and Jim Bob Duggar." Beliefnet.com.

Schultze, Quentin. "Secular Television as Popular Religion." In *Religious Television: Controversies and Conclusions*. Edited by Robert Abelman and Stewart M. Hoover. Norwood, NJ: Ablex Publishing, 1990.

Sterk, Helen. "How Rhetoric Becomes Real: Religious Sources of Gender Identity." *Journal of Communication and Religion* 12 (1989): 24–33.

Wheat, Ed, with Gloria Okes Perkins. *Staying in Love for a Lifetime*. Nashville, TN: Thomas Nelson, 2001.

Wilson, Nancy. *The Fruit of Her Hands: Respect and the Christian Woman*. Moscow, ID: Cannon Press, 1997.

PART II

Film

Chapter 6

Punishing Unfaithful Wives and Working Mothers: Messages of Postfeminism in Contemporary Film

by Erika M. Thomas

Following the successes of second-wave feminism, American society was bombarded by messages from mass media, advertising, and the government blaming social problems such as the breakdown of the American family on the women's liberation movement. Statements that the feminist movement is dead, no longer necessary, or making life worse for American women became recognized as the rhetoric of "postfeminism." Amelia Jones defines postfeminism as the phenomenon of antifeminism, or the backlash against feminism and the beliefs and rights forwarded in the second wave of feminism.[1]

Dominant postfeminist messages began appearing in the 1980s and early 1990s. Suzanna Danuta Walters explains that the term "postfeminism" was first used in public discourse in the October 1982 *New York Times* cover article "Voices from the Post-Feminist Generation." The article includes testimonials from women saying they are unsatisfied and that the "happy" women are those who chose a family over a career. The article sends the message that having a career and raising a family are incompatible goals and that women who try to have it all feel miserable, the supposed condition of the feminist population.[2] Examining the same phenomenon in *Backlash: The Undeclared War Against American Women*, Susan Faludi traces the development of postfeminist, or backlash, messages that portray feminism as negative and harmful to society because it rejects conservative values.[3]

Despite nearly thirty years of feminist scholarship exposing the myths and fallacies at the heart of postfeminist discourse, postfeminist media images and messages still persist. I define the term "postfeminism" as the messages of backlash against feminism, which Angela McRobbie describes as the "active process by which feminist gains of the 1970s and 80s come to be undermined."[4] I distinguish the term "postfeminism" from "postmodernist feminism," "riot grrrls," and "third-wave feminism."[5] Some debate remains over whether we are in an "age" of postfeminism, but regardless, analysis of recent mainstream media reveals postfeminist messages are still dominant. Hollywood films, through their plots and character developments, are responsible for portraying many of the messages that reinforce postfeminism.

This chapter identifies contemporary postfeminist messages by first exploring the classic postfeminist film *Fatal Attraction*,[6] followed by two films released in the twenty-first century: *Unfaithful*[7] and *The Devil Wears Prada*.[8] These films portray various female characters—single, unfaithful, and career-driven respectively—as unhappy women who are ultimately punished for their choices. These representations endorse and perpetuate the images of a "good" mother and wife—married, loyal, and family-oriented. I argue that messages of postfeminism continue to plague American culture through many films' portrayals of "passionate," "liberated," and "career-driven" women and the negative consequences that accompany their decisions.

Postfeminist Theory

Before examining postfeminist messages in contemporary films, we must distinguish what is meant by "postfeminism" and understand the characteristics of films that endorse a postfeminist message. Scholars such as Suzanna Walters[9] and Chris Holmlund[10] have identified multiple strands of postfeminism, distinguishing between the type that occurs within popular culture from that within the academy. This chapter focuses on the trend of postfeminism within popular culture.

The concept of postfeminism encompasses many themes. The feminist movement is described as failing to provide women with happiness and equality. This trend in media coverage first began in the 1970s, when "dismissive and derogatory" headlines and stories constructed feminism as a dead movement.[11] Walters describes "popular postfeminism" as:

> predictably located within generalized antifeminist backlash that has been given free rein in the last ten years. Sources as diverse as the *New York Times*, the film *Baby Boom*, bestsellers about "career women gone wrong," and television series about troubled single women . . . present a somewhat contradictory image of a movement devoid of currency and at the same time responsible for the sad plight of millions of unhappy and unsatisfied women who, thinking that they could have it all, have clearly "gone too far" and jeopardized their chances at achieving the much valorized American Dream.[12]

Walters identifies a second theme in postfeminist films: false dichotomies for women. Many 1980s films and television series dichotomize the mother and working woman, sending the message that women can either succeed in their career or in their role as "Supermom"; rarely do they portray women achieving success in both realms. Walters writes, "In this age of *Fatal Attraction* and *Baby Boom*, feminist struggles and gains are reduced to personal choices, choices that, we are now informed, have created a no-win situation: we cannot have it all."[13] The only films of that era that valorize strong women also strive to emphasize the woman's maternal identification, as in the films *Aliens* and *Terminator 2*.[14] Postfeminist films portray the feminist movement as failed, claiming it only resulted in endorsing the myth that women can have it all. Implying that the feminist movement made women's lives more difficult, these films argue that women must choose between roles or revert to their traditional positions as housewife and mother to be happy.

A third discursive theme found in postfeminist texts is the complications caused by a woman's personal freedom. Many postfeminist films create a text void of social and political contexts. According to Yvonne Tasker and Diane Negra, such films have "frequently taken the form of a prepackaged and highly commodifiable entity, so that discourses having to do with women's economic, geographic, professional, and perhaps most particularly sexual freedom are effectively harnessed to individualism and consumerism."[15] Thus, female agency becomes packaged as a commodity. Women are given the "freedoms" to cook or shop, but any other use of agency is prohibited. Women who deviate from this course by trying to achieve everything are punished accordingly.

Postfeminist messages are overwhelmingly present in films throughout the 1980s and early 1990s. According to Jones:

> The politics of postfeminism takes a violent and explicit turn in the recent spate of films exploring the deviance and ultimate expendability of women who are sexually and/or professionally powerful; examples include the notorious *Fatal Attraction* (1987) by Adrian Lyne, *Presumed Innocent* (1990) by Alan. J. Pakala, *Single White Female* (1992) by Barbet Schroeder, *The Hand that Rocks the Cradle* (1992) by Cirtis Hanson, and the recent, virulently misogynistic and homophobic *Basic Instinct* (1992) by Paul Verhoeven.[16]

These films are grouped together because they all reaffirm postfeminist messages, specifically backlash for trying to achieve it all. According to Elayne Rapping, modern films' portrayals of female characters being denied freedom are more deplorable than the antifeminist messages prevalent in 1940s films because women's inability to make personal choices or acquire personal liberation was a fact of life then. Rapping states, "The world didn't even hint at the possibility of success for women, and those who went for it were doomed. Today, however, there's no such realistic explanation for why women keep losing out. Therefore, the only women we are allowed to see even challenging the status quo . . . are larger-than-life demons."[17] Despite the acceptance of women's liberation ideologies by the American public, portrayals of feminist goals and women's liberation rhetoric are accompanied by messages of resentment, backlash, and punishment in popular culture.

Postfeminist themes are still common in contemporary films. Tasker and Negra argue postfeminism language has become a pronounced feature of popular discourse.[18] Themes of "dissatisfaction" and "retreatism" (the scenario of a well-educated White woman who displays her "empowerment" by retreating from the workforce to care for her husband and family) remain familiar plots, often skewing the representation of choice. "Although a variety of films and genres of the late 1990s and early 2000s hype empowerment, these texts do not sustain any easy or straightforward relationship to women's experiences and social health. Indeed, scholars, popular critics, and mass audiences often report a 'hollow quality' at the heart of many postfeminist texts."[19]

Walters[20] and McRobbie[21] further support the contention that postfeminism continues in our culture, which, they argue, encounters postfeminist discourse in students who resist the label of feminist and the role of activists. Walters observes, "the backlash sentiment has never been so strong."[22] Despite some normalization of postfeminist anxieties and denunciations of feminism, other films (e.g., *Bridget Jones's Diary*) embrace and champion the changing representations of Western young women. Rhetorical strategies such as irony, constructions of new "gender regimes," and modifications to women's genres become the means for a new generation to invoke the principles of women's liberation by celebrating an "ethic of freedom" and discourse of personal choice. McRobbie recognizes a "double entanglement" in the more sophisticated version of today's antifeminism.[23] Western women have been granted some degree of liberation—equality in the classroom, encouragement in the world of work, and financial and sexual freedoms—but they are still excluded from political participation. McRobbie warns, "Women's power to contest the terms of political power is substantial and for this reason it is constantly, though often in a behind-the-scenes way, subjected to interventions designed to limit its potential . . . examples demonstrate just how much ground is lost to women when active feminism goes into abeyance, as it has done so in recent years. . . . Without a strong and vocal women's movement—with all the factions and internal disputes characteristic of a popular movement—the clock does indeed turn backwards."[24]

I analyze the films *Unfaithful* and *The Devil Wears Prada* to illustrate the continuing prevalence of postfeminist messages. I will show how these films form representations of the duties of *wife* and *mother* according to conservative gender roles. While many single women are portrayed as having personal choices in recent films, the demise of the family is still attributed to married or single women who choose personal values such as passion and work over their responsibility to their family. Representations of wives and mothers in postfeminist films suggest that the duty of upholding and protecting one's family remains the primary responsibility of the wife and mother. Before examining *Unfaithful* and *The Devil Wears Prada*, I revisit *Fatal Attraction* to illustrate how films successfully construct and endorse postfeminism, thus creating a double standard for married women since married men are not held equally accountable for the damage their family suffers because of their choices.

Fatal Attraction, Detrimental Representations

Adrian Lyne's *Fatal Attraction* remains one of the most frequently referenced films in postfeminist critiques of American popular culture. The film depicts the wrath of a vengeful woman who terrorizes her lover's family in an attempt to either regain love or enact revenge for her lover's ill treatment toward her. The plot revolves around Dan Gallagher, who is introduced as a lawyer and family man. He and his wife, Beth, have a six-year-old daughter named Ellen and appear happily married. Shortly after meeting a mysterious and attractive editor named Alex Forest at a business event, Dan begins an affair with her. Although he views his relationship with Alex as a one-night stand, Alex grows obsessed with Dan and becomes pathological in her methods to win Dan's affection. After experiencing Alex's rage, incessant phone calls, acts of vandalism, and most heinous act—killing and boiling Ellen's pet rabbit on their kitchen stove—Dan seeks help from the police and eventually confesses his adulterous behavior to Beth. The family is further terrorized when Alex kidnaps Ellen. Later, Alex breaks into the Gallaghers' home and attacks Beth. Together, Dan and Beth fight back, eventually killing Alex in their bathroom. In the final scene, as the police leave the Gallaghers' home, Dan and Beth hug and the camera pans to a family portrait of Dan, Beth, and Ellen.

The characters and plot highlight the problematic representations of women created by filmmakers. There are many reasons this film is seen as postfeminist. First, there is a clear contrast between the characteristics and roles of the two women, Beth Gallagher and Alex Forrest. Beth is a stereotypical housewife. In almost every scene, she is either cooking or cleaning in the kitchen, doing laundry, or caring for her daughter. In the opening scene, she balances everything *but* a career. As Beth prepares for an evening with her husband, she is shown finishing the laundry, managing her husband, and meticulously dressing and grooming. Beth primps nearly naked in front of her vanity mirror as Dan watches her get ready. Her smile indicates she is well aware that Dan is watching her. Caught in the gaze of her husband, Beth appears beautiful, feminine, and embraced by her husband, reaffirming her role as the "good" wife. According to Walters, "The good woman is, like in old times, the good *mother*, who significantly is the sophisticated housewife."[25] Although Beth is also a victim throughout the story, the audience registers with her horror, feels sympathy toward her, and cheers at the triumph of good over evil.

Alex Forrest is the opposite of the "good woman." She is powerful and career-driven, evidenced by her status as an editor at a New York City publishing company. Although thirty-six years old, Alex is still single and childless; she has clearly chosen her career over family. Walters describes her as "a single woman from hell," embodying everything evil: living in a rough neighborhood in the meat district of Manhattan, smoking and drinking, and wearing wild, flowing blonde hair.[26] Alex is uniquely dangerous because she is a free agent sexually. She incites the affair and therefore is viewed as the one to blame. Alex is identified as the seductive *home wrecker* while Dan and Beth become the saviors of the home. In light of Alex's evil, Dan's role in the adultery is largely overlooked and excused, even though his choices as a married man are far more devastating to the home than Alex's initial actions as a single woman.

Additionally, we come to fear Alex because of her frightening, monstrous, and irrational behavior. Although her actions are radical, her justifications and requests outside of the horrific acts are legitimate and merit personal respect. In an angry encounter, Alex asks why Dan is angry with her. "Is it because I won't let you treat me like a slut?" After revealing she is pregnant, Alex continues to demand "respect" as the mother of his child and asks him to live up to his responsibilities. Independent from the plot, these demands do not sound dangerous or evil; on the contrary, they sound like healthy, self-respecting, and empowering requests in line with feminist ideologies. The audience and Dan remain fearful of her, however. Alex uses many catchphrases of the feminist movement, further portraying her as a feminist. According to Kathie Davis, Alex insists on rights to reciprocity, respect, and shared responsibility, yet her actions discredit her feminist language. Davis states, "Alex maintains a lexicon of equality while her behavior grows steadily more outrageous, so her feminist rhetoric seems more and more out of sync with her actions and contributes further to the same lack of credibility that invalidates it."[27]

Portraying Alex as a feminist sends a clear warning: if we fear Alex, we should fear *becoming* Alex. Alex teaches the audience that she longs for a family. Dan assumes she will have an abortion, but she corrects his assumption:

DAN: The abortion. I'll take care of it. I'll pay for it.

ALEX: What makes you think I want an abortion?

DAN: You're not gonna have the baby.

ALEX: Why not? There are plenty of one-parent families.

DAN: I don't have a say in this?

ALEX: I want this child. It has nothing to do with you. I want it whether you're a part of it or not.

DAN: Then why are you telling me? Why not just go ahead and do it?

ALEX: I was hoping that you would want to be a part of it.

DAN: This is crazy. This is totally insane.

ALEX: I'm thirty-six years old. It may be my last chance to have a child.

The dialogue indicates that even the independent, sexually ambitious, and career-driven woman desires to be a wife and mother. The audience not only associates the single, career woman with evil, but the film shows that women who do not choose the path of Beth—the "good" woman—will become crazed and psychotic in their attempt to achieve both career and family.

At the end of the film, Beth prepares her bath, unaware that Alex has broken into her home. She wipes the steam off the mirror and finds Alex standing behind her. Alex's reflection in the Gallaghers' bathroom mirror is juxtaposed with Beth's image in the vanity, thereby reaffirming Alex as the "bad" and "evil" woman. Alex is not sexualized through this reflection; instead, she becomes the literal monster. Her frightening and unexpected appearance mimics the shocking entrance of a monster or psycho killer in a horror film. Her image is feared and hated; thus, audiences come to fear and hate the image of the liberated woman in the same way.

Finally, the audience is positioned to choose between the two women. Even before the "battle scene" in the Gallaghers' bathroom, there is always the risk that Dan may choose Alex over Beth. Audience members are encouraged to identify with and cheer on Beth, the "good" wife, mother, and victim. If the audience sides with Alex, they must reject Beth since the two relationships are mutually exclusive.[28] Thus, Alex's death is a necessity. Disturbed by the loss of the Gallagher family unit, audiences become even more discomfited by the thought of psychotic Alex raising a child on her own. Davis states, "Were Alex to demonstrate her biological power at the social level . . . giving birth to and raising a child in cheerful independence of its father . . . the sea of female power would be washing at the foundations of the patriarchal citadel."[29] Thus, Alex's death is necessary to reward Beth, the "good" and loyal wife, and to eliminate the final danger to the Gallagher family: Alex's unborn child. Her death demonstrates that protection of the family must come at the expense of the "feminist" figure and liberating values.

Unchanging Images in *Unfaithful*

Fifteen years after the release of *Fatal Attraction*, Adrian Lyne directed *Unfaithful*, which has a similar premise. Surprisingly, this film remains largely ignored by feminist critics.[30] According to one review, *Unfaithful* is "a gender-switched *Fatal Attraction*." *Unfaithful* is inspired by the 1969 film *La Femme Infidele*, which tells the story of a wife who cheats on her husband.[31]

In *Unfaithful*, suburban housewife Constance "Connie" Sumner lives a comfortable and stable life with her husband, Edward, and their son, Charlie, in Westchester County. One windy day, Connie takes the train to New York City to help organize a Julliard fund-raising auction. She literally bumps into a French stranger, who invites her to his nearby apartment. Accepting his offer, Connie learns the stranger's name is Paul Martel and that he is a book dealer temporarily living in New York. Obviously attracted to him and encouraged by his flirtation, Connie finds Paul's business card the next day and calls him from a payphone in New York City. Despite some initial hesitations, an affair ensues. Connie begins a regular pattern of visiting Paul during the day and spending evenings and weekends at home with her family. Shortly thereafter, Connie loses control of the balance between her family life and her secret affair. This situation comes to a peak when her husband leaves town for business and she forgets to pick up Charlie from school.

Meanwhile, Edward begins to doubt his wife's loyalty. He hires a private investigator to follow Connie and learns of the affair. Edward eventually visits Paul, emotionally breaks down, and murders Paul. That same evening, Connie somewhat reluctantly ends the affair by leaving a message on Paul's answering machine. After the police visit and she discovers pictures of her and Paul taken by the private investigator, Connie questions Edward. After learning of Paul's fate and Edward's role in his death, Connie and Edward begin to mend their relationship. During a scene with police sirens howling in the distance, it is implied they will always live in a state of uncertainty and fear. The film ends with Connie and Edward embracing after the auction and fundraising party.

Unfaithful exposes the double standard that exists for the "cheating wife." In *Unfaithful*, Connie is surrounded by different representations and subtexts than Dan Gallagher's in *Fatal Attraction*. Throughout the film, Connie is seen as the "problem," the reason why her family falls apart. In *Fatal Attraction*, however, the threat to Dan's family is not his affair but his psychotic lover. Without Alex's interference, Beth and Ellen probably would never know about Dan's affair, for although his actions are despicable, his weekend with Alex does not disrupt his interactions with his family or his love for his wife. Dan is not held responsible for the demise of his family while Alex is feared, hated, and blamed for her actions.

In *Unfaithful*, Connie's choices are directly associated with the demise of her family. She is portrayed as a "bad" wife because she is unfaithful, and more specifically, because she seems unsatisfied in her role as a suburban housewife and mother. In *Fatal Attraction*, Beth and Dan unite to fight Alex, the monster blamed for their problems. In *Unfaithful*, on the other hand, Connie receives the blame as the home wrecker. She has responsibilities to her husband, her son, and her home, yet she fails her family by having an affair and disturbing her role in the private sphere. Although the consequences of Connie's affair do not seem as radical as those experienced by the Gallaghers, Connie's affair noticeably disrupts her maternal role: she burns supper, forgets to pick up her son at school, and denies sex to her husband. Although the impacts seem mild, they are enough to trigger suspicion, and in turn they "hurt" both her son and her husband.

Additionally, Connie is directly blamed for the larger problems that ensue. Her choice to have an affair causes Paul's death and Edward's murderous behavior. When Connie questions Edward about his involvement in Paul's disappearance, she extracts Edward's confession. The conversation quickly turns against Connie. Edward is not asked to explain or justify himself, but Connie is expected to explain her reasons for cheating.

> CONNIE: Tell me what *you* did.
>
> EDWARD: No, you tell me what you did. How you fucked him over and over and over. You lied to me . . . over and over and over.
>
> CONNIE: Edward, please.
>
> EDWARD: No, you don't talk to me now. I gave everything for this family. Everything . . . and what did you do? You threw it all away like it was nothing. For what? To a fucking kid.

Edward concludes, "I know you, and I fuckin' hate you! I didn't want to kill him, I wanted to kill you!" The conversation never returns to Edward and his guilt. Connie's adultery is constructed as more significant than the murder. Although Edward claims he has given up everything for the family, it appears Connie has given up the most to identify as a wife and mother.

Finally, Connie's character development in *Unfaithful* leads to her portrayal as the person most harmed and traumatized by her own choices. In *Fatal Attraction*, the hurt resulting from Dan's affair is primarily physical. His family is almost physically harmed and taken away from him by Alex's physical violence, but they remain emotionally intact despite Dan's adulterous behavior. This is juxtaposed against *Unfaithful*, where Connie's affair weighs heavily on her psyche. In multiple scenes, she is crying, miserable, angry, sad, and conflicted. Edward's guilt over the murder of Paul seems minimal compared to Connie's shame. The film places the role of the family's survivability in the hands of the wife/mother. Connie's affair provides a greater threat to her family than even her husband's decision to murder. Furthermore, it acts as a warning to women about not straying far from the safety of the suburbs or venturing outside the family for happiness because such behavior causes harm to others, pain, and regret.

Unfaithful does not leave audiences with the same sense of justice felt at the end of *Fatal Attraction*. I attribute this to the film's failure to identify Connie's source of happiness. Although her affair with Paul triggers much of her unhappiness, the montage of photos taken by the private investigator captures only earnest moments of feeling happy. Escaping her life in the suburbs and spending time with her passionate lover incites more joy in Connie than the time spent with her family. According to a review by Mike Clark in *USA Today*, "The characters here aren't particularly fleshed out, but Lyne leaves room for viewers to fill in some blanks. Gere's character, for instance, is shown to be testy at work, so maybe he's a tough case at home, too. Though we never specifically see this, the household is filled with tension from the first scene."[32] Despite choosing her family over her lover, Connie and Edward are never shown resolving their subtle but apparent problems. While tension in the home and an unhappy marriage provide insight into Connie's affair, they only make the film's ending more problematic: Connie settles for an unhappy marriage due to guilt, shame, and fear or simply because it is emotionally easier to play the role of the "good" wife. In the end, Connie appears happy, but it is difficult to know for sure. She never articulates her love for Edward in the same way Dan articulates his love for Beth in *Fatal Attraction*. Despite her breakup with Paul, Connie is clearly distressed and saddened by the news of his death. Audiences are left to question whether she truly loves Edward or Paul, yet the family unit is restored, so the film ends.

Unfaithful reinforces postfeminist messages such as the double standard that exists when a woman cheats on her husband versus when a husband cheats on his wife. Connie is held more accountable for her behavior than Dan and Edward. Connie is further disempowered because she does not demand positive changes in her relationship with Edward; instead, she seeks to return to her "normal" and "accepted" roles as trophy wife and homemaker. If Connie is really happy in the end, the film reinforces the belief that she is only happy because she chose a family-oriented life.

The Devil Wears Prada

Dramas and thrillers like *Fatal Attraction* and *Unfaithful* are not the only films sending postfeminist messages. The comedy *The Devil Wears Prada* is also guilty of perpetuating postfeminist backlash.

The Devil Wears Prada is the story of a young woman named Andy Sachs who becomes the second assistant to Miranda Priestly, editor of the New York fashion magazine *Runway*. Andy and first assistant Emily serve as Miranda's personal "whipping girls." They are asked to do everything from picking up skirts and scarves from top fashion designers to completing Miranda's daughters' science fair project. Each day, Andy works hard to satisfy Miranda, but Miranda is continually disappointed in her assistants, especially after they fail to find her a flight out of Miami during a hurricane, causing Miranda to miss her daughters' recital. Now on a mission to succeed at every task while not allowing Miranda to get to her, Andy works yet harder, even changing her appearance and style to please Miranda. Andy, over time, becomes Miranda's ideal assistant.

As Andy begins to meet the expectations of Miranda, her relationships with her family, friends, and boyfriend, Nate, deteriorate, and she soon finds herself isolated. Nonetheless, this does not persuade Andy to quit her job. As a reward for her loyalty, Andy is asked to accompany Miranda to Paris for Fashion Week, a job that traditionally falls to Emily. Coerced to go, Andy shares the news with Emily, who feels betrayed and angry.

Once in Paris, Andy begins to defend, understand, and befriend Miranda more than ever. She also learns two valuable pieces of information: 1) Nigel, one of Miranda's star employees, was picked by Miranda to work with world-famous designer James Holt and 2) Miranda is being replaced as *Runway* editor-in-chief by a young woman named Jacqueline Follet. Andy tries to inform Miranda of the chair's intention but is ignored. The climax of the film occurs at a dinner where Miranda is supposed to appoint Nigel to his new position and learn she has been replaced. During the opening speech, however, Miranda surprises everyone by announcing that she has chosen Jacqueline Follet to be James Holt's new partner, thus occupying her supposed replacement and ensuring she will keep her position as editor-in-chief. Andy realizes she does not want to follow in Miranda's footsteps, so she walks away from Miranda and the job "a million girls would die for." The film ends with Andy finding a new job in journalism, finally beginning the career she always wanted.

The most obvious postfeminist myth perpetuated by the film is women cannot have it all. There are numerous scenes depicting Andy and Miranda failing to maintain healthy relationships with loved ones and their family. We first experience signs of the conflict between work and family when Andy's father visits New York. Instead of enjoying dinner and the musical *Chicago* with her father, Andy spends the evening on her cell phone with Miranda and airlines attempting to find a flight for Miranda back to New York City. This scene is significant because Andy, by choosing work over their time together, causes her father to feel angry toward her rather than her job. Furthermore, Andy is not the only one missing time with her family; Miranda, because she remains trapped in Miami due to a hurricane, misses her daughters' recital. Just as Andy's job prevents her from acting like a "good" daughter, Miranda's career prevents her from fulfilling her role as a "good" mother.

The first time Andy delivers a mock-up of *Runway* to Miranda's house, she walks in on an argument between Miranda and her husband, Stephen, who says to Miranda, "And I sat there waiting for you for almost an hour . . . I knew what everyone in that restaurant was thinking: there he is waiting for her again." This quotation is significant for many reasons. First, it sounds like a line a wife would say to her husband, illustrating Miranda's work ethic and dedication to the job is too much like a man's and that she is subsequently not satisfying her husband. Secondly, Stephen appears embarrassed that others see him as "waiting for her" because this behavior is not traditionally enacted by a man in a heterosexual relationship. This scene indicates Miranda not only threatens her husband's masculinity but risks losing her husband altogether.

A similar event occurs toward the end of the film when Andy and Miranda are in Paris. Andy walks into Miranda's hotel room and finds her crying on the sofa. Miranda tells Andy that Stephen is no longer coming to Paris and has asked for a divorce. Miranda states, "Another divorce . . . splashed across page six. I can just imagine what they are going to write about me. 'The dragon lady, career-obsessed.' 'Snow-queen drives away another Mr. Priestly.'" Miranda takes on the blame for sacrificing family life for her career. Additionally, Miranda is never shown mothering her two daughters. Although she loves her daughters, she does not act as the primary parent and instead has her assistants run errands and attend to other "mothering duties" for the girls. Miranda says, "Anyway, I don't really care what anyone writes about me. But my, my girls—it's just so unfair to the girls. Another disappointment, another letdown, another father figure . . . gone." This scene illustrates the stereotypical punishment for a "career-obsessed" woman: loss. Although Miranda is empowered in her job at *Runway*, she loses control of her family. Furthermore, Miranda perpetuates the negative stereotypes that surround career-driven women. Her choice to succeed at the expense of her family and the title of the film itself reinforce the dangerous assumption that all "bad" mothers and wives are "devils."

As Andy becomes a better assistant and her sense of fulfillment from her job grows, audiences view parallel consequences for Andy in the continued deterioration of her personal life. Andy misses social gatherings with her closest friends, Lily and Doug, and her boyfriend, Nate, and she experiences conflicts with them as a result. In one scene, Andy leaves a dinner party with her friends shortly after arriving because Miranda needs her to run an errand. In that same scene, she snaps at her friends for throwing her phone around and not taking her job as seriously as she does. Andy takes the pressures of her job out on her friends rather than blaming Miranda. On the night she is asked to attend Miranda's benefit dinner, Andy assumes she will be late to Nate's birthday party but ends up missing the party entirely. With each success at work, Andy grows more detached from her friends and Nate. Eventually, the stress on their relationship causes Andy and Nate to break up. During the break-up conversation, Nate tells Andy, "The person whose calls you always take—that's the relationship you are in. I hope you two are very happy together." Nate's comment implies Andy's job is mutually exclusive with their romantic relationship, once again reaffirming the postfeminist myth that there is a dichotomous relationship between one's career and personal life.

The recurring conflicts between career and personal life reaffirm the notion that women cannot possibly "have it all." Most alarming is that Miranda's actions teach Andy to take a different path, a realization that occurs at the end of the film:

> MIRANDA: I see a great deal of myself in you. You can see beyond what people want and what they need . . . and you can choose for yourself.
>
> ANDY: I don't think I'm like that. I, I couldn't do what you did to Nigel, Miranda. I couldn't do something like that.
>
> MIRANDA: Mm. You already did. To Emily.
>
> ANDY: No that was different. I didn't have a choice.

MIRANDA: Oh no, you chose. You chose to get ahead. You want this life, those choices are necessary.

ANDY: But what if this isn't what I want? I mean, what if I don't wanna live the way you live?

At the conclusion of this scene, Andy walks away from Miranda and the position she worked hard to earn. By taking an alternative path, Andy accepts that she can choose a different life for herself. The implication is she does not want to make the same "mistakes" as Miranda.

Feminists Wear Prada: A More Complex Message

Despite the postfeminist implications of Andy's decision to choose a different path from Miranda and the scenes implying "women cannot have it all," this film contains hopeful messages consistent with the ideologies of women's liberation. At the end of the film, Andy does not give up her ambitions and simply accept a position as a wife or mother. After returning to New York, Andy continues to pursue her career. This time, she enters the field of journalism, her original passion. Although she attempts to mend her relationship with Nate, the outcome is ambiguous. It is not clear whether they are dating or that they will begin dating again. Andy is more content working at her passion than settling for romance and a family. Furthermore, Andy's choice is liberating since it is what she really desires rather than an action to please someone else.

Additionally, *The Devil Wears Prada* identifies the double standards embedded in the representations of powerful, career-driven women. This is illustrated in a scene where Andy defends Miranda to a reporter. Although the reporter wants Andy to concede hateful feelings toward Miranda, Andy insists on showing respect to her boss. She states, "Okay, she's tough, but if Miranda were a man, no one would notice anything about her except how great she is at her job." Through this statement, Andy exposes the postfeminist double standard within our culture: successful women are seen as "devils" and home wreckers while successful men are merely viewed as "successful," free from backlash and exonerated from unfavorable consequences. Andy's ability to regain her agency at the end of the film and the recognition of society's gendered double standards potentially work to counterbalance some of the postfeminist messages. The audience sees new interpretations and representations of cultural messages consistent with feminist ideologies.

Conclusion

The analyses in this essay prove postfeminist messages continue to thrive in contemporary films. Recognizing these messages helps us understand how antifeminist beliefs are perpetuated and disseminated throughout American culture. Until mainstream films highlight alternative endings and instances of female empowerment, "feminist," "career-driven," and "unfaithful" wives and mothers will continue to receive a bad reputation. As critique of the double standards women encounter becomes more pervasive, society will begin to alter the images and representations that qualify women as "bad" wives and mothers.

Notes

1. Amelia Jones, "Feminism, Incorporated: Reading 'Postfeminism' in an Anti-Feminist Age," in *The Feminism and Visual Cultural Reader*, ed. Amelia Jones (London: Routledge, 2003), 314.

2. Suzanna Dunata Walters, *Material Girls: Making Sense of Feminist Cultural Theory* (Berkeley: University of California Press, 1995), 117–18.

3. Susan Faludi, *Backlash: The Undeclared War Against American Women* (Crown, 1991); Jones, "Feminism, Incorporated," 314–15.

4. Angela McRobbie, "Post-Feminism and Popular Culture," *Feminist Media Studies* 4 (2004): 255.

5. Chris Holmlund, "Postfeminism from A to G," *Cinema Journal* 44 (2005): 116–21.

6. *Fatal Attraction*, directed by Adrian Lyne (1987; Hollywood: Paramount Pictures).

7. *Unfaithful*, directed by Adrian Lyne (2002; Beverly Hills: Fox 2000 Pictures).

8. *The Devil Wears Prada*, directed by Wendy Finerman (2006; Beverly Hills: Fox 2000 Pictures).

9. Walters, *Material Girls*.

10. Holmlund, "Postfeminism from A to G."

11. Jennifer L. Pozner, "The 'Big Lie': False Feminist Death Syndrome, Profit, and the Media," in *Catching a Wave: Reclaiming Feminism for the 21st Century*, ed. Rory Dicker and Alison Piepmeier (Boston: Northeastern University Press, 2003), 31–56.

12. Walters, *Material Girls*, 119.

13. Walters, *Material Girls*, 122.

14. Walters, *Material Girls*, 132.

15. Yvonne Tasker and Diane Negra, "In Focus: Postfeminism and Contemporary Media Studies," *Cinema Journal* 44 (2005): 107.

16. Jones, "Feminism, Incorporated," 321.

17. Elayne Rapping, "Gender Politics on the Big Screen," *Progressive* 56 (1992): 36.

18. Tasker and Negra, "In Focus," 107.

19. Tasker and Negra, "In Focus," 107.

20. Walters, *Material Girls*.

21. McRobbie, "Post-Feminism and Popular Culture."

22. Walters, *Material Girls*, 141.

23. Angela McRobbie, "Beyond Post-Feminism," *Public Policy Research* 18 (2011): 179–84.

24. McRobbie, "Beyond Post-Feminism," 183–84.

25. Walters, *Material Girls*, 123.

26. Walters, *Material Girls*, 123.

27. Kathie Davis, "The Allure of the Predatory Woman in *Fatal Attraction* and Other Current American Movies," *Journal of Popular Culture* 26 (1992): 53.

28. Sandra R. Joshel, "Fatal Liaisons and Dangerous Attraction: The Destruction of Feminist Voices," *Journal of Popular Culture* 26 (1992): 65.

29. Davis, "The Allure of the Predatory Woman," 55.

30. Searches completed in prominent databases did not acquire results.

31. Mike Clark, "'*Unfaithful*' Turns Torrid Affair Scary," *USA Today*, May 8, 2002.

32. Mike Clark, "Torrid Affair," 6D.

Bibliography

Clark, Mike. "'*Unfaithful*' Turns Torrid Affair Scary." *USA Today*. May 8, 2002.

Davis, Kathie. "The Allure of the Predatory Woman in *Fatal Attraction* and Other Current American Movies." *Journal of Popular Culture* 26 (1992): 47–57.

Faludi, Susan. *Backlash: The Undeclared War Against American Women*. Crown, 1991.

Fatal Attraction. Directed by Adrian Lyne. 1987. Hollywood: Paramount Pictures.
Holmlund, Chris. "Postfeminism from A to G." *Cinema Journal* 44 (2005): 116–21.
Jones, Amelia. "Feminism, Incorporated: Reading 'Postfeminism' in an Anti-Feminist Age." In The Feminism and Visual Cultural Reader, edited by Amelia Jones, 314–29. London: Routledge, 2003.
Joshel, Sandra R. "Fatal Liaisons and Dangerous Attraction: The Destruction of Feminist Voices." *Journal of Popular Culture* 26 (1992): 59–70.
McRobbie, Angela. "Beyond Post-Feminism." *Public Policy Research* 18 (2011): 179–84.
———. "Post-Feminism and Popular Culture." *Feminist Media Studies* 4 (2004): 255–64.
Pozner, Jennifer L. "The 'Big Lie': False Feminist Death Syndrome, Profit, and the Media." In *Catching a Wave: Reclaiming Feminism for the 21st Century*, edited by Rory Dicker and Alison Piepmeier, 31–56. Boston: Northeastern University Press, 2003.
Rapping, Elayne. "Gender Politics on the Big Screen." *Progressive* 56 (1992): 36–37.
Tasker, Yvonne, and Diane Negra. "In Focus: Postfeminism and Contemporary Media Studies." *Cinema Journal* 44 (2005): 107–10.
The Devil Wears Prada. Directed by Wendy Finerman. 2006. Beverly Hills: Fox 2000 Pictures.
Unfaithful. Directed by Adrian Lyne. 2002. Beverly Hills: Fox 2000 Pictures.
Walters, Suzanna Dunata. *Material Girls: Making Sense of Feminist Cultural Theory. Berkeley: University of California Press*, 1995.

Chapter 7

Love and Lack: Media, Witches, and Normative Gender Roles

by Victoria L. Godwin

Rhetorical use of the witch has been extremely effective at justifying normative gender roles. One result of the medieval witchcraze was a more passive image of woman. Whereas medieval women had reputations as "scolds and shrews, bawdy and aggressive," after the witchcraze, "women began to change into the passive, submissive type that symbolized them by the mid-nineteenth century."[1] They protested less, and even their sexuality was seen as passive.[2] Women were confined to and defined by the domestic sphere. No longer suspected as witches, they were safe as girlfriends, wives, and mothers. Medieval rhetoric justified the torture and execution of thousands of women as witches,[3] and their survivors learned to conform to patriarchal gender norms. Analyzing the witch symbol in media representations offers insight into how certain cultural and rhetorical operations intersect in attempts to dominate women.

Witches are not the most beloved of media monsters. Vampires, werewolves, zombies, and extraterrestrials receive far more popular and scholarly attention and analysis. Witches, however, provide an excellent tool for examining gender roles due to their traditional association with women. Medieval rhetoric constructs witches specifically as women. The *Malleus Maleficarum* offers extensive justifications for why women are more often witches than men.[4] Modern texts and viewers avoid calling males "witches"; they are "wizards," "warlocks," or "sorcerers"—even when they use exactly the same spells as their female counterparts.

Susan Douglas discusses witches as part of her larger analysis of supernatural women in *Bewitched, I Dream of Jeannie, The Addams Family,* and other 1960s series as indicative of reactions to feminism and changing gender roles. Men begged these women not to use their magical powers. The narratives allowed three exceptions, however: "to complete domestic chores, to compete over men, and to help the men out of embarrassing situations, which usually had been created by the woman's unauthorized use of her magic powers in the first place."[5]

Decades later, similar rhetorical strategies address feminism and changing gender roles via witches and related supernatural women. Susan Faludi traces cyclical recurrences of reactions against feminism and changing gender roles. She also examines the backlash against feminism in the 1980s and 1990s.[6] There have been no studies, however, of the media representations of witches accompanying that specific backlash, including those found in *The Craft*; *Practical Magic*; *The Witches of Eastwick*; *Hocus Pocus*; *Buffy the Vampire Slayer*; *Charmed*; *Sabrina, the Teenage Witch*; and even less popular examples such as *Poltergeist: The Legacy* and *Teen Witch*. Patriarchal rhetorical strategies within these media representations either discipline witches into normative gender roles as girlfriends, wives, or mothers, or else they punish the women for transgressions of patriarchal norms. Even in a supposedly postfeminist twenty-first century, witches and other supernatural women in the *Harry Potter* series, *The Secret Circle*, *The Vampire Diaries*, *Once upon a Time*, *The Wizards of Waverly Place*, *Being Human*, *Lost Girl*, and other films and television shows indicate similar tensions. This chapter calls attention to these cycles of changing gender roles and the patriarchal rhetorical strategies that attempt to discipline witches and ultimately women.

Media monsters represent the Other, "that which bourgeois ideology cannot recognize or accept but must deal with . . . in one of two ways: either by rejecting and if possible annihilating it, or by rendering it safe and assimilating it, converting it as far as possible into a replica of itself."[7] Assimilation incorporates non-normative ideas such as feminism into the mainstream. In media representations of witches, partial versions of feminism downplay the radical potential to construct women's apparent power as a means to gaining and maintaining normative gender roles. Whether as heroes or villains, the witches reinforce patriarchal control through their frequent use of love spells and glamours as well as by their reliance on external sources of power. Both of these rhetorical strategies construct women as only gaining identity or power from their relationships with patriarchal males or their representatives.

Yet witches simultaneously expose the limitations of patriarchal gender roles. Labeling and punishing such outsiders simultaneously reveals that patriarchal control is not the only option available. Even as patriarchy disciplines those who oppose it, it highlights the fact that it can be opposed. Patriarchy is not a "natural," "universal," or invincible social system, and its attempts to purify itself only expose the constructed nature of its carefully defended gender norms. Furthermore, resistant readings reinterpret these patriarchal rhetorical strategies. Viewers praise media witches' opposition to oppressive societal norms and encouragement of independent thought.[8] Assimilation is not guaranteed.

Love Spells: Happily Ever After

Love spells are a mainstay of media representations of witches. Whether cast by heroes or villains to gain romance or control, love spells define witches by their relationship to a male and thus contribute to patriarchal discipline. A desire for romance motivates the first type of love spells. These most obviously reinforce normative gender roles since witches appear as potential heterosexual girlfriends and eventual wives and mothers. Even publicity material emphasizes these domestic roles. For example, a *TV Guide* article on the television series *Charmed* mainly focuses on the actresses' personal lives, especially past husbands or boyfriends.[9] Alyssa Milano, an actress portraying one of the three witches in the series, "dabbled in magic" of a most acceptable sort: a love-spell kit.[10] Shannen Doherty claims, "I'm the marrying kind and want children *so* badly." When she bought the same love-spell kit, she "had a run of bad luck. . . . So I decided that somebody was tapping me on the shoulder and saying, 'Shannen, calm down. Be happy with the place you are now.'"[11] Although Doherty eventually wants to live a domestic life, such narratives construct her as deferential to a higher power.

Despite temptations to cast love spells to gain the coveted gender roles of girlfriend or wife, media witches often passively wait for their desired male mate to come to them willingly. For example, the Charmed Ones regularly use "feminine" wiles to flirt with men, often competing with their own sisters for the same man. Despite typical television statements that family is more important than any man, it is obvious from their actions what these sisters really value. In "The Fourth Sister,"[12] Prue resents that her duties as one of the Charmed Ones sidetrack her dates and lead to a breakup. Such media representations construct protecting the world as less important than having a boyfriend.

Both *The Witches of Eastwick*[13] and *Practical Magic*[14] feature love spells describing an impossibly perfect man. The witches of Eastwick describe the man of their dreams and then passively wait to see whether anyone arrives. Apparently, what these women really want is the devilish, controlling patriarch Daryl Van Horne. The witches find and use their own inner power to free themselves of Daryl's direct oppression. He is not entirely defeated, however. He returns to tempt his sons through television screens—appropriate given the prevalence of media representations offering patriarchal gender norms. Unless the witches switch off every screen for the rest of their sons' lives, Daryl's influence remains a threat.

In *Practical Magic*, Sally describes in her love spell a perfect man she believes cannot exist, deliberately attempting to protect men from the family curse that kills every man the women marry. Yet she still describes a burning emptiness inside her and believes a man's love will fulfill her dream of being whole. To her surprise, Sally's love spell brings her impossible man to her. Then she breaks the family curse so they can marry. Such narratives construct messages that a woman without a man is not a complete and fulfilled person. She needs a "he" to live happily ever after. Even a seemingly active role such as casting a spell to summon a man is constructed as a passive act, with the witches then waiting for him to arrive in his own sweet time.

In *Sabrina, the Teenage Witch*,[15] Sabrina complains when she learns witches relinquished the ability to cast love spells. She doesn't see any point to being a witch if she lacks that power. She eventually realizes the value of "true love" over magic, however. Likewise, Louise refuses to cast a love spell on Brad in *Teen Witch*[16] since his love would not be "real." Although much is made of the fact that Louise does not force a love spell on Brad, she still basks in the attention he gives her after her magically improved clothes, makeup, and hair make her the most popular girl in school. Louise channels her magical power into a normative form of female influence: physical beauty. She does so for the socially acceptable goal of attracting a boyfriend. Yet Brad still appears as a willing partner who chooses her of his own free will instead of as a victim entrapped by an overly aggressive witch. Although Louise bends the rules, she still demonstrates proper "feminine" behavior by waiting for Brad to notice her and choose her to go to the dance with him. Like many media witches, she never asks him out on a date. Her role is essentially passive. Such passivity is rewarded when a desired male discovers "true love" for a witch and rewards her with a normative role such as girlfriend, wife, or mother.

The second type of love spells cast a witch in an aggressive role, pursuing the one she desires. These love spells are punished. For example, Sabrina will be transformed into a witch's familiar if she forces a human who does not love her to kiss her. In the *Charmed* episode "The Wedding from Hell,"[17] villainous Jade magically forces Alison's fiancé to love her instead. The counter spell requires Alison to "want to do everything in your power to keep the man you love from marrying someone else." Even though Alison steals her fiancé back from Jade, her actions appear acceptable because Jade's magic stole him first. Alison and the Charmed Ones protect the sanctity of marriage and male free will from Jade's aggression by sending Jade back to hell.

In *The Craft*,[18] Sarah's spell to make Chris love her spins out of control. First, Chris attracts ridicule for his excessive fawning behavior. Then he prompts fear as he attempts to force himself on the object of his desire. In response, Sarah dispels her enchantment. Later, Nancy casts a spell to make herself look like Sarah so she can seduce Chris. Sarah appears misguided, whereas Nancy is cast as a villain, even though both girls cast their spells to gain a male's attention. The difference is that Sarah seeks a relationship with a male who is interested in her, while Nancy appears focused on forcing a sexual union with a male who does not desire her. Rather than controlling Chris's behavior, Sarah chooses to wait passively for Chris to love her without magical manipulation. She is the film's heroine, safely disciplined into a passive normative "feminine" gender role. Even after Chris's death, she still is defined by her obedient relationship to Manon, the male source of all witches' power in the film. In contrast, Manon punishes disobedient Nancy with insanity and the loss of magical power.

Whether they are originally cast to pursue romance or control, love spells define witches primarily if not exclusively by their (usually romantic) relationship to a male. Such media representations contribute to patriarchal discipline by constructing women's most desirable—or even sole—gender role as a potential or actual girlfriend, wife, or mother. An independent woman with power of her own does not belong in the happily-ever-after ending of these narratives. Media representations of witches underscore the necessity and benefits of female dependence on a more capable male, whether mortal or divine. This rhetorical strategy also connects the use of love spells in media representations with the tendency to attribute witches' magical power to external sources.

External Sources of Power: Deities and Demons

Media representations frequently depict witches' magical abilities as coming from demons, spell books, or other external (usually patriarchal) sources. Witches' power is borrowed, again casting these women in normative roles defined by their relationship to more powerful sources. Such media representations construct women as lacking any real power of their own. There are medieval precedents for such rhetorical strategies. Medieval priest Martin de Castanega claimed women, "being powerless, have no way other than witchcraft to get what they want."[19] Even as witches, women still have no power of their own, however. Although the *Malleus Maleficarum* recounts fantastic tales of witches who collect stolen penises,[20] the authors then claim witches are only able to conceal the penis "with some glamour."[21] Only the devil himself can actually remove the male member.[22] The witch's power is an illusion generated by a male source of power: the devil acts through her. Such explanations are more reassuring than the possibility that women as witches can have any power over men or any power at all. These themes of borrowed female power continue in mainstream media representations.

The teen witches in *The Craft* are ineffectual until they gain tacit divine or demonic male approval from Manon. Nancy, Bonnie, and Rochelle call themselves witches but are unable to cast spells until Sarah completes their coven. Although much is made of Sarah's maternal magical heritage, it alternatively is inconsequential (precariously balancing pencils) or out of control (accidentally bursting water pipes). Likewise, once Sarah joins, the coven's spells also whirl out of control. A car hits a man when they wish him dead. Sarah's love spell turns Chris into a stalker. Rochelle's protection spell becomes petty revenge instead. Only after a dramatic ritual invocation of Manon do the girls gain some semblance of magical power and control.

Sarah's confrontation of Nancy thoroughly dispels that illusion, however, and exposes the patriarchal discipline at the heart of *The Craft*. During her preparations, the shop owner tells Sarah that to defeat her enemy she will have to surrender herself to a greater power: Manon. Sarah has to rely on a male source of power to succeed. More importantly, she has to obey his will. During their battle, Sarah tells Nancy that Manon "says you abused the power he gave to you, and now you're going to pay the price." Nancy, Bonnie, and Rochelle have no power of their own. What their male master gives, he also takes away when they disobey and displease him. Sarah's obedience is rewarded when she is allowed to keep the greater power Manon granted her. Such media representations undermine the witch by presenting real power as coming only via a relationship with an external male source. Patriarchal social systems limit power; it is only for males or their representatives.

Even as patriarchal rhetoric portrays powerful women as threats, it simultaneously tries to deny them any real power of their own, presenting them as only using or misusing power given to them by external male sources like Manon, Christianity's devil, or various demons serving that patriarchal devil. In "The Wedding from Hell," a demon grants two witches a wish apiece. Grace asks for wealth and power but gains them by marrying wealthy and powerful men. Grace's only power comes from a demon and her relationships as wife and mother to various men. Meanwhile, Jade asks for eternal youth and then tries to marry Grace's son, who will inherit the wealth and power of Grace's husband. Even demons cannot usurp patrilinear inheritance to bestow wealth and power directly on either witch.

In such mainstream media representations, whether witches, demons, or demoted deities, females must draw on external sources of power to cast their spells. The power source need not always be male, so long as it lies outside the witch. In "The Wedding from Hell," Jade must invoke the aid of "Asteria" and "Perses" to summon a storm. This episode also erroneously labels Greek goddess Hecate a demon. This rhetorical strategy robs a goddess of her power and authority. Instead of ruling her own domain, Hecate becomes a servant of a patriarchal deity in another mythos. Aviva invokes "Kali" in "The Fourth Sister," again using the name of another culture's goddess as the name of a demon. Kali even says she will give Aviva power, making it blatantly obvious that this witch has no power of her own, only what others allow her to have. When Aviva tells her aunt to leave her room, she gestures to cast a spell, but the camera's focus on Kali simultaneously making a similar gesture indicates it is Kali who really pushes the aunt away, not Aviva. Aviva has no power of her own but uses Kali's instead. Like the girls in *The Craft*, Aviva also loses her magical powers after she disobeys their source. Even witches' apparent power is borrowed, again casting them in normative gender roles defined solely by their relationship to more powerful sources.

Witches invoke a variety of external sources for their magical power in media representations. The resurrection spell in *Practical Magic* invokes Hecate. In the *Buffy the Vampire Slayer* episode "Bewitched, Bothered, and Bewildered,"[23] Amy invokes the goddess Diana when she casts a spell. Later, she must invoke Hecate to transform Buffy back into a human. Although Amy invokes a female deity, this rhetorical strategy highlights the fact that she has no power of her own—only what others deign to give her. At the end of "Gingerbread,"[24] Willow's spell to restore Amy invokes both Diana and Hecate but does not succeed. Amy remains a rat for several seasons despite multiple attempts. In "Witch,"[25] Catherine invokes "the laughing gods" to "give [her] the power." Not only does she have no power of her own, but she has to make others suffer to gain whatever power "the laughing gods" deign to bestow on her. Catherine must also invoke "Korseth" and "the Dark" to "take" her enemies. She cannot defeat them by herself. Sabrina, the Teenage Witch's attempt at a love spell invokes "the power of all the stars above me." In "The Painting,"[26] Miranda invokes the classical elements: fire, earth, air, and water. A witch asks the "Ancient One" to "protect this space" in the *Charmed* episode "Something Wicca This Way Comes."[27] Even after invoking an outside source of power, her protections are not strong enough to prevent her death at the hands of a single determined male. Such media representations construct women as ultimately lacking any real power of their own.

External Sources of Power: Symbols

Media representations also position symbols, whether words or inanimate objects, as containing more power than the women who wield them. Kerr Cuhulain, author of *The Law Enforcement Guide to Wicca*, explains this perspective as a result of patriarchal systems' attempts to explain how a male god could create even though "in nature the male does not give birth. . . . In Judaism and Christianity, Jehovah begat the universe by uttering specific words."[28] The resulting emphasis on words as magical tools underlies Occidental Ceremonial Magick, which in turn influences media representations of magic. According to this system, power is external and is controlled by "names and words of power" in imitation of Jehovah's act of creation. For these incantations to succeed, "specific words must be said in a specific order."[29] Media reliance on this conception of magic positions witches as merely conduits for power, much as Aristotle claimed women were only conduits for childbirth.[30] According to such misogynistic concepts, a woman may contain a child or magical power, but both come from an outside source (male sperm or magical entities, books, or words) and she contributes nothing of her own.

In many media representations, spells are specific phrases that must be memorized and repeated accurately to produce the desired result. When the sisters resurrect Jimmy in *Practical Magic*, they practice the words to the spell repeatedly, obsessing about reciting them correctly. In *Poltergeist: The Legacy* episode "The Painting," Kat cannot break an enchantment because she did not copy the spell she needs into her notebook. Miranda insists Kat memorize the proper words for a spell and states that spells must rhyme, a tendency that also appears in other media texts such as *Sabrina, the Teenage Witch* and *Charmed*. In such representations, the power lies in the words themselves instead of in the witches who recite them.

Not only are words more powerful than the women who speak them, media witches often are unable to control the consequences of a careless comment. Even if a witch does not intend to cast a spell, her words alone can do so. Spoken wishes grant Sabrina, the Teenage Witch the ability to throw a javelin out of the stadium and lower the pricetag of a swimsuit. She also makes a boy notice her through a casual comment wishing for his attention. Likewise, in *Teen Witch*, Louise wishes for Brad's attention and promptly receives it. Unintentional spells, however, also wreak havoc. In *Practical Magic*, Sally's daughter angrily inflicts chicken pox on a boy who teases her. When Teen Witch Louise tells an actress in the school play to "break a leg," the girl does just that. Also, when the undesirable date Louise's parents force on her makes unwelcome advances, Louise wishes he would leave her alone. He promptly vanishes, leaving their car without a driver. He is never seen again. These accidents emphasize a warning from Louise's spell book: "The power is in the word. Be careful what you say." Such media representations warn women to be careful what they wish for. Better yet, they should remain silent; if they aspire to power, their inability to control it properly will hurt themselves and others.

The spell book, or grimoire, is a related example of an external source of power. Sabrina, the Teenage Witch officially becomes a witch only after she receives the "ancient book." In the episode "Witch," Buffy the Vampire Slayer learns she can reverse all of Catherine's spells by acquiring her spell book. In the *Charmed* episode "Something Wicca This Way Comes," the *Book of Shadows* invokes "the oldest of Gods" and "the Ancient Power" to "give us the power." This Ancient Power will "bring" or "give" that power to the three sisters, but only after they ask for it. Until then, they have no power of their own despite their status as the "Chosen Ones." Even their title emphasizes that some outside power chose them for their role as protectors of the innocent. Furthermore, the spell has to be read at midnight to work; the timing, feeling, and phase of the moon all have to be "just so." The spell does not succeed because of Phoebe's inherent power or ability but because of a string of coincidences. She lacks any power of her own until one outside source, the *Book of Shadows*, gives her access to another: the "Ancient Power." Even after their infusion of power grants the sisters one innate "gift" apiece, their *Book of Shadows* still has all the spells and answers. In "The Wedding from Hell," the sisters must reference their book to discover how to break Jade's spell. Likewise, in *Hocus Pocus*,[31] the Sanderson sisters' most powerful spells can only be cast from their spell book. In addition, the devil gave it to Winifred, once again positing a male source for female power. In *Practical Magic*, the Owens family also has a spell book. The aunts have to consult it to cast a love spell, and the sisters must read it to resurrect Jimmy. Although the Owens women are able to cast minor spells such as stirring coffee and lighting candles without reading them from the book, the real power still resides not in the woman but in the book.

In addition to spoken and written verbal symbols, witches also rely on visual symbols such as pentagrams and amulets. Power comes from these inanimate objects; witches only act as a conduit. The *Poltergeist* episodes in which Miranda appears make it obvious that her power comes from outside sources. In "The Initiation,"[32] Miranda claims her "magic can affect everything" and lets her do anything she wants. Miranda then reveals her pentagram amulet is "where the real power comes from" since it steals and stores other people's power. This witch is a thief who cannot even steal without the aid of her amulet. Miranda's reliance on pentagrams as sources of power undermines her frequent claims of witches' power. One of Miranda's chants attributes all of her knowledge to this symbol: "What I know and what I am is inspired by the pentagram." Indeed, destroying her pentagram leaves her powerless, unable to cast spells.

Louise also relies on an amulet for her power in *Teen Witch*. Her necklace is described as the symbol of her power, yet sometimes her power seems to literally come from the necklace instead of her. Louise magically forces cheerleaders to tell the truth by concentrating on her pendant. At the Moonlight Magic dance, Louise removes her necklace and throws it to Serena. Brad does not dance with her until after she discards the symbol of her power. The song lyrics playing while they dance say this is her "finest hour" and she has "the power." Yet Louise no longer has any power of her own. She surrenders it to gain Brad's affection. A patriarchal relationship as a girlfriend and potential wife and mother is more important than magic. Interestingly, this film seems to be the least popular media text analyzed in this study, rarely mentioned or defended. *Teen Witch* offers an uncomplicated reading in which being a witch is nothing more than a way to attract a boyfriend. Louise briefly assumes a witch identity but quickly abandons it to live happily ever after in a more desirable normative gender role.

Conclusion

Patriarchal rhetorical strategies of witches discipline women into normative gender roles of girlfriends, wives, and mothers. First, witches use love spells and other magic to make themselves more attractive to males. Such media representations construct an independent woman with power of her own as a less desirable gender role than girlfriend, wife, or mother. Whether cast by a hero or villain to gain romance or control, love spells define witches by their relationship to a male and thus contribute to patriarchal discipline. Secondly, media representations demonstrate that witches' magical abilities actually come from demons, deities, spell books, amulets, and other external sources. Both of these rhetorical strategies construct women as only gaining identity and power from a relationship. Although this relationship is usually with a patriarchal male, the various substitutes in media representations drive home the same message. These rhetorical strategies construct women as lacking any real power of their own; their only power is borrowed.

Medieval witch hunts use similar rhetorical strategies. Positioning witches as servants and lovers of the Christian devil denies women power or agency; they are merely channels for his patriarchal power. Medieval rhetoric rejects non-patriarchal gender roles and justifies the annihilation of women as witches. More recent media representations instead attempt to assimilate witches. Aptly, *The Craft*; *Buffy the Vampire Slayer*; *Sabrina, the Teenage Witch*; *Poltergeist: The Legacy*; and *Teen Witch* all focus on teenage witches, as do many of their twenty-first century successors. Just as adolescence is constructed as an acceptable and even expected time for rebellion, so too are witches offered as acceptable forms of feminism. Teenagers are expected to grow up and out of their rebellion. Likewise, witches are constructed as using their feminist power to gain and maintain normative gender roles. Media witches allow women to explore different gender roles with the understanding that traditional roles as girlfriends, wives, and mothers await protagonists. Villains remain outside these normative roles and are punished accordingly.

Audiences take their own meanings from these texts, however. A patriarchal reading of *Practical Magic* emphasizes the need for an entire coven of women to overcome one man's ghost. In a resistant reading, Sally's improvised coven expands the roles available to her neighbors to include "the witch in every woman." Fans use this tagline as an example and explanation of why they like the film. A mother's connection to her injured daughter ties her to her coven mates and a previously unrecognized power within herself. The role of witch also expands as Sally's family members finally cast spells in public. Now they are friends and neighbors, members of the community instead of outcasts. Their roles include but are not limited solely to girlfriends, wives, and mothers.

Such resistant readings of *Practical Magic* and other media texts use the symbol of the witch in more complex ways than patriarchal rhetorical strategies, which oversimplify and limit humanity's choices. Ironically, the same patriarchal rhetorical strategies that discipline witches and women simultaneously reveal the constructed nature of these carefully defended gender norms. Witches in these media representations do not live happily ever after as girlfriends, wives, and mothers because those are natural, universal, and inevitable gender roles. Patriarchal rhetorical strategies guide witches and women into normative gender roles and away from consideration of alternative social norms. Even so, assimilation is not guaranteed. The cycle of media representations of witches continues.

Notes

1. Anne Llewellyn Barstow, *Witchcraze: A New History of the European Witch Hunts* (San Francisco: HarperCollins, 1995), 158.
2. Barstow, *Witchcraze*, 159.
3. Barstow, *Witchcraze*, 21–23.
4. Heinrich Kramer and James Sprenger, *Malleus Maleficarum* (New York: Dover, 1971), 41–48.
5. Susan J. Douglas, *Where the Girls Are: Growing up Female with the Mass Media* (New York: Random House, 1994), 126–27.
6. Susan Faludi, *Backlash: The Undeclared War Against American Women* (New York: Crown Publishers, 1991).
7. Robin Wood, *Hollywood from Vietnam to Reagan* (New York: Columbia University Press, 1986), 73.
8. John Gorman, "Buffy and Angel Are Charmed to Find Xena in the X-Files," *Connections* (Spring 2001): 46; Chad Anctil, "Witches on the Silver Screen," *PanGaia* (Autumn 2000): 30–32; Oberon Zell-Ravenheart, "A Real Wizard on *Harry Potter*," *PanGaia* (Autumn 2000): 36.
9. Janet Weeks, "Charmed Life," *TV Guide*, December 12–18, 1998, 24–29.
10. Weeks, "Charmed Life," 22.
11. Weeks, "Charmed Life," 29.
12. "The Fourth Sister," *Charmed*, directed by Gil Adler (1998; Burbank: 20th Century Fox Home Entertainment, 2005), DVD.
13. *The Witches of Eastwick*, directed by George Miller II (1987; Burbank: Warner Home Video, 1997), DVD .
14. *Practical Magic*, directed by Griffin Dunne (1998. Burbank: Warner Home Video, 2004), DVD.
15. *Sabrina, the Teenage Witch*, directed by Tibor Takacs (1996; Burbank: Lionsgate/Fox, 2003), DVD.
16. *Teen Witch*, directed by Dorian Walker (1989; Burbank: MGM, 2005), DVD.
17. "The Wedding from Hell," *Charmed*, directed by R. W. Ginty (1998; Burbank: 20th Century Fox Home Entertainment, 2005), DVD.
18. *The Craft*, directed by Andrew Fleming (1996; Burbank: Columbia TriStar Home Video, 1997), DVD.
19. Barstow, *Witchcraze*, 93.
20. Kramer and Sprenger, *Malleus Maleficarum*, 121.
21. Kramer and Sprenger, *Malleus Maleficarum*, 118.
22. Kramer and Sprenger, *Malleus Maleficarum*, 122.
23. "Bewitched, Bothered, and Bewildered," *Buffy the Vampire Slayer*, directed by James A. Contner (1998; Burbank: 20th Century Fox, 2005), DVD.

24. "Gingerbread," *Buffy the Vampire Slayer*, directed by James Whitmore Jr. (1999; Burbank: 20th Century Fox, 2005), DVD.

25. "Witch," *Buffy the Vampire Slayer*, directed by Stephen Cragg (1997; Burbank: 20th Century Fox, 2005), DVD.

26. "The Painting," *Poltergeist: The Legacy*, directed by Allan Kroeker (1999; Sci Fi Channel), broadcast.

27. "Something Wicca This Way Comes," *Charmed*, directed by John T. Kretchmer (1998; Burbank: 20th Century Fox Home Entertainment, 2005), DVD.

28. Kerr Cuhulain, *The Law Enforcement Guide to Wicca*, 3rd ed. (Victoria, BC, Canada: Horned Owl Publishing, 1997), 29.

29. Cuhulain, *Law Enforcement*, 29–30.

30. Aristotle, *Politics*, Benjamin Jowett, trans., Constitution Society, accessed November 2, 2000, http://www.constitution.org/ari/polit_01.htm.

31. *Hocus Pocus*, directed by Kenny Ortega (1993; Burbank: Walt Disney Home Video, 2003), DVD.

32. "The Initiation," *Poltergeist: The Legacy*, directed by Bill Fruet (1999; Sci Fi Channel), broadcast.

Bibliography

Anctil, Chad. "Witches on the Silver Screen." *PanGaia* (Autumn 2000): 30–32.

Aristotle. *Politics*. Benjamin Jowett, trans. Constitution Society. Accessed November 2, 2000. http://www.constitution.org/ari/polit_01.htm.

Barstow, Anne Llewellyn. *Witchcraze: A New History of the European Witch Hunts*. San Francisco: HarperCollins, 1995.

"Bewitched, Bothered, and Bewildered." *Buffy the Vampire Slayer*. Directed by James A. Contner. 1998. Burbank: 20th Century Fox, 2005. DVD.

The Craft. Directed by Andrew Fleming. 1996. Burbank: Columbia TriStar Home Video, 1997. DVD.

Cuhulain, Kerr. *The Law Enforcement Guide to Wicca*. 3rd ed. Victoria, BC, Canada: Horned Owl Publishing, 1997.

Douglas, Susan J. *Where the Girls Are: Growing up Female with the Mass Media*. New York: Random House, 1994.

Faludi, Susan. *Backlash: The Undeclared War Against American Women*. New York: Crown Publishers, 1991.

"Forget Me Not." *Poltergeist: The Legacy*. Directed by Jerry Ciccoritti. 1999. Sci Fi Channel. Broadcast.

"The Fourth Sister." *Charmed*. Directed by Gil Adler. 1998. Burbank: 20th Century Fox Home Entertainment, 2005. DVD.

"Gingerbread." *Buffy the Vampire Slayer*. Directed by James Whitmore Jr. 1999. Burbank: 20th Century Fox, 2005. DVD.

Gorman, John. "Buffy and Angel Are Charmed to Find Xena in the X-Files." *Connections* (Spring 2001): 30, 46.

Hocus Pocus. Directed by Kenny Ortega. 1993. Burbank: Walt Disney Home Video, 2003. DVD.

"The Initiation." *Poltergeist: The Legacy*. Directed by Bill Fruet. 1999. Sci Fi Channel. Broadcast.

Kramer, Heinrich, and James Sprenger. *Malleus Maleficarum*. New York: Dover, 1971.

"The Painting." *Poltergeist: The Legacy*. Directed by Allan Kroeker. 1999. Sci Fi Channel. Broadcast.

Practical Magic. Directed by Griffin Dunne. 1998. Burbank: Warner Home Video, 2004. DVD.

Sabrina, the Teenage Witch. Directed by Tibor Takacs. 1996. Burbank: Lionsgate/Fox, 2003. DVD.

"Something Wicca This Way Comes." *Charmed*. Directed by John T. Kretchmer. 1998. Burbank: 20th Century Fox Home Entertainment, 2005. DVD.

Teen Witch. Directed by Dorian Walker. 1989. Burbank: MGM, 2005. DVD.

"The Wedding from Hell." *Charmed*. Directed by R. W. Ginty. 1998. Burbank: 20th Century Fox Home Entertainment, 2005. DVD.

Weeks, Janet. "Charmed Life." *TV Guide*, December 12–18, 1998.

"Witch." *Buffy the Vampire Slayer*. Directed by Stephen Cragg. 1997. Burbank: 20th Century Fox, 2005. DVD.

The Witches of Eastwick. Directed by George Miller II. 1987. Burbank: Warner Home Video, 1997. DVD.

Wood, Robin. *Hollywood from Vietnam to Reagan*. New York: Columbia University Press, 1986.

Zell-Ravenheart, Oberon. "A Real Wizard on *Harry Potter*." *PanGaia* (Autumn 2000): 36.

Chapter 8

Head Above *Water*: Applying Nussbaum's "Capabilities Approach" to Deepa Mehta's 2005 Film

by Lauren J. DeCarvalho

Assessing a culture's treatment of women is one of the best ways to understand how that culture operates. Through this analysis, we can better comprehend a culture's attitudes, norms, values, and belief systems. Specifically, the roles and status of women in a society reveal the structure under which a culture functions. Many feminist philosophers such as Martha C. Nussbaum have made it their mission to study the conditions in which women of other cultures live and work as a way of bringing awareness to these concerns at the global level. Nussbaum has dedicated substantial time to dissecting gender and sexual politics in India, culminating in several published works that have garnered both positive and negative attention. Her critics' primary argument is that Nussbaum is an "outsider" critiquing a culture other than her own. Nussbaum disregards this notion of cultural relativism and remains committed to spotlighting injustices perpetrated against women worldwide.

Many film scholars argue that reading films as texts offers a critical reflection of a culture. With this in mind, I apply Nussbaum's political critique to Deepa Mehta's *Water*[1] in an effort to better understand the unimaginable oppression of the film's central characters: a group of Hindu widows living in forced seclusion and poverty. The purpose of this application is trifold: 1) to examine the film as an exemplar of feminist activism on the part of Deepa Mehta; 2) to apply Nussbaum's political critique as a means of understanding why Mehta's widows are oppressed in their particular circumstances; and 3) to identify the strengths and weaknesses of Nussbaum's approach.

Water: Mehta's Controversial Film

Arguably one of the most controversial films of the 2000s, Deepa Mehta's film *Water* made its debut on September 8, 2005, at the Toronto International Film Festival.[2] Prior to its release, the production was met with anger and hostility due to the candid nature of its content: a social commentary on the treatment of Hindu widowed women in India. While it was set to be filmed in 2000 as the third and final installment of Mehta's *Fire/Earth/Water* trilogy,[3] protests and backlash forced production to a standstill for over four years. According to a *New York Times* article, when the film was officially released, "Hindu nationalists protested that the film was anti-Hindu. Some 500 demonstrators took to the streets, ransacked the set and burned Ms. Mehta in effigy. She appealed to the state government for help, but fearing more violence, local officials asked the film crew to leave."[4] Despite this delay in production, Mehta did not let this backlash deter her from giving a voice to those who have long suffered from antiquated religious traditions. Filming picked up again four years later, moving from India to Sri Lanka.[5] Accompanying this change, Mehta had to recast her main characters and film under a working title to avoid drawing attention.

As Tutun Mukherjee explicates, "The trilogy represents in its totality a powerful and significant cultural challenge to the dominating masculine values and practices of oppression, subjugation, and exploitation of women."[6] The first film, *Fire*, shifts issues of lesbianism, oppression, and patriarchy from the private realm into the public sphere.[7] The second film, *Earth*, situates partition issues of the past in a way that questions those affecting the present.[8] Particular public attention was paid to *Water*'s production because of the heated controversy stemming from the first two films' resistance of patriarchal norms. As the final film in the series, *Water* concludes a trilogy that comments on sensitive political issues in India: *Fire* questions the politics of sexuality; *Earth* dissects the politics of nationalism; and *Water* critiques the politics of religion.[9]

In the film, an eight year-old Hindu girl named Chuyia is sent by her family to live in an ashram for widows after her husband dies. Chuyia is too young to understand why she is sent away as she does not even remember meeting her husband. At the ashram, Chuyia quickly learns the politics of living in such an institution. Her living environment is a tense one as Madhumati, an elder woman and the head of the group, insists that Chuyia thoroughly play the role of the "mourning" widow. Despite the poor living conditions, Chuyia is befriended by a young woman named Kalyani, who appears to be unusual among the group of widows. Kalyani is the only one, aside from Madhumati, who is allowed to have her own separate living quarters. Unlike the rest of the women, she is also granted permission to keep her hair. In a costly exchange, however, Madhumati forces Kalyani into prostitution and uses the profits to cover the ashram's expenses.

With the exception of Madhumati, the bonds between Chuyia and the rest of the women (particularly with an elder woman nicknamed Auntie and a middle-aged woman named Shakuntala) evolve and begin to positively affect the atmosphere of the ashram. Chuyia's refusal to abandon her childlike ways enables her to grow as an individual. Her reluctance to blindly accept the ways of the ashram provokes others such as Kalyani and Shakuntala to begin questioning these rules as well.

Kalyani's conflict is another instance in which blind acceptance of the ashram's rules is questioned. After realizing Narayan (the man she falls in love with) is the son of one of her more prominent patrons, Kalyani decides she cannot live with the shame and ends her own life. Shakuntala takes action for the first time and acknowledges Kalyani's forced prostitution. She is prompted to act after learning Madhumati has identified a replacement for Kalyani: Chuyia. Shakuntala attempts to rescue Chuyia from the pain of (unknowingly) giving her body to a male patron, but she arrives too late, finding Chuyia after the traumatizing experience. With Chuyia in her arms, Shakuntala goes to hear Gandhi say a prayer at a nearby train station. She is so moved by his words that she gives Chuyia to fellow train passenger Narayan and asks him to place the young girl under Gandhi's care. Shakuntala stays behind, and this is where the film concludes.

Despite the film's 1938 setting, the messages are still pertinent today. Most importantly, the film elucidates the harsh conditions in which women are forced to live each day. Institutions like the ashram where Chuyia resides wear the guise of religion. Consequently, the women are less likely to question whether things are as they should be or if there is an alternative way of living that would better suit their personal needs and desires. The few women who are skeptical of their circumstances and who do speak out are usually depicted as rebellious radicals to silence and diminish their voices.[10] Today, women still suffer as a result of these religious façades. According to a *New York Times* article written around the time of filming in 2000, some Hindu widows are still being forced to live in seclusion: "[S]ome say the film fairly reflects what social workers call the worst form of discrimination against women in India. Under ancient Hindu tradition, widows are considered bad luck, even blamed for their husbands' deaths. It is frowned upon for them to remarry—though no such social barriers exist for men. As a result many are left homeless and destitute. About 2,000 abandoned widows are thought to live in Varanasi, an ancient holy city 420 miles southeast of New Delhi."[11] Given this reality, it is not a far stretch to view the protests from Hindu fundamentalist groups—who were adamant that Mehta's film should never be released—as acts of silencing.

Nussbaum on Religion and the Bearer of Rights

Feminist philosopher Martha Nussbaum writes that religions have, time and again, endangered the basic rights of all humans. She affirms that "religious discourse is often powerfully colored by issues of political power."[12] Just as Mehta hints in *Water*, Nussbaum says Hinduism's "traditions contain views of female whorishness and childishness that derive from the Laws of Manu."[13] She also questions cases where widowed women like Metha Bai in India are unable to work outside the home due to religious traditions and thus run the risk of starvation for themselves and their families.[14] Specifically, she asks, "What, then, is 'the culture' of a woman like Metha Bai? Is it bound to be that determined by the most prevalent customs in Rajasthan, the region of her marital home? Or, might she be permitted to consider with what traditions or groups she wishes to align herself, perhaps forming a community of solidarity with other widows and women, in pursuit of a better quality of life?"[15]

In Mehta's film, Chuyia and the other widows enact the conflict between the predominant Hindu culture and the choice of communal resistance.

On the subject of how families operate, Nussbaum first details Gary Becker's "maximization of utility" approach, which states that everyone in a household should put aside their own feelings and do what they can to benefit the family as a whole.[16] In response, Nussbaum argues that "in real life, however, the economy of the family is characterized by pervasive 'cooperative conflicts,' that is, situations in which the interests of members of a cooperative body split apart, and some individuals fare well at the expense of others."[17] Therefore, Nussbaum suggests that more focus be placed on the rights of the individuals who comprise that household. In other words, "the fundamental bearer of rights is the individual human being. This seems right: A violation of a person is no better when it comes from some group to which the person belongs than when it comes from the state."[18] The individual bears at least ten rights, described in Nussbaum's list of capabilities.

Mehta's *Water* and Nussbaum's "Capabilities"

In *Sex & Social Justice*, Nussbaum outlines ten rights she feels every human is entitled to. If any of these "functional capabilities" are compromised, she argues, a person will be denied a "good human life."[19] Applying Nussbaum's list of capabilities to Mehta's film illuminates the oppression of this particular group of widows as well as revealing beneficial and problematic areas of Nussbaum's suggested approach. The aim of this section is to highlight specific scenes from the film that exemplify Nussbaum's list.

Life

The first capability pertains to life in general. As Nussbaum sees it, every human being has a right to live a long life devoid of factors that may cause it to end prematurely. In the film, viewers learn there are essentially three options for Hindu widows in India: burning with their deceased husbands; leading a life of self-denial; or, if the family permits it, marrying the late husband's younger brother. The women in the ashram are obviously following the second option; however, they were not given a choice in the matter, as most were either too young to make a decision or were simply forced into the ashram by their families. Their lack of appropriate shelter and adequate nourishment contributes to their overall poor living conditions. As the holy man in the film later reveals, a new law was passed that enables Hindu widows to remarry. The women of the ashram are not aware of this news concerning remarriage, however. This painful juxtaposition demonstrates how religious traditions trump the basic needs of individuals, particularly women.

Bodily Health

Nussbaum identifies the second capability as the right to various types of good health (including but not limited to reproduction, nourishment, and sufficient living conditions). The ashram women are restricted to one meal a day. Mehta describes the rationale behind these restrictions in her audio commentary on the film: "They're only allowed one meal a day, and that meal has to be without oil, onions, tomatoes, salt, in order to keep them pure. I mean the whole idea was, not to keep them pure but, to actually make them completely desexualized and not alive. . . . When we go further into the film, I can tell where it all came from because really this is all a misinterpretation of Hinduism to benefit a patriarchal society."[20]

Additionally, the women are essentially homeless outside the ashram because the religious custom that they must remain in mourning bars them from employment. They beg for food and money whenever they can, which is usually on their way to and from visiting the holy man by the river. This depiction of women suffering due to compromises to bodily heath illustrates the pressing nature of this particular capability.

Bodily Integrity

The third capability is an extension of the second. Nussbaum states that people should be able to live where they choose, wander where they wish, make decisions concerning reproduction and sexual satisfaction on their own, and be protected against assault (e.g., domestic violence, marital rape, and sexual assault). Since the widows have no money to pay for their religious seclusion, Madhumati is forced to make ends meet any way she can. She decides to compromise Kalyani's quality of life by forcing Kalyani to sell her body to wealthy businessmen. Any money that Kalyani receives from her patrons goes to Madhumati, who then uses it to pay for the ashram's expenses. When Kalyani refuses to work for Madhumati anymore, stating that "this is an ashram, not a brothel," Madhumati turns to eight-year-old Chuyia to fill the position. Nussbaum's description of bodily integrity condemns Madhumati's forcing prostitution onto the other women as a violation of their rights as human beings.

Senses, Imagination, Thought

The fourth capability Nussbaum calls "senses, imagination, thought."[21] By this, she means all humans should be able to think (or imagine) for themselves. This includes having a sufficient education and being able to choose words and thoughts as a person wishes to articulate and think them. Most of the ashram's widows are illiterate since they arrived when they were very young. Additionally, many of these women are denied freedom of expression by Madhumati, who keeps a tight rein over the ashram. Early on, when Chuyia inquires where the ashram with "male widows" is located, the women respond angrily, "What a horrible thing to say! God protect our men from such a fate. May your tongue burn. Pull out her tongue and throw it in the river." Thus, her thoughts are punished by the remarks of the other women. Chuyia is continually reprimanded throughout the film for wanting to enjoy herself and act like the child she is. These women are denied pleasurable experiences of any kind which, as Nussbaum asserts, inhibits their thought processes and imagination.

Emotions

For the fifth capability, Nussbaum argues all humans should be able to display their emotions (e.g., love, grief) as they see fit, particularly in regards to showing affection toward other people and things outside one's own body. After Chuyia arrives at the ashram and realizes what her new life will be like, she stubbornly insists on going home. Chuyia is told to forget about her old life and concentrate on her new life in the ashram. In response to Chuyia's pleas, Madhumati explains, "Our Holy Books say a wife is part of her husband while he's alive. Right? And when husbands die, God help us, wives also half die. So how can a half-dead woman feel pain?" Chuyia replies, "Because she's half alive." By preventing Chuyia from grieving the loss of her family as she transitions to ashram life, Madhumati is met with anger and disrespect from the little girl, who illustrates the significance of emotional expression.

Practical Reason

Nussbaum's sixth capability—that all people have a right to "practical reason"—includes being able to both plan one's life and critically reflect on it. The violation of this functional capability is seen in the film when Madhumati denies Kalyani the right to remarry. According to Hindu tradition, widows are not supposed to remarry; doing so is considered a sin. (As pointed out earlier, however, the law had recently changed to allow remarriages.) In response to Kalyani's request, Madhumati locks her away until Shakuntala comes along to release her. Kalyani abandons her forced position as a prostitute and goes to meet her new love, at which point she realizes his father is a prominent patron of hers. Rather than explaining the problem to Narayan, she finds the shame so unbearable she takes her own life.

This functional capability is also demonstrated by Shakuntala, who decides she can no longer hide her knowledge of the forced prostitution occurring in the ashram, particularly after learning widows can remarry. She acts on her judgment and reason to release Kalyani from imprisonment and send Chuyia away from the ashram, where she would no longer be placed in the arms of patrons by Madhumati. The contrast between violating and upholding the capability for practical reasons demonstrates why humans should be entitled to it in the first place.

Affiliation

For the seventh functional capability, Nussbaum explains that all humans beings should be entitled to affiliate with one another if they so decide. In other words, they should not be subjected to alienation and discrimination within a community. In the film, the widows are segregated from the rest of the world. With the exception of praying with the holy man by the river, they are not allowed to associate with men at all. They come across like lepers to everyone outside the ashram's walls. In one scene, Kalyani and Chuyia are bathing in the river. Viewers notice that a nearby woman, who is also bathing, gives them a dirty look, at which point Kalyani tells Chuyia to stop laughing. Later in the scene, Kalyani accidentally bumps into another woman while she's following Chuyia, who is trying to catch a runaway dog. The woman shouts, "What are you doing? Widows shouldn't run around like unmarried girls. You've polluted me! I have to bathe again." Her reaction is typical of those suffered by the widows throughout the film. In a later scene, when Shakuntala is collecting water from the river where a wedding ceremony is taking place, a man tells her, "Watch it! Don't let your shadow touch the bride!" This man's comment disturbs the holy man, who says angrily to himself: "Such ignorance. It's this ignorance that is our misfortune." Viewers side with the holy man as they witness these widows endure discrimination from the world outside the ashram.

Other Species

Extending her notion of the seventh capability, Nussbaum explains that, for the eighth capability, people should have the right to live "in relation to animals, plants, and the world of nature" if they wish to do so.[22] In addition to being shunned by the rest of the world, the widows do not have much contact with nature, other than the river where they bathe and pray. Nussbaum argues that all humans should have the right to choose, if they wish, to live amongst other species. As depicted in the film, however, the widows' culture looks down on such a decision. Despite this, Kalyani breaks this rule and hides a puppy in her living quarters. Her dismissal of this rule shows the importance of humans interacting with other living things.

Play

For the ninth item, Nussbaum states that everyone deserves a right to play and do as they like in terms of leisure and recreational activities. The widows are never allowed to do as they wish, particularly when it comes to leisure. Kalyani constantly reprimands Chuyia for smiling and playing with the puppy as the child is supposed to be in mourning. In a later scene, Chuyia is dropped off at a house, where she is told to stay and play. Chuyia enters the house and announces that she has "come to play." Regrettably, this takes on an entirely different meaning she is unaware of: her forced prostitution.

Control over One's Environment

Nussbaum describes the tenth capability as the right of every human to make both political and material decisions, thereby having "control over one's environment."[23] In the ashram, the widows have no say over how they live. Both politically and materially, they are denied the right to make decisions concerning their surroundings; in essence, they are denied their own agency. Their lack of financial support causes them to be vulnerable. Any money the widows do manage to gather goes directly to Madhumati for the ashram's rent and other expenses. Thus, they cannot even save up for their own cremation (as was the case with "Auntie"). Nussbaum would argue that every human is entitled to exert control over her environment and lifestyle. This functional capability is demonstrated by Shakuntala, who takes a stand against Madhumati, releases Kalyani, and rescues Chuyia from the ashram's harsh lifestyle. Now free to do as she pleases, Shakuntala decides to see Gandhi speak at a nearby train station following his recent release from jail.

A Critique of Nussbaum's List

The application of Nussbaum's list to Mehta's film elucidates both affirming and problematic areas of the capabilities approach. The greatest strength in adopting such an approach is that Nussbaum (and Mehta) allows viewers to see that these widows are living in the ashram for all the wrong reasons. They are denied food, happiness, and freedom of expression—all under the guise of religion, which Mehta further explicates in her audio commentary on the film: "A lot of women were sent to Varanasi to live out their lives in renunciation usually because of property. So religion, you know, was traditionally used, or misused, rather . . . to get rid of women so they would not be a part of the property dispute." Kalyani's beloved, Narayan, makes this injustice blatant for Mehta's audience in his dialogue with Shakuntala shortly after Kalyani's suicide:

> SHAKUNTALA: Why are widows sent here? There must be a reason for it.
>
> NARAYAN: One less mouth to feed. Four saris saved, one bed, and a corner is saved in the family home. There is no other reason why you are here. Disguised as religion, it's just about money.

Additionally, the mannerisms the women display in "mourning" the loss of their husbands reveal the true nature of the situation: many were too young to remember them or never even met them in the first place. Furthermore, those who do remember their husbands speak harshly of them.

Throughout the film, viewers see Shakuntala struggling to hold tight to her faith, despite the harsh conditions she and the other widows must endure. Their lifestyle of self-denial, combined with alienation and discrimination, forces them to live in "purity," yet survival translates to forced prostitution. Due to their arrival at the ashram at a young age, most of the women are illiterate and uneducated. Consequently, these women do not question religious beliefs and are unaware of new laws promoting remarriage for widows. They are shunned and treated like the diseased. It is human nature to want to live in a society where consensual verbal, physical, and sexual interactions take place amongst its members. Even Madhumati, who appears to be the most hardened to the ashram lifestyle, naturally desires interaction with another living being, a feeling that becomes evident when she cries and genuinely mourns the death of her parrot.

Nussbaum's capabilities approach is geared toward public policy makers. Every person is capable of having their ten human rights, but only to the extent that public policy makers and the government inform them of how to access and develop these "capabilities." Measures need to be taken to grant individuals access to developing these resources. Nussbaum states, "It just asks us to concern ourselves with the distribution of resources and opportunities in a certain way, namely, with concern to see how well *each and every one of them* is doing, seeing each and every one as an end, worthy of concern."[24] With this in mind, it appears Nussbaum's approach, if integrated into the world of the film, would have made living a lot easier for the widows. Nussbaum argues that it is the duty of public policy makers to ensure a society's individuals know how to *use* resources as opposed to just being *given* them. In Mehta's film, a law was recently passed that grants and promotes remarriage for widows. Government officials, however, made no effort to visit ashrams and inform the widows of this new law.

The biggest weakness in Nussbaum's philosophy does not pertain to her list of functional capabilities but rather to the reasoning behind it, which places the needs of an individual over the needs of a social or familial unit. This is to say that Nussbaum's approach gets complicated once children are involved. In the case of Shakuntala and Chuyia, Shakuntala sacrifices her own needs (loving Chuyia almost as if she were her daughter) to provide the young girl with a better life. Mehta details this sacrifice in the film's audio commentary: "So, the film, you know, sort of ends with Shakuntala's conflict. It's redemption. It's about ending with her ultimate sacrifice because on a personal level, it is a sacrifice. I mean she's giving away the person that she loves the most, Chuyia, but she also realizes that to leave Chuyia here as a widow in this ashram, in this life, is tantamount to murder."[25] Shakuntala's sacrifice is crucial in that it reveals her answer to a question she posed earlier during a dialogue with the holy man:

> HOLY MAN: Gandhi is one of the few people in the world who listens to the voice of his conscience.
>
> SHAKUNTALA: But . . . what if our conscience conflicts with our faith?

Shakuntala's decision is also important to assess as it demonstrates where Nussbaum and Mehta diverge in their beliefs. According to Nussbaum, individuals should concentrate on developing their own capabilities, first and foremost, before attempting to help others achieve the same thing. This contradicts Mehta's vision, however, particularly of Hinduism. In her audio commentary, Mehta discusses how her film is essentially about the "misinterpretation of Hinduism," not about the religion itself. She clarifies her viewpoint by asserting that Mahatma Gandhi was the closest thing to a perfect individual, if there was such a notion, particularly since he did not "misinterpret" Hinduism for his own personal gains. Mehta quotes a line from one of Gandhi's favorite hymns, which has been translated into English: "'The good human being is one who understands the pain of others.' So that's the true line through this song. So it's not about yourself, it's about someone else."[26] By letting Chuyia go with Narayan, Shakuntala is putting her own needs aside to ensure Chuyia never has to endure the pain of forced prostitution again. This is one instance where Nussbaum's capabilities approach does not fit with Mehta's perspective.

Conclusion

Mehta's *Water* is inspirational as it embodies feminist resistance to injustices continually inflicted on women globally, often under the guise of religious traditions. As pointed out in "The Story Behind the Making of *Water*" featurette, Mehta's filmmaking persisted despite numerous acts of silencing.[27] Similarly, feminist philosopher Martha C. Nussbaum has studied the injustices perpetrated against women, specifically in terms of their poor living and working conditions. In her attempt to inhibit these injustices with her own feminist activism, Nussbaum outlines ten capabilities that all human beings should have. As stated earlier, Nussbaum's approach is directed toward public policymakers who, as she argues, should do more than just grant resources to individuals; instead, they should ensure these individuals know how to develop these resources to better their lives. In this chapter, I have applied Nussbaum's list of functional capabilities to Mehta's film as a way of understanding how the denial of basic human rights is oppressive. In *Water*, those most affected are Mehta's group of widows. I hope this analysis will encourage feminist philosophers and filmmakers like Nussbaum and Mehta to continue exposing brutal injustices and amplifying the voices of women who continue to endure harsh living and working conditions worldwide.

Notes

1. *Water*, directed by Deepa Mehta (2005; Fox Searchlight Pictures, 2006), DVD. The film was nominated for the 2007 Academy Award for Best Foreign Language Film.

2. Fincina Hopgood, "The Politics of Melodrama in Deepa Mehta's *Water*," *Metro Magazine: Media and Education Magazine* 149 (2006): 145, accessed April 22, 2012, http://connection.ebscohost.com/c/articles/21816463/politics-melodrama-deepa-mehtas-water.

3. *Fire*, directed by Deepa Mehta (1996; Trial by Fire Films), DVD. This film also incited violent Hindu fundamentalist protests in India.; *Earth*, directed by Deepa Mehta (1998, Cracking the Earth Films), DVD.

4. Elisabeth Bumiller, "Film Ignites Wrath of Hindu Fundamentalists," *New York Times*, accessed April 22, 2012, http://www.nytimes.com/2006/05/03/movies/03wate.html?_r=1.

5. Bumiller, "Film Ignites Wrath," paragraph 8.

6. Tutun Mukherjee, "Deepa Mehta's Film *Water*: The Power of the Dialectical Image," *Canadian Journal of Film Studies* 17 (August 2008): 36, accessed April 22, 2012, http://www.filmstudies.ca/journal/cjfs/archives/articles/mukherjee-deepa-mehta-water.

7. Gary Morris, "Burning Love: Deepa Mehta's *Fire*," *Bright Lights Film Journal* 30 (October 2000), accessed April 22, 2012, http://www.brightlightsfilm.com/30/fire.html.

8. Jeanette Herman, "Memory and Melodrama: The Transnational Politics of Deepa Mehta's *Earth*," *Camera Obscura* 20 (2005): 109, accessed April 22, 2012, http://cameraobscura.dukejournals.org/content/20/1_58/107.citation.

9. Hopgood, "The Politics of Melodrama," 144.

10. bell hooks, *Teaching to Transgress: Education as the Practice of Freedom* (New York: Routledge, 1994), 178–79.

11. "Protests Halt Shooting of Film on Trials of Indian Widowhood," *New York Times*, accessed April 22, 2012, http://www.nytimes.com/2000/02/11/world/protests-halt-shooting-of-film-on-trials-of-indian-widowhood.html.

12. Martha C. Nussbaum, *Sex and Social Justice* (New York: Oxford University Press, 1999), 86.

13. Nussbaum, *Sex and Social Justice*, 36.

14. Nussbaum, *Sex and Social Justice*, 29.

15. Nussbaum, *Sex and Social Justice*, 37.

16. Nussbaum, *Sex and Social Justice*, 33.

17. Nussbaum, *Sex and Social Justice*, 33.

18. Nussbaum, *Sex and Social Justice*, 102.

19. Nussbaum, *Sex and Social Justice*, 41–42.

20. "Audio Commentary," *Water*, directed by Deepa Mehta (2005; Fox Searchlight Pictures, 2006), DVD.

21. Nussbaum, *Sex and Social Justice*, 41.

22. Nussbaum, *Sex and Social Justice*, 41.

23. Nussbaum, *Sex and Social Justice*, 42.

24. Nussbaum, *Sex and Social Justice*, 63.

25. "Audio Commentary."

26. "Audio Commentary."

27. "The Story Behind the Making of *Water*," *Water*, directed by Deepa Mehta (2005; Fox Searchlight Pictures, 2006), DVD.

Bibliography

"Audio Commentary." *Water*. Directed by Deepa Mehta. 2005. Fox Searchlight Pictures, 2006. DVD.

Bumiller, Elisabeth. "Film Ignites Wrath of Hindu Fundamentalists." *New York Times*. Accessed April 22, 2012. http://www.nytimes.com/2006/05/03/movies/03wate.html?_r=1.

Earth. Directed by Deepa Mehta. 1998. Cracking the Earth Films. DVD.

Fire. Directed by Deepa Mehta. 1996. Trial by Fire Films. DVD.

Herman, Jeanette. "Memory and Melodrama: The Transnational Politics of Deepa Mehta's *Earth*." *Camera Obscura* 20 (2005): 106–42. Accessed April 22, 2012. http://cameraobscura.dukejournals.org/content/20/1_58/107.citation.

hooks, bell. *Teaching to Transgress: Education as the Practice of Freedom*. New York: Routledge, 1994.

Hopgood, Fincina. "The Politics of Melodrama in Deepa Mehta's *Water*." *Metro Magazine: Media and Education Magazine* 149 (2006): 142–47. Accessed April 22, 2012. http://connection.ebscohost.com/c/articles/21816463/politics-melodrama-deepa-mehtas-water.

Morris, Gary. "Burning Love: Deepa Mehta's *Fire*." *Bright Lights Film Journal* 30 (October 2000). Accessed April 22, 2012. http://www.brightlightsfilm.com/30/fire.html.

Mukherjee, Tutun. "Deepa Mehta's Film *Water*: The Power of the Dialectical Image." *Canadian Journal of Film Studies* 17 (August 2008): 35–47. Accessed April 22, 2012. http://www.filmstudies.ca/journal/cjfs/archives/articles/mukherjee-deepa-mehta-water.

Nussbaum, Martha C. *Sex and Social Justice*. New York: Oxford University Press, 1999.

"Protests Halt Shooting of Film on Trials of Indian Widowhood." *New York Times*. Accessed April 22, 2012. http://www.nytimes.com/2000/02/11/world/protests-halt-shooting-of-film-on-trials-of-indian-widowhood.html.

"The Story Behind the Making of *Water*." *Water*. Directed by Deepa Mehta. 2005. Fox Searchlight Pictures, 2006. DVD.

Water. Directed by Deepa Mehta. 2005. Fox Searchlight Pictures, 2006. DVD.

PART III
News Coverage

Chapter 9

Feminine Style and Militant Motherhood in Antiwar Discourse: Cindy Sheehan as Grieving Mother and/or Left-Leaning Radical

by Heidi E. Hamilton

When Cindy Sheehan began her protests outside President George W. Bush's Crawford, Texas, ranch in August 2005, media latched onto her as a sympathetic symbol of a war gone badly. For a few weeks, Sheehan galvanized the anti-Iraq war movement; her role as grieving mother of a fallen soldier provided the movement with a legitimate public symbol, one more easily accepted by mainstream America than those antiwar figures often perceived as unpatriotic or unsupportive of America's soldiers. The media, however, soon began characterizing Sheehan's rhetoric and actions—including her arrests and controversial visit to Venezuela—as increasingly radical.

How are the two conflicting portraits of Sheehan to be understood? This chapter explores these two discordant rhetorical personas: the grieving mother who should be listened to based on her status as a mother and the left-leaning radical who alienates the public with her politicization. I analyze both her rhetoric and mediated public discourse to determine not only how she characterizes herself but also how others shape public perceptions of her. This analysis examines the efficacy of Sheehan's rhetoric as well as revealing insights into the intersection of rhetoric, gender, and politics operating today. I argue that Sheehan uses motherhood appeals and elements of what Campbell calls the "feminine style"[1]—particularly what other scholars such as Tonn have termed "maternal militancy,"[2]—to ground her rhetoric against the Bush Administration and the war in Iraq. These choices open up opportunities for her rhetoric to be heard and to make arguments that mobilize others, but they also limit her when public discourse characterizes Sheehan's rhetoric and actions as radical, questioning her right to speak in the name of "mother."

Feminine Style and the Rhetoric of Motherhood

Sheehan's reliance on personal experience as a mother warrants further examination of the literature on feminine style and motherhood appeals, particularly given that her development of these appeals calls into question how far a rhetor can go and remain effective. While we might assume theorizing about a feminine style rightfully has reached a standstill, Sheehan's case illustrates that while the feminine style enables, it also limits. Revisiting how this style plays out—especially when used with motherhood appeals and radical politics—reveals where rhetorical scholarship is at in terms of gender and politics.

Stemming from women's experiences in the private sphere, the feminine style developed by Karlyn Kohrs Campbell includes such attributes as personal tone, use of personal experience, use of examples as evidence, inductive reasoning, and the encouragement of audience participation and identification.[3] Bonnie J. Dow and Mary Boor Tonn argue that, given women's traditional restriction to the private sphere, "women are encouraged to exhibit communicative patterns that correspond to the tasks that women are expected to perform in the private sphere . . . female communication is characterized as concrete, participatory, cooperative, and oriented toward relationship maintenance."[4] Sara Hayden (2003), in applying Campbell's theory to the Million Mom March, identifies the functions this style achieves, including "its ability . . . to offer alternative modes of political reasoning" and "promoting an empathic response from audience members."[5] In these instances, much of the research has considered sympathetic audiences. Sheehan exhibits characteristics of this style not only to like-minded audiences but also to those supporting the war. Exploring how elements of the style appear and are received within this dual context of sympathetic and oppositional audiences yields greater insights into the style's strengths and limitations than previous research.

To further understand how the style operates rhetorically, we also must consider the invocation of motherhood as a rhetorical appeal. Christine Woyshner argues that American women have often used understandings about mothers "as selfless, caring, and nurturing people" as a basis for social reform.[6] Women's influence is necessary to change the world because women take care of things. Woyshner states that the use of motherhood as an argument for reform escalated in the nineteenth century, when men and women's roles became more divided due to the effects of industrialization, immigration, and urbanization. As women[7] became more limited to the private sphere, motherhood emerged as an important avenue that allowed them a voice in the public sphere. Meghan Gibbons points out that "the right to maternal expression and protest" is not confined to the United States.[8] Referring to examples from antiwar and peace groups in the United States, El Salvador, and Argentina, Gibbons states, "Belief in the sacred role of mother gives political mothers' groups a power. . . . They have used it to argue that they are better qualified than others to make decisions about which causes are worth the ultimate sacrifice of life."[9] For instance, the 1960s organization Women Strike for Peace used maternal appeals to protest the Vietnam War, enlarging their scope beyond the war and draft to join international efforts calling for an end to violence and war in general.[10] Nancy Scheper-Hughes cautions that these arguments from motherhood are "by intentional design, rather than by any natural predisposition."[11] Women choose to use their motherhood as a rhetorical tactic; to talk about maternal appeals does not necessarily imply an essentialist view of women as inherently more peaceful and nurturing of life. She comments, "Women have just as often used the moral claims of motherhood to launch campaigns to support war as they have to support peace."[12] This chapter's analysis primarily focuses on how Sheehan utilizes motherhood as an argumentative claim and how that claim is turned against her.

Why choose the invocation of motherhood as a rhetorical appeal? Swerdlow argues that positioning oneself as a mother speaking allows admission into the public sphere because one is "acting in the service of others," which is what mothers do.[13] It confronts the prohibition on women speaking out in protest of governmental actions. Because the military and war have traditionally been seen as masculine public spheres, this invocation of motherhood offers a way of subverting another gender stereotype (women do not belong in military rhetoric) in an area where few avenues exist for women to justify their right to speak on this topic.[14]

There are limits, however, on the ability to effectively use these appeals. Woyshner states that status as a mother is only an argumentative strategy in issues dealing with the care of children.[15] Of course, which issues this area includes can be part of the rhetorical maneuvering. The rhetor must define the subject as one in which her children's lives are affected, thus falling within her purview as a mother. Gibbons stresses the need to stick to this message: "Preserving the purity of the average mother's voice has always been essential to motherhood groups. The most influential have coached mothers not to pontificate on subjects beyond their expertise. They have stuck to reciting their personal stories with a mind-numbing consistency and presenting a self-deprecating attitude about their potential to influence social change."[16] So the reliance on personal experience—a primary hallmark of the feminine style—as evidence for the mother's appeals restricts the ability to venture beyond these experiences. Experiencing caring for children under certain conditions provides the mother rhetor with the arguments, but if she moves into a larger debate on the issue, her arguments no longer fall within the feminine style or the pure mother's voice. Even more so, audience perception plays a role in determining whether the mother is viewed as sufficiently "self-deprecating," rather than "pontificating," as illustrated by Sheehan's case.

Combining the invocation of motherhood with the feminine style, one option is what Tonn identifies as a "militant motherhood."[17] In this conception, while nurturing is often a characteristic of motherhood, the mother as social activist also may need to be confrontational in her approach. For example, Mother Jones, while telling stories and interacting with the audience, would use "profanity, creative name-calling, and caustic wit."[18] While dominant images usually ignore a mother's militant side, when conditions threaten children, "the need for maternal protectiveness is most pronounced . . . while a maternal persona may be warmly nurturing, it also may be confrontational."[19] In the framework of militant motherhood, the self-deprecating attitude mentioned previously marks powerlessness; power instead is enacted through "bawdy, rowdy, and irreverent personal expression."[20] This approach alters the motherhood appeal by playing with societal expectations of mothers. Rather than portraying demure homebodies who humbly assert themselves when their children are threatened, militant motherhood enacts a different persona of the mother. The militant mother, however, must walk a fine line between that confronting spirit and a mother's *nurturing* nature from which confrontation arises.

Other scholars have applied this combination of feminine style and maternal militancy to various case studies. For instance, the mothers of the Million Mom March attempted to stir up a collective anger in their audience against Congress's failure to act against gun violence.[21] Women within the environmental justice movement use their roles as mothers to argue against harmful environmental policies.[22] Peeples and DeLuca make two insightful observations about these motherhood appeals. In both cases, the women use their personal experiences "to rhetorically construct the 'truth' of the matter," not allowing oppositional presentations of scientific, objective knowledge to negate the power of their own arguments.[23] Secondly, the mothers argue that their move into the public sphere is not a choice but a necessity given the rhetorical situation. Peeples and DeLuca explain, "The rhetoric of Environmental Justice leaves no other options for being a good mother than to be a militant one. Their children are endangered, and no other course of action will save them. . . . It is not only of dire importance to do so, but the militant activist persona is already embedded in motherhood and just needs to be released."[24] In this way, the power that stems from motherhood roles in the private sphere is preserved, as the women do not seek out public attention for their own sake (which would indicate a lack of concern for the home). Instead, the exigency requires seeking out attention in order to be a good mother—and doing so in a way that calls forth fierce maternal protectiveness (i.e., the militant stance).

Examples of previous movements suggest that the feminine style combined with maternal appeals opens up possibilities for women's arguments within the public sphere. The added dimension of maternal militancy allows that feminine, maternal rhetoric to move beyond traditional images of meekness to confrontation. In this chapter, I examine how Cindy Sheehan's rhetoric enacts elements of both feminine style and militant motherhood. I also analyze how this rhetoric is received within public discourse, suggesting that while these rhetorical tactics provide opportunities to make particular arguments, Sheehan also encounters limits on how far these appeals can leverage her arguments. This case study analysis also indicates the opportunities and limitations provided to other rhetors who utilize motherhood appeals in challenging both sympathetic and oppositional audiences.

To examine her rhetoric, I look at statements posted or reprinted on the Gold Star Families for Peace website (an antiwar group Sheehan cofounded) and comments given to the media. I located mediated public discourse from August 2005 through July 2008 by using her name as a search term within the Lexis-Nexis database of major newspaper articles. Popular discourse provides an indication of how she was perceived and portrayed as well as how successful she was at promoting her own message. Media discourse from her opponents, including op-ed pieces and quotations within other stories, indicates how they use her arguments and actions to undermine her claims and how they attempt to refute the motherhood appeal.

The Potential in Sheehan's Militant Motherhood Appeals

Sheehan grounds her basis for public speech in the death of her son, Specialist Casey Austin Sheehan, who was killed in April 2004. She began her antiwar protest in August 2005, when she went to Crawford, Texas, stating that she would remain outside President Bush's ranch for the duration of his five-week vacation unless he agreed to meet with her. Sheehan characterizes her actions as "that of a broken-hearted mom sitting down in front of George Bush's ranch wanting to know why my son died."[25] In this statement, reprinted widely, she positions herself primarily as a mother and reminds the public of her story, her son's death.

As her rhetoric persisted beyond this initial protest, she invoked the right of mothers to protect their children as the basis for her actions. For instance, in a letter to Bush, she writes of the killing of Iraqi and Afghani children and states, "I feel like you are killing *my precious* babies to further your greed for power and riches."[26] In this instance, she moves from claiming to be the mother of one fallen soldier to being a mother to many children. Zeina Zaatari argues that women's roles create networks of relationships, which allow women to enter the public sphere as "mothers of all."[27] Grounding her political activism within a larger community, Sheehan thus claims a larger responsibility to speak out.

She also characterizes her actions as "matriotically dissenting."[28] Notice Sheehan's provocative play on words here. Twisting the term "patriotic"—particularly the idea that dissent is often viewed as unpatriotic—Sheehan trumps the conception of patriotism as love and loyalty to country with a mother's love and loyalty to her child. The subtle implication is that not only is she granted the right to speak but that she should not be criticized for her dissent.

Invoking motherhood as rhetorical authorization, Sheehan uses several elements of the feminine style. Repeatedly, she tells the personal story of her reaction to Casey's death. For instance, she is quoted, "Every day is like April 4, 2004, all over again. . . . Every morning, I wake up, and I ask myself, 'How in the hell am I going to get through another day without him with me?' And then I go to bed at night, and I say, 'Wow, I made it through another day without Casey.'"[29] She draws on her personal, everyday experience as a grieving mother, and her comments are emotional, designed to evoke sympathy and convey her heartache. One aspect of the feminine style is to create audience identification; in this respect, Sheehan's rhetoric conjures an image that other mothers can relate to even if only hypothetically (e.g., imagining the grief of losing a child). In doing so, she shifts the rhetorical ground away from the abstract, emotionless rhetoric associated with militaristic masculinity, a move that offers sympathetic audiences an alternative way to view the war that deviates from the Bush Administration's narrative.

Sheehan also draws on examples to support her arguments. She tells an anecdote of being accosted in a parking lot while with her daughter and her daughter's friends. The "probably inebriated" man accused her of not caring about her son because she speaks out against what he died for. Sheehan uses this example to prove how stubborn some people remain, despite increasing evidence that the rationale for war was deceptive.[30] She also uses examples of others to illustrate that she is not alone in experiencing loss. Sheehan relates the story of another mother whose son was killed, stating, "I know what that mom has been going through since her son flew off to this misguided and evil occupation of Iraq."[31] Her example indicates that more mothers feel this way; rhetorically, she positions herself as the one speaking on behalf of them.

Initially, public discourse generally accepted Sheehan's invoking of motherhood as a basis for her right to speak. One *Washington Post* editorial comments, "As the parent of a dead soldier, Sheehan has so much moral authority precisely because so few Americans . . . risk sharing her plight."[32] Even those disagreeing with her recognized the power of the maternal argument. While simultaneously labeling her arguments "vile nonsense," Reinhard writes, "Cindy Sheehan is a grieving, distraught mother who lost a good son. She has every right to make her views known. . . . In fact, a parent of a dead soldier has secured that right in a way most Americans have not."[33] So not only does she have a right to speak, but she has a greater right than others. The feminine style works in this context as well, according to supporters: "Sheehan succeeded in personalizing opposition to the war."[34] This personalization is a hallmark of the feminine style, and it takes on increased relevance within the war context. More than an abstract body count and the absence of images of the deceased (given Administration's blockage of media coverage of soldiers' caskets returning to the United States) possibly can, Sheehan's telling of her own story, of her son-soldier Casey, brings the impact of the war home to her audience.

Sheehan's style is not all personal stories and grief, however. She also evidences maternal militancy in attacking Bush and others, showing not just loss but anger over the death of her son and other "children." In a letter to Bush holding him, not the enemy, responsible for the deaths, she states, "you are killing our children." Additionally, she calls Bush a "disgrace and a danger to our country."[35] He is "an out of control criminal that needs to be impeached for his lies; removed from office for his transgressions; and imprisoned for his crimes against humanity."[36] She thus uses anger to call out Bush for what she clearly sees as illegal actions. She enlarges the blame to include companies profiting from the war. Her rhetoric can hardly be described as meek or mild: "The Halliburtons, Bechtels, Blackwater Securities, KBR's, Standard Oils are raking the billions at a clip that would make Barberry Coast pirate ship Captains' heads spin. The no-bid profiteers are cronies and/or former companies of the vice president and most of the Bush regime. I don't know how can the blood-monied devils look at their own children or grandchildren and not be ashamed and appalled that their insatiable greed killed someone else's flesh and blood!"[37] Here, her rhetoric clearly moves from personal stories to personal attacks. Repeatedly referring to "BushCo," she draws connections between the Administration and corporations to impugn their motives for war, holding them responsible for the killing of children. In this way, employing language that relies on name-calling (e.g., "pirates," "devils," "regime"), she attempts to construct a "truth" about the war's immorality while also undermining appeals to patriotic support of the war allowed by purer motives.

Sheehan utilizes this militant rhetoric to encourage action (to mobilize her constituency, in Tonn's words). She argues, "War will finally have to stop when we mothers (and fathers, spouses, etc.) stop allowing our leaders to march our children off to wars that are to feed the ravenous war monster. . . . Whether the wars are covert or overt they are always being waged with our babies' blood."[38] Importantly, even as her rhetoric becomes militant, it also remains grounded in the motherhood appeal as she talks about "our children" and "our babies' blood." Her militancy stays rooted in her constructed persona of the concerned mother speaking on behalf of all children. Even the title to the call suggests action while it invokes motherhood. In a play on words,[39] Sheehan titles her piece "Mamas Don't Let Your Babies Grow up to Be Soldiers," directly confronting the masculine sphere of soldiering by suggesting that mothers must take responsibility for their children.

Sheehan thus employs elements of the feminine style even as she relies on a militant version of motherhood to support her arguments. In characterizing herself as the grieving mother, she effectively utilizes personal experience and identification to demonstrate why she deserves the right to speak and be listened to (i.e., her stance will protect children's lives). Her maternal militancy tactics follow a similar pattern. While engaging in name-calling and more descriptive rhetoric, she continuously reminds her audience of her role as mother, keeping in line with the persona that her rhetoric constructed for herself. These rhetorical tactics are successful for her in terms of calling attention to this issue and claiming a right to speak on this issue.

Limits to Sheehan's Militant Motherhood Rhetoric

Sheehan's militant rhetoric also opens her up to oppositional arguments, however. When her rhetoric and actions stray from the motherhood appeal into more politically charged territory, they both undercut the basis of her appeals and allow war supporters to create an alternative persona of her as the left-leaning radical. In this sense, not only does the socially constructed image of mother become problematic, but her aggressive stances also provide ammunition for opponents to shape perceptions of her. Tonn, commenting on the competing expectations of women's roles and their public mission, states, "Some critics have argued that invoking motherhood may help neutralize this paradox for women speakers. . . . Yet while symbolic motherhood may ease this reconciliation, this analysis reveals that motherhood itself may require skillful rhetorical negotiation."[40]

Providing another example, Fabj's analysis of the Mothers of Plaza de Mayo suggests that this group's effectiveness is linked to their decision to voice their requests through symbols of motherhood instead of more threatening political rhetoric.[41] In other words, the feminine style along with maternal appeals may be effective, but only if the rhetor avoids overly political rhetoric *that disassociates her* from her role as mother.

In this section, I focus on mediated discourse surrounding Sheehan, examining how it views her more political rhetoric and actions vis-à-vis her claims to grieving motherhood and how her opponents use her stances to construct an alternative persona of her by undercutting her claims to maternal authority.

As protests shifted away from the focus of meeting with President Bush, Sheehan's actions moved beyond the feminine style into what some would describe as more radical territory. These actions include her January 2006 visit to Venezuela to attend a world peace conference and meet with Venezuelan President Hugo Chavez, a controversial figure within the United States. During this meeting, she called Bush a terrorist. While she certainly had called Bush names before, this occasion was marked by the fact that she was on foreign soil in the company of a leader with whom the United States had been at odds. She also was arrested several times, including during the State of the Union address and at a protest outside the United Nations. Each of these actions appears beyond the boundaries that speaking as a mother of a fallen soldier would allow.

Public discourse thus also distinguishes between Sheehan as grieving mother and activist. For example, one article points out that she is "an aggrieved mother whose son had died in Iraq. Plainspoken and unscripted, Sheehan delivered an easily relatable story that gave her a kind of moral authority. Since then, some have questioned whether Sheehan has strayed too far politically."[42] The author points out that Sheehan's personal experience as a mother of a fallen soldier gave her authority; when her actions seem to go beyond those of grieving mother to outspoken woman, her authority is questioned. Other articles put the problem much more bluntly: "[She] has morphed from being a grieving mother with a smattering of media coverage to one of the most visible—and polarizing—figures."[43] In one sense, this polarization fits the role of the militant mother, whose rhetoric is not expected to remain polite or uncontroversial.

Sheehan's perceived shift to a more radical stance, however, provides her opponents with easy targets for attacks against her. They move from calling her a mother to calling her other names, displacing her maternal authority. Akerman describes her as a "pin-up girl for the loopy Left, global terrorists."[44] In pointing to a number of actions she engaged in—such as refusing to pay income taxes and supporting a lawyer who had been convicted in a terrorist plot—Rosen argues that Sheehan is "a veritable supermarket of rants, clichés, and conspiracy theories about President Bush and the United States."[45] Using gendered metaphors ("pinup girl," "supermarket"), these statements illustrate the backlash over her growing public presence. Rather than remaining tied to the symbols of motherhood—as Fabj indicates would be a wise rhetorical maneuver[46]—Sheehan transitions to a more politicized stance, one in which she loses moral authority to speak according to public discourse perceptions. In this way, her militant mother stance hurts her cause as she shifts from a strict focus on her son and protecting children to politicizing the war and engaging in controversial actions, leaving her open to attacks from others.

Furthermore, even her ability to speak as a mother is called into question by some. If her position as a grieving mother provides her with credibility, then attacking her role as a mother undermines her rhetorical appeal. Three particular lines of argument recur in the mediated discourse: She profited from her son's death, she neglected to support Casey, and she did not speak for all parents.

The first argument suggests that rather than speaking out of grief, she was profiting from her son's death. In terms that evoke gendered hysteria, Akerman describes her as "using her soldier son Casey's coffin as a soapbox . . . *shrilly* exploiting her son Casey's death."[47] Those protesting her shouted, "Media whore!" at an event to discuss her decision to run against Representative Nancy Pelosi.[48] This gendered chant maligns her motives and questions her authenticity, implying she acts not on behalf of her son but to gain attention for herself. Several articles point to the fact that she works with political consultants and public relations professionals.[49] *The American Spectator* suggests that she is "more antiwar protester than grieving mother," disputing the possibility of being both protester and mother.[50] Venturing too far into the public while using Casey's death as evidence and working on her image as a mother (as opposed to just being one), Sheehan abandons the private sphere role that had given her the credibility to speak. Within this argument, lines are redrawn between the public (protester) and the private (mother) spheres. She can invoke mothering as long as she stays "self-deprecating" and "selfless," traditional gender stereotypes. The attention and professionalism taint her, causing the loss of her pure, moral authority as a mother.

The second line of argument states that she neglected to support her son as a mother should, suggesting that Casey would not agree with her public stances. Casey willingly joined the military, re-enlisted, and then volunteered for the mission during which he was killed. Given these facts, opponents argue, "It seems unlikely that he would have warmed to either this characterization [being sent into a 'raging, insurgent uprising'] or the manner in which his mother has so enthusiastically embraced a broad coalition of left-wing American groups."[51] This line of argument particularly challenges Sheehan's credibility because the appeal to motherhood is based on a mother's responsibility to protect her children. If Casey made his own choices, different from his mother's, he did so as an adult, not a child. Because he acted as a man, Sheehan now seems to fit the societal stereotype of the *overbearing*, rather than the protective, mother. Furthermore, Sheehan's arguments are characterized as an "infantilization of the military," which is "deeply insulting to America's warriors."[52] Arguing that she has a responsibility to speak out on behalf of her children identifies soldiers as children, a rhetorical move her opponents resist. Hayden posits that maternal appeals become less effective when advocating change that protects adults; the power in the appeal comes from "their duty to protect children."[53] Unlike other maternal appeals focusing on young children (e.g., the Million Mom March about gun violence against children[54] and the environmental justice movement protesting environmental hazards affecting children[55]), Sheehan's appeals do not, in an age sense, involve literal children. While Sheehan attempts to frame her appeal as a protection of children—such as when she refers to wars "being waged with our *babies'* blood"[56]—the military presents a challenge to this framing because soldiers are not often viewed as children in need of protection. Quite the contrary, in the most positive light, we view them as the heroes and protectors of innocents.

The third line of argument attacks Sheehan's characterization as a universal mother by suggesting that she does not speak for all parents or on behalf of all children. The media quotes Gold Star families (referring to the designation for those who have lost children in war) who support the war. For example, Elfriede Plumondore states, "As a mom, I say that you've got to let them finish the job . . . I feel that as much now, maybe even more. Otherwise it would all be for nothing."[57] Gary Qualls, who lost a son, emphatically states, "Cindy Sheehan does not speak for America. And she does not speak for me. . . . She is destroying the morale of the service members that are protecting us all."[58] Here, contrary to the public stance Sheehan took, these parents argue for the continuation of the war. For them, Sheehan's stance dishonors the memory of fallen soldiers, making death just death and not heroic sacrifice, and thus denigrates the very soldiers she claims to protect.

In August 2005, a group consisting of parents of soldiers serving in Iraq and Afghanistan and calling themselves the "You Don't Speak for Me, Cindy" Tour, traveled to Crawford, Texas.[59] Using support-the-troops rhetoric, they argued that not all parents feel protecting children means pulling out of Iraq. This line of argument also addresses the public sphere/private sphere distinction. Sheehan's position suggests that she was forced into the public sphere because of Casey's death but that her public stance was rooted in her private role as a mother. The fact that other families spoke out against her suggests that her private sphere experience was not their private sphere experience; while her loss led to anger against Bush, their losses led to more support for finishing the job as a way to honor their sons and daughters. If she cannot speak for others, then hers is a singular experience, one that resists being used as evidence for a wider public argument.

Thus we see in these three lines of argument direct responses to the maternal appeal. Whether questioning her right to speak or implying that she is not acting as a mother should, these arguments attempt to undermine the rhetorical basis for her authority to take on public issues.

Conclusion

For Cindy Sheehan, invoking her experience as a mother through the rhetorical tactics of feminine style and maternal militancy presents both opportunities and limitations. Her rhetoric works carefully to craft a persona of the grieving mother. Her ability to attract attention stems from a mother's loss, and the authority granted to her to speak is grounded in the perception that she paid a sacrifice. Using these advantages, Sheehan crafts rhetorical appeals that remind her audience that she speaks on behalf of the children whose lives were being lost. Her militancy calls out those whom she views as responsible for their lost lives and allows her to stir up her audience to anger against those parties in order to motivate them toward action.

Peeples and DeLuca suggest, however, that "using motherhood may be more effectual or lasting when used to motivate one's own constituency rather than to influence the opposition."[60] Here is where Sheehan's militancy results in limitations. Supporters as well as detractors were viewing her appearance in the public spotlight. A position of militant motherhood opens her, and by association the antiwar movement, up to criticisms of being too radical for mainstream America. The feminine style's reliance on personal experience to justify the rhetor's place in the public rather than the private sphere can be turned against the rhetor when she is attempting to persuade those who are not sympathetic. The opposition's personal experiences become equally valid. Additionally, Peeples and DeLuca comment on the "tension between taking action and maintaining the appearance of femininity."[61]

This case study suggests that the feminine style, combined with a militant motherhood stance, requires even more negotiation. The context and subject matter become particularly important: While the feminine style as indicated through the sharing of personal experience and identification may allow entry into the public sphere, if what one talks about while there seems "unladylike" or beyond the bounds of maternal cares, the rhetor may lose the audience. Merely playing the role of the grieving mother cannot sway public opinion (sympathy alone will not translate to action on the part of others); yet, for Sheehan, venturing beyond this role allows public discourse to discount her credibility. She appears to have problems negotiating the expectations of how a mother is supposed to act with what she wishes to accomplish in a public role.

Furthermore, while it would seem obvious that maternal appeals allow a rhetor to achieve a degree of legitimacy, as seen in this case study, there is a risk of over-relying on these appeals. If the basis for motherhood can be undercut, then the basis for moral authority is also undermined. Sheehan's opponents reframe motherhood as a cultural rather than a biological relationship. They cannot deny that she is Casey's mother, but they can characterize her as not acting like a mother. The three lines of argument prevalent in media discourse illustrate this point. Each suggests that Sheehan's protest activities and rhetoric crossed a line. The cultural archetype of the "good mother" comes in many forms and appears differently across contexts, war being just one of them. While a rhetor may draw on this archetype to justify her claims, opponents may also draw from its polysemic nature to delegitimize the mother-rhetor's argument. In this regard, the power of the maternal appeal is called into question and suggests a rhetor cannot merely claim the mantle of motherhood to be successful but must also be seen as acting like a mother.

Notes

1. Karlyn Kohrs Campbell, *Man Cannot Speak for Her: A Critical Study of Early Feminist Rhetoric*, Vol. 1 (New York: Greenwood Press, 1989).

2. Mari Boor Tonn, "Militant Motherhood: Labor's Mary Harris 'Mother' Jones," *Quarterly Journal of Speech* 82 (1996): 1–21.

3. Campbell, *Man Cannot Speak for Her.*

4. Bonnie J. Dow and Mari Boor Tonn, "'Feminine Style' and Political Judgment in the Rhetoric of Ann Richards," *Quarterly Journal of Speech* 79 (1993): 288.

5. Sara Hayden, "Family Metaphors and the Nation: Promoting a Politics of Care Through the Million Mom March," *Quarterly Journal of Speech* 89 (2003): 203.

6. Christine Woyshner, "Motherhood, Activism, and Social Reform," *USA Today*, March 1, 2002, 66.

7. Woyshner carefully delineates that she is talking about middle-class white women. Within other races and classes, gender roles developed differently, particularly given the constraints on

working women's time and racial prejudices, thus restricting women's roles even more in the public sphere.

8. Meghan Gibbons, "On the Home Front: The Politics of Motherhood," *Washington Post*, October 16, 2005, B3.

9. Gibbons, "On the Home Front," B3.

10. Amy Swerdlow, *Women Strike for Peace: Traditional Motherhood and Radical Politics in the 1960s* (Chicago: University of Chicago Press, 1993).

11. Nancy Scheper-Hughes, "Maternal Thinking and the Politics of War," in *The Women and War Reader*, ed. Lois A. Lorentzen and Jennifer Turpin (New York: New York University Press, 1998), 233.

12. Scheper-Hughes, "Maternal Thinking," 233.

13. Swerdlow, *Women Strike for Peace*, 186.

14. An alternative avenue is seen with women's increasing military involvement as evidenced by a growing percentage of women in the military and the opening up of some combat roles. The fact that war is no longer a solely male experience provides another justification for women's right to speak, albeit limited to women who have participated in these roles.

15. Woyshner, "Motherhood, Activism, and Social Reform."

16. Gibbons, "On the Home Front," B3.

17. Tonn, "Militant Motherhood."

18. Tonn, "Militant Motherhood," 2.

19. Tonn, "Militant Motherhood," 3.

20. Tonn, "Militant Motherhood," 6.

21. Hayden, "Family Metaphors and the Nation."

22. Jennifer A. Peeples and Kevin M. DeLuca, "The Truth of the Matter: Motherhood, Community and Environmental Justice," *Women's Studies in Communication* 29 (2006): 59–87.

23. Peeples and DeLuca, "The Truth of the Matter," 62.

24. Peeples and DeLuca, "The Truth of the Matter," 73.

25. Christopher Caldwell, "The Mother of Smoke Screens," *Financial Times*, August 20, 2005, 9.

26. Cindy Sheehan. "Hey George," *Gold Star Families for Peace*. September 12, 2006, accessed October 23, 2006, http://www.gsfp.org/article.php?id=262, para. 5; italics in original.

27. Zeina Zaatari, "The Culture of Motherhood: An Avenue for Women's Civil Participation in South Lebanon," *Journal of Middle East Women's Studies* 2 (2006): 34.

28. Cindy Sheehan. "A Nation Still at War," *Gold Star Families for Peace*. October 7, 2006, accessed October 23, 2006, http://www.gsfp.org/article.php?id=266, para. 10.

29. Robert Seltzer, "Crawford Snub Another Stab in Mom's Aching Heart," *San Antonio Express-News*, August 21, 2005, 1H.

30. Cindy Sheehan. "It's Personal," *Gold Star Families for Peace*. September 5, 2006, accessed October 23, 2006, http://www.gsfp.org/article.php?id=261.

31. Sheehan. "A Nation Still at War," para. 5.

32. Peter Beinart, "When the War Won't Stay at Bay; With Bush and the Public Insulated from Iraq, Cindy Sheehan Has Moral Authority," *Washington Post*, August 18, 2005, A21.

33. David Reinhard, "Actions Only a 'Peace Mother' Could Love," *Sunday Oregonian*, August 28, 2005, B4.

34. Linda Feldmann, "Did the Cindy Sheehan Vigil Succeed?" *Christian Science Monitor*, August 29, 2005, 1.

35. Sheehan. "Hey George," para. 7.

36. Cindy Sheehan. "Me, Hugo and George," *Gold Star Families for Peace*. July 15, 2006, accessed October 23, 2006, http://www.gsfp.org/article.php?id=232, para. 17.

37. Cindy Sheehan. "Mamas Don't Let Your Babies Grow up to Be Soldiers," *Gold Star Families for Peace*. July 10, 2006, accessed October 23, 2006, http://www.gsfp.org/article.php?id=227, para. 7.

38. Sheehan. "Mamas Don't Let Your Babies," para. 11.

39. The reference is to the song "Mamas Don't Let Your Babies Grow up to Be Cowboys," made famous by Waylon Jennings and Willie Nelson. The song bemoans the life of the cowboy while simultaneously romanticizing it. Moreover, the intended audience elevates cowboys and denigrates "doctors and lawyers and such." In co-opting this cultural reference, Sheehan hopes the audience will respond to the title while ignoring the complicated insertion of mothers into the military realm.

40. Tonn, "Militant Motherhood," 16.

41. Valeria Fabj, "Motherhood as Political Voice: The Rhetoric of the Mothers of Plaza de Mayo," *Communication Studies* 44 (1993): 1–18.

42. Mark Sommer, "Politics Is Clouding Message of Antiwar Activist Sheehan," *Buffalo News*, June 15, 2006, A1.

43. Marjie Lundstrom, "It's Free Speech, Even If You Don't Like What Sheehan Is Saying," *Sacramento Bee*, October 13, 2005, A3.

44. Piers Akerman, "Flawed Ideology Comes to Grief," *Daily Telegraph* (Australia), May 23, 2006, 14.

45. Mike Rosen, "Tide Turning on Sheehan," *Rocky Mountain News*, August 26, 2005, 39A.

46. Fabj, "Motherhood as Political Voice."

47. Akerman, "Flawed Ideology Comes to Grief"; italics added.

48. Larry Eichel, "Voices, Tempers Rise over War; Peace Activist Cindy Sheehan Came to Phila. for Rally. Her Opponents Turned out, Too," *Philadelphia Inquirer*, July 25, 2007, B1.

49. Michael A. Fletcher, "Cindy Sheehan's Pitched Battle; In a Tent Near Bush's Ranch, Antiwar Mother of Dead Soldier Gains Visibility," *Washington Post*, August 13, 2005, A1, and Vicki Haddock, "Cindy Sheehan's Year of Living Famously," *San Francisco Chronicle*, March 19, 2006, D1.

50. As quoted in Fletcher, "Cindy Sheehan's Pitched Battle."

51. Akerman, "Flawed Ideology Comes to Grief."

52. Mark Steyn, "'Peace Mom's' Marriage a Metaphor for Dems," *Chicago Sun-Times*, August 21, 2005, 7.

53. Hayden, "Family Metaphors and the Nation," 212.

54. Hayden, "Family Metaphors and the Nation."

55. Peeples and DeLuca, "The Truth of the Matter."

56. Sheehan. "Mamas Don't Let Your Babies."

57. David Reinhard, "War and Remembrance: Why Gold Star Families Now Fight for Their Fallen," *Sunday Oregonian*, February 26, 2006, E5.

58. Nancy Dillon, "Dad of Slain G.I. Rips 'Peace Ma,'" *Daily News* (New York), September 19, 2005, 12.

59. Kathleen Parker, "Cindy Sheehan and the Bona Fides of Grief: The 'You Don't Speak for Me, Cindy' Tour is Headed for Crawford with Another Story to Tell," Pittsburgh Post-Gazette, August 24, 2005, B7, and Joe Garofoli, "She Reopened Debate About War, and Boy, Is She Hearing About It," *San Francisco Chronicle*, August 18, 2005, A1.

60. Peeples and DeLuca, "The Truth of the Matter," 82.

61. Peeples and DeLuca, "The Truth of the Matter," 64.

Bibliography

Akerman, Piers. "Flawed Ideology Comes to Grief." *Daily Telegraph* (Australia), May 23, 2006.

Beinart, Peter. "When the War Won't Stay at Bay; With Bush and the Public Insulated from Iraq, Cindy Sheehan Has Moral Authority." *Washington Post*, August 18, 2005.

Caldwell, Christopher. "The Mother of Smoke Screens." *Financial Times*, August 20, 2005.

Campbell, Karlyn Kohrs. *Man Cannot Speak for Her: A Critical Study of Early Feminist Rhetoric*, Vol. 1. New York: Greenwood Press, 1989.

Dillon, Nancy. "Dad of Slain G.I. Rips 'Peace Ma.'" *Daily News* (New York), September 19, 2005.

Dow, Bonnie J., and Mari Boor Tonn. "'Feminine Style' and Political Judgment in the Rhetoric of Ann Richards." *Quarterly Journal of Speech* 79, no. 3 (1993): 286–302.

Eichel, Larry. "Voices, Tempers Rise over War; Peace Activist Cindy Sheehan Came to Phila. for Rally. Her Opponents Turned Out, Too." *Philadelphia Inquirer,* July 25, 2007.

Fabj, Valeria. "Motherhood as Political Voice: The Rhetoric of the Mothers of Plaza de Mayo." *Communication Studies* 44 (1993): 1–18.

Feldmann, Linda. "Did the Cindy Sheehan Vigil Succeed?" *Christian Science Monitor,* August 29, 2005.

Fletcher, Michael A. "Cindy Sheehan's Pitched Battle; In a Tent Near Bush's Ranch, Antiwar Mother of Dead Soldier Gains Visibility." *Washington Post,* August 13, 2005.

Garofoli, Joe. "She Reopened Debate About War, and Boy, Is She Hearing About It." *San Francisco Chronicle,* August 18, 2005.

Gibbons, Meghan. "On the Home Front: The Politics of Motherhood." *Washington Post,* October 16, 2005.

Haddock, Vicki. "Cindy Sheehan's Year of Living Famously." *San Francisco Chronicle,* March 19, 2006.

Hayden, Sara. "Family Metaphors and the Nation: Promoting a Politics of Care Through the Million Mom March." *Quarterly Journal of Speech* 89 (2003): 196–215.

Lundstrom, Marjie. "It's Free Speech, Even If You Don't Like What Sheehan Is Saying." *Sacramento Bee,* October 13, 2005.

Parker, Kathleen. "Cindy Sheehan and the Bona Fides of Grief: The 'You Don't Speak for Me, Cindy' Tour is Headed for Crawford with Another Story to Tell." *Pittsburgh Post-Gazette,* August 24, 2005.

Peeples, Jennifer A. and Kevin M. DeLuca. "The Truth of the Matter: Motherhood, Community and Environmental Justice." *Women's Studies in Communication* 29 (2006): 59–87.

Reinhard, David. "Actions Only a 'Peace Mother' Could Love." *Sunday Oregonian,* August 28, 2005.

———. "War and Remembrance: Why Gold Star Families Now Fight for Their Fallen." *Sunday Oregonian,* February 26, 2006.

Rosen, Mike. "Tide Turning on Sheehan." *Rocky Mountain News,* August 26, 2005.

Scheper-Hughes, Nancy. "Maternal Thinking and the Politics of War." In *The Women and War Reader.* Edited by Lois A. Lorentzen and Jennifer Turpin, 227–33. New York: New York University Press, 1998.

Seltzer, Robert. "Crawford Snub Another Stab in Mom's Aching Heart." *San Antonio Express-News,* August 21, 2005.

Sheehan, Cindy. "Hey George," *Gold Star Families for Peace.* September 12, 2006. Accessed October 23, 2006. http://www.gsfp.org/article.php?id=262.

———. "It's Personal," *Gold Star Families for Peace.* September 5, 2006. Accessed October 23, 2006. http://www.gsfp.org/article.php?id=261.

———. "Mamas Don't Let Your Babies Grow up to Be Soldiers," *Gold Star Families for Peace.* July 10, 2006. Accessed October 23, 2006. http://www.gsfp.org/article.php?id=227.

———. "Me, Hugo and George," *Gold Star Families for Peace.* July 15, 2006. Accessed October 23, 2006. http://www.gsfp.org/article.php?id=232.

———. "A Nation Still at War," *Gold Star Families for Peace.* October 7, 2006. Accessed October 23, 2006. http://www.gsfp.org/article.php?id=266.

Sommer, Mark. "Politics Is Clouding Message of Antiwar Activist Sheehan." *Buffalo News,* June 15, 2006.

Steyn, Mark. "'Peace Mom's' Marriage a Metaphor for Dems." *Chicago Sun-Times,* August 21, 2005.

Swerdlow, Amy. *Women Strike for Peace: Traditional Motherhood and Radical Politics in the 1960s.* Chicago: University of Chicago Press, 1993.

Tonn, Mari Boor. "Militant Motherhood: Labor's Mary Harris 'Mother' Jones." *Quarterly Journal of Speech* 82 (1996): 1–21.

Woyshner, Christine. "Motherhood, Activism, and Social Reform." *USA Today,* March 1, 2002.

Zaatari, Zeina. "The Culture of Motherhood: An Avenue for Women's Civil Participation in South Lebanon." *Journal of Middle East Women's Studies* 2 (2006): 33–64.

Chapter 10

Grisly Mama: Carnivorous Media Coverage of Sarah Palin[1]

by Alena Amato Ruggerio

Former Governor of Alaska Sarah Palin has been objectified, sexualized, and parodied since capturing the national spotlight in 2008, but it would be an oversimplification to reduce her public persona just to these depictions. Palin has also used the media for her own purposes, calling out political commentators for being sexist elitists—and then becoming one herself. Why is it so difficult to pin her down? Why does she remain a public figure long after her direct participation in executive governance waned? This chapter explains her longevity with a rhetorical criticism of Sarah Palin's complex public persona as interpreted through the systemic metaphor of meat. Simultaneously, she is the fierce grizzly mama and the simpering pageant queen; the folksy populist and the censor of democratic participation. Although she worked to her advantage the metaphor of the carnivore embedded in her public image as a mother, politician, and celebrity, she was also victimized by the patriarchal implications of "dead meat" underlying this discourse.

Sarah Palin, Mediated Mother

Palin's performance of femininity[2]—and the media's commentary on it—illustrates the misogyny of political coverage. In a discussion about forms of "gendered mediation," Gidengil and Everitt describe how the media cover politics according to a male-oriented agenda that effectively subordinates female candidates to "novelty" status.[3] Similarly, the media covertly and continuously present an ideology of White males as the dominant group in the United States, in turn perpetuating a hegemony that devalues and debases women. Indeed, many analyses of the 2008 presidential campaign point to both anecdotal and observed evidence of gender bias in media coverage of Hillary Clinton and Sarah Palin in contrast to that of their opponents.[4] Specifically, some criticized those in the news media for presenting decidedly more negative coverage of the two women than their male counterparts, and in the case of Clinton, blatant hostility. In their study of media coverage of Clinton and Palin, Carlin and Winfrey find evidence of the gendered organizational stereotypes of mother, sex object, and child originally developed by Rosabeth Moss Kanter and Julia Wood.[5] Carlin and Winfrey conclude that not only do these sexist portrayals objectify women, but they also potentially impact audience perceptions of the candidates' ability to lead the country.

Scholarly analysis of Sarah Palin has focused almost exclusively on her gendered representation, as in Bradley and Wicks's analysis of the balance between bloggers' commentaries on personal matters like her wardrobe and pregnant teenage daughter and her stance on political issues.[6] Online conversations about Palin's ability to be both a politician and a mother of five children allow women to publicly discuss the choices of working mothers, but McCarver points out that the discourse of these choices is often individualized rather than systematized.[7] Avance, Crocco, and Marvin use myth to connect Palin's politics with her fecundity, actually framing the 2008 presidential election as a fertility rite in which the power of her sexuality was not enough to prevent the inevitable sacrifice of her warrior-man, John McCain.[8] Gibson and Heyse identify a "faux maternal persona" in Palin's vice presidential nomination acceptance speech to the Republican National Convention on September 3, 2008. This persona makes manifest the conflict between the motherly content and language of her speech versus her complicity in the "continuation of a conservative masculine script."[9] What Gibson and Heyse conceptualize as a contradiction, Harp, Loke, and Bachmann see as a blend, categorizing Palin as a hybrid of both feminine and masculine performance.[10] Oles calls the same phenomenon an "inarticulate gender-bending," a blundering attempt to blur the categories of frontier maverick and slick urban candidate.[11] The complex gender performances communication scholars grapple with are enacted in the underlying double-sided metaphor of meat in discourse by and about Sarah Palin.

The Metaphor of Meat

Kenneth Burke led the transformation of metaphor treatment from elocutionist-era ornamental flourish to an epistemological tool of *inventio*, a means for discovering and creating meaning in arguments.[12] Metaphor, as one of Burke's four master tropes,[13] has the power to name and constitute our perceptions and interpretations of reality.[14] In particular, metaphor can shape political discourse in four ways, as identified by Charteris-Black:[15]

> 1. Conveying political arguments to the audience. In the context of media information overload, metaphors turn complex political issues into easily digested simplifications for voters.[16]
>
> 2. Using political mythology to communicate ideology. Metaphors activate unconscious symbols, as in the previously mentioned fertility rite,[17] tapping into a deeper audience narrative that can help the speaker meet persuasive goals.
>
> 3. Increasing the effect of emotional appeals. In a later study, Charteris-Black takes this notion further, arguing that metaphors in political communication unite unconscious emotion and conscious reason by legitimizing the anxieties of the voting public into a reassuring sense of the rightness of their convictions.[18]
>
> 4. Convincing an audience of the *ethos* of the political rhetor. Mio, Riggio, Levin, and Reese link metaphors to the charisma and inspiration of presidential leaders.[19]

Metaphors provide the frame through which gender is depicted in media representations of political candidates. Karrin Vasby Anderson describes the importance of metaphors to the construction and recreation of the public personae of women running for high public office.[20] Specifically, both the politicians themselves and the media coverage of them assert metaphors of pioneering, puppetry, beauty pageantry, and unruliness.[21]

Sarah Palin's public persona is inscribed by those four metaphors,[22] but it is also significantly shaped by a controlling but often unconscious metaphor of meat invoked by Palin herself as an image of empowered motherhood. Reinterpreted in media coverage as sexist objectification of the idealized Republican "MILF," metaphoric references to meat inhabit the intersection of political power and gender performance. Howe's analysis of 1980s American political speeches documents the prevalence of masculine root metaphors of sports and warfare.[23] The metaphorical vehicle of meat—with its cluster of hunting, carnivore, mass slaughter, blood, and gun images—combines both the sporting and killing metaphors of patriarchally dominated politics.

Ecofeminist critics have called attention to the connection between the metaphor of meat and masculine gender performance. Eating meat is an act of dominance, a symbol of the male human hunter's control over the lives of animals. Eating meat—the muscle of an animal—is equated with building large, strong human muscles.[24] Carol J. Adams highlights the ominous side of masculine performance vis-à-vis meat: "Images of butchering suffuse patriarchal culture," which she connects to symbolic male violence: "Sexual butchering is a basic component of male pornographic sexuality."[25] Despite its aggressive and misogynist overtones, the association of meat consumption and patriarchal power resists reframing: "To reject such messages is to reject human as omnivore on top of the food chain, or what has been constructed as an essential part of U.S. culture."[26]

Rogers argues that recent depictions of beef eating in television advertisements not only reinscribe the patriarchal model of masculinity, but they also re-entrench a hegemonic system of male dominance under perceived threat from feminists and environmentalists.[27] Meat consumption is constructed symbolically as a locus of power and masculine strength within a larger American belief system.[28] Wesley Buerkle's analysis of burger commercials identifies the heteronormativity and homophobia of the meat-eating symbol as retaliation against the rise of the metrosexual 1990s man.[29]

The case of Sarah Palin's media coverage both typifies and problematizes the gender implications of the meat metaphor in political discourse as it is performed in the context of domestic gender roles. This chapter asserts that the political messages from Palin herself and the media are circumscribed by an underlying carnivorous metaphor.

Blood-Soaked Hunter vs. Sexualized Prey

Photographs of Sarah Palin sitting in her Anchorage office with a dead bear flung over the sofa behind her or hunched over a dead caribou she had presumably just killed surfaced soon after she became a vice presidential candidate. Media sources frequently quoted Palin's hunting references, most notably "I eat, therefore I hunt."[30] The sheer force of hunting imagery in political discourse is apparent in the following excerpt from an article by *Washington Post* columnist Kathleen Parker:

> Republicans are determined to demonstrate their political virility by displaying not just their hunting trophies, but their fearlessness in carving up a fresh kill for the family table. . . . it's impossible to avert one's gaze from the puddles of blood surfacing in certain politicians' photo albums. . . . 'Show me the blood' seems to be the mantra in some quarters of the GOP. It started with you-know-who from Alaska, who won carnivore hearts when it became known that she could field dress a moose.[31]

Parker goes on to link Palin's image as a hunter with her identity as a different kind of mother, in effect a female father:

> The new coin of the realm was gore and the message was clear: The Democratic "mommy" party of swooning dependents can't stand the sight of blood (and therefore can't be trusted to protect America). The Republican "father party" of virile (and fertile) warriors is strong, self-sufficient and unafraid. No one who eats suffers any illusions about what precedes the cuisine. Something has to die, as Palin noted. . . . Gutting and gore are obviously part of the game.[32]

Palin took the masculine performance of the underlying meat metaphor to a further extreme by trumpeting her hunting and consumption of *wild* rather than farm-raised meat. As Nick Trujillo describes, frontiersmanship is a defining characteristic of the patriarchal performance of masculinity.[33] Media coverage during and after the 2008 presidential campaign magnified the hunter trope Palin offered to the public.

In another manifestation of carnivore discourse, headlines containing references to Palin's identity as an attack dog such as "Attack Dog: Palin and Simple"[34] and "Mad Dog Palin"[35] were ubiquitous in media reactions to her RNC acceptance speech. Numerous articles carried references to Palin as an attack dog,[36] attack puppy,[37] or pit bull.[38] Harp, Loke, and Bachmann explain that Palin's pit bull reference in her RNC address was made in the context of her maternal identity as a "hockey mom"; if she had instead called herself a pit bull when referring to a more masculine-associated fight against political corruption in Alaska, they ask, would the audience have responded to this metaphor with as much applause?[39]

As images of bloodthirsty pursuit of prey, the hunter and pit bull[40] are examples of carnivorous metaphors that move beyond political forcefulness into physical aggression. Palin invites her audience into a perspective of meaning based on the patriarchal conceptualization of agency: strong, independent, self-sufficient, powerful, and potentially violent. Drawing on the American audience's associations of meat as vigor, meat as power, Palin's identity as a hunter and attack dog qualified her for high political office as a person strong enough to decide life and death.

Capitalizing on the secondary association of the meat metaphor with significance and substance (e.g., "put the *meat of your argument* in the body of the speech," "*flesh out* this main point with examples"), Palin also portrays herself as focusing on political issues rather than superficialities. Perhaps this explains her mystified response when her competence and intelligence were questioned by opponents and pundits in the 2008 campaign; unconsciously, she could not grasp why some people rejected the transference of the meat metaphor from her hunting practices to her claims to well-considered political positions.

Palin successfully perpetuated her feminine performance of bloodthirstiness before a conservative audience because it was couched in the patriarchally approved language of motherhood, especially in the carnivorous metaphor of the mama grizzly. In her May 14, 2010, address to the conservative women's political group the Susan B. Anthony List, Palin jumped from the pit bull of the presidential election campaign to the mama grizzly of her post-political celebrity: "There in Alaska, I always think of the mama grizzly bears that rise up on their hind legs when somebody's coming to attack their cubs, to do something adverse toward their cubs. No, the mama grizzlies, they rear up. And, you know, if you thought pit bulls were tough, you don't want to mess with the mama grizzlies."[41]

Palin's grizzly bear ferocity is tolerated because it is not for herself but for the protection of her children; it matters that she characterized herself and the female candidates she endorsed as *mama* grizzlies not responsible for the figurative violence perpetrated in defense of their cubs. In comparing then-Governor Palin's pregnancy in office to Massachusetts Governor Jane Swift's pregnancy, Loke, Harp, and Bachmann conclude that Palin's experience was depicted more sympathetically in the media in part because Palin publicly accepted the culturally mandated version of motherhood, a performance she would later dub the mama grizzly.[42] She participated enthusiastically in the masculine sphere as a frontier hunter, a blood-sporting pit bull, and a protective grizzly bear[43] without really threatening prevailing gender norms.[44]

Even as a willing participant in patriarchy using carnivorous metaphors to her advantage, Palin still triggered consequences on the opposite side of the dialectical coin, invoking meat language that objectified her not as the hunter but as the prey.[45] Some of the coverage of Palin during her vice presidential run either made direct reference to the fact that she was a former beauty pageant contestant or more indirectly described her in beauty pageant terms. The following examples typify this construct: "A well-delivered [speech] with an appealing combination of charm and bite"[46] and Palin may be a "political lightweight," but she's "a charming lightweight."[47] Palin's *Newsweek* cover on November 23, 2009, was further evidence of cheerleader/beauty queen imagery. Beyond the argument that it was sexist because the editors transferred her image from *Runner's World* magazine to a political cover, I believe that part of the sexism lies within the male gaze invited by her pose. Palin's body orientation, with her weight on the straight back leg and her front leg bent, is a classic pageant pose meant to show off the feminine figure. Her smile, hands on hips, and arms akimbo invite the gaze of the patriarchal eye and signal her assumed receptiveness to being evaluated as an object of desire and fertility. The fact that the controversy over this *Newsweek* cover dominated the public conversation reinforces the dialectical tension between Palin as an assertive predator and Palin as "Caribou Barbie,"[48] the beauty contestant all grown up into the ultimate "MILF." The *Newsweek* headline "How Do You Solve a Problem Like Sarah?" points to the inherent inability of the media to resolve the dialectic.

Palin's choice to use the language of meat triggered the hyperhetero, hypersexual masculine response embedded in the metaphor. The associations of wildness in her hunting references to moose meat, caribou meat, and fishing rather than domestically farmed hogs and cattle invited a sexualized and uninhibited response by the media. Her political messages were so imbued with the meat metaphor that it was not surprising when media depictions of the 2008 election campaign conflated the tenor (Sarah Palin) with the vehicle of the metaphor (meat), transforming Palin from the carnivore to the consumed. The metaphor collapsed into literalness, and Palin became the meat. Anderson identifies the 2008 election as uniquely "pornified," or depicted through a frame of sexual degradation and objectification—a backlash against the political gains of leaders like Sarah Palin and Hillary Clinton.[49] This pornification was likely exacerbated by the discourse of carnivorous consumption in which Palin *became* the corporeal feminine, reduced to the flesh of her body. Palin projected herself in terms of active agency, but her use of the meat metaphor was also inverted in the media, framing her in typical patriarchal terms as a passive object to be symbolically killed and consumed.

Red-Meat Populist vs. Dead-Meat Censor

A "red meat" speech is political rhetoric intended to fire up a party's already committed base of supporters.[50] The use of the red meat metaphor was especially ubiquitous in coverage of Palin, as one political news analyst observed: "Is it just me, or is this year's political 'go-to' word—RED MEAT—getting on anybody else's nerves? . . . On the way to meet our NC delegates this morning, I was listening to CNN on the radio, and I think I heard Soledad [O'Brien] and the guests she was interviewing say RED MEAT about 30 times. They were referring to Gov. Sarah Palin's speech last night."[51]

The following comments are representative of the overwhelming number of red meat references that appeared in media coverage of Palin's RNC speech: "Palin, wearing red, served up the red meat and the crowd ate it up"[52]; "Palin's speech was 'very well done and . . . effective . . . at the red-meat-tossing detail'"[53]; "Thrown some red meat, the Republican Party ate it up"[54]; "Those inside the Xcel Energy Center may have devoured the red meat served up in . . . Palin's speech"[55]; and "She offered some rabble-rousing lines and partisan red meat."[56] Similar headlines read, "Palin Dangles Red Meat to Heated Wisconsin Crowd"[57] and "Palin's Red Meat Obama Roast."[58] The use of this political term so prominently in the media coverage of Palin's vice presidential candidacy helps explain the conflation of the tenor and vehicle of the meat metaphor. So overtly foregrounded, the meat references bring with them the connotative construction of both agency and subjectivity.

Media reports emphasized Palin's red meat populism in their coverage of audience reactions to her RNC speech. *Rolling Stone*'s Matt Taibbi writes, "In the crush to exit the stadium, a middle-aged woman wearing a cowboy hat, a red-white-and-blue shirt . . . gushed to a male colleague . . . 'She totally reminds me of my cousin! . . . She's a real woman! The real thing!'"[59] Related reports pointed out that "She reveled in the goodness of the small-town folks 'who grow our food, run our factories and fight our wars'"[60] and that "she came across as genuine and down-to-earth."[61] Palin's "frontier authenticity"[62] caused her not just to remain on the public scene without holding political office, but it legitimated her position and secured her a television miniseries called *Sarah Palin's Alaska*, in which she continued branding her image as the grassroots mother bathed in metaphorical blood.

The carnivorous imagery of red meat feeds into the populist base of Republican political ideology. Hunting is viewed as an anti-elite (as millionaires are not obligated to hunt for survival) and rural activity. Yet *USA Today* criticized the caribou hunt in *Sarah Palin's Alaska* because Palin and her party violated this folksy vision of hunting when they were shown flying six hundred miles from her home to engage in "the sort of experiential safari popular among high-end, non-resident sport hunters" rather than attempting to fill the family freezer with any genuine skill.[63] Palin as wealthy meat-maker also appeals to the racist strains of populism activated against Barack Obama since hunting has been constructed as a predominantly White pastime from the days of the English foxhunt. Heinz and Lee identify tradition and patriotic piety as one of the associational clusters of meat discourse,[64] congruent with Republican connotations of political populism.

Conversely, the other side of the populist red meat metaphor contains threats of danger and mindlessness. Shooting and eating meat is such a primal biological process that Palin's use of the metaphor encouraged the audience to pay less attention to higher-order cognitions. The metaphor kept the audience mindset focused low on Maslow's hierarchy of needs, shutting down higher-order debate and dissention and making it seem "natural" to focus on emotions of fear. Due to the "deadness" of meat, expectations of Palin's thoughtfulness and intelligence were diminished, and the national audience was encouraged to follow suit.

Consistent with this vacant and menacing half of the red meat dialectic, Palin's fear appeals to the audience base at campaign rallies began to appear in the political discourse. For example, *Washington Post* columnist Clarence Page observes, "The red-meat rhetoric thrown out at McCain's recent rallies stains his good name with a tinge of fear-mongering, anger-baiting and xenophobia."[65]

The anti-intellectual, hate-based side of the populist red meat dialectic was made more prevalent through media accounts of Palin's adversarial relationships with those working in what she repeatedly referred to as the "elite" media. Tom Shales notes that Republicans ran against the media in the 2008 campaign, "portraying themselves as poor, abused victims of media aggression."[66] In her July 26, 2010, speech resigning from the Alaskan governorship, Palin played the mama grizzly by blasting the news media for, among other things, manufacturing stories about her family, and she railed against Hollywood "starlets" who seemed "hell-bent on tearing down our country" and were out to get her.[67] This public feud became the focus of media coverage during and after the campaign, effectively driving a larger ideological wedge between "plain folks" in the audience and the so-called elite media. Palin's rhetoric and the subsequent media coverage of her reality television show focused this anti-elitism upon Barack Obama, painting him as an out-of-touch snob.

While Sarah Palin threw red meat folksiness to her Republican base in her campaign addresses, it was less than nourishing. Her appeal to populism carries within it the undertones of intellectual deadness implied in the meat metaphor. Palin's carnivorous discourse signals danger not only for her portrayal of her mother role but also for the audience's expectations of themselves as a democratic electorate.

Conclusion

Sarah Palin is at once the mama grizzly and the pageant queen, the folksy populist inviting Joe Sixpack to share a steak and the censor of democratic participation, the Madonna and the "MILF." The more she confused pundits, bloggers, and newscasters who were unable to pigeonhole her on just one side of these dialectics, the better off she was. She continues to benefit from a polysemous, ambiguous relationship with the media and their audiences, working the dialectical tensions of the carnivore to her personal and party-wide advantage while at the same time being victimized by the patriarchal implication of "dead meat" underlying the discourse.

Since we pay more attention because we're still not sure what to make of her, Sarah Palin maintains her longevity on the national stage long after her fifteen minutes of fame should have been up. Many factors contribute to her longevity, but her staying power and self-definition are propelled by the media ambiguity of these carnivorous dialectics. In effect, Palin cocreates this dialectical framework (and the media subsequently follow along), beginning with the now-infamous joke from her RNC acceptance speech: "They say the difference between a hockey mom and a pit bull is lipstick."[68] In this case, the rhetoric of the pit bull with red lips connotes both sexualized beauty and dripping blood, two sides of the meat metaphor that serve to contain and complicate Palin's public image as a mother, politician, and celebrity.

Notes

1. An earlier version of this study, coauthored with Susan F. Walsh, was presented to the Feminism and Women Studies Division at the National Communication Association conference in San Francisco, 2010.

2. See Judith Butler, *Gender Trouble: Feminism and the Subversion of Identity* (New York: Routledge, 1990) for the foundational discussion of gender as performance rather than biology.

3. Elisabeth Gidengil and Joanna Everitt, "Talking Tough: Gender and Reported Speech in Campaign News Coverage," *Political Communication* 20 (2003): 210.

4. Diana Carlin and Kelly Winfrey, "Have You Come a Long Way, Baby? Hillary Clinton, Sarah Palin, and Sexism in 2008 Campaign Coverage," *Communication Studies* 60 (2008): 326–43; Marie Cocco, "Misogyny I Won't Miss," *Washington Post*, May 15, 2008, accessed May 1, 2012. http://www.washingtonpost.com/wp-dyn/content/article/2008/05/14/AR2008051403090.html; Susan Estrich, "Media Were Unfair to Hillary," *Mail Tribune* [Medford, OR], February 15, 2008, 5B; Froma Harrop, "White Women Take the Gloves Off," *Mail Tribune* [Medford, OR], June 3, 2008, 6B; Roseann Mandziuk, "Dressing Down Hillary," *Communication and Critical/Cultural Studies* 5 (2008): 312–16; Susan F. Walsh, "Taking Humor Seriously: Gender Matters in Political Cartoons of Hillary Rodham Clinton in the 2008 U.S. Presidential Campaign" (paper presented at the annual meeting of the International Conference on the Arts in Society, Birmingham, England, July 2008).

5. Carlin and Winfrey, "Long Way"; Rosabeth Moss Kanter, *Men and Women of the Corporation* (New York: Basic Books, 1977); Julia T. Wood, *Gendered Lives: Communication, Gender, and Culture* (Boston: Wadsworth Cengage Publishing, 2009).

6. Amy M. Bradley and Robert H. Wicks, "A Gendered Blogosphere? Portrayal of Sarah Palin on Political Blogs During the 2008 Presidential Campaign," *Journalism & Mass Communication Quarterly* 88 (2011): 807–20.

7. Virginia McCarver, "The Rhetoric of Choice and 21st-Century Feminism: Online Conversations About Work, Family, and Sarah Palin," *Women's Studies in Communication* 34 (2011): 20–41.

8. Rosemary Avance, Andrew Crocco, and Carolyn Marvin, "On Making Us Whole: The Dynamics of Fertility in the 2008 Presidential Election" (paper presented at the annual meeting for the International Communication Association, 2010).

9. Katie L. Gibson and Amy L. Heyse, "'The Difference Between a Hockey Mom and a Pit Bull': Sarah Palin's Faux Maternal Persona and Performance of Hegemonic Masculinity at the 2008 Republican National Convention," *Communication Quarterly* 58 (2010): 236.

10. Dustin Harp, Jaime Loke, and Ingrid Bachmann, "First Impressions of Sarah Palin: Pit Bulls, Politics, Gender Performance, and a Discursive Media (Re)contextualization," *Communication, Culture, and Critique* 3 (2010): 291–309.

11. Denise L. Oles, "The Inarticulate Gender-Bending Performance of Vice-Presidential Nominee Sarah Palin," Conference Proceedings of the National Communication Association/American Forensic Association Alta Conference on Argumentation (2010): 353–58.

12. Kenneth Burke, *A Rhetoric of Motives* (Berkeley: University of California Press, 1969 [Original publication 1950]).

13. Kenneth Burke, *A Grammar of Motives* (Berkeley: University of California Press, 1969 [Original publication 1945]).

14. William Franke, "Metaphor and the Making of Sense: The Contemporary Metaphor Renaissance," *Philosophy and Rhetoric* 33 (2000): 138.

15. Jonathan Charteris-Black, *Corpus Approaches to Critical Metaphor Analysis* (Basingstoke: Palgrave-Macmillan, 2004).

16. Jeffery Scott Mio, "Metaphor and Politics," *Metaphor and Symbol* 12 (1997): 113–33.

17. Avance, Crocco, and Marvin, "On Making Us Whole."

18. Jonathan Charteris-Black, "Britain as a Container: Immigration Metaphors in the 2005 Election Campaign," *Discourse and Society* 17 (2006): 567.

19. Jeffery Scott Mio, Ronald E. Riggio, Shana Levin, and Renford Reese, "Presidential Leadership and Charisma: The Effects of Metaphor," *Leadership Quarterly* 16 (2005): 287–94.

20. Karrin Vasby Anderson, "Hillary Rodham Clinton as 'Madonna': The Role of Metaphor and Oxymoron in Image Restoration," *Women's Studies in Communication* 25 (2002): 1–24.

21. Karrin Vasby Anderson and Kristina Horn Sheeler, *Governing Codes: Gender, Metaphor, and Political Identity* (Lanham, MD: Rowman and Littlefield, 2005).

22. Janis L. Edwards and C. Austin McDonald, "Reading Hillary and Sarah: Contradictions of Feminism and Representation in 2008 Political Cartoons," *American Behavioral Scientist* 54 (2010): 313–29.

23. Nicholas Howe, "Metaphor in Contemporary American Political Discourse," *Metaphor and Symbolic Activity* 3 (1988): 87–104.

24. C. Wesley Buerkle, "Metrosexuality Can Stuff It: Beef Consumption as (Heteromasculine) Fortification," *Text and Performance Quarterly* 29 (2009): 77–93.

25. Carol J. Adams, *The Sexual Politics of Meat: A Feminist-Vegetarian Critical Theory* (New York: Continuum, 1990), 58–59.

26. Kimberly A. Powell, "The Great American Meatout: Engaging a Society of Meat-Eaters in Anti-Meat Consumption Rhetoric," *Journal of the Northwest Communication Association* 31 (2002): 81–102.

27. Richard A. Rogers, "Beasts, Burgers, and Hummers: Meat and the Crisis of Masculinity in Contemporary Television Advertisements," *Environmental Communication* 2 (2008): 282.

28. Bettina Heinz and Ronald Lee, "Getting Down to the Meat: The Symbolic Construction of Meat Consumption," *Communication Studies* 49 (1998): 86–99.

29. Buerkle, "Stuff It."

30. Sarah Palin, *America by Heart: Reflections on Family, Faith, and Flag* (Harper, 2010).

31. Kathleen Parker, "Red-Meat Republicans: Pandering to the Base with Blood," *Mail Tribune* [Medford, OR], January 25, 2010.

32. Parker, "Red-Meat Republicans."

33. Nick Trujillo, "Hegemonic Masculinity on the Mound: Media Representations of Nolan Ryan and American Sports Culture," *Critical Studies in Mass Communication* 8 (1991): 290–308.

34. Larry Sabato, "Attack Dog: Palin and Simple" Center for Politics, September 4, 2008, accessed May 1, 2012, http://www.centerforpolitics.org/crystalball/articles/itw2008090402.

35. Matt Taibbi, "Mad Dog Palin," *Rolling Stone*, October 2, 2008, accessed May 1, 2012, http://www.goodsearch.com/Search.aspx?Keywords=rolling+stone&Source=mozillaplugin.

36. Scott Conroy, "Palin Dangles Red Meat to Heated Wisconsin Crowd," CBS News, October 9, 2008, accessed May 1, 2012, http://www.cbsnews.com/8301-502443_162-4512162-502443.html; Sabato, "Attack Dog."

37. Clarence Page, "Red-Meat Blitz Stains McCain," *Chicago Tribune*, October 12, 2008, accessed May 1, 2012. http://articles.chicagotribune.com/2008-10-12/news/0810110372_1_sen-john-mccain-sarah-palin-sen-barack-obama.

38. Kevin Drum, "Sarah Palin's Speech," *Mother Jones*, September 3, 2008, accessed May 1, 2012. http://www.motherjones.com/kevin-drum/2008/09/sarah-palins-speech.

39. Harp, Loke, and Bachmann, "First Impressions," 303.

40. It is not pit bulls who are inherently aggressive, but rather it is their sometimes vicious human companions who train and abuse them to become so. The references to blood sport here are meant to reflect common metaphorical connotations and media usage, not canine reality.

41. Sarah Palin, "Don't Mess with Mama Grizzlies," *Human Life Review*, 2010, accessed May 3, 2012, http://www.humanlifereview.com/index.php/archives/52-2010-summer/111-dont-mess-with-mama-grizzlies.

42. Jaime Loke, Dustin Harp, and Ingrid Bachmann, "Mothering and Governing," *Journalism Studies* 12 (2011): 205–20.

43. Her early basketball nickname, "Sarah Barracuda," even cast her as a meat-eating fish.

44. Operating from an alternative metaphor, Barker-Plummer names this the ideal patriarchal girlfriend. Bernadette Barker-Plummer, "Reading Sarah Palin," *Flow Journal* 8 (2008), accessed May 1, 2012, http://flowtv.org/2008/10/reading-sarah-palin-bernadette-barker-plummer-university-of-san-francisco.

45. Julia Wood's original construct of child/pet involves components of lack of capability, competency, and maturity, leading some women in the workplace to be perceived as cute but not to be taken seriously. Carlin and Winfrey (2009) use this construct in an analysis of media coverage of Palin and Hillary Clinton. The typology has been modified to include the cheerleader and pageant queen stereotypes presented here.

46. "Ms. Palin's Introduction," *Washington Post*, September 4, 2008, accessed May 1, 2012, http://www.washingtonpost.com/wp-dyn/content/article/2008/09/03/AR2008090303516.html.

47. Dan Amira, "Sarah Palin Hurts So Good," *New York Magazine*, September 4, 2008, accessed May 1, 2012, http://nymag.com/daily/intel/2008/09/sarah_palin_hurts_so_good.html.

48. A sobriquet popularized by liberal radio show host Stephanie Miller after seeing it used online at Democratic Underground.com. Tunku Varadarajan, "Airhead Zealot: From A–Z, the Things People Say About Sarah Palin," *Forbes*, October 13, 2008, accessed May 3, 2012, http://www.forbes.com/2008/10/13/sarah-palin-republican-oped-cx_tv_1013varadarajan.html.

49. Karrin Vasby Anderson, "Rhymes with Blunt: Pornification and U.S. Political Culture," *Rhetoric and Public Affairs* 14 (2011): 327–68.

50. Carmen Dixon, "Political Theater—Palin's Red Meat Obama Roast," *Blackvoices*, September 4, 2010, accessed May 1, 2012, http://www.bvblackspin.com/2008/09/04/Sarah-palin-speech.

51. Geof Levine, "Politics Has Turned Me into a Vegetarian," WRAL News [Raleigh, Virginia], September 4, 2008, accessed May 1, 2012, http://www.wral.com/news/local/politics/blogpost/3486555.

52. David Catanese, "Sarah Palin Blasts Mainstream Media in Speech at College of the Ozarks," KY3 News, December 2, 2009.

53. Gale Collins, "Sarah Palin Speaks!" *New York Times*, September 4, 2008, accessed May 1, 2012, http://www.nytimes.com/2008/09/04/opinion/04collins.html?_r=1.

54. Andrew Romano, "Assessing Palin's Big Speech," *Newsweek*, September 4, 2008, accessed May 1, 2012, http://www.goodsearch.com/search.aspx?keywords=newsweek.com.

55. Tim O'Brien, "Palin Doesn't Woo Michigan Independents," *StarTribune* [Minneapolis, MN], September 4, 2008, accessed May 1, 2012, http://www.startribune.com/opinion/27862799.html.

56. Jonathan Martin, "Palin Resigns, Blasts Press, 'Starlets,'" *Politico*, July 26, 2009, accessed May 1, 2012, http://www.politico.com/news/stories/0709/25451.html.

57. Conroy, "Palin Dangles Red Meat."

58. Dixon, "Political Theater."

59. Taibbi, "Mad Dog Palin."

60. Romano, "Assessing Palin's Big Speech."

61. Tom Shales, "She Shoots! She Scores! A Hockey Mom's Moment," *Washington Post*, September 4, 2008, accessed May 1, 2012. http://www.washingtonpost.com/wp-dyn/content/article/2008/09/04/AR2008090400111.html.

62. Robert Mason, "'Pitbulls' and Populist Politicians: Sarah Palin, Pauline Hanson and the Use of Gendered Nostalgia in Electoral Campaigns," *Comparative American Studies* 8 (2010): 185–99.

63. Nick Jans, "What Palin's Show Says About Us," *USA Today*, January 5, 2011, accessed May 3, 2012, http://www.usatoday.com/news/opinion/forum/2011-01-06-column06_ST_N.htm.

64. Heinz and Lee, "Getting Down to the Meat," 91.

65. Page, "Red-Meat Blitz."

66. Shales, "She Shoots!"

67. Martin, "Palin Resigns." A reference to actor and activist Ashley Judd, who excoriated Palin for supporting the use of helicopters to kill wolves.

68. Sarah Palin, "Republican Vice Presidential Nomination Acceptance Speech," September 3, 2008, accessed May 3, 2012, http://americanrhetoric.com/speeches/convention2008/sarahpalin2008rnc.htm.

Bibliography

Adams, Carol J. *The Sexual Politics of Meat: A Feminist-Vegetarian Critical Theory*. New York: Continuum, 1990.

Amira, Dan. "Sarah Palin Hurts So Good." *New York Magazine*. September 4, 2008. Accessed May 1, 2012. http://nymag.com/daily/intel/2008/09/sarah_palin_hurts_so_good.html.

Anderson, Karrin Vasby. "Hillary Rodham Clinton as 'Madonna': The Role of Metaphor and Oxymoron in Image Restoration." *Women's Studies in Communication* 25 (2002): 1–24.

———. "Rhymes with Blunt: Pornification and U.S. Political Culture." *Rhetoric and Public Affairs* 14 (2011): 327–68.

Anderson, Karrin Vasby, and Kristina Horn Sheeler. *Governing Codes: Gender, Metaphor, and Political Identity*. Lanham, MD: Rowman and Littlefield, 2005.

Avance, Rosemary, Andrew Crocco, and Carolyn Marvin. "On Making Us Whole: The Dynamics of Fertility in the 2008 Presidential Election." Paper presented at the annual meeting for the International Communication Association, 2010.

Barker-Plummer, Bernadette. "Reading Sarah Palin." *Flow Journal* 8 (2008). Accessed May 1, 2012. http://flowtv.org/2008/10/reading-sarah-palin-bernadette-barker-plummer-university-of-san-francisco.

Bradley, Amy M., and Robert H. Wicks. "A Gendered Blogosphere? Portrayal of Sarah Palin on Political Blogs During the 2008 Presidential Campaign." *Journalism & Mass Communication Quarterly* 88 (2011): 807–20.

Buerkle, C. Wesley. "Metrosexuality Can Stuff It: Beef Consumption as (Heteromasculine) Fortification." *Text and Performance Quarterly* 29 (2009): 77–93.

Burke, Kenneth. *A Grammar of Motives*. Berkeley: University of California Press, 1969 [Original publication 1945].

———. *A Rhetoric of Motives*. Berkeley: University of California Press, 1969 [Original publication 1950].

Butler, Judith. *Gender Trouble: Feminism and the Subversion of Identity*. New York: Routledge, 1990.

Carlin, Diana, and Kelly Winfrey. "Have You Come a Long Way, Baby? Hillary Clinton, Sarah Palin, and Sexism in 2008 Campaign Coverage." *Communication Studies* 60 (2008): 326–43.

Catanese, David. "Sarah Palin Blasts Mainstream Media in Speech at College of the Ozarks." KY3 News, December 2, 2009.

Charteris-Black, Jonathan. "Britain as a Container: Immigration Metaphors in the 2005 Election Campaign." *Discourse and Society* 17 (2006): 563–81.

———. Corpus Approaches to Critical Metaphor Analysis. Basingstoke: Palgrave-Macmillan, 2004.

Cocco, Marie. "Misogyny I Won't Miss." *Washington Post*, May 15, 2008. Accessed May 1, 2012. http://www.washingtonpost.com/wp-dyn/content/article/2008/05/14/AR2008051403090.html.

Collins, Gale. "Sarah Palin Speaks!" *New York Times*, September 4, 2008. Accessed May 1, 2012. http://www.nytimes.com/2008/09/04/opinion/04collins.html?_r=1.

Conroy, Scott. "Palin Dangles Red Meat to Heated Wisconsin Crowd." CBS News, October 9, 2008. Accessed May 1, 2012. http://www.cbsnews.com/8301-502443_162-4512162-502443.html.

Dixon, Carmen. "Political Theater—Palin's Red Meat Obama Roast." *Blackvoices*, September 4, 2010. Accessed May 1, 2012. http://www.bvblackspin.com/2008/09/04/Sarah-palin-speech.

Drum, Kevin. "Sarah Palin's Speech." *Mother Jones*, September 3, 2008. Accessed May 1, 2012. http://www.motherjones.com/kevin-drum/2008/09/sarah-palins-speech.

Edwards, Janis L., and C. Austin McDonald. "Reading Hillary and Sarah: Contradictions of Feminism and Representation in 2008 Political Cartoons." *American Behavioral Scientist* 54 (2010): 313–29.

Estrich, Susan. "Media Were Unfair to Hillary." *Mail Tribune* [Medford, OR], February 15, 2008.

Franke, William. "Metaphor and the Making of Sense: The Contemporary Metaphor Renaissance." *Philosophy and Rhetoric* 33 (2000): 137–53.

Gibson, Katie L., and Amy L. Heyse. "'The Difference Between a Hockey Mom and a Pit Bull': Sarah Palin's Faux Maternal Persona and Performance of Hegemonic Masculinity at the 2008 Republican National Convention." *Communication Quarterly* 58 (2010): 235–56.

Gidengil, Elisabeth, and Joanna Everitt. "Talking Tough: Gender and Reported Speech in Campaign News Coverage." *Political Communication* 20 (2003): 209–32.

Harp, Dustin, Jaime Loke, and Ingrid Bachmann. "First Impressions of Sarah Palin: Pit Bulls, Politics, Gender Performance, and a Discursive Media (Re)contextualization." *Communication, Culture, and Critique* 3 (2010): 291–309.

Harrop, Froma. "White Women Take the Gloves Off." *Mail Tribune* [Medford, OR], June 3, 2008.

Heinz, Bettina, and Ronald Lee. "Getting Down to the Meat: The Symbolic Construction of Meat Consumption." *Communication Studies* 49 (1998): 86–99.

Howe, Nicholas. "Metaphor in Contemporary American Political Discourse." *Metaphor and Symbolic Activity* 3 (1988): 87–104.

Jans, Nick. "What Palin's Show Says About Us." *USA Today*, January 5, 2011. Accessed May 3, 2012. http://www.usatoday.com/news/opinion/forum/2011-01-06-column06_ST_N.htm.

Kanter, Rosabeth Moss. *Men and Women of the Corporation*. New York: Basic Books, 1977.

Levine, Geof. "Politics Has Turned Me into a Vegetarian." WRAL News [Raleigh, Virginia], September 4, 2008. Accessed May 1, 2012. http://www.wral.com/news/local/politics/blogpost/3486555.

Loke, Jaime, Dustin Harp, and Ingrid Bachmann. "Mothering and Governing." *Journalism Studies* 12 (2011): 205–20.

Mandziuk, Roseann. "Dressing Down Hillary." *Communication and Critical/Cultural Studies* 5 (2008): 312–16.

Martin, Jonathan. "Palin Resigns, Blasts Press, 'Starlets.'" *Politico*, July 26, 2009. Accessed May 1, 2012. http://www.politico.com/news/stories/0709/25451.html.

Mason, Robert. "'Pitbulls' and Populist Politicians: Sarah Palin, Pauline Hanson and the Use of Gendered Nostalgia in Electoral Campaigns." *Comparative American Studies* 8 (2010): 185–99.

McCarver, Virginia. "The Rhetoric of Choice and 21st-Century Feminism: Online Conversations About Work, Family, and Sarah Palin." *Women's Studies in Communication* 34 (2011): 20–41.

Mio, Jeffery Scott. "Metaphor and Politics." *Metaphor and Symbol* 12 (1997): 113–33.

Mio, Jeffery Scott, Ronald E. Riggio, Shana Levin, and Renford Reese. "Presidential Leadership and Charisma: The Effects of Metaphor." *Leadership Quarterly* 16 (2005): 287–94.

"Ms. Palin's Introduction." *Washington Post*. September 4, 2008. Accessed May 1, 2012. http://www.washingtonpost.com/wp-dyn/content/article/2008/09/03/AR2008090303516.html.

O'Brien, Tim. "Palin Doesn't Woo Michigan Independents." *Star Tribune* [Minneapolis, MN], September 4, 2008. Accessed May 1, 2012. http://www.startribune.com/opinion/27862799.html.

Oles, Denise L. "The Inarticulate Gender-Bending Performance of Vice-Presidential Nominee Sarah Palin." Conference Proceedings of the National Communication Association/American Forensic Association Alta Conference on Argumentation. 2010: 353–58.

Page, Clarence. "Red-Meat Blitz Stains McCain." *Chicago Tribune*, October 12, 2008. Accessed May 1, 2012. http://articles.chicagotribune.com/2008-10-12/news/0810110372_1_sen-john-mccain-sarah-palin-sen-barack-obama.

Palin, Sarah. *America by Heart: Reflections on Family, Faith, and Flag*. Harper, 2010.

———. "Don't Mess with Mama Grizzlies." *Human Life Review*. 2010. Accessed May 3, 2012. http://www.humanlifereview.com/index.php/archives/52-2010-summer/111-dont-mess-with-mama-grizzlies.

———. "Republican Vice Presidential Nomination Acceptance Speech." September 3, 2008. Accessed May 3, 2012. http://americanrhetoric.com/speeches/convention2008/sarahpalin2008rnc.htm.

Parker, Kathleen. "Red-Meat Republicans: Pandering to the Base with Blood." *Mail Tribune* [Medford, OR], January 25, 2010.

Powell, Kimberly A. "The Great American Meatout: Engaging a Society of Meat-Eaters in Anti-Meat

Consumption Rhetoric." *Journal of the Northwest Communication Association* 31 (2002): 81–102.
Rogers, Richard A. "Beasts, Burgers, and Hummers: Meat and the Crisis of Masculinity in Contemporary Television Advertisements." *Environmental Communication* 2 (2008): 281–301.
Romano, Andrew. "Assessing Palin's Big Speech." *Newsweek*, September 4, 2008. Accessed May 1, 2012. http://www.goodsearch.com/search.aspx?keywords=newsweek.com.
Sabato, Larry. "Attack Dog: Palin and Simple." Center for Politics, September 4, 2008. Accessed May 1, 2012. http://www.centerforpolitics.org/crystalball/articles/itw2008090402.
Shales, Tom. "She Shoots! She Scores! A Hockey Mom's Moment." *Washington Post*, September 4, 2008. Accessed May 1, 2012. http://www.washingtonpost.com/wp-dyn/content/article/2008/09/04/AR2008090400111.html.
Taibbi, Matt. "Mad Dog Palin." *Rolling Stone*, October 2, 2008. Accessed May 1, 2012. http://www.goodsearch.com/Search.aspx?Keywords=rolling+stone&Source=mozillaplugin.
Trujillo, Nick. "Hegemonic Masculinity on the Mound: Media Representations of Nolan Ryan and American Sports Culture." *Critical Studies in Mass Communication* 8 (1991): 290–308.
Varadarajan, Tunku. "Airhead Zealot: From A–Z, the Things People Say About Sarah Palin." *Forbes*, October 13, 2008. Accessed May 3, 2012. http://www.forbes.com/2008/10/13/sarah-palin-republican-oped-cx_tv_1013varadarajan.html.
Walsh, Susan F. "Taking Humor Seriously: Gender Matters in Political Cartoons of Hillary Rodham Clinton in the 2008 U.S. Presidential Campaign." Paper presented at the annual meeting of the International Conference on the Arts in Society, Birmingham, England, July 2008.
Wood, Julia T. *Gendered Lives: Communication, Gender, and Culture*. Boston: Wadsworth Cengage Publishing, 2009.

Chapter 11

"Stand by Your Man" Revisited: Political Wives and Scandal

by Hinda Mandell

According to the American cultural script, if there is a press conference where an ostensibly heterosexual male politician addresses sexual wrongdoing, his wife is often standing right next to him. The purpose of this chapter is to document media construction of wives at the center of political sex scandals. It represents a first step toward understanding how these often silent—but publicly present—women are represented to the general public as figures within their husbands' scandals.

I researched news coverage of seven political sex scandals that occurred from 2004 to 2009. Articles were taken from *USA Today*, the *New York Times*, *Washington Post*, CNN.com, and the largest-circulating newspaper in the state where each scandal took place. (For the Governor Eliot Spitzer scandal, I used the *Albany Times-Union* as the hometown paper since the *New York Times* represents the largest circulation paper in New York.) The seven scandals involved New Jersey Governor James McGreevey (2004), Louisiana Senator David Vitter (2007), Idaho Senator Larry Craig (2007), New York Governor Eliot Spitzer (2008), Florida Congressional Representative Tim Mahoney (2008), Nevada Senator John Ensign (2009), and South Carolina Governor Mark Sanford (2009). Scandals were selected based on the national exposure they received in the press as well as the occurrence of a news conference. I analyzed 473 articles, including written text and photographs, through microfilm.

Findings indicate that news coverage of political wives has a distinct tone of discomfort, conveyed by both news writers and quotations from the general public. This discomfort—centered on tacit women who support the husbands who appeared to have betrayed them—is connected to the public's fear of the political wife's situation. The political wives, therefore, become symbols of their own personal experiences, which are coopted by a fearful public. Scandals are moralizing events,[1] and the ones featured in this chapter succeeded in producing public discourse on infidelity and conjugal relationships.

Each of the seven wives was constructed as fulfilling a supportive role for her husband, even if she was absent from the politician's press conference or subsequently divorced him. On the surface, this research is about gender and scandal, but at its core, this study reveals the push-and-pull between deeply embedded social norms surrounding "wifeness" (my term for what it means to be a wife) and the discomfort of the news media when depicting a wife "standing by her man." The media reproduce the "stand by her man" construction they simultaneously condemn.

When a political wife stands at her husband's press conference, her face represents for news writers a symbol of female pain as the victim of male, spousal betrayal. Available for all to see, her discomfort is visible on her face, which in turn contributes to the unease of news writers and the public as constructed in the articles. The political wives' motivations for attending the press conference, along with their personal experiences standing at the podium, are co-opted by the news media and subsequently broadened as "bad for women everywhere."[2] Their presence and pain are broadened to reflect the experiences of all scorned wives, not just political ones.

Political Wives and Face-ism

While the political wife's face is given symbolic power, her face is not photographically represented to the same extent as the husband-politician. Indeed, 28.3 percent of all articles feature a standalone photograph of the husband-politician with his face prominently displayed. By contrast, 8 percent of articles feature a standalone photograph of the political wife. These findings support previous literature on "face-ism," the extent to which a face is given prominence in photographs or other visual representations. Credited with naming this phenomenon, Archer, Iritani, Kimes, and Barrios found men's faces were more prominently featured than women's in photographs across cultures. They also found face-ism is a centuries-old phenomenon with painters from the fifteenth and sixteenth centuries more prominently featuring men's faces while focusing more on women's bodies. They speculate that the different rate of facial prominence shapes the way people think about male and female bodies, so men are more closely aligned with the attributes of the face (including the wit and intelligence of the mind), while women are more closely associated with the attributes of their body and attractiveness, including the "emotions located in the metaphorical heart."[3] Face-ism not only reinforces traditional gender stereotypes, but it does so in a seemingly subconscious way. Ideologies on gender are not always consciously reproduced by individuals, but they are reproduced nonetheless.[4] The rate of facial prominence shapes people's perceptions of those photographed. People with higher facial prominence are viewed as smarter and more ambitious than those whose faces are not featured as prominently in photographs.[5] With men's faces more notably displayed in media channels, gender stereotypes are reproduced and reinforced so men are valued for their intelligence and authority while women are valued for their kindness and nurturing, traits more often associated with the female body.[6] This gendered presentation in photographs contributes to the way media consumers think about women as less dominant, driven, and assertive than their male counterparts. "Facial prominence appears to activate gender stereotypes," Levesque and Lowe observe. "Once activated, the stereotype likely influences an array of important judgments regarding a target person."[7] Face-ism research has revealed that the rate of facial prominence reflects patriarchal gendered assumptions: men are more dominant and assertive while women are less so.

The Female Face as a Call to Action

The irony is that while political wives are the subject of significantly less standalone photographs than their husbands, their faces are symbolically leveraged as a metaphorical tool to speak broadly of female pain caused by male infidelity. In contrast, the faces of male politicians in news coverage were not viewed as anything other than the individual faces of James McGreevey, David Vitter, Larry Craig, Eliot Spitzer, Tim Mahoney, John Ensign, and Mark Sanford. Yet news articles commented on the faces of political wives, especially that of Silda Spitzer, as symbols of broader issues such as humiliation caused by cheating husbands, female subjugation, and "standing by your man" in times of trouble. If face-ism mirrors gender stereotypes of women embodying "emotions located in the metaphorical heart,"[8] their very physical presence tugs at the emotional heartstrings of news writers and the general public. This sympathy toward the political wives results in a discomfort with the wives' performance of traditional gender roles within their husbands' scandal. The wives, after all, carry the emotional burden of their husbands.[9] News writers often comment that this burden is apparent in the faces of political wives.

While a number of news writers commented on the faces of the political wives involved in these scandals, one in particular connected the wife's face to Helen of Troy without directly naming the mythological character. "Tear-stained, puffy and frozen in a mask of anguish, Silda Wall Spitzer's was the face that launched a *million* opinions."[10] While the face of Helen of Troy, renowned for her beauty, launched a thousand ships to free the captured woman, Silda Spitzer's face launched a million opinions, indicating the extent to which her face prompted the expression of strong feelings regarding her "captive" situation. Literary scholar Laurie E. MaGuire notes that while Helen of Troy was celebrated for her beauty, descriptions of her were never specific. Writers referenced her beauty without providing details. After all, "if Helen is indisputably the most beautiful woman in the world, as soon as you provide details you make her beauty disputable."[11] Similarly, when writers describe the political wives' faces at their husbands' press conferences, they do so in a way that speaks of pain and emotional suffering—generally. The political wife's pain is easily broadened to a female public. Just as Helen's tale is one of "disruption, of moving from outside to inside,"[12] so too does the perceived marital chaos caused by the politician's sex scandal move from the public domain ("outside" with the press conference) to the ("inside") private domain of conversation and anecdote sharing as the public discusses the consequences of infidelity in their own networks. Political wives have come to symbolize pain and self-subjugation to the husband's professional needs.

Marital Gender Norms and the Press Conference

Articles on political wives question the wife's very presence at the politician's press conference or take special note of her absence.[13] The tone ranges from subconscious criticism by reducing the wife to a prop through references to her being "at her husband's side" to outright derision for "standing by her man." While this criticism may be understandable—and perhaps laudable in some cases because it is uncomfortable to see a silent wife—her press conference attendance should be analyzed within the context of her role as a political wife. This means analyzing her role as an auxiliary political figure and as a woman. While political wives may be people of privilege, considering the power their socioeconomic position and elite status afford them, they are still women. Within the context of the marital dyad, they hold a subordinate position to their husbands.[14] While marital power relations are changing, the overall gendered dynamic persists. It is then reasonable to assume that men of rarified privilege may have even higher expectations of maintaining power in their conjugal relationship.

Generally speaking, a wife is expected to show active interest in her husband's work as part of her supportive duties.[15] When a wife is part of a "two-person single career," she is expected to be even more encouraging of her husband's professional work, since she is an unpaid contributor to its success.[16] A political wife is expected by her husband and the public to actively campaign for her husband-politician, host events, and give her own public speeches.[17] If she does not exhibit her support in a visible way, she is perceived to be uninterested in the marital relationship.[18] Of course, there are many benefits to a wife participating in a two-person single career, and she may indeed view her contributions as a professional partnership.[19]

In the context of both the career-dominated marriage and the gendered power dynamic, the political wife's presence at her husband's press conference is similar in some ways to her presence at his other political events. She participates in public events to show her support for him, demonstrate her investment in the marriage, and vouch for the husband's integrity as a man and a politician. Her "stamp of approval" becomes ever more critical—and controversial—when the husband-politician acts or is accused of acting in a manner that directly calls his integrity into question. Ultimately, her presence at the press conference is not out of character from her participation in her husband's other landmark events since political wives often accompany their husbands in public. Winfield and Friedman found the "escort role" was the most popular media frame for wives of presidential candidates in the 2000 election.[20] It is reasonable to assume, therefore, that if politicians want and need their wives' public support in good times, then most definitely they would seek to secure their wives' support in bad times. The political wife may be compelled to stand next to her husband at the press conference because she feels it is her wifely duty to be supportive of her husband, fulfilling her gender-based role as a traditional wife who takes care of her husband's emotional needs. Additionally, if the wife helped build the edifice of her marriage, she might feel compelled to defend it at its most vulnerable moment. The key difference between the wife's participation in her husband's political events as an auxiliary political figure prior to his sex scandal and her participation in his press conference afterward is how it personally reflects on her. At campaign events and fundraisers, the wife is working to further her husband's career. At the press conference, she is trying to save it, even though he presumably violated the basic marital tenets of monogamy and fidelity.

Scandal and Marital Negotiation

Even if news articles criticize the wife's presence, she clearly has her reasons for attending her husband's press conference. Only one article suggests that private negotiations may have resulted in her attendance, however.[21] This shows the extent to which political sex scandals are about the social institution of marriage as much as they are about power and the values surrounding sex norms. News writers and the public appear to assume that the political marriage is akin to a "civilian" marriage—that the same expectations governing the taboos of sex outside marriage still apply, even as infidelity among politicians is documented as notoriously recurrent.[22] Thus, political wives may be more forgiving of their husband-politicians who engage in extramarital sexual relationships and less naïve about monogamy than the general public. Darlene Ensign was noted in two hometown articles for knowing about her husband's extramarital sexual proclivities and for taking steps to minimize the occurrence of his affairs.[23] The wives of some professional athletes, for instance, are well aware of the likelihood that their athlete-husbands are offered or engage in extramarital sex while traveling during the sports season.[24] Likewise, the political couples in this study may have had an outright agreement about the husband-politicians' sexual freedom. Regardless of any hypothetical agreement between political wife and husband-politician, however, it is reasonable to assume the political wife would be distraught over a *scandal* surrounding her husband's sexual behavior because of the related emotional, financial, and temporal costs to her and her family. When news breaks of a politician's sex scandal, the political wife is forced to decide whether to play her script as the aggrieved but supportive spouse. As part of this script, she is also pushed into the mold of a traditional wife, one who presumably expects monogamy and is betrayed when the husband is "found out." The public's presumption of a traditional, monogamous marriage between the political wife and the husband-politician may magnify the female public's fear of infidelity. The public may view the pain on the wife's face as hurt from the sexual betrayal, while the political wife herself may be irate at her husband for bringing this public humiliation on her and potentially destroying the career she helped build with her sacrifices. In the cases of Silda Spitzer and Jenny Sanford, both wives are described by the news media as giving up their high-profile, white collar positions as an attorney and banker respectively to raise their children and aid their husband's professional work.

A political wife who subordinates her professional needs to her husband's may have negotiated with the husband-politician during his scandal, offering to attend his press conference in exchange for a benefit that remains unknown to the public. While this assertion may appear speculative, the lack of news commentary on marital negotiation is noteworthy. Negotiation is a common exercise within marriage.[25] A key indicator that a political-wife negotiation likely took place can be found in the Tim Mahoney scandal. On October 14, 2008, the congressional representative from Florida held a press conference at which he addressed allegations of sexual impropriety without directly acknowledging his affairs. Terry Mahoney sat next to him, staring down the whole time, her mouth in a pressed, grim line. Six days later, on October 20, 2008, Terry Mahoney filed for divorce from her husband. Why would she attend her husband's press conference, knowing how uncomfortable the media spotlight would be, if she knew—and he likely also knew—that a divorce was immediately to follow? A reasonable answer is that Terry Mahoney's attendance at the press event was the result of a negotiation that offered her greater leverage in divorce proceedings and garnered Tim Mahoney the presence of his wife at the press conference.

With the exception of one mention in a single article,[26] news coverage of political wives does not speculate about—and certainly does not report on—private negotiations that may have taken place between the political wife and the husband-politician for her to attend the press conference. Instead, the wife's presence is read as matter of fact and criticized as such: the political wife "stands by her man" as a supportive "good" wife. News writers judge the politician for taking advantage of his wife, but they also judge the political wife for her apparent passivity as a wife who makes her needs subservient to her husband's. This one-dimensional reading of the political wife assumes she is fulfilling a traditional gender role. This construction belies what may be a more accurate reality in a political wife's life in which she works to bolster her husband's career in pre-scandal times but also conducts her own independent work such as overseeing her own political initiatives, speaking publicly, volunteering, serving on boards, and overseeing domestic issues. In daily life, she is not a political appendage superglued to her husband's side.[27] She is busy with her own (often unpaid) work, even if this work ultimately serves the paid work of her husband. The sex scandal script, however, returns the wife to the public's eye as a stereotype, confining her to the patriarchal mold of the wife "standing by her man," whereas before she may have been in charge of her own staff and running her own initiatives. In this way, the press conference reifies gender norms within the marriage by forcing the wife to decide for herself—or be persuaded by others—whether she will conform to patriarchal expectations surrounding wifeness. Even when two political wives in this study, Darlene Ensign and Jenny Sanford, chose not to attend their husbands' press conferences, they released statements on the same day, thereby putting themselves into play as wives in the scandals. Darlene Ensign constructed herself as a wholly supportive wife, while Jenny Sanford condescended to her husband by stating, "I believe Mark has earned a chance to resurrect our marriage."[28] Therefore, while these two wives deviated from the political-wife script with their physical absence, they reaffirmed it by releasing statements that expressed their commitment to marriage as an institution. As such, each of these political sex scandals exemplifies hegemonic public displays of traditional gender roles and norms. The husband, as the more dominant and powerful figure, acknowledges wrongdoing. His quiet wife supports him with her presence, bolstering both his delicate emotional state and affirming his integrity—although bruised. He is a man ultimately "worthy" of having his wife stand by him.

(Re)Production of Ideology Despite Opposition

The news media and the public were uneasy with the stereotypic gender roles these sex scandals highlighted. They pushed back against them with criticism and discomfort at the image of a political wife often appearing to be aligned with her husband after he appeared to act out against her, causing her personal, emotional, and familial suffering. Since the overwhelming majority of the public does not have a personal relationship with the political couple, the discomfort expressed in feature and trend stories relates more to the public's own fears surrounding infidelity and unease with traditional marital roles. Yet even as news writers pushed back against the hegemonic construction of political wives as passive women failing to assert their better interests, the articles still reproduce deeply embedded constructions of political wives as subordinate to their more powerful husbands. While news writers sometimes use the phrase "stand by your man" in a conscious, tongue-in-cheek—but always critical—way, other times they reproduce latent examples of wifely diminishment. Stuart Hall argues that ideologies are not necessarily consciously reproduced by those who both oppose and support such systems of power. Instead, people pass on ideology through an often unintentional performance.[29] Heider finds this ideological performance by broadcast reporters, whose adherence to news routines and norms diminishes the production of meaningful news coverage for communities of color on the local newscast. He labels this phenomenon "incognizant racism."[30] Incognizant racism occurs when reporters are so socialized by newsroom values they both intentionally and unintentionally overlook stories that highlight the complexities of minority groups. "It is the result of dozens of daily decisions, of years of training and practice, of decades of cultural orientation, and of a well-documented history of systematic and institutionalized neglect."[31]

Incognizant racism is also conceptually useful for analyzing news writers' reproduction of traditional gender norms that often appear to offend them on a conscious level. Such examples occur whenever a news writer describes the wife as being "at" or "by" her husband's "side." This phrasing, often used by news writers when making a passing reference to the political wife, represents a colloquial way of conveying that the wife stood physically next to her husband. Its embedded meaning, however, is that she is an appendage, a supportive one, who is present at his event. Since she is at *his* side, he holds the balance of power over her. In only one instance was a politician described as at his wife's side. While news writers express frustration and disdain at the politician for "using" his wife and at the political wife for allowing herself to be used, the media continue to reproduce patriarchal gender norms by constructing the wife as a passive figure in relation to her husband. Just as incognizant racism, according to Heider, emerges from "decades of cultural orientation" regarding race, so too does this cultural orientation help explain gender bias in news construction of political wives as supplemental to their husbands. News constructions of gender according to normative roles are not necessarily dependent on the writer's own gender. Newsrooms are dominated by Protestant, liberal, middle-class college-educated men.[32] Yet Craft and Wanta found the issues newspapers cover are not dependent on the number of women in high-level managerial newsroom positions because the norms and routines of the newsroom reduce the amount of personal experience that leaks into news coverage.[33] The cultural orientation of news reflects broader system-wide values surrounding race, gender, and ethnicity. The often homogeneous nature of the content—independent of its writer's gender—indicates that cultural norms are often upheld in news coverage. By approaching the production of news as a process that (re-)embeds social norms, it is possible to understand why news writers oppose political wives upholding traditional gender norms on the one hand while furthering these stereotypes in latent rhetorical ways on the other.

An Amended Definition of Scandal

Those who study scandal provide a multidimensional definition of the phenomenon that addresses its complexity.[34] Thompson's articulation of scandal includes the breach of social norms, secret activity, disapproval of the acts, public expression of this disapproval, and a marred reputation for those caught in the transgression.[35] An amended definition would include an additional point: scandals must prompt a vocal segment of the public to talk about these events as they relate to their own lives and affect their own social networks. While this part of the amended definition might appear to be folded into "the public expression of disapproval," it has a more personal dimension. In this study, the scandals (Spitzer and Sanford) that generated the most news coverage also triggered the most trend stories in which members of the public not only express their opinions but also speak from personal experience about being victims of male infidelity.

Scandals cannot blossom into full-blown sensational affairs unless the public feels strongly about what transpired. When people have strong emotions and opinions on a topic, they are often driven by personal experience, fear, and desire. When people are not actively engaged in talking about a scandal, its lack of momentum prevents the scandal from making it to the top of newscasts, the most-emailed sections of online news sites, and the covers of popular tabloid weeklies. When scandals surge as the most-talked-about news events—as measured by the Pew Research Center for the People and the Press—they connect to people's interest in scandal as it relates to their own lives and networks. Since scandal is rooted in the interpersonal dimension, it achieves its power from an audience invested in its narrative.[36] "To become a real scandal, the media accounts must spark the imagination of the public."[37] The public's role in the scandal script is to engage in public discourse about how scandal relates to the lives and communities of news consumers. That public chatter propels forward the scandal's narrative, providing it momentum necessary to remain in the news. The narrative is often highly personal and prompts people to share their own experiences and cautionary tales on the subject. Some scandals particularly strike a nerve with the public because of shock at the scandal itself (e.g., "Spitzer had sex with $3,000/hour prostitutes?!"). The combination of surprise, tinged with the salacious topic of sexual immorality, prompts people to talk freely and personally about the scandal. These reflections and opinions enter the realm of gossip when people connect the scandal to comparable actions in their personal networks. While Bird notes that news stories can emerge from gossip,[38] she does not reflect on the effect of gossip in pushing forward news of scandal after the story "breaks." Gossip, like scandal, is a moral and socially regulating phenomenon.[39] The confluence of the two phenomena (scandal and gossip) helps sustain interest in a scandal. Ultimately, an amended definition of scandal should reflect the role of personal discussions and anecdote-sharing in the wake of mediated scandals, with a common deterioration into gossip. If people do not talk about scandal as it relates to their personal lives, then the scandal itself is not significant enough to engage in personal, moral discourse.

Looking Toward Future Scandals

While this study found news coverage of scandal both opposed and reproduced patriarchal gender roles, future political sex scandals will reveal whether these gender norms continue to be upheld or challenged. I predict future press conferences relating to male political sex scandals will see fewer wives in attendance, but the wives will continue to be written into the scandal script. The traditional traits ascribed to a wife, including her "supportive" nature, are so deeply embedded that even her absence will be spun as spousal support, perhaps through her release of a statement. Additionally, the politician's transgression against the traditional monogamous marriage model is perceived to represent a transgression against his wife. In a career-dominated marriage, the wife is regarded as an extension of her husband's identity.[40] Her work, volunteerism, hosting, and presence at public events reflect on her spouse. Even if the wife chooses to be absent from the press conference—thus resisting the supportive role society ascribes to her—the wife's longstanding identity as an extension of her husband will return her to the script. These culturally embedded norms may also shape her self-perception. As a result, she may release a supportive statement following reports of her husband's affair as Darlene Ensign and Jenny Sanford did, obliquely opting in to the scandal script. Such a statement would attempt to publicly reaffirm her marriage and uphold her identity as a political wife. Ultimately, the hegemonic process will remain intact: while the wife may be absent from her husband's "I have sinned" press conference, she will participate as a figure in the scandal narrative. Her statements will reaffirm the health of the political couple as a unit, thereby reaffirming the prominent social institutions of marriage. The wife will be constructed as "standing by her man," even when she did not literally stand next to him. In this study, every one of the political wives either stood physically next to her husband at his press conference (Dina Matos McGreevey, Wendy Vitter, Suzanne Craig, Silda Spitzer, Terry Mahoney) or released a statement that extended a public olive branch to the offending husband (Darlene Ensign and Jenny Sanford). Hence it is the political wife who reaffirms the unity of marriage in a moment of marital crisis. The irony is that her very presence, intended to reflect well on the husband-politician, may succeed in diminishing his reputation. After all, the "stand by your man" trope appears to be derided by the public on a conscious level even though it is reproduced unconsciously.

Notes

1. John B. Thompson, *The Media and Modernity: A Social Theory of the Media* (Stanford: Stanford University Press, 1995); John B. Thompson, *Political Scandal: Power and Visibility in the Media Age* (Cambridge: Blackwell Publishers, 2000); S. Elizabeth Bird, *The Audience in Everyday Life: Living in a Media World* (New York: Routledge, 2003); James Lull and Stephen Hinerman, eds., *Media Scandals: Morality and Desire in the Popular Culture Marketplace* (New York: Columbia University Press, 1997).

2. Kristi L. Gustafson, "First Comes Love and Now Forgiveness?" *Times-Union*, March 16, 2008, G16.

3. Dane Archer, Bonita Iritani, Debra D. Kimes, and Michael Barrios, "Face-ism: Five Studies of Sex Differences in Facial Prominence," *Journal of Personality and Social Psychology* 45 (1983): 734.

4. Candace West and Don H. Zimmerman, "Doing Gender," *Gender and Society* 1 (1987): 125–51.

5. Maurice J. Levesque and Charles A. Lowe, "Face-ism as a Determinant of Interpersonal Perceptions: The Influence of Context on Facial Prominence Effects," *Sex Roles* 41 (1999): 241–59.

6. Archer, Iritani, Kimes, and Barrios, "Face-ism: Five Studies"; Levesque and Lowe, "Face-ism as a Determinant."

7. Levesque and Lowe, "Face-ism as a Determinant."

8. Archer, Iritani, Kimes, and Barrios, "Face-ism: Five Studies," 734.

9. Janet Finch, *Married to the Job: Wives' Incorporation in Men's Work* (Boston: Allen and Unwin, 1983); Susan Maushart, *Wifework: What Marriage Really Means for Women* (New York: Bloomsbury, 2001).

10. Paul Grondahl, "A Woman Betrayed with a Future to Ponder," *Times-Union*, March 13, 2008, 5.

11. Laurie E. MaGuire, *Helen of Troy: From Homer to Hollywood* (Malden, MA: John Wiley & Sons, 2009).

12. MaGuire, *Helen of Troy*, 48.

13. Monica Hesse, "In One Man's Fall, Bruises for All," *Washington Post*, March 15, 2008, C1; Jan Hoffman, "Public Infidelity, Private Debate: Not My Husband (Right?)," *New York Times*, March 16, 2008, Style 1; Stacey Morris, "Keep Wives out of Public Confessionals," *Times-Union*, March 15, 2008, A7; Gustafson, "First Comes Love," G16; Alessandra Stanley, "Mars and Venus Dissect the Spitzer Scandal on the TV Talk Shows," *New York Times*, March 12, 2008, E1; Fred LeBrun, "A Stunning Journey from Day One to All-But-Done," *Times-Union*, March 11, 2008, A9; Eugene Robinson, "It Wasn't Her Place, the Spotlight Spitzer Should Have Faced Alone," *Washington Post*, March 14, 2008, A17; Michael Gormley and Amy Westfeldt, "Spitzer Hid His Inner Torment," *Times-Union*, March 16, 2008, A5; Grondahl, "A Woman Betrayed," 5.

14. Miriam M. Johnson, *Strong Mothers, Weak Wives: The Search for Gender Equality* (Berkeley: University of California Press, 1988); J. Richard Udry, *The Social Context of Marriage* (Philadelphia: Lippincott, 1971).

15. Finch, Married to the Job.

16. Hanna Papanek, "Men, Women, and Work: Reflections on the Two-Person Career," *American Journal of Sociology* 78 (1973): 852–72.

17. Papanek, "Men, Women, and Work."

18. Finch, *Married to the Job.*

19. Eliza K. Pavalko and Glen H. Elder, "Women Behind the Men: Variations in Wives' Support of Husbands' Careers," *Gender and Society* 7 (1993): 548–67.

20. Betty Houchin Winfield and Barbara Friedman. "Gender Politics: News Coverage of the Candidates' Wives in Campaign 2000," *Journalism and Mass Communications Quarterly* 80 (2003): 548–66.

21. John Lantigua, "Many Factors Test Limits of Loyalty for Political Wives, Therapists Say," *Palm Beach Post*, October 26, 2008, A1.

22. Myra MacPherson, *Power Lovers: An Intimate Look at Politicians and Their Marriages* (New York: Putnam, 1975).

23. Molly Ball, "High Hopes Get Dashed," *Las Vegas Review-Journal*, June 28, 2009.

24. George Gmelch and Patricia Mary San Antonio, "Baseball Wives: Gender and the Work of Baseball." *Journal of Contemporary Ethnography* 30 (2001): 335–56; Ortiz, Steven M., "Using Power: An Exploration of Control Work in the Sport Marriage," *Sociological Perspectives* 49 (2006): 527–57.

25. Robert O. Blood and Donald M. Wolfe, *Husbands and Wives: The Dynamics of Married Living* (New York: Free Press, 1960).

26. Lantigua, "Many Factors," A1.

27. Morris, "Keep Wives," A7.

28. Kevin Justus, "Governor's Wife Releases Statement on Affair," News Channel 7, June 24, 2009, accessed April 8, 2011, http://www2.wspa.com/news/2009/jun/24/jenny_sanford_releases_statement_on_affair-ar-1396.

29. Stuart Hall, "The Whites of Their Eyes: Racist Ideologies and the Media," in *Gender, Race, and Class in Media*, ed. Gail Dines and Jean M. Humez (Thousand Oaks, CA: Sage Publications, 1995), 18–22.

30. Don Heider, *White News: Why Local News Programs Don't Cover People of Color* (London: Lawrence Erlbaum, 2000), 52.

31. Heider, White News, 52.

32. Stephanie Craft and Wayne Wanta, "Women in the Newsroom: Influences of Female Editors and Reporters on the News Agenda," *Journalism & Mass Communication Quarterly* 81 (2004): 124–38.

33. Craft and Wanta, "Women in the Newsroom."

34. Thompson, The Media and Modernity; Lull and Hinerman, Media Scandals; Paul Apostolidis and Juliet A. Williams, eds., *Public Affairs: Politics in the Age of Sex Scandals* (Durham, NC: Duke University Press, 2004); Mark D. West, *Secrets, Sex, and Spectacle: The Rules of Scandal in Japan and the United States* (Chicago: University of Chicago Press, 2006).

35. Thompson, *Political Scandal.*

36. Bird, *The Audience.*

37. Bird, *The Audience*, 31.

38. Bird, *The Audience.*

39. Patricia Meyer Spacks, *Gossip* (Chicago: Knopf, 1985); Robert F. Goodman and Aaron Ben-Ze'ev, eds., *Good Gossip* (Lawrence: University Press of Kansas, 1994).

40. Papanek, "Men, Women, and Work"; Finch, *Married to the Job.*

Bibliography

Archer, Dane, Bonita Iritani, Debra D. Kimes, and Michael Barrios. "Face-ism: Five Studies of Sex Differences in Facial Prominence." *Journal of Personality and Social Psychology* 45 (1983): 725–35.

Apostolidis, Paul, and Juliet A. Williams, editors. *Public Affairs: Politics in the Age of Sex Scandals.* Durham, NC: Duke University Press, 2004.

Ball, Molly. "Ensign Wounds Keep Festering." *Las Vegas Review-Journal*, July 12, 2009.

———. "Ex-Ensign Aide Details Wife's Affair." *Las Vegas Review-Journal*, July 9, 2009.

———. "High Hopes Get Dashed." *Las Vegas Review-Journal*, June 28, 2009.

Bird, S. Elizabeth. *The Audience in Everyday Life: Living in a Media World.* New York: Routledge, 2003.

Blood, Robert O., and Donald M. Wolfe. *Husbands and Wives: The Dynamics of Married Living.* New York: Free Press, 1960.

Craft, Stephanie, and Wayne Wanta. "Women in the Newsroom: Influences of Female Editors and Reporters on the News Agenda." *Journalism & Mass Communication Quarterly* 81 (2004): 124–38.

Finch, Janet. *Married to the Job: Wives' Incorporation in Men's Work.* Boston: Allen and Unwin, 1983.

Gmelch, George, and Patricia Mary San Antonio. "Baseball Wives: Gender and the Work of Baseball." *Journal of Contemporary Ethnography* 30 (2001): 335–56.

Goodman, Robert F., and Aaron Ben-Ze'ev, editors. *Good Gossip.* Lawrence: University Press of Kansas, 1994.

Gormley, Michael, and Amy Westfeldt. "Spitzer Hid His Inner Torment." *Times-Union*, March 16, 2008.

Grondahl, Paul. "A Woman Betrayed with a Future to Ponder." *Times Union*, March 13, 2008.

Gustafson, Kristi L. "First Comes Love and Now Forgiveness?" *Times-Union*, March 16, 2008.

———. "The Whites of Their Eyes: Racist Ideologies and the Media." In *Gender, Race, and Class in Media*, edited by Gail Dines and Jean M. Humez, 18–22. Thousand Oaks, CA: Sage Publications, 1995.

Heider, Don. *White News: Why Local News Programs Don't Cover People of Color.* London: Lawrence Erlbaum, 2000.

Hesse, Monica. "In One Man's Fall, Bruises for All." *Washington Post*, March 15, 2008.

———. "News? Sigh. No Affair to Remember." *Washington Post*, June 18, 2009.

Hoffman, Jan. "Public Infidelity, Private Debate: Not My Husband (Right?)." *New York Times*, March 16, 2008.

Johnson, Miriam M. *Strong Mothers, Weak Wives: The Search for Gender Equality.* Berkeley: University of California Press, 1988.

Justus, Kevin. "Governor's Wife Releases Statement on Affair." News Channel 7, June 24, 2009. Accessed April 8, 2011, http://www2.wspa.com/news/2009/jun/24/jenny_sanford_releases_statement_on_affair-ar-1396.

Lantigua, John. "Many Factors Test Limits of Loyalty for Political Wives, Therapists Say." *Palm Beach Post*, October 26, 2008.

LeBrun, Fred. "A Stunning Journey from Day One to All-But-Done." *Times-Union*, March 11, 2008.

Levesque, Maurice J., and Charles A. Lowe. "Face-ism as a Determinant of Interpersonal Perceptions: The Influence of Context on Facial Prominence Effects." *Sex Roles* 41 (1999): 241–59.

Lull, James, and Stephen Hinerman, editors. *Media Scandals: Morality and Desire in the Popular Culture Marketplace.* New York: Columbia University Press, 1997.

MacPherson, Myra. *Power Lovers: An Intimate Look at Politicians and Their Marriages.* New York: Putnam, 1975.

MaGuire, Laurie E. *Helen of Troy: From Homer to Hollywood.* Malden, MA: John Wiley & Sons, 2009.

Maushart, Susan. *Wifework: What Marriage Really Means for Women*. New York: Bloomsbury, 2001.
Meyer Spacks, Patricia. *Gossip*. Chicago: Knopf, 1985.
Morris, Stacey. "Keep Wives out of Public Confessionals." *Times-Union*, March 15, 2008.
Ortiz, Steven M. "Using Power: An Exploration of Control Work in the Sport Marriage." *Sociological Perspectives* 49 (2006): 527–57.
Papanek, Hanna. "Men, Women, and Work: Reflections on the Two-Person Career." *American Journal of Sociology* 78 (1973): 852–72.
Pavalko, Eliza K., and Glen H. Elder. "Women Behind the Men: Variations in Wives' Support of Husbands' Careers." *Gender and Society* 7 (1993): 548–67.
Robinson, Eugene. "It Wasn't Her Place, the Spotlight Spitzer Should Have Faced Alone." *Washington Post*, March 14, 2008.
Stanley, Alessandra. "Mars and Venus Dissect the Spitzer Scandal on the TV Talk Shows." *New York Times*, March 12, 2008.
Thompson, John B. *The Media and Modernity: A Social Theory of the Media*. Stanford: Stanford University Press, 1995.
———. *Political Scandal: Power and Visibility in the Media Age*. Cambridge: Blackwell Publishers, 2000.
Udry, J. Richard. *The Social Context of Marriage*. Philadelphia: Lippincott, 1971.
West, Mark D. *Secrets, Sex, and Spectacle: The Rules of Scandal in Japan and the United States*. Chicago: University of Chicago Press, 2006.
West, Candace, and Don H. Zimmerman. "Doing Gender." *Gender and Society* 1 (1987): 125–51.
Winfield, Betty Houchin, and Barbara Friedman. "Gender Politics: News Coverage of the Candidates' Wives in Campaign 2000." *Journalism and Mass Communications Quarterly* 80 (2003): 548–66.

Chapter 12

"Taking Care of the Children and the Country": Nancy Pelosi and the Trope of Motherhood in Partisan and Mainstream Media

by Sheryl L. Cunningham

On January 4, 2007, Nancy Pelosi addressed the 110th Congress as the first female Speaker of the U.S. House of Representatives. Regarded as a boundary-breaking woman across most news discourse, Pelosi described herself as such in her first speech to the 110th Congress: "It's an historic moment for the Congress. It's an historic moment for the women of America. It is a moment for which we have waited over two hundred years. Never losing faith, we waited through the many years of struggle to achieve our rights. But women weren't just waiting; women were working. Never losing faith, we worked to redeem the promise of America, that all men and women are created equal."[1]

In her speech, Pelosi explicitly identifies with women, and in her public discourse both before and after her reelection to the House of Representatives, she has consistently referred to herself as a specific kind of woman, a "mother of five." When Pelosi became Speaker, one image—Pelosi holding the Speaker's gavel while surrounded by children—was reproduced in almost every visual news representation of her from that day. Pelosi and those advising her saw a strategic advantage in emphasizing a discourse of motherhood. Yet many women who want to participate in electoral politics must still seriously consider how discourses of motherhood and family may negatively impact their prospects.[2] Such consideration is due, in part, to the fact that throughout U.S. history women have encountered what Minow describes as a "dilemma of difference" made necessary by a separation of spheres: one public and one private, with idealized womanhood solidly grounded in the latter of the two.[3] To gain access to the public sphere, women may attempt to elide that difference by claiming equality with men; the main assumption is that women need to argue that men and women are basically the same and so deserve similar treatment or opportunities. On the other hand, some women become wary of arguments about sameness due to the fact that men's and women's lived experiences are often quite different, and expecting women to focus on sameness is asking them to behave like men. To mark difference, then, a woman may emphasize a characteristic that makes her distinctly female, such as her ability to give birth, as Pelosi does when she calls herself a "mother of five." Such emphasis may harm her chances of being taken seriously in the public sphere, however, because of an essentialist understanding of mother as the primary role for women.

Separation of Spheres

In thinking about women, media, and politics, we must consider the history of women's relationship to the public sphere. This context makes intelligible the "dilemma of difference" because it highlights what is at stake in questions of difference and how sex differences have been used to exclude women from participating in electoral politics. In the United States, women's participation in the public sphere has been constrained in two basic ways. The first constraint was a legal one barring women from voting in political elections, which was overcome when the Nineteenth Amendment for women's suffrage passed in 1920. The second constraint was cultural, and it barred "proper" women from speaking in public. Both had the effect of excluding women from formal politics. Campbell explained this exclusion was largely due to the belief in a separation of spheres and conceptions of an ideal womanhood for White women in particular: a woman was "to remain entirely in the private sphere of the home, eschewing any appearance of individuality, leadership, or aggressiveness. Her purity depended on her domesticity; the woman who was compelled by economic need or slavery to work away from her own hearth was tainted."[4] Due to White women's longtime sequestering in the domestic inside, the public sphere was a masculinized cultural arena to which women did not enjoy easy access. The masculinization of the public sphere is still evident, but women have made inroads into it through one avenue.

Though many women do run for office and win, they are still proportionally underrepresented in terms of actual numbers due to a strong emphasis on masculinity in electoral politics. Huddy and Terkildsen find that candidates who emphasize stereotypically masculine traits are perceived as more competent than those who emphasize feminine traits.[5] Research on the American presidency repeatedly shows that the office itself is often linked with masculinity.[6] In her analysis of gendered discourse in the 1992 presidential campaigns, Wahl-Jorgensen argues that candidates create masculine personas by referencing certain domains of life considered masculine such as the military, fraternity, sports, and the family.[7] While culturally considered the domain of women, the family is often discursively represented in politics through the term "family values," a patriarchal construction by which men are supposed to be the breadwinners, protectors, and final decision makers.[8] In their analysis of presidential campaign films, Parry-Giles and Parry-Giles show that presidential contenders have been aligned with "institutions and cultural practices that define masculinity for American society," including the military and athletic accomplishments.[9]

The military is also a highly masculinized institution. Women are allowed to enter the U.S. military, but in contemporary politics the "appropriate" place of women in the military is unclear, while the place of men is not only fixed but legally marked. For example, male bodies are conscripted while female bodies are exempt in that males are required to register with the government on turning eighteen so as to be eligible for military service should the need for a draft arise. Tosh argues this act of conscription is just one instance in which "the state acts to reinforce masculine norms."[10] The fact that women are not technically allowed to hold combat positions also suggests that the military is still imagined as a masculine space.[11] Hoagland points out that the logic of men protecting women and children rests on the assumption that Other men are predators and so "our" men must provide protection for women and children.[12] This logic is evident, for example, in the George W. Bush administration's rhetoric following the terrorist attacks of September 11, 2001, when military action in Afghanistan was couched in terms of protecting Afghan women from Afghan men.[13] Bystrom and her coauthors point out that the events of September 11 may put female candidates—particularly those running for the U.S. House and Senate—at a disadvantage due to the renewed emphasis on the military and the War on Terrorism; these issues call up a type of masculinity that may be difficult for women to perform without seeming *too* masculine.[14]

Even with the emphasis on masculinity in two aspects of the public sphere—electoral politics and the protection of the nation—women have used discourses of motherhood to enter the public sphere. Tonn argues that labor leader Mary "Mother Jones" Harris used a discourse of motherhood, combined with a rhetorical militancy, to great effect: "As performed by Jones, militant motherhood is grounded both in physical care and protection and in a feminine rhetorical style that is at once affirming and confrontational."[15] Hayden shows how women participating in the Million Mom March, an event organized to advocate for stricter gun control laws, utilize their experiences as mothers "to promote a political and moral order in which the values of caring, empathy, and nurturance [were] privileged."[16] Motherhood can be a potent rhetorical position, yet, as DiQuinzio points out, this relationship can easily become "essential motherhood," an outcome that threatens to reify the essentialist assumption that all women want to mother and should prefer a private sphere role to that of a public sphere role such as senator or representative.[17]

In this chapter, I discuss the image of Pelosi surrounded by children that was reproduced across media discourse as well as a wider range of media coverage in the weeks before and after she became Speaker of the House. One of Pelosi's preferred self-representations is that of a "mother of five," meaning she is the mother of five children. Mainstream media outlets[18] (ABC News and the *New York Times*) accept her role as mother and, in several cases, link her motherhood to her success as a politician: for them, she is an experienced mom who knows how to handle the unruly Democratic Party. Partisan media outlets, however—represented in this study by Fox News, the *National Review*, and the *New Republic*[19]—tend to question and at some points openly reject the characterization of Pelosi as a mother figure. Though she is, in fact, a mother of five children, conservative commentators and journalists consistently try to dissociate her from motherhood. These attempts suggest that the label of "mother" and who has the right to claim it are points of contention between the two major political parties and a particular point of anxiety for conservatives who may be used to ownership of discourses about family and the importance of motherhood. I argue that Pelosi is able to use the trope of motherhood successfully in the public sphere but that use may still be problematic.

The Image of Pelosi as Mother

After Pelosi became the first female Speaker of the House, an image of her holding the Speaker's gavel aloft while surrounded by children dominated the news. The children in the photograph are Pelosi's own grandchildren as well as the children and grandchildren of other politicians. Pelosi functions symbolically in this image as the first *woman* to be Speaker of the House. In the image, Pelosi stands behind the Speaker's desk. Seen from the waist up, she is wearing a dark-colored suit and pearl necklace. I draw attention to her clothing because attention to dress is important for women in politics. Although discussions of how political women dress has been used to trivialize[20] or confine them to the domestic sphere,[21] clothing does affect how one is perceived: "For women in particular, style [of clothing] plays a part in the construction and symbolic expression of social position, being oppositional, subversive or conservative."[22] Pelosi's choice of clothing was appropriate to the occasion: she wore a dark-colored suit, the business uniform of most professionals. The construction of Pelosi's suit visibly marked her difference through the absence of a tie. Her choice of necklace also marked difference. American men, even when they wear necklaces, are not likely to wear the style Pelosi chose: large pearls.

She smiles broadly as she holds the Speaker's gavel in her right hand and raises it above her head. Studies in nonverbal communication have shown the importance of smiling; a smile often leads to positive perceptions of the person who is smiling, particularly for women.[23] In this case, Pelosi's smile conveys feelings of happiness. Off-center behind Pelosi is a huge American flag that dwarfs both her and the children around her. She is surrounded by small male and female children, both children of color and White children. By holding the gavel above her head, Pelosi becomes the tallest figure in the image and serves as the immediate focal point. Pelosi's body and the gavel are in vertical alignment with the American flag, so the viewer sees Pelosi, the gavel, and then the flag, which continues beyond the edited space of the image. This is an image of a woman in politics at a moment of triumph, her hand raised in victory. The raised gavel, however, does not only make Pelosi the focal point, but it also shows her in a posture of power and confidence.

The flag, gavel, and children are each elements with their own symbolic potential. First and foremost, both the American flag and the Speaker's gavel are representations of American power. They are not powerful in and of themselves but as Barthes argued become powerful through a process of signification.[24] The power of the flag as a symbol is nowhere better exemplified than in the debate over flag-burning and free expression, in which the flag becomes an extension of the nation—so much so that, like the nation, it must be protected from those who would do it harm.[25] The gavel is most closely associated with the judiciary and symbolizes justice and judgment, individual power to call to order, and the power to end or dismiss. That the person standing in front of the American flag and holding the gavel is a woman speaks potently of gender equality. This image says women have "made it." Pelosi argued for exactly this interpretation in her speech: "For our daughters and our granddaughters today we have broken the marble ceiling. For our daughters and our granddaughters now the sky is the limit. Anything is possible for them."[26] Pelosi claims equality for all women based on her success and also claims young women and girls—daughters and granddaughters—will no longer face such difficult obstacles to political power.

The inclusion of children in the image further marks Pelosi's gender difference by invoking the trope of motherhood. Here, there was a double identification with women—one explicit, embodied by Pelosi *as* a woman, the other implicit and suggested by the history of motherhood being conceptualized as a woman's primary role. A skeptical reader might ask how this photo is about motherhood when male politicians also pose for photos with children, and those images do not necessarily invoke a discourse of fatherhood. Consider one example. On January 8, 2002, George W. Bush signed the No Child Left Behind Act. At this signing, children were included in the photo, though not as many as in Pelosi's, and there were also other politicians. In Bush's case, however, the children "made sense" in a different way. They were meant to represent the children who would benefit from passage of the bill. When Pelosi became the Speaker of the House, there was no direct or logical relationship to children. Her speech did not focus on children, other than the two lines mentioning daughters and granddaughters, and yet in the photos and video coverage of post-speech Pelosi, she is surrounded by children. There was no need to mention children in her speech or position herself in the middle of them, but Pelosi's choice to do so connected her with children in such a way that the viewer must try to make sense of their presence.

Viewers did try to make sense of the children's presence, and they did not agree on how the image ought to be interpreted. BagNews, a "progressive site dedicated to visual politics and the analysis of news images," posted the image of Pelosi with the children, and an online discussion ensued.[27] BagNews is a partisan website used by people likely to be sympathetic to Pelosi, but the comments on the blog were instructive in seeing how the image of Pelosi with the children could be read in many different ways, even by progressives. The site's publisher, Michael Shaw, posted the image and had a negative interpretation of it, arguing, "Sure, sure, apologists can say it's endearing, or even promotional, indicative of a new Congressional focus on Americans, their families and the future. And to that, I say: you're rationalizing. As the political creatures that we are, the first connection here involves Nancy Pelosi associated with little children and babies and the sense of a Congressional delegation made up of the same."[28] Shaw reads the image as saying Pelosi will now be in charge of a bunch of children, thus infantilizing House members and trivializing her own role as a political leader. Later in his post, he shifts away from a motherhood frame when he asks, "Is [Pelosi] being pigeon-holed into the gender-bent role of mommy or unbaked first grade teacher?"[29] Here Shaw suggests another interpretation for the image, elementary teacher rather than mother. Though both are gendered roles, his question suggests that the image is polysemous, able to be interpreted in several different ways.[30] Even if viewers accept that the image is about motherhood, whether this association is one that helps or hurts Pelosi and the Democrats is still open to interpretation and further complicates the use of the trope. The responses to Shaw's question and the photograph were varied, with the first commenter (of a total of fifty-seven) writing: "Just another mom in tennis shoes. Patty Murray is serving her 3rd term in the Senate and is 4th ranked. You would think the MSM [mainstream media] would figure it out that being a mom has a lot more real constructive power in it than being a fat old dude with big hair."[31] This poster's comment suggests Pelosi was evoking motherhood in the image and that motherhood is a powerful rhetorical position for women in politics. Another commenter, however, offers this view: "Democrats = not serious, not powerful. Therefore not worthy of respect."[32] This commenter seems to agree with Shaw's reading that the image trivialized Pelosi and, more broadly, the whole Democratic Party. Another commenter writes that a reader's sex likely influences perceptions of the image: "I think it's a bit much that it was used as the main picture, but otherwise it's wonderful. It was a day of celebration and acknowledgement that families and the future matter. Maybe women who view it have less trouble with this image than men do."[33] I argue that this textual moment calls for what Ceccarelli describes as a reading of "hermeneutic depth" in which "both an interpretation and its opposite are sustained by the text."[34] First, viewers do not necessarily accept that this image is about motherhood, and even when they do, the readings are oppositional: the image is potentially both trivializing and empowering. Pelosi exemplifies the constraints as well as the possibilities for a woman speaking as a mother figure in politics.

What is it about being a woman in a position of power, such as Speaker of the House, that compels Pelosi to surround herself with children in the first photo opportunity she has as Speaker? The complexity of the image speaks to the position in which many female politicians find themselves should they choose to use motherhood as a source of rhetorical invention in the public sphere. The image shows a successful political woman, but it also shows how strategic constructions of women in positions of power are patriarchally constrained. To take on the role of "mother" in politics may be a necessary strategic maneuver in some rhetorical situations,[35] while at the same time it depends on a relationship that has often been oppressive in its rearticulation of the public/private divide. It is a rhetorical construction fraught with tension because it risks an essentialism many women have long fought against, and yet it proves to be a compelling source of inspiration for women who do not want to accept the continuation of the public/private dichotomy still used to keep women out of public life.

Media Coverage in Partisan and Mainstream Press

In the image, Pelosi's relationship to the nation is articulated through the trope of motherhood. This representation is common across news discourse about Pelosi. She is often described as a mother figure for the Democratic Party. Her experience of motherhood is even offered as explanation for her leadership style. She is described as the tough mother or grandmother who cares for the country and disciplines the unruly Democratic Party. On ABC News, Anchor Charlie Gibson describes her this way: "Nancy Pelosi, Democrat from California, took the gavel. But in a picture, perhaps, even more symbolic, the new Speaker was on the floor for a time, holding her six-year-old grandson all the while, giving directions on how events were to proceed. It seemed the ultimate in multitasking. Taking care of the children and the country."[36] In this discourse, the power of the mother trope in politics is evident: Pelosi becomes the ultimate female multitasker able to handle both children and the nation with ease. Throughout her campaign, Pelosi often referred to herself as having a "mother of five voice," and this presentation of self was taken up by ABC and the *New York Times*. Consider the following exchange between Pelosi and ABC News Anchor Terry Moran:

> PELOSI: When the mics are off, yeah, the mother-of-five voice comes in handy. My colleagues hear it coming, they, they know.
>
> MORAN: And that voice works. Nancy Pelosi somehow managed to instill real discipline in the Democratic ranks and that famously fractious party. She'll need to keep that up as the country looks to her and Democrats as they take power in Congress.[37]

This exchange suggests Pelosi's experiences as a mother made her into a good leader, one able to bring the Democrats in line. ABC News again emphasizes Pelosi's disciplinary skills in another segment: "A few minutes in the store with Pelosi and her daughter, and you can see how she got the unruly Democrats whipped into shape. Because whatever the GOP thinks of her, Pelosi has brought an almost Republican-style order to the Democrats. Under her leadership, they've voted lockstep against Republicans nearly 90 percent of the time."[38]

The *New York Times* also suggests her leadership skills are the result of her experiences as a mother, describing Pelosi as a famous parent who "know[s] that the experience of raising children and managing a household is not just maddening and delicious: it can also serve to develop skills that are central to successful management."[39] The *Times* further states that she "guided her caucus to victory by enforcing remarkable party discipline" and quotes Representative Anna G. Eshoo, another mother of five children, who says: "I'll say to her, 'Nancy, I'd blow up if I had to deal what you deal with,'" followed by, "If there wasn't discipline in her house, there would have been chaos. She knows how important that is."[40] What is most notable about this coverage is the positive linking of motherhood to her position of national leadership and the explicit references to how motherhood made Pelosi a good disciplinarian for the Democratic Party. The implication is that her ability to discipline her party will be good for the political system.[41]

Conservative media outlets tend to reject the characterization of Pelosi as a mother. When commenting on an image shown in the mainstream media of Pelosi holding a baby, a Fox News analyst complains the image was spin and little else: "That's the total home run for the spin doctors. They put a picture in front of it, and some dumb TV reporter just said, 'Oh yes, well I guess she's taking care of the country.'"[42] In other words, viewers should not think of Pelosi as a mother who can care for the country. The *National Review* openly scoffs at Pelosi's attempt to position herself as a mother or grandmother figure, saying that asking the Republicans to cooperate with her after she was unwilling to cooperate with them in the past is like saying, "Do as I say, not as I do. That is counsel unworthy of any loving grandmother."[43] The conservative commentary also focuses more on Pelosi's age by repeatedly marking her as grandmother and not just a mother. A Fox News commentator expresses incredulity at the characterization of Pelosi in these gendered roles: "Look, I think this really stems from this Democratic Party right now where they have Nancy Pelosi please [sic] being heralded as this grandmother and mother and the most powerful woman in the world and sort of embracing motherhood when for decades liberal Democrats have done nothing but denigrate motherhood through movements like the radical feminism movement, pro abortion movements and attacks on the traditional family value. It's absolutely ridiculous."[44] The speaker indicates that Democratic or liberal women who position themselves as mothers will be dissociated from that position if they can be linked to feminism and abortion rights. This commentator suggests that liberals or feminists cannot be considered good mothers because anyone who supports a pro-choice position does not value motherhood. Even though Pelosi is, in reality, a mother and grandmother, much of the conservative media commentary suggests she should not have access to this discourse because she does not behave as a conservatively imagined mother ought to. For these media outlets, Pelosi's motherhood is not authentic but rather a ploy about which viewers should remain skeptical; Fox News commentator Bill O'Reilly puts the question this way to a guest on his show: "So you're not buying Nancy Pelosi as the kindly Italian grandmother?"[45]

In the mainstream news outlets, Pelosi's skills as a politician who can discipline and control her party are often linked to her experiences as a mother. It should be noted, however, that when her skills as a disciplinarian are acknowledged in the *National Review*, they are not linked to her mothering skills: "She enforced a party loyalty that had House Democrats deliver 'the most unified voting record in fifty years' according to the *Washington Post*. In 2005, her caucus voted along strict party lines 88 percent of the time. In 1997, fifty-one House Democrats supported a Republican budget that significantly reduced domestic spending. Last year, there wasn't a single Democratic vote for a five-year GOP budget plan with far more modest reductions."[46] There is an admission that she is a leader who disciplines her party, but the positive association with motherhood as the reason for her skills is missing. The *National Review* further questions her ability to control her party: "Complicating the picture for Pelosi will be the ideological diversity in her caucus. If her margin of control is small and her moderate/conservative members are not acquiescent, Pelosi will have found a kind of diversity that she does not like."[47] Here, Pelosi is controlled by her party, and particularly by Democratic moderates and conservatives. There is no indication that her experiences as a mother have helped her build the skills necessary to discipline her party. Even the center-left *New Republic* points out Pelosi's potential problems with the Democratic Party, unfavorably comparing the incoming Democratic majority to the 1994 Republican majority: "And, unlike the Contract-toting newcomers of '94, who marched in devoted lockstep with their leader, Pelosi's troops—who include everyone from Barbara Lee, a Berkeley-based sponsor of a 'Department of Peace,' to Heath Shuler, a culturally conservative rural populist—have dueling agendas of their own."[48] Instead of shoring up Pelosi's problems by pointing to her mothering skills, Crowley calls her "grudge-bearing Pelosi," suggesting a much different and more damaging characterization than that of the multitasking mother.

The difference between the partisan and mainstream coverage of Pelosi as Democratic mother is striking. The positive articulations of motherhood are virtually absent from all partisan publications, even the center-left publication analyzed, suggesting that a discourse of motherhood does not mesh with a discourse of nation in these news outlets. Pelosi's motherhood is often reproduced in mainstream media content as the reason for her success both in her career and her role as a manager of the Democrats. Such coverage shows taking on the role of mother is politically powerful, offering one way women can get their own representations of self reproduced in news discourse (or at least in mainstream news).[49] The left-leaning publication in this analysis ignores motherhood altogether. Pelosi's motherhood, in the right-leaning press, is seen as a violation of partisan turf and conservative norms regarding who should have access to symbolic representations of the family. Put simply, journalists and commentators at the *National Review* and Fox News did not want Pelosi to be represented as a mother in media discourse.

What's a Woman to Do?

In these news outlets, motherhood is a contested discursive space and one conservative media outlets are unwilling to give up to Pelosi, although mainstream media outlets seem to celebrate motherhood and acknowledge how mothering skills in the private sphere translate into leadership skills in the public sphere. Such coverage suggests the trope of motherhood remains a powerful rhetorical position from which women can speak, but the position is not unassailable and could easily devolve into questioning whether a particular politician is a good mother or bad mother. Even among those who consider themselves progressive and likely to support the Democratic Party, the image creates differing and strong responses: some of pride and happiness regarding motherhood as well as those of disappointment and frustration that the image makes the Democrats seem childlike and not to be taken seriously.

Such complexity raises several issues for women politicians who may want to emphasize motherhood in their public discourse. First, the trope of motherhood may rearticulate the idea of the separation of spheres and through this, the idea of "essentialist motherhood." Second, some women may be more able to access this discourse than others. Clearly, women without children are put at a disadvantage. But women with children should also proceed with caution. Sarah Palin is an instructive counterexample to Pelosi in this regard. For example, when Palin was nominated for the vice presidency, she was sometimes critiqued by both Republicans and Democrats for her role as a mother. Some questioned who would take care of her young children if Palin became vice president. It seems Pelosi's age and lack of young children at home allow her to emphasize motherhood without the same risk a younger woman with younger children might experience, at least when it comes to mainstream media coverage. Third, though Democrats are unlikely to be covered positively in conservative press, Democratic women must understand they may become targeted because they articulate motherhood in a way that violates partisan turf. This does not mean they should not articulate notions of mothering and care, but it likely does mean their mothering will be highly scrutinized and critiqued. Finally, even given these constraints, many women and men are inspired by a politician who is also a "mom in tennis shoes." The articulation of an ethic of care, mothering, or, perhaps just parenting, might help show that the public and private spheres are not mutually exclusive, but they can and do inform one another.

Notes

1. Nancy Pelosi, "First Speech to 110th Congress," accessed February 18, 2007, http://www.cnn.com/2007/POLITICS/01/04/pelosi.transcript/index.html.

2. Mary Banwart, Dianne Bystrom, and Terry Robertson, "From the Primary to the General Election: A Comparative Analysis of Media Coverage of Candidates in Mixed-Gender Races for Governor and U.S. Senate in 2000," *American Behavioral Scientist* 46 (2003): 658–76; Linda Witt, Glenna Matthews, and Karen Paget, *Running as a Woman: Gender and Power in American Politics* (New York: The Free Press, 1995).

3. Martha Minow, *Making All the Difference: Inclusion, Exclusion, and the American Law* (Ithaca, NY: Cornell University Press, 1990).

4. Karlyn Kohrs Campbell, *Man Cannot Speak for Her: A Critical Study of Feminist Speakers* (New York: Greenwood Press, 1989), 10.

5. Leonie Huddy and Nayda Terkildsen, "The Consequences of Gender Stereotypes for Women Candidates at Different Levels and Types of Offices," *Political Research Quarterly* 46 (1993): 503–25.

6. Suzanne Daughton, "Women's Issues, Women's Place: Gender-Related Problems in Presidential Campaigns," in *Presidential Campaign Discourse: Strategic Communication Problems*, ed. Kathleen E. Kendall (Albany, NY: State University of New York Press, 1995), 221–40; Stephen Ducat, *The Wimp Factor* (Boston: Beacon Press, 2004); Caroline Heldman, Susan Carroll, and Stephanie Olson, "She Brought Only a Skirt: Print Media Coverage of Elizabeth Dole's Bid for the Republican Presidential Nomination," *Political Communication* 22 (2005): 315–35; Karen Wahl-Jorgensen, "Constructing Masculinities in U.S. Presidential Campaigns: The Case of 1992," in *Gender, Politics, and Communication*, ed. Annabelle Sreberny and Liesbet van Zoonen (Cresskill, NJ: Hampton Press, 1999), 79–100; Marcia Lynn Whicker and Todd W. Areson, "The Maleness of the American Presidency," in *Women in Politics: Outsiders or Insiders?*, ed. Lois Duke, 2nd edition (Upper Saddle River, NJ: Prentice Hall, 1996), 175–86.

7. Wahl-Jorgensen, "Constructing Masculinities."

8. Daughton, "Women's Issues"; Shawn Parry-Giles and Trevor Parry-Giles, "Gendered Politics and Presidential Image Construction: A Reassessment of the 'Feminine Style,'" *Communication Monographs* 63 (1996): 337–53; Wahl-Jorgensen, "Constructing Masculinities."

9. Parry-Giles and Parry-Giles, "Gendered Politics," 343.

10. John Tosh, "Hegemonic Masculinity and the History of Gender," in *Masculinities in Politics and War: Gendering Modern History*, ed. Stefan Dudnik, Karen Hagenamm, and John Tosh (Manchester, UK: Manchester University Press, 2004), 41.

11. Levitz reports that women are in combat positions and the rule that they are not allowed to be there functions as rhetorical appeasement rather than as a statement about the reality of who is fighting in combat zones in Iraq. Jennifer Levitz, "The War in Iraq: Under Fire: Female Soldiers Are Fighting and Dying in Iraq, Even Though U.S. Policy Allows Only Men in Frontline," *Providence Journal*, August 7, 2005, A1. At the time this book is going to press, the Department of Defense's position on women in combat is in flux. Currently, following a Pentagon study conducted at the request of Congress that confirms Levitz' findings, the roles female soldiers have already been performing with battalions close to the front lines in Iraq and Afghanistan are being formalized. See Elisabeth Bumiller, "Pentagon Allows Women Closer to Combat, but Not Close Enough for Some," *New York Times*, February 9, 2012, http://www.nytimes.com/2012/02/10/us/pentagon-to-loosen-restrictions-on-women-in-combat.html?_r=2.

12. Sarah Hoagland, "Moral Revolution: From Antagonism to Cooperation," in *Feminism and Philosophy: Essential Readings in Theory, Reinterpretation, and Application*, ed. Nancy Tuana and Rosemarie Tong (Boulder, CO: Westview, 1995), 175–86.

13. Elizabeth F. Randol, "Homeland Security and the Cooptation of Feminist Discourse," in *Women and Children First: Feminism, Rhetoric, and Public Policy*, ed. Sharon Meagher and Patrice DiQuinzio (Albany, NY: SUNY Press, 2005), 17–36; Kevin Coe, David Domke, Meredith Bagley, Sheryl Cunningham, and Nancy Van Leuven, "Hyper-Masculinity as Ideology and Strategy: George W. Bush, the 'War on Terrorism,' and an Echoing Press," *Journal of Women, Politics, and Policy* 29 (2007): 31–56.

14. Dianne Bystrom, Mary Banwart, Linda Kaid, and Terry Robertson, *Gender and Candidate Communication* (New York: Routledge, 2004).

15. Mari Boor Tonn, "Militant Motherhood: Labor's Mary Harris 'Mother' Jones," *Quarterly Journal of Speech* 82 (1996): 3.

16. Sara Hayden, "Family Metaphors and the Nation: Promoting a Politics of Care Through the Million Mom March," *Quarterly Journal of Speech* 89 (2003): 200.

17. Patrice DiQuinzio, "Love and Reason in the Public Sphere: Maternalist Civic Engagement and the Dilemma of Difference," in *Women and Children First: Feminism, Rhetoric, and Public Policy*, ed. Sharon Meagher and Patrice DiQuinzio (Albany, NY: SUNY Press, 2005), 228.

18. Articles and transcripts were collected from ABC News and *New York Times* from September 29, 2006, to January 18, 2007, from the Lexis-Nexis database, using the search term "Pelosi."

19. Articles and transcripts were collected from Fox News, the *National Review*, and the *New Republic* from September 29, 2006, to January 18, 2007, from the Lexis-Nexis database using the search term "Pelosi."

20. Rebecca Ann Lind and Colleen Salo, "Framing of Feminists and Feminism in News and Public Affairs Programs in U.S. Electronic Media," *Journal of Communication* 52 (2002): 211–28.

21. Ellen Reid Gold and Renee Speicher, "Marilyn Quayle Meets the Press: Marilyn Loses," *Southern Communication Journal* 61 (1995): 93–103.

22. Tara Brabazon, "What Will You Wear to the Revolution? Thatcher's Genderation and the Fashioning of Change," *Hecate* 22 (1996): 115.

23. Eva Krumhuber, Anthony Manstead, and Arvid Kappas, "Temporal Aspects of Facial Displays in Person and Expression Perception: The Effects of Smile Dynamics, Head-Tilt, and Gender," *Journal of Nonverbal Behavior* 31 (2007): 39–56.

24. Roland Barthes, *Mythologies* (New York: Hill and Wang, 1972).

25. Carolyn Marvin, "Theorizing the Flag Body: Symbolic Dimensions of the Flag," *Critical Studies in Mass Communication* 8 (1991): 119–38.

26. Pelosi, "First Speech."

27. BagNews is a blog about visual media literacy. It is also defines its agenda as partisan with the intention of analyzing "images and framing for an underlying conservative or commercial agenda." The Pelosi posting is at Michael Shaw, "Opening Shots," BagNews, accessed January 19, 2007, http://www.bagnewsnotes.com/2007/01/opening-shots.

28. Shaw, "Opening Shots."

29. Shaw, "Opening Shots."

30. Leah Ceccarelli, "Polysemy: Multiple Meanings in Rhetorical Criticism" *Quarterly Journal of Speech* 84 (1998): 395–415; Celeste Condit, "The Rhetorical Limits of Polysemy," *Critical Studies in Mass Communication* 6 (1989): 103–22.

31. PT, "Opening Shots," BagNews, accessed April 25, 2012, http://www.bagnewsnotes.com/2007/01/opening-shots.

32. Ebie, "Opening Shots," BagNews, accessed April 25, 2012, http://www.bagnewsnotes.com/2007/01/opening-shots.

33. itwasntme, "Opening Shots," BagNews, accessed April 25, 2012, http://www.bagnewsnotes.com/2007/01/opening-shots.

34. Ceccarelli, "Polysemy," 408.

35. Tonn, "Militant Motherhood."

36. *World News with Charles Gibson*, January 4, 2007, ABC News, accessed August 5, 2007, from the Lexis-Nexis database.

37. *Nightline*, November 8, 2006, ABC News, accessed August 5, 2007, from the Lexis-Nexis database.

38. *Good Morning America*, October 26, 2006, ABC News, accessed August 5, 2007, from the Lexis-Nexis database.

39. Kelley Holland, "Among Your Qualifications, an M.B.A. at Household U." *New York Times*, December 31, 2006.

40. Kate Zernike, "Ready to Be Voice of the Majority," *New York Times*, November 9, 2006.

41. This does not mean Pelosi was not characterized negatively in these mainstream media outlets but that articulations of motherhood and Pelosi as a mother were overwhelmingly positive.

42. *Fox News Watch*, January 6, 2007, Fox News, accessed August 3, 2007, from the Lexis-Nexis database.

43. Kate O'Beirne, "Beware of Bi: What Do Democrats Mean When They Talk up 'Bipartisanship?'" *National Review*, December 18, 2006.

44. *The Big Story with John Gibson*, January 12, 2007, Fox News, accessed August 3, 2007, from the Lexis-Nexis database.

45. *The O'Reilly Factor*, November 8, 2006, Fox News, accessed December 20, 2007, from the Lexis-Nexis database.

46. O'Beirne, "Beware of Bi."

47. Robert Moran, "After the Deluge," *National Review*, November 7, 2006.

48. Michael Crowley, "Full House," *New Republic*, December 11, 2006.

49. Sondra Cappuccio, "Mothers of Soldiers and the Iraq War: Justification Through Breakfast Shows on ABC, CBS, and NBC," *Women & Language* 29 (2006): 3–9; David Niven and Jeremy Zilber, "'How Does She Have Time for Kids and Congress?' Views on Gender and Media Coverage from House Offices," *Women and Politics* 23 (2001): 147–65.

Bibliography

Banwart, Mary, Dianne Bystrom, and Terry Robertson. "From the Primary to the General Election: A Comparative Analysis of Media Coverage of Candidates in Mixed-Gender Races for Governor and U.S. Senate in 2000." *American Behavioral Scientist* 46 (2003): 658–76.

Barthes, Roland. *Mythologies*. New York: Hill and Wang, 1972.

Brabazon, Tara. "What Will You Wear to the Revolution? Thatcher's Genderation and the Fashioning of Change." *Hecate* 22 (1996): 114–27.

Bumiller, Elisabeth. "Pentagon Allows Women Closer to Combat, but Not Close Enough for Some." *New York Times*, February 9, 2012. http://www.nytimes.com/2012/02/10/us/pentagon-to-loosen-restrictions-on-women-in-combat.html?_r=2.

Bystrom, Dianne, Mary Banwart, Linda Kaid, and Terry Robertson. *Gender and Candidate Communication*. New York: Routledge, 2004.

Campbell, Karlyn Kohrs. *Man Cannot Speak for Her: A Critical Study of Feminist Speakers*. New York: Greenwood Press, 1989.

Cappuccio, Sondra. "Mothers of Soldiers and the Iraq War: Justification Through Breakfast Shows on ABC, CBS, and NBC." *Women & Language* 29 (2006): 3–9.

Ceccarelli, Leah. "Polysemy: Multiple Meanings in Rhetorical Criticism." *Quarterly Journal of Speech* 84 (1998): 395–415.

Coe, Kevin, David Domke, Meredith Bagley, Sheryl Cunningham, and Nancy Van Leuven. "Hyper-Masculinity as Ideology and Strategy: George W. Bush, the 'War on Terrorism,' and an Echoing Press." *Journal of Women, Politics, and Policy* 29 (2007): 31–56.

Condit, Celeste. "The Rhetorical Limits of Polysemy." *Critical Studies in Mass Communication* 6 (1989): 103–22.

Crowley, Michael. "Full House." *New Republic*, December 11, 2006.

Daughton, Suzanne. "Women's Issues, Women's Place: Gender-Related Problems in Presidential Campaigns." In *Presidential Campaign Discourse: Strategic Communication Problems*, edited by Kathleen E. Kendall, 221–40. Albany, NY: State University of New York Press, 1995.

DiQuinzio, Patrice. "Love and Reason in the Public Sphere: Maternalist Civic Engagement and the Dilemma of Difference." In *Women and Children First: Feminism, Rhetoric, and Public Policy*, edited by Sharon Meagher and Patrice DiQuinzio, 227–46. Albany, NY: SUNY Press, 2005.

Ducat, Stephen. *The Wimp Factor*. Boston: Beacon Press, 2004.

Ebie. "Opening Shots." BagNews. Accessed April 25, 2012. http://www.bagnewsnotes.com/2007/01/opening-shots.

Fox News Watch. January 6, 2007. Fox News. Accessed August 3, 2007, from the Lexis-Nexis database.

Gold, Ellen Reid, and Renee Speicher. "Marilyn Quayle Meets the Press: Marilyn Loses." *Southern Communication Journal* 61 (1995): 93–103.

Good Morning America. October 26, 2006. ABC News. Accessed August 5, 2007, from the Lexis-Nexis database.

Hayden, Sara. "Family Metaphors and the Nation: Promoting a Politics of Care Through the Million Mom March." *Quarterly Journal of Speech* 89 (2003): 196–216.

Heldman, Caroline, Susan Carroll, and Stephanie Olson. "She Brought Only a Skirt: Print Media Coverage of Elizabeth Dole's Bid for the Republican Presidential Nomination." *Political Communication* 22 (2005): 315–35.

Hoagland, Sarah. "Moral Revolution: From Antagonism to Cooperation." In *Feminism and Philosophy: Essential Readings in Theory, Reinterpretation, and Application*, edited by Nancy Tuana and Rosemarie Tong, 175–86. Boulder, CO: Westview, 1995.

Holland, Kelley. "Among Your Qualifications, an M.B.A. at Household U." *New York Times*, December 31, 2006.

Huddy, Leonie, and Nayda Terkildsen. "The Consequences of Gender Stereotypes for Women Candidates at Different Levels and Types of Offices." *Political Research Quarterly* 46 (1993): 503–25.

itwasntme. "Opening Shots." BagNews. Accessed April 25, 2012. http://www.bagnewsnotes.com/2007/01/opening-shots.

Krumhuber, Eva, Anthony Manstead, and Arvid Kappas. "Temporal Aspects of Facial Displays in Person and Expression Perception: The Effects of Smile Dynamics, Head-Tilt, and Gender." *Journal of Nonverbal Behavior* 31 (2007): 39–56.

Levitz, Jennifer. "The War in Iraq: Under Fire: Female Soldiers Are Fighting and Dying in Iraq, Even Though U.S. Policy Allows Only Men in Frontline." *Providence Journal*, August 7, 2005, A1.

Lind, Rebecca Ann, and Colleen Salo. "Framing of Feminists and Feminism in News and Public Affairs Programs in U.S. Electronic Media." *Journal of Communication* 52 (2002): 211–28.

Marvin, Carolyn. "Theorizing the Flag Body: Symbolic Dimensions of the Flag." *Critical Studies in Mass Communication* 8 (1991): 119–38.

Minow, Martha. *Making All the Difference: Inclusion, Exclusion, and the American Law*. Ithaca, NY: Cornell University Press, 1990.

Moran, Robert. "After the Deluge." *National Review*, November 7, 2006.

Nightline. November 8, 2006. ABC News. Accessed August 5, 2007, from the Lexis-Nexis database.

Niven, David, and Jeremy Zilber. "'How Does She Have Time for Kids and Congress?' Views on Gender and Media Coverage from House Offices." *Women and Politics* 23 (2001): 147–65.

O'Beirne, Kate. "Beware of Bi: What Do Democrats Mean When They Talk up 'Bipartisanship?'" *National Review*, December 18, 2006.

Parry-Giles, Shawn, and Trevor Parry-Giles. "Gendered Politics and Presidential Image Construction: A Reassessment of the 'Feminine Style.'" *Communication Monographs* 63 (1996): 337–53.

Pelosi, Nancy. First Speech to 110th Congress. Accessed February 18, 2007. http://www.cnn.com/2007/POLITICS/01/04/pelosi.transcript/index.html.

PT. "Opening Shots." BagNews. Accessed April 25, 2012. http://www.bagnewsnotes.com/2007/01/opening-shots.

Randol, Elizabeth F. "Homeland Security and the Cooptation of Feminist Discourse." In *Women and Children First: Feminism, Rhetoric, and Public Policy*, edited by Sharon Meagher and Patrice DiQuinzio, 17–36. Albany, NY: SUNY Press, 2005.

Shaw, Michael. "Opening Shots." BagNews. Accessed January 19, 2007. http://www.bagnewsnotes.com/2007/01/opening-shots.

The Big Story with John Gibson. January 12, 2007. Fox News. Accessed August 3, 2007, from the Lexis-Nexis database.

The O'Reilly Factor. November 8, 2006. Fox News. Accessed December 20, 2007, from the Lexis-Nexis database.

Tonn, Mari Boor. "Militant Motherhood: Labor's Mary Harris 'Mother' Jones." *Quarterly Journal of Speech* 82 (1996): 1–21.

Tosh, John. "Hegemonic Masculinity and the History of Gender." In *Masculinities in Politics and War: Gendering Modern History*, edited by Stefan Dudnik, Karen Hagenamm, and John Tosh, 41–60. Manchester, UK: Manchester University Press, 2004.

Wahl-Jorgensen, Karen. "Constructing Masculinities in U.S. Presidential Campaigns: The Case of 1992." In *Gender, Politics, and Communication*, edited by Annabelle Sreberny and Liesbet van Zoonen, 79–100. Cresskill, NJ: Hampton Press, 1999.

Whicker, Marcia Lynn, and Todd W. Areson. "The Maleness of the American Presidency." In *Women in Politics: Outsiders or Insiders?*, edited by Lois Duke, 2nd edition, 175–86. Upper Saddle River, NJ: Prentice Hall, 1996.

Witt, Linda, Glenna Matthews, and Karen Paget. *Running as a Woman: Gender and Power in American Politics*. New York: The Free Press, 1995.

World News with Charles Gibson. January 4, 2007. ABC News. Accessed August 5, 2007 from the Lexis-Nexis database.

Zernike, Kate. "Ready to Be Voice of the Majority." *New York Times*, November 9, 2006.

Chapter 13

Local Media Madness: How One City's Media Helped Perpetuate the Myth of the "Perfect" Coach's Wife

by Diana L. Tucker

I grew up in a college football coaching family. I spent most of my time dressed in school colors for whichever team my dad was coaching. Weekends were spent in a frenzy of football-related activities. When fall was over, football and its activities did not cease. There were end-of-the-season parties and bowl games. After Christmas, the recruiting season began, and I spent every Friday and Saturday with a babysitter while Mom and Dad schmoozed with recruits.

This gave me the sense that my father had an important job and was an important person. As I reflect on this part of my life, however, I realize it all focuses around my father. My mother's absence from my memory is curious because it was my father who was seldom around. My mother was a constant figure, but her efforts often went unacknowledged. As a feminist rhetorical scholar, I am not surprised by this lack of attention to my mother. What men do in the sports industry is highly valued, and women's participation in and contributions to the world of sports is greatly undervalued.[1]

Before college football became such a lucrative industry, the coach of a large university, his staff, and their families could lead fairly normal lives. Some schools had more pressure than others, but the money and fame for coaches did not go as high or reach as far as they do today. With the emergence of all-sport media outlets, that has changed. Now, head football coaches of Division I universities are major celebrities in their towns, states, and sometimes even the nation.

Urban Meyer, Nick Saban, Jim Tressel, and Joe Paterno are examples of Division I head coaches who have achieved national recognition. The scrutiny by local and national media of the head football coach and his staff at schools such as Ohio State, Florida, Alabama, and Penn State is extreme. Shelley Meyer, Terry Saban, Ellen Tressel, and Sue Paterno may not be household names around the country, but they are well-known in their own backyards because their local media target them for stories. The level of "media madness" for a college team—and subsequently the coach and his wife—grows exponentially with its success. If the state or city does not have a professional football team or if their pro team is not very successful, the likelihood that the media will focus on the closest Division I college team is even higher.

Take one such town, Columbus, Ohio, and its college team, The Ohio State University Buckeyes. The Ohio State University (OSU) football team has developed into the favorite in Ohio, surpassing all pro sports teams[2] and making the head coach a household name. The year 2011 was a tumultuous one for the Buckeyes. Jim Tressel had been the head coach for ten years when he resigned in May 2011 after a violation of NCAA rules. Luke Fickell (Tressel's assistant head coach) was named the interim head coach and coached the team through the 2011 season. In late November 2011, Urban Meyer (University of Florida head coach until he resigned after the 2010 season due to health issues) was named the new head coach.

For a decade, Ellen Tressel made headlines in the local media for her endeavors as "Mrs. Coach." When Luke Fickell was named head coach, the media bombarded his wife, Amy, with requests for interviews and questions about her husband. Shelley Meyer was quoted extensively in the media concerning her husband's hire as the new OSU head football coach. This chapter examines the rhetorical implications of this "local media madness" surrounding these three women and their status as "Mrs. Coach."

A community of football coaches' wives called the American Football Coaches' Wives Association (AFCWA) meets yearly in conjunction with the American Football Coaches' Association (AFCA).[3] In addition to providing me with their newsletters and publications, the AFCWA allowed me access to their members at the 1999 meeting in Nashville, Tennessee. I interviewed thirty members and participated in scheduled events while there. My previous research also included a rhetorical analysis of football coaches' autobiographies and how they talk about their wives' roles in their careers. The key thematic focus on wives in the coaches' autobiographies and AFCWA publications was that "wife" is someone who must "sacrifice," and she does so by being a "surrogate for the coach," a "caregiver," and part of a "support staff."[4] It is through this lens that I will analyze Ohio media depictions of Ellen Tressel, Amy Fickell, and Shelley Meyer.

Coach's Wife as Surrogate, Caregiver, and Support Staff

Coaches ask wives to be surrogates in numerous ways, particularly as "scapegoats."[5] In their autobiographies, when football coaches describe their wife's activities, behaviors, and reactions, they often make her seem "too good for this world," positioning her for the role of scapegoat. Kenneth Burke explains that a scapegoat becomes "worthy" of sacrifice because of his or her high value, because he or she is the "most perfect sacrifice."[6] Because she is "too good for this world," the wife becomes the scapegoat upon whom others heap their burdens, and she is expected to accept these burdens willingly. The coach's wife often finds herself in surrogate roles as father for her children, mother to players, and even a substitute for the coach at various functions.[7]

In these autobiographies, the theme of "caregiver" functions to relieve the coach's guilt over being absent from home or slightly impersonal with the public; the excuse is that his wife is the more perfect person to do these things.[8] She becomes the sacrifice and ultimately the caregiver because she does it well. The coaches place their wives on a pedestal, which allows them to heap surrogate and caregiver burdens on the women. Because so many of the coaches' autobiographies mention their own irritability and their wives' cheerfulness, readers may be discouraged from seeking out discrepancies; indeed, readers are more likely to look for wives who confirm the status quo. According to the autobiographies, the football coach expects his wife to exist in a world of paradoxes. She is to lead the family, be independent, and do most of the work for the family, yet she has no voice in major decisions about the family (such as when they move to a new job).[9] This is true outside the home as well. Evidence in the autobiographies indicates that while the coach's wife is expected to adhere to constraints of a more Victorian idea of "true womanhood"[10] behind the scenes, she is also expected to step out and be a more public caregiver by hosting social functions and becoming a surrogate mom to players as well as other coaches and their wives.

The coach mentioning his wife in the autobiography functions rhetorically as praise, but it simultaneously reifies her "proper" role to readers. Many of the coaches describe their wives' independence, assertiveness, and toughness, but only when she is taking on the role of surrogate. By describing their wives this way, the coaches help to keep their wives on a pedestal.

Until now, I have discussed only how the husbands have described their wives' role in their coaching career, but the women of the AFCWA also have much to say on the subject of being a "surrogate," "caregiver," and coach's "support staff." In their own publications (newsletters and a cookbook), the AFCWA women rhetorically construct themselves in the role of "support" rather than focusing on being a "surrogate" or a "caregiver."[11] "Supporting" their husbands still includes surrogacy and caregiver functions, however.

In *The Support Staff* (the AFCWA newsletter) and the *Winning Seasons* AFCWA cookbook, the coaches' wives introduce the idea of support for one another. Indeed, the name of the newsletter exemplifies this concept. Yet support for each other is often figuratively tied into the support of football. Sports metaphors abound. For example, one AFCWA member writes in the cookbook, "Just holler and someone can offer suggestions because they have been in the same 'fourth down and a yard to go' situation."[12] These metaphors emphasize the women's connection to football: it permeates all they do.

One discrepancy between how coaches describe their wives' roles and how the AFCWA women describe their roles is in the use of the term "independent." Football coaches see their wives as independent and then equate independence with words such as "leadership."[13] In their publications, however, the AFCWA members tend to equate independence with being alone.[14] The cookbook especially is full of poems and statements on loneliness because the football coach is rarely home. Between long hours during the season, recruiting in winter, spring practice, and summer football camps, a coach's job is never done. This, of course, means the wife's job is also never done.

"Lovelywives" and Media Interviews

In addition to the standards for being a "good" wife set by football coaches in their autobiographies and the standards set by the members of the AFCWA, media representatives have also set standards for coaches' wives to meet. Women connected to men engaged in football are relegated to the literal and figurative sidelines: "Lovely wives—as TV commentators invariably call us—women whose lives are intimately affected by the vicissitudes of sports. We are expected to be present at all the games, we sometimes lead the cheering, we welcome sports (personified as players, fans, sportswriters, coaches) into our homes. Many coaches' wives are lovely, but sports announcers use it as if it were a single word—"*lovelywife*"—used to stand for a certain kind of woman: trivial, irrelevant, interchangeable."[15]

There are clear rhetorical implications for local media's use of the coach's wife for a story's focus. In earlier research, I explored the idea of American football fans seeing "their" coach as a godlike figure.[16] J. Clark Roundtree discusses a similar phenomenon in an article analyzing the 1992 presidential election. He argues that Americans view the president as "ever present," meaning the president is never NOT the president.[17] Americans have a similar view of sports coaches, especially the more famous ones.[18] Of course, coaches are made famous by the media. The "ever-present" status of a coach—along with the view of him as not just a leader of a team but a leader and role model for everyone—creates a public burden for the coach. In turn, those putting the coach on a pedestal also see him as omniscient and invincible. The more popular a coach is, the more pressure there is for him and the team to succeed, thus relegating the coach to longer working hours geared toward achieving that success. The desire fans and reporters may have for getting the coach to grant interviews is mutually exclusive to the coach's desire for time alone to work or to be with family. Thus, the cycle of success begets media attention, which begets less time for a coach to do what he wants. Enter the coach's wife.

Finch describes how "certain features of the content and organization of men's work typically impose structures and constraints upon wives' lives, obliging wives to construct their own lives within the consequent limitations."[19] Finch was referring to an earlier era when financial implications and the patterns of home life revolved around the husband and thus around his job. Such antiquated practices are not in play formally today, yet the coach's family *does* still revolve around his life and his job. Many women who happen to be married to a football coach have careers of their own, but just like in the era Finch examines, the structure of football family life centers around the coach and his schedule.

The wife as surrogate for her coaching husband is a key feature of this study. A number of local news articles referenced the reporter being unable to interview the coach, so he or she went to the wife instead. One reporter wrote that Coach Tressel "declined to be interviewed for his story," but Ellen Tressel "was more than willing to shed some light on her husband's off-the-field behavior."[20] Many articles covering Ellen at various functions stated she was there because her husband could not be.[21] While the media outlet is trying to make the wife significant enough to report on, they simultaneously ensure she is "put in her place" as the surrogate for the coach because they would really rather talk to him. In other articles, the coach's wife is sought out for her opinion on things such as her husband's game day attire,[22] what he is like on game day, or how his health is faring.[23]

I collected nineteen articles from Ohio newspapers and online magazines along with six video segments from Ohio newscasts. After reading and watching all of the sources, I opted to use ten articles for this study as the other items simply repeated the same information. My analytical method is Burkeian cluster analysis, which I used earlier when analyzing the football coaches' autobiographies. Kenneth Burke was enchanted by a rhetor's word choices and the way a rhetor would position words to persuade a reader. He wanted to understand the rhetor's worldview, and because he believed most writings were representational, he felt critics have license to interpret the hidden meanings of a text.[24] Burke devised a method of analyzing language that Foss and other rhetorical scholars call "cluster criticism." Burke believed if one were to tally up or track the number of ways an author refers to a certain term, one can understand the symbolism behind those words.[25] The word choices of the media coverage of the three Ohio State head football coaches' wives form clusters, and I will be interpreting the symbolism behind them.

When describing the procedure for conducting a cluster analysis, Foss explains that the critic must identify key terms in the artifact.[26] I have chosen to use key themes rather than sticking solely to terms. My cluster analysis of four different artifacts—news reports on coaches and their wives, football coaches' autobiographies, the wives' statements to the press, and AFCWA publications—all revealed the same rhetorical clusters.

Reporters' Rhetoric

The reporters' rhetoric repeatedly mentions the women's responsibilities and burdens as coaches' wives, but those are the only times the reporter frames the coach's wife as a person. All other questions and details focus on what she thinks about her husband or about what her husband said to her about some event. When the reporters do discuss aspects of the wife and her life, their rhetoric echoes that found in coaches' autobiographies.

In their autobiographies, the coaches' descriptors for physical attributes and character might lead a reader to believe the proper football coach's wife has never had a bad day.[27] It seems she is always beautiful and cheerful. Coaches Chuck Knox, Bill Reid, Jerry Glanville, and Joe Paterno use such terms as "cute," "little," "fair," "lovely," and "womanly" when referencing their wives.[28] Similarly, when describing Amy Fickell, one reporter writes, "Amy Fickell is fit and pretty, with soft blond hair, exquisite skin, ocean eyes and an easy smile."[29] This was the opening line for the interview article. The second line: "But make no mistake: The wife of Ohio State University's new head football coach is no Barbie doll."[30] While the reporter may be telling us NOT to think of Amy Fickell as a Barbie doll, referencing this standard against which females have measured themselves for decades automatically leads readers to think about traditionally feminine roles. This continues with the reporter asking Fickell about her thoughts on "spa time" and "chores."

In various interviews with Ellen Tressel and Amy Fickell, reporters ask how the women prepared to take on the responsibilities of a football coach's wife. In their autobiographies, the coaches also discuss the "duties" their wives carry because of their jobs. Ralph Sabock explains the challenges inherent to the job of football coach's wife: "Most of the unhappiness that occurs with coaches' wives arises because they never really understood what is involved in coaching and what kind of demands this profession makes on the coach and the family. It takes a special kind of wife to cope with this."[31] Statements such as this help verify the status of the coach and what he says about the wife's role in football.

Reporters disclose that "Ellen Tressel plays a major role speaking with recruits and their families before home games, gets to know the players each season, works with several charities and sees her husband for date nights every Thursday during the fall."[32] A number of articles make mention of a coach's wife doing all the finances for the family.[33] Reporters describe the wife's role in terms such as "order of business," "keeping a busy schedule," "married to the game of football," "juggling schedules," "making game plans," and being a "civic leader," a "decision-maker," and a "host." The reporters see the role as a job in many cases; interestingly, they even mention duties such as "juggling schedules" and being a "host," activities often performed by wives and mothers of any family. Of course, it would not be suitable to have a football coach depicted as doing such mundane things. But when the media shows his wife as being "just like everyone else," it allows fans to keep the coach on a pedestal while making him seem more human. On the other hand, there are three instances in which the coach's wife is referred to as the "First Lady of Football."[34] This affords her the status one might give to the presidential First Lady, thus giving the story more backbone.

The last theme concerning burdens occurs less frequently in the coaching autobiographies, but it is present. For instance, Coach Earl Blaik informs readers that his wife, Merle, "has been the perfect football wife . . . if it is possible, [she] suffered even more anguish and was even more intolerant of defeat. She paid the price."[35] The burdens coaches refer to are football-related, such as the burden of defeat. While the coaches mention their wives taking care of the family alone or attending functions in his stead, they rarely describe these instances as burdens. Conversely, reporters seem to understand the coach's wife's life can be burdensome, but they do not link that burden to football. They instead link it to the absence of the coach from the home. Commentary about the wife's responsibilities being a burden are most often clustered around comments about the coach being "away," "working endless hours," or the "overwhelming life . . . where the stakes are obviously high" (meaning the coach's win and loss record).[36] Another article, however, makes it clear that much of what is expected of Amy Fickell leaves her "unfazed by its stresses."[37]

When reporters comment on the wives' imperturbable demeanor, there seems to be a hint of surprise. Even reporters with some celebrity status in the community can be star-struck by a famous football coach. Thus, they are surprised that the coach's wife treats her husband, his coaching, and the lifestyle that job creates as an everyday occurrence. In their autobiographies, the coaches elevate their wives to a pedestal, making them a "perfect sacrifice" upon whom they heap burdens. Meanwhile, reporters put the coaches on a pedestal but still acknowledge the burdens heaped on the wives. They also seem incredulous that the wife does not put herself on a pedestal. On the contrary, the coaches' wives reveal they truly are unfazed by big-time celebrity status.

Wives' Rhetoric

The published comments of Ellen Tressel, Amy Fickell, and Shelley Meyer mirror those made by the AFCWA members. The main theme of the AFCWA rhetoric is that of support for one another and their husbands, in addition to their responsibilities as coaches' wives.[38] In my analysis of the AFCWA's rhetoric, I was curious to see how the women might be rhetorically constructing their gender role in football culture. I was interested in the same for this study of OSU head coaches' wives and discovered the themes of "support" and "responsibilities" in conjunction with their talk about traditional feminine gender roles.

The AFCWA equates "support of one another" with "being sisterly" and "support of husbands" as akin to "caregiver" and "sacrifice" roles.[39] As mentioned above, "independence" tends to mean "loneliness" for the AFCWA members and thus is part of their sacrifice.[40] This sentiment can best be summed up by a poem written by a group of members published in the AFCWA cookbook *Winning Seasons*, which describes the husband missing family events such as the birth of a baby and a birthday party because he is out recruiting or at practice.[41] Similarly, Amy Fickell explains, "I have to step up and be both parents much of the time. That's kind of how I can support him—by taking the weight of the family."[42]

Most coverage of Shelley Meyer depicts her discussing her husband's return to coaching after a year's hiatus due to health issues. While she admits she wanted him to take more time off before returning to coaching, she is firm in her statements that he is ready, and she believes in him and his ability to manage the job and his health. For instance, she says, "He's been there [poor health and overstressed about the job]. And he knows what he needs to do to not go there. He's done a lot of work, talking to a lot of people the last eleven months and working at it spiritually."[43] Meyer goes on to reaffirm she will support him and hopes he will take more time for the family, but that she will be there when he can't.[44]

Ellen Tressel explains, "You have to be fairly independent. There are times you get lonely. But it's not all about you."[45] This quotation demonstrates that being independent and being lonely go hand in hand, and that is a sacrifice coaches' wives must be willing to make to support their husbands' careers. Tressel also reveals that part of the sacrifice is giving up privacy and even worrying about her own safety. "They [OSU administrators] took us on a tour of the stadium . . . and took me to a place where I was to sit for the games and described it to me as, 'This is the safe place for you,' and that was a little unnerving because I didn't realize that I was going to be in any danger."[46] A possible threat to one's safety or life gives new meaning to "perfect sacrifice."

In addition to "true woman" duties and managing the household finances, coaches' wives are often expected to perform other jobs for their husband's team for the "usual coach's wife charge of zero."[47] The AFCWA members give examples that stretch from being "requested to choose, organize and coach the first ever squad of women cheerleaders"[48] at the Naval Academy to playing hostess for recruits and their families.[49] Similarly, in Columbus, Ellen Tressel and Amy Fickell mention a number of responsibilities they carry as head coaches' wives. As chief financial officer of the family, Fickell reports, "My husband doesn't even know what his paycheck is. He does not know how to write a check out, I think."[50] And Tressel reveals that her husband "doesn't even know where the checkbook is!"[51] All three women reiterate that their job is to "take care of everything that happens at home—everything with the home and the children" and to constantly play host to guests coming in for games.[52]

These three women talk more about their duties outside the home than the members of the AFCWA do. Ellen Tressel especially took on a substantial role in working with players and for charities important to her husband.[53] She attended many functions and even team practices so she could get to know the players. "They're special and he [husband] talks about them and I want to see what their special features are that he's so excited about."[54] While Jim Tressel was head coach at Ohio State, Ellen Tressel worked for at least five different charities on her and her husband's behalf.[55] Because Coach Tressel is not an avid golfer, Ellen Tressel often steps in to play at golfing charity functions.[56] It is evident that at least in this Ohio community, the head coach's wife is expected to be seen publicly and get involved in the community. Amy Fickell also volunteers time at her husband's foundation for illiteracy and teaches vacation Bible school at their church.[57] At the time of this writing, Shelley Meyer has not yet moved to Columbus since her husband was only recently hired, but surely she will get involved with the community and become just as popular a figure in the media as her predecessors.

In analyzing the AFCWA rhetoric, I determined that football coaches' wives tended to communicate in a "feminine rhetorical style." That is, they rely on personal experience and encourage identification between audience and rhetor.[58] They use personal narratives to bond with one another and to demonstrate their "sisterhood" to outsiders. In addition, their constant reminders that they do not want their "sisters" to have to lose games (even though they may be on the other side of that game as the victor) encourages audiences to identify with the women as compassionate, nurturing, and caring—all feminine qualities.[59]

In their interviews with local media, Ellen Tressel, Amy Fickell, and Shelley Meyer demonstrate similar rhetorical actions. In all of the interviews, the women share personal experiences, and the topics and wording they use encourage identification between the audience and themselves. For example, they discuss their children and how they make their children's lives their focus and help make the coaching father more present in the children's lives. Amy Fickell repeatedly expresses how she makes sure there are routine times when the children get to see their father, even if it is part of his work day: "Sometimes during the season we try to sneak down to practice on Wednesday nights. The kids love it. [On game day,] usually the kids and I drive him to The Blackwell [hotel on campus] and drop him off. And after the game, it is my favorite point in time during the day: The kids and I wait and go onto the field with him and sing 'Carmen Ohio' [OSU Alma Mater] with the band. It's fun to see the kids get to be part of it."[60]

In Shelley Meyer's early days as the new "First Lady of Buckeye Football," she repeatedly told the story of how she and her children wrote up a contract Urban Meyer had to sign before he could sign the one with Ohio State.[61] She wanted to make it clear to fans that they might have expectations of their new coach, but his family did, too, and that she regarded theirs as more important.[62] She might be inviting other "protective wives and mothers" in her audience to identify with her. Ellen Tressel did not have younger children at home when Jim Tressel joined Ohio State in 2001. Thus, she did not discuss working children into her husband's schedule. Instead, she tried to emphasize other family activities such as "date night" and a superstitious tradition she shared with her husband on game day.[63] Sports fans are a superstitious bunch, and providing insight into her own and her husband's superstitions definitely encourages readers to identify with her. Ellen Tressel did demonstrate how important children are in a football family's life when she orchestrated a drive to get needed items for one of the assistant coaches whose wife had quadruplets.[64]

At no point in any interview do any of the women complain about their lives. The closest they came was, "Sure, there are times you wish you could say, 'No, I'm not going to speak at a school or whatever.' But it is not all about you. It's about, how much do you care?"[65] Even this slight negative admission ends with a call for compassion and caring. This rhetorical choice invites audiences not only to feel some sympathy for the coach's wife but to know they do not *have* to feel sympathy. It invites fans to feel their coach is in good hands and does not have worries outside his job, thus leaving him free to lead their team to victory. Finally, the rhetoric from the three OSU coaches' wives in this study of local media coverage demonstrates that a woman married to a football coach has much on her plate but that it is all in a day's work—work that is rewarding even when difficult.

Conclusion

This chapter has compared earlier rhetorical analyses of football coaches' autobiographies and AFCWA members' publications with data collected from news sources in Ohio concerning the most recent head coaches' wives of the OSU football program. I have demonstrated the similarities between football coaches' expectations for their wives and local reporters' rhetorical construction of the duties for OSU head football coaches' wives in their articles and newscasts. I then compared the rhetorical implications of the AFCWA publications with how Ellen Tressel, Amy Fickell, and Shelley Meyer communicated about their lives publicly, illustrating the analogous themes in the two studies. Not only did the coaches expect their wives to become surrogates for them in many ways, but the AFCWA members also expected and willingly became surrogates for their husbands. That surrogacy is also visible in the lives of contemporary Ohio State football coaches' wives. The "local media madness" feeds on this need for surrogacy because the coach is rarely available for interviews himself or can't allow himself to be as candid for reporters as his wife might be. Thus, the football spouse must be willing to be public, stand in for her husband, and demonstrate her aptitude at being the "perfect coach's wife."

Notes

1. Nick Trujillo, "Hegemonic Masculinity on the Mound: Media Representations of Nolan Ryan and American Sports Culture," *Critical Studies in Mass Media* 8 (1991): 290–308.

2. Amy Daughters, "College Football: 7 Teams That Are More Popular Than Their NFL Counterparts," Bleacher Report, accessed February 18, 2012, http://bleacherreport.com.

3. Diana L. Tucker, "A Rhetorical Analysis of Women's Role in American Sport Culture: The Case of the Football Coach's Wife" (PhD diss., Southern Illinois University Carbondale, 2003): 89.

4. Tucker, "A Rhetorical Analysis."

5. Diana L. Tucker, "The Making of a Perfect Sacrifice: A Rhetorical Analysis of Football Coaches' Descriptions of Their Wives," in *Sport, Rhetoric and Gender: Historical Perspectives and Media Representations*, ed. Linda K. Fuller (New York: Palgrave Macmillan, 2006), 241.

6. Kenneth Burke, *Philosophy of Literary Form* (Berkeley: University of California Press, 1941), 40.

7. Tucker, "Perfect Sacrifice."

8. Tucker, "Perfect Sacrifice."

9. Tucker, "Perfect Sacrifice."

10. Karlyn Kohrs Campbell, *Man Cannot Speak for Her: A Critical Study of Feminist Speakers* (Westport, CT: Greenwood Press, 1989).

11. Diana L. Tucker, "A Gender Drama in American Football Culture: The Case of the Coach's Wife," *Football Studies* 4 (2001): 67.

12. AFCWA, *Winning Seasons: A Collection of Recipes and Memories* (Louisville: *Ad Craft Sports Marketing*, 1996), 94.

13. Tucker, "Perfect Sacrifice," 241.

14. Tucker, "A Gender Drama," 71.

15. Tereasa Goodwin Phelps, *The Coach's Wife: A Memoir* (New York: W. W. Norton, 1994), 11.

16. Tucker, "A Rhetorical Analysis," 89.

17. J. Clark Roundtree III, "The President as God, the Recession as Evil: Actus, Status, and the President's Rhetorical Bind in the 1992 Election," *Quarterly Journal of Speech* 81 (1995): 325.

18. Tucker, "A Rhetorical Analysis," 89.

19. Janet Finch, *Married to the Job: Wives' Incorporation in Men's Work* (London: George Allen & Unwin, 1983), 21.

20. Rob Oller, "Behind the Vest," *Columbus Dispatch* (Columbus, OH), January 7, 2008, accessed February 18, 2012, http://www.dispatch.com/content/stories/sports/2008/01/06/Tresslife.ART_ART_01-06-08_A1_ER8V9JJ.html

21. For example, "Acts of Charity," *Columbus Dispatch* (Columbus, OH), October 20, 2007, accessed February 18, 2012, http://www.dispatch.com/content/stories/life_and_entertainment/2007/10/20/1AA_CHARITY20_--_THEME_OF_DA.ART_ART_10-20-07_D2_MP87RCV.html.

22. Jeffrey Sheban and Kevin Joy, "In Choosing Game-Day Attire, OSU's Fickell Might Consider Those Who Coached Before Him," *Columbus Dispatch* (Columbus, OH), September 2, 2011, accessed February 18, 2012, http://www.dispatch.com/content/stories/life_and_entertainment/2011/09/02/what-should-he-wear.html.

23. Jon P. Spencer, "The Mrs. Makes It a Done Deal," *Mansfield News Journal* (Mansfield, OH), November 29, 2011, accessed February 18, 2012, http://pqasb.pqarchiver.com/mansfieldnewsjournal/access/2522065961.html?FMT=ABS&date=Nov+29%2C+2011.

24. Sonja K. Foss, *Rhetorical Criticism: Exploration and Practice*, 2nd ed. (Prospect Heights, IL: Waveland Press, 1996).

25. Burke, *Philosophy of Literary Form*, 20.

26. Foss, *Rhetorical Criticism*, 65.

27. Tucker, "Perfect Sacrifice," 243.

28. Jerry Glanville with J. David Miller, *Elvis Don't Like Football: The Life and Raucous Times of the NFL's Most Outspoken Coach* (New York: Macmillan, 1990); *Chuck Knox with Bill Plaschke, Hard Knox: The Life of an NFL Coach* (San Diego: Harcourt, Brace, Jovanovich, 1988); Bill Reid, *Big-Time Football at Harvard*, 1905: *The Diary of Coach Bill Reid*, ed. Ronald A. Smith (Urbana: Illinois University Press, 1994); Joe Paterno with Bernard Asbell, *Paterno: By the Book* (New York: Random House, 1989).

29. Kristy Eckert, "Into the Spotlight: Meet the New First Lady of Buckeye Nation," *Capital Style*, accessed February 18, 2012, http://www.capital-style.com/content/stories/2011/09/YC-coachs-wife-amy-fickell.html.

30. Eckert, "Into the Spotlight."

31. Ralph J. Sabock, *The Coach* (Philadelphia: W. B. Saunders, 1973), 78.

32. Doug Lesmerises, "Ellen Tressel Discusses Her Husband, Ohio State Football Coach Jim Tressel, and Their Life away from the Football Field," *Plain Dealer* (Cleveland, OH), October 7, 2010, accessed February 18, 2012, http://www.cleveland.com/osu/index.ssf/2010/10/post_21.html.

33. Such as Eckert, "Into the Spotlight."

34. Kristy Eckert, "Life on the Sidelines: Wives of Three Ohio State Coaches Talk About Their Lives in and out of the Spotlight," *Capital Style*, accessed February 18, 2012, http://www.capital-style.com/content/stories/2009/09/01/0901_trendsetter_sides.html; Eckert, "Into the Spotlight."

35. Earl Blaik with Tim Cohane, *The Red Blaik Story* (New Rochelle, NY: Arlington House, 1960), 69.

36. Eckert, "Life on the Sidelines."

37. Eckert, "Into the Spotlight."

38. Tucker, "A Gender Drama."

39. Tucker, "A Gender Drama," 67.

40. Tucker, "A Gender Drama," 71.

41. AFCWA, *Winning Seasons*, 108.

42. Eckert, "Into the Spotlight."

43. Spencer, "The Mrs."

44. Spencer, "The Mrs."

45. Eckert, "Life on the Sidelines."

46. Lesmerises, "Ellen Tressel Discusses Her Husband."

47. AFCWA, *Winning Seasons*, 200.

48. AFCWA, *Winning Seasons*, 200.

49. Tucker, "A Gender Drama," 73.

50. Eckert, "Into the Spotlight."
51. Eckert, "Life on the Sidelines."
52. Eckert, "Life on the Sidelines."
53. Lesmerises, "Ellen Tressel Discusses Her Husband."
54. Lesmerises, "Ellen Tressel Discusses Her Husband."
55. Eckert, "Life on the Sidelines."
56. "See Who Ellen Tressel Eliminated in This Week's Shootout," 10TV.com (Columbus, OH), accessed February 18, 2012, http://www.10tv.com/content/stories/2008/06/30/shootout_week_3.html.
57. Eckert, "Into the Spotlight."
58. Campbell, *Man Cannot Speak for Her*, 13.
59. Tucker, "A Rhetorical Analysis," 187.
60. Eckert, "Into the Spotlight."
61. "Shelley Meyer Reluctant to Resume Role of Coaching Wife," 10TV.com (Columbus, OH), accessed February 18, 2012, http://www.10tv.com/content/stories/2012/02/02/columbus-shelley-meyer-reluctant-her-husband-returned-to-coaching-so-soon.html.
62. Spencer, "The Mrs."
63. Eckert, "Life on the Sidelines."
64. "Well-Known Buckeyes Make Life Easier for Quads," 10TV.com (Columbus, OH), accessed February 18, 2012, http://www.10tv.com/content/stories/2008/06/30/quad_squad.html.
65. "Well-Known Buckeyes."

Bibliography

"Acts of Charity." *Columbus Dispatch* (Columbus, OH). October 20, 2007. Accessed February 18, 2012. http://www.dispatch.com/content/stories/life_and_entertainment/2007/10/20/1AA_CHARITY20_--_THEME_OF_DA.ART_ART_10-20-07_D2_MP87RCV.html.

AFCWA. *The Support Staff.* American Football Coaches' Wives Association Newsletter, 1998.

———. *Winning Seasons: A Collection of Recipes and Memories.* Louisville: Ad Craft Sports *Marketing*, 1996.

Blaik, Earl, with Tim Cohane. *The Red Blaik Story*. New Rochelle, NY: Arlington House, 1960.

Burke, Kenneth. *Philosophy of Literary Form*. Berkeley: University of California Press, 1941.

Campbell, Karlyn Kohrs. *Man Cannot Speak for Her: A Critical Study of Feminist Speakers*. Westport, CT: Greenwood Press, 1989.

Daughters, Amy. "College Football: 7 Teams That Are More Popular Than Their NFL Counterparts." Bleacher Report. http://bleacherreport.com.

Eckert, Kristy. "Into the Spotlight: Meet the New First Lady of Buckeye Nation." Capital Style. Accessed February 18, 2012. http://www.capital-style.com/content/stories/2011/09/YC-coachs-wife-amy-fickell.html.

———. "Life on the Sidelines: Wives of Three Ohio State Coaches Talk About Their Lives in and out of the Spotlight." *Capital Style*. Accessed February 18, 2012. http://www.capital style.com/content/stories/2009/09/01/0901_trendsetter_sides.html.

Finch, Janet. *Married to the Job: Wives' Incorporation in Men's Work*. London: George Allen & Unwin, 1983.

Foss, Sonja K. *Rhetorical Criticism: Exploration and Practice*, 2nd ed. Prospect Heights, IL: Waveland Press, 1996.

Glanville, Jerry, with J. David Miller. *Elvis Don't Like Football: The Life and Raucous Times of the NFL's Most Outspoken Coach*. New York: Macmillan, 1990.

Knox, Chuck, with Bill Plaschke. *Hard Knox: The Life of an NFL Coach*. San Diego: Harcourt, Brace, Jovanovich, 1988.

Lesmerises, Doug. "Ellen Tressel Discusses Her Husband, Ohio State Football Coach Jim Tressel, and Their Life away from the Football Field." *Plain Dealer* (Cleveland, OH), October 7, 2010. Accessed February 18, 2012. http://www.cleveland.com/osu/index.ssf/2010/10/post_21.html.

Oller, Rob. "Behind the Vest." *Columbus Dispatch* (Columbus, OH), January 7, 2008. Accessed February 18, 2012. http://www.dispatch.com/content/stories/sports/2008/01/06/Tresslife.ART_ART_01-06-08_A1_ER8V9JJ.html.

Paterno, Joe, with Bernard Asbell. *Paterno: By the Book*. New York: Random House, 1989.

Phelps, Tereasa Goodwin. *The Coach's Wife: A Memoir*. New York: W. W. Norton, 1994.

Reid, Bill. *Big-Time Football at Harvard, 1905: The Diary of Coach Bill Reid*. Edited by Ronald A. Smith. Urbana: Illinois University Press, 1994.

Roundtree III, J. Clark. "The President as God, the Recession as Evil: Actus, Status, and the President's Rhetorical Bind in the 1992 Election." *Quarterly Journal of Speech* 81 (1995): 325–52.

Sabock, Ralph J. *The Coach*. Philadelphia: W. B. Saunders, 1973.

"See Who Ellen Tressel Eliminated in This Week's Shootout." 10TV.com (Columbus, OH). Accessed February 18, 2012. http://www.10tv.com/content/stories/2008/06/30/shootout_week_3.html.

Sheban, Jeffrey and Kevin Joy. "In Choosing Game-Day Attire, OSU's Fickell Might Consider Those Who Coached Before Him." *Columbus Dispatch* (Columbus, OH), September 2, 2011. Accessed February 18, 2012. http://www.dispatch.com/content/stories/life_and_entertainment/2011/09/02/what-should-he-wear.html.

"Shelley Meyer Reluctant to Resume Role of Coaching Wife." 10TV.com (Columbus, OH). Accessed February 18, 2012. http://www.10tv.com/content/stories/2012/02/02/columbus-shelley-meyer-reluctant-her-husband-returned-to-coaching-so-soon.html.

Spencer, Jon P. "The Mrs. Makes It a Done Deal." *Mansfield News Journal* (Mansfield, OH), November 29, 2011. Accessed February 18, 2012. http://pqasb.pqarchiver.com/mansfieldnewsjournal/access/2522065961.html?FMT=ABS&date=Nov+29%2C+2011.

Trujillo, Nick. "Hegemonic Masculinity on the Mound: Media Representations of Nolan Ryan and American Sports Culture." *Critical Studies in Mass Media* 8 (1991): 290–308.

Tucker, Diana. L. "A Gender Drama in American Football Culture: The Case of the Coach's Wife." *Football Studies* 4 (2001): 58–76.

———. "The Making of a Perfect Sacrifice: A Rhetorical Analysis of Football Coaches' Descriptions of Their Wives." In *Sport, Rhetoric and Gender: Historical Perspectives and Media Representations*, edited by Linda K. Fuller, 241–51. New York: Palgrave Macmillan, 2006.

———. "A Rhetorical Analysis of Women's Role in American Sport Culture: The Case of the Football Coach's Wife." PhD diss., Southern Illinois University Carbondale, 2003.

"Well-Known Buckeyes Make Life Easier for Quads." 10TV.com (Columbus, OH). Accessed February 18, 2012. http://www.10tv.com/content/stories/2008/06/30/quad_squad.html.

Chapter 14

Who's Framing Whom? Michele Bachmann and the (Primary) Politics of Motherhood

by Ann E. Burnette

The 2012 presidential election offered dramatic stories and clashes among the Republican primary candidates. One of the most compelling figures was U.S. Congresswoman Michele Bachmann, who, after two terms representing the sixth district of Minnesota, jumped into the fray by launching her own presidential campaign. As a conservative Republican, avid Tea Party supporter, and evangelical Christian, she appeals to many Republican voters who express a desire for an authentically conservative alternative to President Barack Obama. Bachmann officially entered the race on June 27, 2011, and quickly demonstrated she was a serious contender for the nomination. She was the first woman ever to win the Ames Straw Poll conducted by the Iowa Republican Party on August 13, 2011. She also had strong performances in the Republican presidential primary debates held throughout the rest of 2011. Like the other candidates, however, Bachmann suffered setbacks as well as triumphs, and when the Iowa Caucuses were held on January 3, 2012, she finished in sixth place. The next day, she suspended her campaign.

During her active candidacy, Bachmann seemed poised to challenge and extend the legacy of Democratic presidential primary candidate Hillary Clinton and Republican vice presidential nominee Sarah Palin in the 2008 presidential campaign. Scholarship on female political candidates indicates that women who run for office face different perceptions and expectations from mass media sources and the public than do male candidates. As the most recent woman to run for national office, Bachmann offers a timely case study as to how women can negotiate these perceptions as they seek election to the nation's highest offices. This study evaluates newspaper coverage of Bachmann during her primary campaign. Newspapers frequently framed Bachmann according to her status as a mother and defined her political history, accomplishments, and goals in those terms. The motherhood frame performed the function of feminizing Bachmann and presenting her activities as appropriate maternal pursuits. While some journalists speculated on the effectiveness of Bachmann's appeal as a mother, none questioned the legitimacy of the motherhood frame. The media framing of Bachmann, however, is only part of the equation. Bachmann herself often describes her political history, accomplishments, and goals in terms of her status as a mother. This raises the questions, Who's framing whom, and what are the implications?

Media Frames

Mass media news cannot convey everything pertaining to a given event or issue, so reporters, editors, and organizations must decide what gets covered and what does not. The news media thus frame events. Robert Entman explains, "To frame is to select some aspects of a perceived reality and make them more salient in a communication text, in such a way as to promote a particular problem, definition, causal interpretation, moral evaluation and/or treatment recommendation for the item described."[1] The frames appearing in news media have ideological implications. As Katie Gibson contends, "Media frames invite the audience to understand issues, events, and individuals in particular ways."[2] Entman notes that media frames' ideological messages appear to audiences to be natural and neutral.[3] This makes their ideological dimensions all the more powerful.

The framing function of news is crucial to political campaigns. This importance increases as political races move from local campaigns to national ones. James Devitt notes, "Only a small proportion of the electorate has the opportunity to meet candidates in person, so voters rely on news coverage . . . in forming their opinions of those running for office."[4] The majority of voters will only know political candidates through mass media frames.

One frequent category of media frames of political news is gender norms and gender expectations. Scholars of media coverage of female political candidates have found news reports more frequently call attention to women's appearance, family relationships, and emotional states than they do when covering men.[5] This reporting results in a frame that assesses how these women adhere to or violate accepted gender norms. Gibson notes the existence of "dominant or stock media frames that shape the coverage of women who challenge gender norms."[6]

Many of the media frames are based on categories scholars first observed among professional women. In *Men and Women of the Corporation*, Rosabeth Kanter identifies four "stereotyped informal roles" through which token women could fit into corporate culture.[7] They are "mother," "seductress," "pet," and "iron maiden."[8] Kanter argues that these roles serve a highly functional purpose because "men could respond to and understand" representatives of these categories.[9] Julia Wood updated these categories in 1994 and noted that the role of mother "has both indirect and literal forms."[10] Members of an organization often expect the women of the organization to attend to the emotional and support needs of the organization's men. In addition, women who are also mothers face harsh judgment as to whether they can fulfill both their professional and maternal responsibilities. Wood reminds us that using these stereotypes frames our perceptions of people within these stereotypes when she notes, "the language we use in defining others may function to blind us to seeing them outside of categories to which we assign them."[11] Rhetorical and media scholars have identified these categories as themes that appear within media frames of women politicians.

For this study, I reviewed newspaper articles that reported on any aspect of Bachmann's presidential primary campaign from June 13, 2011—when she announced during a Republican primary debate that she had filed her papers to run for president—to January 5, 2012, the day after she suspended her primary campaign. I analyzed articles from the *New York Times*, the *Washington Post*, the *Los Angeles Times*, and the *Christian Science Monitor* to achieve editorial and geographical diversity. I included news as well as opinion pieces. I will discuss how the newspapers framed: 1) Bachmann as a mother, 2) the link between Bachmann's motherhood and her politics, and 3) the strategic implications of Bachmann's motherhood.

Framing Bachmann as a Mother

Newspaper coverage of Michele Bachmann illustrates that the motherhood frame for women in public life is alive and well. Throughout her primary campaign, Bachmann's status as a mother was a reliable frame for the coverage she received. The discussion of Bachmann's motherhood was particularly vivid because of the size and nature of her family. Within the frame of mother, Bachmann appeared as both a heroic and reassuringly ordinary mother.

When Bachmann indicated during the June 13, 2011, Republican primary debate that she would be running for president, reporters filed articles that introduced her as a presidential candidate and a mother. The framing of Bachmann's status as mother emphasized her five biological children as well as the children Bachmann and her husband fostered. In one write-up of the June 13 debate, the author called attention to "the most eye-popping point on Bachmann's resume: She and her husband have been foster parents to 23 children, in addition to raising five children of their own."[12] Weeks later, another reporter mentioned Bachmann's "brood, which includes the staggering number—23!—of foster kids."[13] Bachmann was not only a mother but a heroic mother who willingly took on a large number of children, some of whom presented difficulties for the family. One article quoted Bachmann's brother, Dr. Paul Amble, observing that the foster children had "a lot of challenges" and had experienced "difficult home lives" before concluding, "I think Michele and Marcus both had a real heart for that."[14] This heroic mother frame did not go uncontested. Some critics argued that, while the Bachmanns had indeed worked with twenty-three foster children, many of those children—all were girls—spent only months with the Bachmann family and regarded the Bachmann house as a place to live while they were being treated at the University of Minnesota. In response, one article quoted the head of the private foster agency, George Hendrickson, who confirmed, "From our agency's perspective, I thought they did a very nice job."[15]

Bachmann's heroism as a mother of biological and foster children is inspiring. In this frame, however, Bachmann was also portrayed as a reassuringly ordinary mother. One profile noted, "Friends remember her planning neighborhood picnics and organizing bicycle parades."[16] One of Bachmann's sons, Lucas Bachmann, recalled approvingly of one period of his childhood, "We did a lot of bingo and buffets."[17] In these depictions, Bachmann is an ordinary mother who is concerned with domestic activities. This portrayal makes it clear that motherhood, rather than a political career, is Bachmann's priority. As one reporter wrote, "Bachmann's life was dominated by her family, not by political ambitions."[18] The motherhood frame provides a nonthreatening interpretation of Bachmann as a political figure.

Framing Motherhood and Politics

The media's framing of Bachmann as a mother strongly affected how she was framed as a politician. The newspaper coverage often framed her political accomplishments and potential in terms of her motherhood. Newspaper accounts reported how Bachmann's experience as a mother led her to pursue politics, framed Bachmann's political platforms in terms of her status as mother, and explained how her status provided an automatic connection with voters.

The media repeated the narrative that Bachmann's motherhood and advocacy for her children led her into politics. One reporter made the causal link explicit: "It was her role as a mother, both to her biological children and to her adolescent foster daughters, that spurred her to seek public office."[19] Many accounts of Bachmann's political career traced her involvement as a mother in local education issues and how this work led her to politics. Bachmann joined the board of a Stillwater, Minnesota, charter school and parlayed that experience into speaking to groups of parents, lobbying to change education policies, and ultimately running for her local school board (a race she lost) and then for the state senate (a seat she won). In these accounts, journalists framed Bachmann's status as a mother as crucial. As one article observed, "Mrs. Bachmann cut her political teeth on an issue that concerns nearly all mothers: education."[20] Her passion for the charter school led her to enroll one of her children in it. In her speaking and advocacy, she talked about her desires for her children and her experiences homeschooling them. In this frame, her status as a foster mother is also important. One reporter observed that Bachmann was "dismayed by the lack of rigor"[21] her foster daughters encountered in their public schools, and this further fueled her desire to reform education. At times the motherhood frame was so strong that Bachmann's political work did not even represent a natural evolution of her concerns as a mother but an incidental, secondary outcome. One journalist describes Bachmann's autobiography as telling the story of "her five biological children and 23 foster children; and her accidental foray into politics."[22] Bachmann's status as a mother is a defining feature in her political biography; it was a path to a political career she would not have otherwise entered. Again, the motherhood frame blunts any question of whether Bachmann had purely political ambitions.

In reporting on Bachmann's primary campaign, the media continued to draw freely on the motherhood frame. Newspaper coverage of Bachmann's race framed Bachmann's political platforms in terms of her status as mother, including the assumption that Bachmann's motherhood gave her expertise in the area of education. The media also reported on her association with conservative "family values" political platforms consistent with the motherhood frame. When Bachmann, along with Texas Governor Rick Perry and former Pennsylvania Senator Rick Santorum, signed the pledge put forward by the Family Leader group to earn the group's endorsement, one reporter noted she "was the first to sign a pledge to support traditional marriage" and observed "she has held firm" on the issue.[23] The pledge required candidates to "block same-sex marriage and [put] women 'in forward combat roles,' while being faithful to their spouses and supporting 'robust childbearing and reproduction.'"[24] Often the media framed her opposition to same-sex marriage as a measure to protect children. One article described a rally at which Bachmann spoke, saying, "In our public schools, whether they want to or not, they'll be forced to start teaching that same-sex marriage is equal, that it is normal and that children should try it."[25] One commentator flatly equated Bachmann's references to her mothering experiences with her qualities as a candidate: "Her biographical and political message are the same."[26]

The most famous instance of candidate Bachmann exercising the power conferred on her by the mother frame was the stand she took against Rick Perry in the September 12, 2011, Republican primary debate. Bachmann took Perry to task for mandating that twelve-year-old girls in Texas be vaccinated against the human papillomavirus (HPV), which can cause cervical cancer. News sources widely quoted Bachmann's accusation, "To have innocent little twelve-year-old girls be forced to have a government injection through an executive order is just flat-out wrong."[27] In this scenario, the frame of Bachmann as a mother and foster mother to girls lent considerable strength to her political stance. On the morning after the debate, Bachmann, in an interview on the NBC *Today* show, argued that the vaccine could also cause mental illness. As the press reported it, Bachmann based this claim on the assertion of a mother who spoke to her after the debate. The *New York Times* reported that Bachmann "made the link between the vaccine and mental illness after meeting a tearful woman following Monday night's debate. . . . The woman said her daughter had developed mental retardation after being vaccinated."[28] As a presidential candidate who was a mother, Bachmann was sanctioned to protect innocent children and to voice the fears of other mothers. Mothers are not only allowed but expected to perform this type of advocacy. The motherhood frame casts this as maternal rather than political zeal, which again softens the image of a woman engaged in aggressive political debate.

Finally, the media frame of Bachmann as mother enabled newspapers to explore another dimension of Bachmann's motherhood: the bond she could build with voters who fit the motherhood frame. One such group of voters consisted of parents who home-schooled their children. As one reporter wrote, "Bachmann, who home-schooled her five children, has been courting such families for months."[29] Another account noted that Bachmann's "coalition included home-schooling parents."[30] Bachmann's homeschooling fit easily within the media motherhood frame, which provided a natural and expected way for Bachmann to build a political base. This was another way of depicting Bachmann's political efforts as an extension of appropriate maternal concerns. In this way, necessary political activities, such as building coalitions and getting votes to defeat opponents, are feminized as relational rather than being viewed as competitive or masculine.

The Strategic Value of Motherhood

In reporting on Michele Bachmann's presidential primary run, the media often commented on how motherhood functioned rhetorically and politically. Reporters, opinion writers, and bloggers sometimes considered the implications of Bachmann playing the "mom card."[31] While a few articles questioned whether the media coverage of Bachmann could be construed as sexist, none critically evaluated how the media generated and used the frame of motherhood. But journalists did discuss how Bachmann was using the frame and to what degree she was effective. Reports also made it clear the narrative could be misapplied. In that case, the media engaged in disciplining Bachmann for not subscribing appropriately to the motherhood frame.

Most of the media discussion of Bachmann's use of the motherhood narrative concluded that it was positive and appealing. When Bachmann first indicated she would seek the Republican presidential nomination, GOP strategist Ron Bonjean observed that Bachmann "did a great job of weaving in her experiences as a foster mother, a congresswoman, and an attorney."[32] In a piece entitled, "Bachmann's Story Helps Her Connect with Voters," Chris Cillizza argued, "Bachmann's candidacy is heavily premised on her personal story—she is the only woman (and mother) in the race and mentions the fact that she has raised five children and 23 foster children at nearly every campaign stop."[33] Cillizza described a campaign appearance in which Bachmann recounted a miscarriage she suffered and tied the story to her opposition to abortion. Cillizza noted, "Bachmann's decision to reveal something so personal . . . provides a window into her unique appeal in the race."[34] Bonjean argued Bachmann's appeal was so strong it would have an impact on the way other candidates would need to campaign: "The other candidates are now forced to personalize their stories more."[35]

One profile of Bachmann, "Bachmann Plays the Mom Card in Campaign,"[36] analyzed exactly what kind of a mom Bachmann represented. Reporter Melinda Henneberger argued, "Bachmann plays the mom card differently than others have."[37] The reporter noted that "Instead of the warm-and-worried 'mom in tennis shoes' that Patty Murray (D-Wash.) ran as for the Senate, or the ferocious, angry 'mama grizzly' that her friend Sarah Palin is, Bachmann is running as the disciplinarian mom, who says no all the time."[38] This analysis, while evaluating different expressions of motherhood, assumes the legitimacy of the motherhood frame.

The coverage of Bachmann did acknowledge her appeal as a mother had specific overtones and implications stemming from her evangelical Christian beliefs. Bachmann's conservative religious values were consistent with the motherhood frame and thus invited other women with similar beliefs to identify even more strongly with Bachmann as a mother. One commentator described the new definition of "feminism" conservative women were embracing and speculated, "It is their focus on motherhood, I think, that makes these new Christian feminists so appealing to millions—their unflinching insistence that their families come first, that even the most ambitious among them occasionally have spit-up on their blouses."[39] This commentator argued that the focus on motherhood evidenced by Bachmann and other conservative Christian females "appeals to America's working mothers" and would satisfy "a void created by the political left."[40]

While there was positive media coverage of Bachmann's use of the motherhood frame, journalists also indicated it was possible to overplay the motherhood card. In September, *New York Times* columnist Gail Collins posed the possibility that Bachmann self-identified as a mother too often. Collins asked, "How often should a female candidate with children bring that up?"[41] Collins answered, "frequently enough that we can appreciate a special sympathy for issues like early childhood education. But not so often that you could imagine it being her first comment during negotiations with North Korea over plutonium processing."[42] Other journalists found fault with Bachmann's attempt to argue that the HPV vaccine was potentially dangerous to children by invoking one mother's story. The media reported favorably on Bachmann's attack on Perry in defense of twelve-year-old girls during the September 12, 2011, debate: "Bachmann had scored debate points Monday when she slammed Perry."[43] But journalists cried foul when Bachmann circulated the story of the mother who claimed her daughter had been hurt by the vaccine. Most accounts of the interaction between Bachmann and the mother described the mother as emotionally overcome. This mother was variously characterized as "crying,"[44] "weeping,"[45] and "tearful."[46] The *Washington Post* described Bachmann's reliance on such emotional and unreliable testimony as "Ms. Bachmann's hysterics about hapless little girls being forced to get injections."[47] The motherhood frame, while advantageous for Bachmann in many regards, also has its limits, and the media were quick to discipline Bachmann for misusing it.

Bachmann on Bachmann

The media clearly constructed Michele Bachmann's frame by relying heavily on the frame of mother. This served the purpose of making Bachmann's story understandable and socially acceptable because her political experiences and ambitions could be fit within the template of a mother who was by turns heroic, ordinary, outraged—and sometimes hysterical. The motherhood frame explained and feminized Bachmann as she competed against her male opponents. But Bachmann is also an exemplar of the female politician who seeks to fit her own persona within acceptable gender roles by displaying standard markers of femininity to counteract any perceived harsh or masculinizing dimensions of competing in the public sphere. While the media relied heavily on the motherhood frame to interpret Bachmann, she framed her own experiences within the parameters of motherhood and thus gave the media plenty of material to work with.

Bachmann frequently spoke about the importance of motherhood to her life in a variety of campaign venues. In interviews, speeches, and debates, she often led with her status as wife and mother in describing her qualifications to be president. In a late 2011 interview, Bachmann said, "My number one job description for my whole life was to be a happy mother at home raising our children."[48] Bachmann introduced herself to many Americans during the June 12, 2011, Republican primary debate by saying, "I'm a former federal tax litigation attorney. I'm a businesswoman. We started our own successful company. I'm also a member of the United States Congress. I'm a wife of 33 years. I've had five children, and we are the proud foster parents of 23 great children."[49] When reports circulated in July that Bachmann suffered from possibly debilitating migraines, she released a statement that began: "I am a wife, a mother, a lawyer who worked her way through law school, a former state senator who achieved the repeal of a harmful piece of educational policy in Minnesota, and a congresswoman who has worked tirelessly fighting against the expansion of government and wasteful spending."[50] Whether speaking generally of her qualifications or responding to possible obstacles to her campaign, Bachmann privileged her identity as a mother.

Bachmann also claimed it was her role as mother and foster mother that led her unexpectedly into politics. When she officially announced her candidacy on June 27, 2011, she said, "I hadn't planned on getting into politics. I loved the law and went to law school. I went on to William and Mary to become a tax lawyer. Together with my husband we started a successful small business. When I saw the problems with our local school district and how academic excellence was being eroded by federal government interference with the local schools, I decided to do more than just complain about it."[51] She listed her traditional professional qualifications for high public office while making it clear it was her concern for children in the educational system that led her to politics. In her announcement speech, she also said, "I didn't seek public office for fortune or power but simply to make life better in our community and education better for our children."[52]

Bachmann regularly linked her stances on political issues to her role as a mother. She told the audience at one political rally, "It's time for tough love" and described the members of Congress as a "dysfunctional family."[53] In some cases, she injected a good deal of emotion into her appeals by assuming the role of mother. In her announcement speech, she contrasted the United States with "those who sacrifice others, like terrorists who use little children as human shields."[54] In the aftermath of her face-off with Rick

Perry over the governor's HPV vaccine mandate, Mitt Romney said in a subsequent debate that Perry should get a "mulligan." Bachmann responded, "Little girls who have a negative reaction to this potentially dangerous drug don't get a mulligan. They don't get a do-over."[55]

This rhetorical strategy on the part of Bachmann is not unusual for women who run for public office. Kathleen Hall Jamieson describes the double bind faced by women who strive for achievement that challenges traditional gender expectations: "femininity and competence in the public sphere are mutually exclusive."[56] She cautions, "It can still be hazardous for a woman to venture out of her 'proper sphere.'"[57] Numerous rhetorical and media scholars have described the feminine rhetorical style as a series of rhetorical strategies that enable women to frame arguments in terms of the feminine gender role.[58] These strategies stem from, among other things, the propriety of women communicating in a way that strengthens relationships and conveys an ethic of care. While the feminine style may have evolved as a way for women to find a public voice, men as well as women can adopt components of the style in political communication. More recent studies of female political figures have addressed the ways in which feminine style may reinforce gender stereotypes.[59]

Conclusion

In 1978, Gaye Tuchman argued that newspapers "engage in the symbolic annihilation of women" by minimizing the coverage of women in the professional world, adapting to female readers through stories that "cater to a traditional view of women's interest," and ignoring issues such as sex discrimination.[60] More than three decades later, women in politics have forced an expansion of perceptions and discussion of gender roles. Yet even as women are launching credible runs for top national offices, news media coverage continues to rely on explanatory frames such as motherhood to represent female political candidates to the American public. This frame, as Diana Carlin and Kelly Winfrey observe, "has potential to elevate women's political standing but also poses pitfalls."[61] On the one hand, it can be a source of rhetorical strength for mothers because it explains women's political ambitions and agendas in a way that makes them understandable and palatable to potential voters. Yet the frame also limits the argumentative appeals that women can make and limits their perceived credibility to issues that can be construed as a maternal. And, of course, the frame marginalizes the arguments of women who are not mothers.

The importance and influence of media representations of political candidates are difficult to overemphasize since most American voters rely on these representations to form their own perceptions of candidates, issues, and campaigns. Moreover, media frames such as the frame of motherhood appear to be natural and complete; voters are not encouraged to question or challenge these frames or to evaluate candidates according to different priorities.

There is a further problem, however, because at the same time female candidates are being defined and normalized by mass media frames, they also often make rhetorical choices that reify the stereotypes on which these frames are based. In many cases, women may feel compelled to do so—the media can and does discipline women who violate feminine frames.[62] This pressure leaves female politicians and candidates in a bind. Some find themselves trying to utilize the rhetorical power of the frames and also chafing against their limitations. Carlin and Winfrey note that Hillary Clinton and Sarah Palin were caught in this bind: "Both clung to stereotypical portrayals of women when it appeared to suit their needs, and both demanded that they be considered 'candidates who happen to be women' rather than women candidates when sexism surfaced."[63] Michele Bachmann benefitted from the motherhood frame but was also bound by its restrictions. Future female candidates will undoubtedly also face this dilemma. Perhaps the best way to challenge the assumptions of the motherhood frame is to make the frame visible by identifying it as it influences news coverage and as women invoke it in their own rhetoric. Women—whether they are mothers or not—must be able to make unlimited rhetorical contributions to the political domain.

Notes

1. Robert M. Entman, "Framing: Toward Clarification of a Fractured Paradigm," *Journal of Communication* 43 (1993): 53.

2. Katie L. Gibson, "Undermining Katie Couric: The Discipline Function of the Press," *Women and Language* 32 (2009): 51.

3. Entman, "Framing: Toward Clarification," 53.

4. James Devitt, "Framing Gender on the Campaign Trail: Female Gubernatorial Candidates and the Press," *Journalism & Mass Communication Quarterly* 79 (2002): 445–46.

5. See Sean Aday, and James Devitt, "Style over Substance: Newspaper Coverage of Elizabeth Dole's Presidential Bid," *The Harvard International Journal of Press/Politics* 6 (2001): 52–73; Devitt, "Framing Gender on the Campaign Trail"; Dianne Bystrum, "Advertising, Web Sites, and Media Coverage: Gender and Communication Along the Campaign Trail," in *Gender and Elections: Shaping the Future of American Politics*, eds. Susan J. Carroll and Richard L. Fox (Cambridge: Cambridge University Press, 2006): 169–88; Diana B. Carlin and Kelly L. Winfrey, "Have You Come a Long Way, Baby? Hillary Clinton, Sarah Palin, and Sexism in 2008 Campaign Coverage," *Communication Studies* 60 (2009): 326–43; Gibson, "Undermining Katie Couric."

6. Gibson, "Undermining Katie Couric," 51.

7. Rosabeth Moss Kanter, *Men and Women of the Corporation* (New York: Basic Books, 1977), 233.

8. Kanter, *Men and Women of the Corporation*, 233–36.

9. Kanter, *Men and Women of the Corporation*, 233.

10. Julia T. Wood, *Gendered Lives: Communication, Gender, and Culture* (Belmont, CA: Wadsworth Publishing Company, 1994), 263.

11. Wood, *Gendered Lives*, 264.

12. Linda Fedmann, "New Hampshire GOP Debate Belonged to Mitt Romney, Michele Bachmann," *Christian Science Monitor*, June 15, 2011, http://www.csmonitor.com.

13. Lisa Miller, "Evangelical Women Create Their Own Brand of Feminism," *Washington Post*, July 30, 2011, http://www.washingtonpost.com.

14. Quoted in Sheryl Gay Stolberg, "A Presidential Hopeful's Calling Began with Foster Children," *New York Times*, June 22, 2011, http://www.nytimes.com.

15. Quoted in Stolberg, "A Presidential Hopeful's Calling."

16. Stolberg, "A Presidential Hopeful's Calling."

17. Quoted in Stolberg, "A Presidential Hopeful's Calling."

18. Donna St. George, "Consistent Conservative," *Washington Post*, December 12, 2011, http://www.washingtonpost.com.

19. Stolberg, "A Presidential Hopeful's Calling."

20. Stolberg, "A Presidential Hopeful's Calling."

21. St. George, "Consistent Conservative."

22. Seema Mehta, "It's Not Just Democrats Who Anger Bachmann; In a New Book, She Criticizes Bush and Other Republicans for Embracing 'Bailout Socialism,'" *Los Angeles Times*, November 21, 2011, http://www.latimes.com.

23. St. George, "Consistent Conservative."

24. Susan Saulny, "'The Marriage Pledge': Endorsing but Not Signing," *New York Times*, December 13, 2011, http://www.nytimes.com.

25. Stolberg, "For Bachmann, Gay Rights Stand Reflects Mix of Issues and Faith," *New York Times*, July 17, 2011, http://www.nytimes.com.

26. Melinda Henneberger, "Bachmann Plays the Mom Card in Campaign," *Washington Post*, November 23, 2011, http://www.washingtonpost.com.

27. Quoted in "The Wrong Prescription," *Washington Post*, September 14, 2011, http://www.washingtonpost.com.

28. Trip Gabriel, "With Stakes for Bachmann Higher Now, Her Words Get in the Way," *New York Times*, September 16, 2011, http://www.nytimes.com.

29. Seema Mehta, "Bachmann Tries to Widen Appeal: The Niche Candidate Works to Become a Plausible General Election Competitor," *Los Angeles Times*, July 30, 2011, http://www.latimes.com.

30. Jeff Zeleny, "Iowa Poll Goes to Bachmann; Paul is Second," *New York Times*, August 14, 2011, http://www.nytimes.com.

31. Henneberger, "Bachmann Plays the Mom Card."

32. Quoted in Amy Gardner and Sandyha Somashekhar, "Basking in New Momentum, Bachmann Plots Path Ahead," *Washington Post*, June 15, 2011, http://www.washingtonpost.com.

33. Chris Cillizza, "Bachmann's Story Helps Her Connect with Voters," *Washington Post*, July 1, 2011, http://www.washingtonpost.com.

34. Cillizza, "Bachmann's Story."

35. Quoted in Gardner and Somashekhar, "Basking in New Momentum."

36. Henneberger, "Bachmann Plays the Mom Card."

37. Henneberger, "Bachmann Plays the Mom Card."

38. Henneberger, "Bachmann Plays the Mom Card."

39. Miller, "Evangelical Women."

40. Miller, "Evangelical Women."

41. Gail Collins, "The Bachmann Chronicles," *New York Times*, September 15, 2011, http://www.nytimes.com.

42. Collins, "The Bachmann Chronicles."

43. Robin Abcarian and Seema Mehta, "Leno Can't Budge Bachmann from Stance on Gays, Vaccine," *Los Angeles Times*, September 17, 2011, http://www.latimes.com.

44. Abcarian and Mehta, "Leno Can't Budge Bachmann."

45. Michael Gerson, "Time for a Dose of Reality," *Washington Post*, September 16, 2011, http://www.washingtonpost.com.

46. Trip Gabriel, "With Stakes for Bachmann Higher Now, Her Words Get in the Way," *New York Times*, September 16, 2011, http://www.nytimes.com.

47. "The Wrong Prescription."

48. Quoted in Sarah Pulliam Bailey, "Michele Bachmann: It's High Time We Have a Mother in the White House," *Christianity Today*, November 22, 2011. http://www.christianitytoday.com.

49. "Transcript of Republican Debate on June 13, 2011," CNN, accessed January 26, 2012, http://transcripts.cnn.com/TRANSCRIPTS/1106/12/se.02.html.

50. "Bachmann's Headaches." *Washington Post*, July 21, 2011, http://www.washingtonpost.com.

51. Michele Bachmann, "Bachmann Officially Announces Her Run for the Presidency of the United States in Waterloo, Iowa," Michele Bachmann for President, accessed June 27, 2011, http://www.michelebachmann.com.

52. Bachmann, "Bachmann Officially Announces."

53. Quoted in Jeff Zeleny and Carl Hulse, "Candidates Warn about Debt-Deal Compromise," *New York Times*, July 10, 2011, http://www.nytimes.com.

54. Bachmann, "Bachmann Officially Announces."

55. Quoted in Gabriel, "With Stakes for Bachmann Higher Now."

56. Kathleen Hall Jamieson, *Beyond the Double Bind: Women and Leadership* (New York: Oxford University Press, 1995), 127.

57. Jamieson, *Beyond the Double Bind*, 4.

58. See Karlyn Kohrs Campbell, "The Rhetoric of Women's Liberation: An Oxymoron," *Quarterly Journal of Speech* 59 (1973): 74–86; Kathleen Hall Jamieson, *Eloquence in an Electronic Age: The Transformation of Political Speechmaking* (New York: Oxford University Press, 1988); Bonnie J. Dow and Mari Boor Tonn, "'Feminine Style' and Political Judgment in the Rhetoric of Ann Richards," *Quarterly Journal of Speech* 79 (1993): 286–302; Jane Blankenship and Deborah C. Robson, "A 'Feminine Style' in Women's Political Discourse: An Explanatory Essay," *Communication Quarterly* 43 (1995): 353–66; Karlyn Kohrs Campbell, "The Discursive Performance of Femininity: Hating Hillary," *Rhetoric & Public Affairs* 1 (1998): 1–19.

59. See Shawn J. Parry-Giles and Trevor Parry-Giles, "Gendered Politics and Presidential Image Construction: A Reassessment of the 'Feminine Style,'" *Communication Monographs* 63 (1996): 337–53; Katie L. Gibson and Amy L. Heyse, "'The Difference Between a Hockey Mom and a Pit Bull': Sarah Palin's Faux Maternal Persona and Performance of Hegemonic Masculinity at the 2008 Republican National Convention," *Communication Quarterly*, 58 (2010): 235–56.

60. Gaye Tuchman, "The Symbolic Annihilation of Women by the Mass Media," in *Hearth and Home: Images of Women in the Mass Media*, ed. Gaye Tuchman et al. (New York: Oxford University Press, 1978), 29.

61. Carlin and Winfrey, "Have You Come a Long Way, Baby?" 332.

62. See Gibson, "Undermining Katie Couric."

63. Carlin and Winfrey, "Have You Come a Long Way, Baby?" 327.

Bibliography

Abcarian, Robin, and Seema Mehta. "Leno Can't Budge Bachmann from Stance on Gays, Vaccine." *Los Angeles Times*, September 17, 2011. http://www.latimes.com.

Aday, Sean, and James Devitt. "Style over Substance: Newspaper Coverage of Elizabeth Dole's Presidential Bid." *The Harvard International Journal of Press/Politics* 6 (2001): 52–73.

Bachmann, Michele. "Bachmann Officially Announces Her Run for the Presidency of the United States in Waterloo, Iowa." Michele Bachmann for President. http://www.michelebachmann.com.

"Bachmann's Headaches." *Washington Post*, July 21, 2011. http://www.washingtonpost.com.

Bailey, Sarah Pulliam. "Michele Bachmann: 'It's High Time We Have a Mother in the White House.'" *Christianity Today*, November 22, 2011. http://www.christianitytoday.com.

Blankenship, Jane, and Deborah C. Robson. "A 'Feminine Style' in Women's Political Discourse: An Explanatory Essay." *Communication Quarterly* 43 (1995): 353–66.

Bruni, Frank. "Much Ado About Michele." *New York Times*, July 24, 2011. http://www.nytimes.com.

Bystrum, Dianne. "Advertising, Web Sites, and Media Coverage: Gender and Communication Along the Campaign Trail." In *Gender and Elections: Shaping the Future of American Politics*, edited by Susan J. Carroll and Richard L. Fox, 169–88. Cambridge: Cambridge University Press, 2006.

Campbell, Karlyn Kohrs. "The Discursive Performance of Femininity: Hating Hillary." *Rhetoric & Public Affairs* 1, (1998): 1–19.

———. "The Rhetoric of Women's Liberation: An Oxymoron." *Quarterly Journal of Speech* 59 (1973): 74–86.

Carlin, Diana B., and Kelly L. Winfrey. "Have You Come a Long Way, Baby? Hillary Clinton, Sarah Palin, and Sexism in 2008 Campaign Coverage." *Communication Studies* 60 (2009): 326–43.

Cillizza, Chris. "Bachmann's Story Helps Her Connect with Voters." *Washington Post*, July 1, 2011. http://www.washingtonpost.com.

Collins, Gail. “The Bachmann Chronicles.” *New York Times*, September 15, 2011. http://www.nytimes.com.

Continetti, Matthew. “No American Left Behind: In the 2012 Presidential Race, the Republicans Should Favor Human Capital Over Investment Capital.” *Los Angeles Times*, August 31, 2011. http://www.latimes.com.

Devitt, James. “Framing Gender on the Campaign Trail: Female Gubernatorial Candidates and the Press.” *Journalism & Mass Communication Quarterly* 79 (2002): 445–63.

Dow, Bonnie J., and Mari Boor Tonn. “‘Feminine Style’ and Political Judgment in the Rhetoric of Ann Richards.” *Quarterly Journal of Speech* 79 (1993): 286–302.

Entman, Robert M. “Framing: Toward Clarification of a Fractured Paradigm.” *Journal of Communication* 43 (1993): 51–58.

Feldmann, Linda. “New Hampshire GOP Debate Belonged to Mitt Romney, Michele Bachmann.” *Christian Science Monitor*, June 14, 2011. http://www.csmonitor.com.

———. “Next, Iowa Straw Poll: Why It Matters to GOP Presidential Candidates.” *Christian Science Monitor*, August 8, 2011. http://www.csmonitor.com.

Gabriel, Trip. “In Iowa, Religious Right Is Now a Force Divided.” *New York Times*, October 11, 2011. http://www.nytimes.com.

———. “With Stakes for Bachmann Higher Now, Her Words Get in the Way.” *New York Times*, September 16, 2011. http://www.nytimes.com.

Gardner, Amy, and Sandyha Somashekhar. “Basking in New Momentum, Bachmann Plots Path Ahead.” *Washington Post*, June 15, 2011. http://www.washingtonpost.com.

Gerson, Michael. “Time for a Dose of Reality.” *Washington Post*, September 16, 2011. http://www.washingtonpost.com.

Gibson, Katie L. “Undermining Katie Couric: The Discipline Function of the Press.” *Women and Language* (2009): 51–59.

Gibson, Katie L., and Amy L. Heyse. “‘The Difference Between a Hockey Mom and a Pit Bull’: Sarah Palin’s Faux Maternal Persona and Performance of Hegemonic Masculinity at the 2008 Republican National Convention.” *Communication Quarterly* 58 (2010): 235–56.

Henneberger, Melinda. “Bachmann Plays the Mom Card in Campaign.” *Washington Post*, November 23, 2011. http://www.washingtonpost.com.

Jamieson, Kathleen Hall. *Beyond the Double Bind: Women and Leadership*. New York: Oxford University Press, 1995.

———. *Eloquence in an Electronic Age: The Transformation of Political Speechmaking*. New York: Oxford University Press, 1988.

Kanter, Rosabeth Moss. *Men and Women of the Corporation*. New York: Basic Books, 1977.

Knickerbocker, Brad. “Michele Bachmann ‘The One to Watch’ as She Kicks off Her Presidential Campaign.” *Christian Science Monitor*, June 26, 2011. http://www.csmonitor.com.

Mehta, Seema. “Bachmann Tries to Widen Appeal: The Niche Candidate Works to Become a Plausible General Election Competitor.” *Los Angeles Times*, July 30. 2011. http://www.latimes.com.

———. “Bachmann’s Facts Often Aren’t: The GOP Candidate’s Frequent Miscues May Be Starting to Weigh on Her Campaign.” *Los Angeles Times*, October 24, 2011. http://www.latimes.com.

———. “It’s Not Just Democrats Who Anger Bachmann; In a New Book, She Criticizes Bush and Other Republicans for Embracing ‘Bailout Socialism.’” *Los Angeles Times*, November 21, 2011. http://www.latimes.com.

Miller, Lisa. “Evangelical Women Create Their Own Brand of Feminism.” *Washington Post*, July 30, 2011. http://www.washingtonpost.com.

Parry-Giles, Shawn J., and Trevor Parry-Giles. “Gendered Politics and Presidential Image Construction: A Reassessment of the ‘Feminine Style.’” *Communication Monographs* 63 (1996): 337–53.

Saulny, Susan. “Embattled but Confident, Bachmann Says She Is the ‘Complete Package.’” *New York Times*, January 2, 2012. http://www.nytimes.com.

———. "The 'Marriage Pledge': Endorsing but Not Signing." *New York Times*, December 13, 2011. http://www.nytimes.com.

Shear, Michael D. "Bachmann Wins over Some Skeptics." *New York Times*, June 15, 2011. http://www.nytimes.com.

———. "The Spouses: Marcus Bachmann's Message." *New York Times*, December 17, 2011. http://www.nytimes.com.

St. George, Donna. "Consistent Conservative." *Washington Post*, December 13, 2011. http://www.washingtonpost.com.

Stolberg, Sheryl Gay. "A Presidential Hopeful's Calling Began with Foster Children." *New York Times*, June 22, 2011. http://www.nytimes.com.

———. "For Bachmann, Gay Rights Stand Reflects Mix of Issues and Faith." *New York Times*, July 17, 2011. http://www.nytimes.com.

———. "Where God and Justice Were Once Intertwined." *New York Times*, October 14, 2011. http://www.nytimes.com.

"Transcript of Republican Debate on June 13, 2011." CNN. Accessed January 26, 2012. http://transcripts.cnn.com/TRANSCRIPTS/1106/12/se.02.html.

"Transcript of Republican Debate at the Reagan Library." *New York Times*. http://www.nytimes.com.

Tuchman, Gaye. "The Symbolic Annihilation of Women by the Mass Media." In *Hearth and Home: Images of Women in the Mass Media*, edited by Gaye Tuchman, Arlene Kaplan Daniels, and James Benet, 3–38. New York: Oxford University Press, 1978.

West, Paul. "Bachmann Hammers Perry over HPV Vaccination Requirement; She Accuses the GOP Front-Runner of 'Crony Capitalism' Following a Test Debate Exchange." *Los Angeles Times*, September 14, 2011. http://www.latimes.com.

"The Wrong Prescription." *Washington Post*, September 14, 2011. http://www.washingtonpost.com.

Wood, Julia T. *Gendered Lives: Communication, Gender, and Culture*. Belmont, CA: Wadsworth Publishing Company, 1994.

Zeleny, Jeff. "Iowa Poll Goes to Bachmann; Paul is Second." *New York Times*, August 14, 2011. http://nytimes.com.

Zeleny, Jeff, and Carl Hulse. "Candidates Warn About Debt-Deal Compromise." *New York Times*, July 10, 2011. http://www.nytimes.com.

Zeleny, Jeff, and Michael D. Shear. "Republican Rivals Unleash Broadside on Paul in Iowa." *New York Times*, December 28, 2011. http://www.nytimes.com.

PART IV

Internet

Chapter 15

Momtinis, Not Martyrs: Examining 'Anti-Mom' Blogs, Muted Groups, Standpoints, and the Struggle over Motherhood

by Rita L. Rahoi-Gilchrest

Readers of this chapter already know something about the emergence of blogs as a medium for personal expression, and it is hardly likely today that a reader has *never* accessed an online blog for personal enjoyment. If you have not, however, let's begin with an essential and scholarly definition of blogging as "the reverse-chronological posting of individually-authored entries which includes the capacity to provide hypertext links and often allow comment-based responses from readers."[1] Even though blogs have become part of our daily lives, the sheer volume of the blog phenomenon is still impressive to consider. One 2010 article in *Business Wire* magazine estimates that nearly eighty thousand new blogs are being launched every day; that number will only continue to grow exponentially.[2]

Given this amassing of online expression, one area deserving closer attention is the extent to which women have embraced blogging. Lenhart and Fox reported in the *Journal of Computer-Mediated Communication* in 2009 that even six years ago, studies indicated more than half of the blogging population was under the age of thirty, with blogging being almost evenly divided between men and women.[3] *Business Wire* magazine estimates that the popular New York BlogHer conference currently attracts more than one thousand women bloggers who write on everything from motherhood to lifestyle and from politics to health and wellness.[4]

Writing in a recent issue of the public relations journal *PRism*, Katie Stansberry clarifies that the term "mommy blogging" was originally a term of disrespect intended to trivialize the online posts of housewives who wrote exclusively about their children, homemaking, and day-to-day lives.[5] Despite the corresponding public perception reported by Mia Lövheim that "girl bloggers" write about private life, fashion, and gossip,[6] the business world is paying attention to this blogging boom. Recently, Bryan McCleary, director of external relations for Procter & Gamble's baby care division, announced to *Advertising Age* magazine, "It's official: Mom bloggers are the new influencers."[7] In 2011, *Advertising Age* magazine listed twenty-five women who have just signed up with a new PR talent agency specializing in representing their mommy blogs.[8] Marketing pull and PR ventures aside, the phenomenon of women bloggers deserves feminist/scholarly attention as well.

The Shift in Women's Blogging: From "Mommy Blogs" to the Anti-Mom Phenomenon

Early on in the emergence of "women's blogs," many sites and authors took one of two distinct directions. Bloggers generally focused on either "lifestyle" issues or "mommy" issues, with clear distinctions between the two types of sites. Mommy blogs became so popular a form of online expression that one writer created a satirical mock-mommy blog called *Seriously So Blessed*,[9] featuring all of the self-praising, typo-riddled posts; cutesy font choices; and pink-dominated color schemes critics claim typify "traditional" mommy blogs.[10]

More recently, however, women bloggers have been feeling a need to express their views in more varied ways. As the previously cited *Business Wire* article indicates, "Today's top 'mommy' bloggers are moving beyond the talk of diapers and baby photos that first defined them."[11] This growing diversity in women's online expression is directly in line with Armstrong and McAdams's earlier 2009 observation predicting that "we will come to speak primarily not of blogging per se, but of . . . many other specific subgenres which are variations on the overall blogging theme."[12] Nowhere has this explosion of digital diversity been more evident than in the growing number of women's blogs concerning nontraditional approaches to motherhood.

These sites are often self-labeled as "anti-mom" blogs;[13] even when they are not listed as such, they usually contain numerous references to "not being a *regular* mom" in a sort of definition by negation. Anti-mom sites are hosted by women who openly argue with traditional expectations for mothers, especially stay-at-home moms. These women don't claim to be perfect; they don't have perfect children; and they don't have perfect houses (and some even have cocktail hour, or "momtini time," during their kids' play dates).

This chapter examines the emergence of "anti-mom" blogs from a communication-based perspective to establish that these sites represent situated struggle—the struggle for women to define themselves and their views not only against male perspectives but also in contrast to other more "traditional" mommy bloggers. These newer anti-mom blogs, although they do not actually oppose all that motherhood traditionally stands for, represent an effort to open up perspectives on women's experiences and "challenge dominant representations of motherhood within our society."[14] The next section of this chapter provides a brief overview of two communication frameworks—muted group theory and feminist standpoint theory—to help frame the discussion that follows.

Muted Group Theory

Inspired by 1970s social anthropological research, muted group theory was developed by Cheris Kramarae in the early 1980s. The theory's essential premise is that although men and women experience the world differently, women are often forced to fit their ideas and issues into a male-developed framework. This forces women either to use male language (which often does not fit their experience) or to remain silent ("muted").

This problem is complicated by the fact that women have to invent language to reflect their reality (e.g., the term "date rape") as well as by the phenomenon that women sometimes suppress or silence other women to maintain some measure of power. The theory identifies methods of silencing that can range from ridicule, ritual, and gatekeeping to harassment. The author then identifies possible responses to silencing, which include identifying the problem, rediscovering/reclaiming women's experiences, and reinventing/elevating language to reflect women's lives more accurately.[15]

As Julia Wood discusses, these two theories obviously have some underlying similarities in their critical approach to understanding human communication.[16] In this chapter, both perspectives have value; muted group theory certainly applies to the earlier discussion of how many women have sought to find a voice through blogging to express their own unique experiences, particularly the experiences of motherhood. Standpoint theory, however, offers a way to look more deeply at the issues of how anti-mom bloggers are expressing their feeling of being the "outsider within" not only the community of mothers but also, perhaps, the community of women who blog.

Feminist Standpoint Theory

Based on the work of the German philosopher Georg Hegel[17] and adapted by scholar Nancy Hartsock,[18] feminist standpoint theory is a framework to help us discuss what disempowered groups lack. The theory posits that our material possessions and class standing have a marked influence on the way we understand society. Generally speaking, when people from different backgrounds come into conflict, the more privileged group is able to determine the grounds of the argument and set the rules of engagement. The less privileged group, though members often have a broader perspective on the issue than those in power, struggles to have its viewpoint heard and considered.

In this theory, "standpoint" is defined as an achieved position based on social location that leads to reflection/political activity. Concepts important to this theory involve the idea of the "outsider within" (the person from a disempowered group who manages to rise to privilege but feels uncomfortable in that position), "bottom-up knowledge" (the term for the broader understanding members of disadvantaged groups must possess to live by the "rules," let alone have any opportunity for advancement), and "situated knowledge" (the term for a person's perspective, given her own economic and social standing).[19] With these brief definitions of the three theories in mind, we can now examine excerpts from anti-mom blogs—and the reactions to them—from each perspective in turn.

"What Is Cradle Cap, and How to Get Rid of It"[20]: Women Bloggers as Muted Groups

The initial motivation for the creation of women's blogs appears to have been the need to talk about experiences not expressed in everyday discourse. Muted group theory purports that dominant-group (in this case, male) experiences shape both the language and opportunities for speaking offered to nondominant group members and that men and women are further led to perceive the world differently by the traditional division of labor. Because blogging can be done privately in the home (often during breaks from the "women's work" that inspires blog posts), it is a medium that allows women not only to talk about their experiences but also to connect with other women regardless of physical proximity. As Amy S. S. writes on her *Snarky Mommy* blog:

> If there's anything we've learned over the last few years, it's that social media makes a difference. Some of the best support I've gotten as a parent is from a group of moms I "met"

> through an online group when I was pregnant. This group of women, all due in February 2006, has supported each other through pregnancy, childbirth, postpartum depression, sleepless nights, births of other children and even a near-death experience in one of these families. When I say these women are my friends, there's no "online" modifier in front of that word. Social media brought us together and I am so glad to have all of their support. The same with this little ole blog. I have "met" (and physically met) some amazing women because of it. I have learned things I would never have known and found that I'm not alone when it comes to the practice of raising small people with a healthy dose of humor. Twitter, Facebook, you name it—it connects us.[21]

Male critics, however, did not take long to begin attacking mommy blogs. One such critic, Matt Armstrong, comments on his *One Off* blog that of the blogs he regularly reads:

> The great majority . . . are . . . run by women. And a great majority of those are run by what the blogosphere has termed 'Mommy Bloggers.' The term came about, as one could imagine, as a large contingent of stay-at-home moms turned to the internet to share their stories and show off pictures of their adorable children.
>
> In my tracking of the mommy blog phenomenon, I have noticed a few similarities between the blogs. In fact, these similarities are so steady that I follow several blogs of people who aren't mothers, but whose blogs still fit within the mommy blog philosophy. (Before I continue, I would like to point out that I'm not going to be criticizing, but I still read dozens of these blogs every day. I'm just making observations.)
>
> A few common traits:
>
> 1. They are usually hosted at blogger.com.
>
> 2. They have very feminine templates, usually consisting of flowers, lace, pink, and other super-frilly, girly stuff.
>
> 3. It seems as most of them are written by Mormon women, and contain all of the cultural references thereto.
>
> 4. despite the fact that the writers are usually quite educated the blogs are replete will spelling errors completely lack capitalization and use extremely emphatic punctuation! (if they use any at all, lol)
>
> 5. They are written in a very colloquial speech type pattern, or, even worse, use text-speak as a real language.
>
> 6. They often use HUGE capitalized letters at the beginning of their paragraphs, change the colors of their text, and otherwise use **unusual** *typesetting* tricks.
>
> 7. Often-times, they are center aligned.
>
> 8. They gush about husbands, boyfriends, lack of boyfriends, their best friends at school, etc. There's a lot of love in these blogs.
>
> 9. They are usually filled with supportive comments from other mommy bloggers. These comments often echo the exact same traits listed above. They are all relentlessly, unrealistically, sickeningly positive.[22]

Perhaps this kind of negative male response has also contributed to the reinvention of the traditional mommy blog. Katie Stansberry, writing in the previously mentioned issue of *PRism*, claims the term "mommy blogging" has been reclaimed by "a community of active writers who are challenging existing notions of motherhood through their public blogs."[23] And, given the fact that the term is showing up so frequently today in marketing and advertising magazines, it seems clear the phrase "mommy blogging" has earned some measure of respect (from potential profiteers, at least). This is exactly the kind of reclaiming of language Cheris Kramarae identified as one of the means by which a muted group can respond to a dominant group's attempts at silencing.[24]

"I'm Not a Typical Mom": Standpoints of Anti-Mom Blogs

If traditional mommy bloggers write about diaper wipes and cradle cap, what do anti-mommy bloggers write about? Well, diaper wipes and cradle cap, sometimes, but they also write about Thirsty Thursdays and momtinis. For instance, Alexis raves about piña coladas and their attendant calories on her *The Exhausted Mom* blog, but she offers hope with a "skinny" version.[25] AntiMomAmanda must have been at the same holiday parties, posting earlier that month: "Although still extremely hung over from New Years, I had to find ways to get rid of the four Asti bottles I have left over in my fridge. I came across the 'Old Capri Long Drink' on yummly.com. It must be my Italian blood that was drawn to this but anything that has Asti Spumante AND Limoncello as its main ingredients is a winner in my book."[26] Other anti-mom bloggers have followed this lead. Melissa Sommers, author of the *Suburban Bliss* blog, created a momtini logo for her site featuring a pacifier tilted rakishly in a martini glass,[27] and author Amy Smith has actually titled her blog *The Momtini Lounge*.[28]

In addition to the pro-drinking stance, many anti-mom blogs exhibit a backlash reaction to the holistic childrearing practices their authors feel pressured to follow. Anti-mom bloggers often profess their deep love of cheap plastic toys, fast food, and quick parenting fixes (in addition to those frosty momtinis during play dates). One blogger who identifies herself simply as "Me" and her youngest son as "The Cool Cucumber" on her anti-mom blog comments: "The Cucumber and I started baby yoga this week. When I whipped out a formula bottle to feed him and then proceeded to change his non-cloth diaper, some of the harpies in the class audibly gasped. Screw you, hippies. Mama has her hands full and the last thing I need is to carry around is a shitty diaper all day to make you feel better. I recycle, so there."[29] As a side note, she also offers a 'Confessional' on her site as a safe space for other women who feel the same way. One young blogger goes so far as to admit she might actually not even *want* children, titling the home page of her blog, "Welcome to My Not-a-Mommy Blog: My Future Babies Scare Me."[30]

Perhaps anti-mom blogger Amy Morrison has taken the boldest step of all—one that resulted in a viral sensation. On her *Pregnant Chicken* blog, she created images of what she calls "pregnancy porn," featuring photos of handsome stars such as Jon Hamm and Ryan Reynolds and captioned comments such as, "Hey, Babe, let's celebrate your gestational diabetes coming back normal by eating Skittles off my abs" and "Use me as your body pillow. You know I find your pregnancy-induced snoring adorable." Morrison writes: "Pregnant ladies *should* have their very own candy to look at! We have needs! We have desires! So after seeing a bunch of these [blogs] for crafting and new moms online, I thought about some of the wonderful words many pregnant women might like to hear."[31] Morrison's images are rapidly becoming popular posts and reposts on many Facebook pages.

Not all anti-mom bloggers are this openly defiant. Some worry they will suffer a negative reaction to their writing because they are expressing a view of motherhood that does not align with traditional mommy blogs. This is similar to the "outsider within" phenomenon Patricia Hill Collins writes about when applying standpoint theory to her experiences as an African American female academic.[32] Although these women consider themselves good mothers, they are aware that talking about cocktail play dates, disposable diapers, and porn for pregnant ladies might not endear them to more traditional mommies.

There might well be reason for anti-mom bloggers to fear a virulent response. Last year, the author of the *Mom365* site posted a photograph of a woman giving birth on her Facebook page. Facebook then deleted the photo and all of the comments, posting a message that the post violated Facebook's Statement of Rights and Responsibilities. After the incident, the author seemed genuinely concerned and puzzled, posting on the *Mom365* blog:

> The photo, by Lynsey Stone Photography, upset some of our Facebook followers—a few moms were outraged and several found the photo disgusting or too private for sharing. But many others found the picture to be beautiful and a tribute to womens' strength. We're sorry if we offended some of our followers. We believe that an artistically strong image of a woman birthing naturally, with her partner catching the baby, tells a powerful story.
>
> What do you think? Was Facebook right to remove the photo in order to protect some people from material they might not want to see? (Facebook also routinely removes breastfeeding photos posted in breastfeeding groups.) Is the picture pornographic (and in that case, is National Geographic wrong to consider it for an award)? Or is Facebook overly sensitive to strong images of women as mothers?[33]

Writers on traditional mommy blogs such as *Strollerderby* are also responding to the "momtini" craze as aberrant and detrimental to women, pointing out that Stephanie Wilder-Taylor, a writer and blogger who published the book *Sippy Cups Are Not for Chardonnay*, quit drinking and renounced her cocktail play dates for the straight mom life.[34]

Given so much controversy over determining the "right" way to mother, when readers who share nontraditional sentiments find an anti-mom blog, their response is immediate, expressing both identification and relief. In a post on the *BlogHer* site titled, "Avoiding and Embracing Anti-Mommy Blogging," the writer notes:

> There's a sub-niche of mommy bloggers that some may not be aware of. We are the writers who tell it like it is. Or was. We're about penning real accounts, thoughts and philosophies. Sometimes those are in regards to parenting, sometimes we'll throw some photos of our broods online, but the overwhelming response we often get is: "Yes. Thank you. I feel like this too and didn't know that other people did—I'm so happy you were willing to write about it." We are not unique in mommy blogging, except for the simple fact that there's a higher probability of coming across a stray f-bomb in one of our posts. Also, we'll probably tell you about that time we attempted suicide, ran away from home, or decided to have an abortion. And why. And before you know it, you're telling *us* about that time you ________. We are real. We're women who see the line and step over it, just in case someone needs to see a friendly face on the other side. *We often get email responses*

> *to posts instead of comments—not everyone's ready to put their name on their own truth.* And that's okay, too. Because we are. We're not driving mini-vans with Chopin gracefully wafting out the smear-free windows, and we're not afraid to say it. Hell, some of us have Weezer replaying on our store-brand mp3 players while we wait for the bus. But we're here, part of the crowd—even if we are a tad unrepresented.[35]

When anti-mommy bloggers do post something they believe is more traditional, they often offer an apology of sorts. For instance, AntiMomAmanda describes her emotional reaction when her daughter fell in love with a new toy. She then immediately notes, "I know what your [sic] thinking, this is awfully similar to a cheesy mom post that I tend to stray from."[36] This raises the question of whether or not readers of an anti-mom blog might actually feel betrayed if the author tries to express a more complex standpoint that blends traditional and nontraditional approaches to motherhood.

A slightly different reason to consider standpoint theory in relationship to anti-mom blogs comes, ironically, from a cross-cultural study by Yi-Ning Katherine Chen. Although Chen compared Taiwanese and American blogs, she makes the relevant claim that "cultural factors, such as the way that popular bloggers relate to others, may contribute to how they present themselves and their social relations in blogs."[37] Moreover, a woman who finds herself in an environment where she feels constrained by social expectations of motherhood and uncomfortable expressing her views to those around her might be less likely to write an anti-mom blog than someone who already has a supportive social network of educated, affluent friends—even though the first woman might feel just as strongly about the same issues. Pedersen and Macafee are among the scholars who argue that women generally have a greater desire for anonymity than men, which can discourage women even further from establishing the public online self successful blogging requires.[38]

We cannot assume, then, even if we read both traditional and anti-mom blogs, that the entirety of all women's feelings about motherhood is represented. We need to read each blog mindful of the circumstances each author describes. Only then can we compare those experiences to our own and understand the role that standpoint plays in the depiction of attitudes toward motherhood.

Can Blogging About Motherhood Make a Difference?

Having spent some time considering the emergence of anti-mom blogs, we would find it comforting but simplistic to believe the growing presence of these blogs will result in more enlightened and tolerant perspectives on motherhood. But just because a medium exists to challenge traditional expectations, it does not mean the medium will itself enact change.

As Hamilton observes in her article on feminist testimony in the Internet age, "Although feminist blogs provide new fora for the dissemination of female testimony, in many ways they replay older debates within feminism."[39] The ability of readers to disagree openly, and even vehemently, with a blog's author raises the possibility that those who support traditional motherhood will attempt to suppress anti-mom bloggers. This issue came to the fore in 2009 when it was revealed that a blog supposedly authored by a woman who was pregnant and decided against a late-term abortion was a fraud created by political conservatives. In response to the incident, a woman named Veronica wrote this on the *BitchMedia* blog: "What I find the most troubling about this story is that it throws all bloggers back into 'how do I trust you' mode? I blogged my pregnancy, the death of my mother and the birth of my daughter. How do you know anything I said was true? How do I know anything you say is true?"[40]

If dominant groups manipulate blogs to reify their values, we are back to the same problem Kramarae originally identified in shaping muted group theory—that a group maintains its dominance "by stifling and belittling the speech and ideas of those they label as outside the privileged circle."[41] In other words, the fact that mommy and anti-mom blogs can manifest the dichotomy between the real and the ideal versions of motherhood risks encouraging readers to take one side versus the other or to frame their own opinions in terms of this dichotomy instead of engaging in transformative dialogues.

The medium of blogging itself might also lead to a devaluing of all women's varied perspectives on what constitutes motherhood and the importance of that discussion. Kramarae points out that male domination of language and media originally led women to find private ways of expressing themselves—from diaries, letters, and sewing circles to the first women's novels.[42] Dale Spender, studying women's use of email and other technologies in the workplace, discovered that women's messages were still being "dismissed as 'nattering,' rather than being valued as legitimate message constructions."[43] If women want their views of motherhood understood, but men (and perhaps other women as well) dismiss their blogged messages as trivial—and especially if only like-minded peers follow these blogs, whether they espouse traditional or nontraditional views on motherhood—then nothing is gained.

We must also remember that despite its popularity, blogging still remains an activity available largely to those on the "empowered" side of the digital divide, which means many other diverse perspectives on motherhood are never aired online. What about the mothers who can't afford momtinis, let alone the leisure time and the laptop to create blogs? The marketing angle cannot be ignored, either: the blogs with the most links and the most sponsorship are, as Harp and Tremayne note, the blogs with the most traffic and the most mainstream attention.[44] If we extend this argument further, it is possible that in gaining voice for the realities of motherhood through blogging, women compromise their perspectives as they seek to promote their sites (e.g., by accepting sponsorship from companies selling products perceptually linked with traditional motherhood such as diapers and baby food).

Finally, the reality of blogging is that even when an author's writing has political overtones, bloggers are generally most interested in self-expression. Myers describes blogging strategies as all being "ways of presenting one's own contribution as distinctive, *showing one's entitlement to a position*."[45] If anti-mom bloggers are grounding their experience in the personal—which, after all, is the nature of blogging—and respondents are basing their posts on their own personal experiences in turn, we are not moving together toward a greater truth.

Obviously, there is value in a medium that offers the opportunity for different standpoints to be aired, especially the standpoints of members of a previously muted group: women who are mothers, speaking about motherhood as a unique experience. Nevertheless, if those experiences are continually defended as being unique and each blog's worldview is presented as being unlike the views of others (therefore more deserving of attention), what greater understanding do we gain as we read these sites? Lu Wei points out the links back to muted group and standpoint theory on this issue, noting bloggers with higher socioeconomic status tend to have more politically than personally oriented blogs and that less personal political bloggers are perceived to have greater social influence.[46] Ultimately, then, as we examine these sites through the frameworks of muted group and standpoint theories, blogs about motherhood—whether traditional or anti-mom in nature—might raise just as many questions about the reality and universality of the motherhood experience as they seek to answer.

Notes

1. Axel Bruns and Joanne Jacobs, introduction to *Uses of Blogs*, ed. Axel Bruns and Joanne Jacobs (New York: Peter Lang, 2006), 1.

2. "'Mommy Blogs' Increasing in Influence by Moving Beyond Talk of Diapers and Baby Photos," *Business Wire*, accessed January 24, 2012, http://www.businesswire.com/news/home/20100728005558/en/%E2%80%9CMommy-Blogs%E2%80%9D-Increasing-Influence-Moving-Talk-Diapers.

3. Lenhart and Fox, 2006, as cited in Cory L. Armstrong and Melinda J. McAdams, "Blogs of Information: How Gender Cues and Individual Motivations Influence Perceptions of Credibility," *Journal of Computer-Mediated Communication* 14 (April 2009): 435–56.

4. "'Mommy Blogs' Increasing," para. 1.

5. Katie Stansberry, "Mapping Mommy Bloggers: Using Online Social Network Analysis to Study Publics," *PRism* 8 (2011): 1–14, accessed January 6, 2011, http://www.prismjournal.org/homepage.html.

6. Mia Lövheim, "Personal and Popular: The Case of Young Swedish Female Top-Bloggers," *Nordicom Review* 32 (2011): 3–16.

7. Jack Neff, "P&G Relies on Power of Mommy Bloggers," *Advertising Age* 79 (July 14, 2008): 4.

8. Alexandra Bruell, "Now, Mommy Bloggers Have Their Own Talent Agency," *Advertising Age* 72 (2011): 6.

9. *Seriously So Blessed* (blog), accessed April 10, 2012, http://seriouslysoblessed.blogspot.com.

10. Examples of what I term 'traditional' mommy blogs, some of which are popular enough to have considerable product placement and sponsorship, include *Metropolitan Mama* (http://metropolitanmama.net/), *An Island Life: Hawaii Mom Blog* (blog) (http://islandlife808.com/), *The Happiest Mom* (blog) (http://thehappiestmom.com/), *Mom It Forward: Where Mom Is a Verb* (blog) (http://momitforward.com/), and Simcha Fisher's blog for the National Catholic Register (http://www.ncregister.com/blog/simcha-fisher/).

11. "'Mommy Blogs' Increasing," para. 3.

12. Armstrong and McAdams, "Blogs of Information," 435–36.

13. See, for instance, *The Anti-Mom Blog* (blog) (http://antimomblog.com/) and *Anti-SuperMom* (http://www.antisupermom.com/).

14. Lori Kido Lopez, "The Radical Act of 'Mommy Blogging': Redefining Motherhood Through the Blogosphere," *New Media & Society* 11 (August 2009): 729.

15. A review of the theory's framework and general concepts can be found in Timothy Borchers, *Rhetorical Theory: An Introduction* (Belmont, CA: Thomson Higher Education, 2006).

16. Julia T. Wood, "Feminist Standpoint Theory and Muted Group Theory: Commonalities and Divergences," *Women & Language* 28 (Fall 2005): 61–64.

17. Georg Wilhelm Friedrich Hegel, *Phenomenology of Spirit*, trans. A. V. Miller (Oxford: Oxford University Press, 1977).

18. Nancy C. M. Hartsock, "The Feminist Standpoint: Developing the Ground for a Specifically Feminist Historical Materialism," in *Feminism and Philosophy: Essential Readings in Theory, Reinterpretation, and Application*, ed. Nancy Tuana and Rosemarie Tong (Boulder: Westview Press, 1995).

19. A complete discussion of the theory—including uses and applications as well as strengths and limitations—can be found in Richard West and Lynn H. Turner, *Introducing Communication Theory: Analysis and Application* (Boston: McGraw-Hill, 2010).

20. The title of a typical "mommy blog" post. "What Is Cradle Cap and How to Get Rid of It," *Digital Mom Blog* (blog), accessed January 25, 2012, http://blogs.babble.com/babys-first-year-blog/2012/01/25/what-is-cradle-cap-and-how-to-get-rid-of-it.

21. Amy S. S., "Looking for Donors," *Snarky Mommy* (blog), accessed January 26, 2012, http://snarkymommy.com/?gclid=CN_H6cW_6a0CFQQBQAodMmiA4g.

22. Matt Armstrong, "The Anti-Mommy Blogger," *One Off* (blog), accessed April 10, 2012, http://blog.mattarmstrongmusic.com/2009/02/10/the-anti-mommy-blogger.

23. Stansberry, "Mapping Mommy Bloggers," 2.

24. Cheris Kramarae, "Muted Group Theory and Communication: Asking Dangerous Questions," *Women & Language* 28 (Fall 2005): 55–61; Cheris Kramarae, *Women and Men Speaking: Frameworks for Analysis*. (Rowley, MA: Rowley, 1981).

25. Alexis, *The Exhausted Mom* (blog), "Thirsty Thursday," accessed January 26, 2012, http://exhaustedmomdiary.blogspot.com.

26. *AntiMomAmanda: The Anti Mom Blog* (blog), "Thirsty Thursday—New Year's Edition," accessed January 5, 2012, http://antimomblog.com.

27. Melissa Sommers, *Suburban Bliss* (blog), accessed April 10, 2012, http://www.suburbanbliss.net.

28. Amy Smith, *The Momtini Lounge* (blog), accessed April 10, 2012, http://momtinilounge.com.

29. "Postpartum my Eggo, Week 4," *I Like Beer and Babies* (blog), accessed January 19, 2012, http://www.ilikebeerandbabies.com.

30. Carlie Crash, "Welcome to My Not-a-Mommy Blog: My Future Babies Scare Me," *Carlie Crash* (blog), accessed April 10, 2012, http://carliecrash.com/2010/02/15/welcome-to-my-not-a-mommy-blog-my-future-babies-scare-me.

31. Amy Morrison, "Porn for Pregnant Ladies," *Pregnant Chicken* (blog), http://www.pregnantchicken.com.

32. Patricia Hill Collins, "Learning from the Outsider Within: The Sociological Significance of Black Feminist Thought," *Social Problems* 33 (1986): 14–32.

33. "Facebook Removes *Mom365* Content: Anti-Mom or Pro-Family?" *Mom365* (blog), accessed April 10, 2012, http://community.mom365.com/profiles/blogs/facebook-removes-mom365-content-anti-mom-or-pro-family-1.

34. "Are Moms Drinking Too Much?" *Strollerderby* (blog), accessed April 10, 2012, http://blogs.babble.com/strollerderby/2011/06/30/are-moms-drinking-too-much.

35. "Avoiding and Embracing Anti-Mommy Blogging," *BlogHer* (blog), accessed April 10, 2012, http://www.blogher.com/avoiding-and-embracing-anti-mommy-blogging. Italics added.

36. AntiMomAmanda, "A Toy Every Baby Should Have," *AntiMomAmanda: The Anti Mom Blog* (blog), accessed January 25, 2012, http://antimomblog.com.

37. Yi-Ning Katherine Chen, "Examining the Presentation of Self in Popular Blogs: A Cultural Perspective," *Chinese Journal of Communication* 3 (March 2010): 28.

38. Sarah Pedersen and Caroline Macafee, "Gender Differences in British Blogging," *Journal of Computer-Mediated Communication* 12 (July 2007): 1472–92.

39. Carrie Hamilton, "Feminist Testimony in the Internet Age: Sex Work, Blogging, and the Politics of Witnessing," *Journal of Romance Studies* 9 (Winter 2009): 87.

40. Veronica, "Anti-Abortion Mommy Blog Hoax Exposed," *Bitch Magazine*, accessed January 24, 2012, http://bitchmagazine.org/post/anti-abortion-mommy-blog-hoax-exposed.

41. Kramarae, "Muted Group Theory and Communication," 55.

42. Kramarae, *Women and Men Speaking*.

43. As quoted in Judith D. Hoover, Sally O. Hastings, and George W. Musambira, "Opening a Gap in Culture: Women's Uses of the Compassionate Friends Website," *Women & Language* 32 (Spring 2009): 83.

44. Dustin Harp and Mark Tremayne, "The Gendered Blogosphere: Examining Inequality Using Network and Feminist Theory," *Journalism & Mass Communication Quarterly* 83 (Summer 2006): 247–64.

45. Greg Myers, "Stance-Taking and Public Discussion in Blogs," *Critical Discourse Studies* 7 (November 2010): 263, italics added.

46. Lu Wei, "Filter Blogs vs. Personal Journals: Understanding the Knowledge Production Gap on the Internet," *Journal of Computer-Mediated Communication* 14 (April 2009): 532–58.

Bibliography

Alexis. "Thirsty Thursday." *The Exhausted Mom* (blog). Accessed January 26, 2012. http://exhaustedmomdiary.blogspot.com.

Amy S. S. "Looking for Donors." *Snarky Mommy* (blog). Accessed January 26, 2012. http://snarkymommy.com/?gclid=CN_H6cW_6a0CFQQBQAodMmiA4g.

AntiMomAmanda. "A Toy Every Baby Should Have." *AntiMomAmanda: The Anti Mom Blog* (blog). Accessed January 25, 2012. http://antimomblog.com.

———. "Thirsty Thursday—New Year's Edition." Accessed January 5, 2012. http://antimomblog.com.

Armstrong, Cory L., and Melinda J. McAdams. "Blogs of Information: How Gender Cues and Individual Motivations Influence Perceptions of Credibility." *Journal of Computer-Mediated Communication* 14 (April 2009): 435–56.

Armstrong, Matt. "The Anti-Mommy Blogger." *One Off* (blog). Accessed April 10, 2012. http://blog.mattarmstrongmusic.com/2009/02/10/the-anti-mommy-blogger.

Beth. Accessed April 10, 2012. *Anti-Supermom* (blog). http://www.antisupermom.com.

BlogHer. "Avoiding and Embracing Anti-Mommy Blogging." *BlogHer* (blog). Accessed April 10, 2012. http://www.blogher.com/avoiding-and-embracing-anti-mommy-blogging.

Borchers, Timothy. *Rhetorical Theory: An Introduction*. Belmont, CA: Thomson Higher Education, 2006.

Bruell, Alexandra. "Now, Mommy Bloggers Have Their Own Talent Agency." *Advertising Age* 72 (2011): 6.

Bruns, Axel and Joanne Jacobs. Introduction to *Uses of Blogs*. Edited by Axel Bruns and Joanne Jacobs, 1–8. New York: Peter Lang, 2006.

Business Wire. "'Mommy Blogs' Increasing in Influence by Moving Beyond Talk of Diapers and Baby Photos." Accessed January 24, 2012. http://www.businesswire.com/news/home/20100728005558/en/%E2%80%9CMommy-Blogs%E2%80%9D-Increasing-Influence-Moving-Talk-Diapers.

Chen, Yi-Ning Katherine. "Examining the Presentation of Self in Popular Blogs: A Cultural Perspective." *Chinese Journal of Communication* 3 (March 2010): 28–41.

Collins, Patricia Hill. "Learning from the Outsider Within: The Sociological Significance of Black Feminist Thought." *Social Problems* 33 (1986): 14–32.

Crash, Carlie. "Welcome to My Not-a-Mommy Blog: My Future Babies Scare Me." *Carlie Crash* (blog). Accessed April 10, 2012. http://carliecrash.com/2010/02/15/welcome-to-my-not-a-mommy-blog-my-future-babies-scare-me.

Digital Mom. "What Is Cradle Cap and How to Get Rid of It." *Digital Mom Blog* (blog). Accessed January 25, 2012. http://blogs.babble.com/babys-first-year-blog/2012/01/25/what-is-cradle-cap-and-how-to-get-rid-of-it.

Fisher, Simcha. *Simcha Fisher National Catholic Register Blog* (blog). Accessed April 10, 2012. http://www.ncregister.com/blog/simcha-fisher.

Francis, Megan. *The Happiest Mom* (blog). Accessed April 10, 2012. http://thehappiestmom.com.

Hartsock, Nancy C. M. "The Feminist Standpoint: Developing the Ground for a Specifically Feminist Historical Materialism." In *Feminism and Philosophy: Essential Readings in Theory, Reinterpretation, and Application*, edited by Nancy Tuana and Rosemarie Tong. Boulder: Westview Press, 1995.

Hamilton, Carrie. "Feminist Testimony in the Internet Age: Sex Work, Blogging, and the Politics of Witnessing." *Journal of Romance Studies* 9 (Winter 2009): 86–101.

Harp, Dustin, and Mark Tremayne. "The Gendered Blogosphere: Examining Inequality Using Network and Feminist Theory." *Journalism & Mass Communication Quarterly* 83 (Summer 2006): 247–64.

Hegel, Georg Wilhelm Friedrich. *Phenomenology of Spirit*. Translated by A. V. Miller. Oxford: Oxford University Press, 1977.

Hoover, Judith D., Sally O. Hastings, and George W. Musambira. "Opening a Gap in Culture: Women's Uses of the Compassionate Friends Website." *Women & Language* 32 (Spring 2009): 82–90.

I Like Beer and Babies (blog). "Postpartum my Eggo, Week 4." Accessed January 19, 2012. http://www.ilikebeerandbabies.com.

Kramarae, Cheris. "Muted Group Theory and Communication: Asking Dangerous Questions." *Women & Language* 28 (Fall 2005): 55–61.

———. *Women and Men Speaking: Frameworks for Analysis*. Rowley, MA: Rowley, 1981.

Lopez, Lori Kido. "The Radical Act of 'Mommy Blogging': Redefining Motherhood through the Blogosphere." *New Media & Society* 11 (August 2009): 729–47.

Lövheim, Mia. "Personal and Popular: The Case of Young Swedish Female Top-Bloggers." *Nordicom Review* 32 (2011): 3–16.

Myers, Greg. "Stance-Taking and Public Discussion in Blogs." *Critical Discourse Studies* 7 (November 2010): 263–75.

Mom365. "Facebook Removes Mom365 Content: Anti-Mom or Pro-Family?" *Mom365* (blog). Accessed April 10, 2012. http://community.mom365.com/profiles/blogs/facebook-removes-mom365-content-anti-mom-or-pro-family-1.

Mom It Forward: Where Mom Is a Verb (blog). Accessed April 10, 2012. http://momitforward.com.

Morrison, Amy. "Porn for Pregnant Ladies." *Pregnant Chicken* (blog). http://www.pregnantchicken.com.

Neff, Jack. "P&G Relies on Power of Mommy Bloggers." *Advertising Age* 79 (July 14, 2008): 4–24.

Okamoto, Kailani. *An Island Life: Hawaii Mom Blog* (blog). Accessed April 10, 2012. http://islandlife808.com.

Pedersen, Sarah, and Caroline Macafee. "Gender Differences in British Blogging." *Journal of Computer-Mediated Communication* 12 (July 2007): 1472–92.

Seriously So Blessed (blog). Accessed April 10, 2012. http://seriouslysoblessed.blogspot.com.

Sheaffer, Stephanie. *Metropolitan Mama* (blog). Accessed April 10, 2012. http://metropolitanmama.net.

Smith, Amy. *The Momtini Lounge* (blog). Accessed April 10, 2012. http://momtinilounge.com.

Sommers, Melissa. *Suburban Bliss* (blog). Accessed April 10, 2012. http://www.suburbanbliss.net.

Stansberry, Katie. "Mapping Mommy Bloggers: Using Online Social Network Analysis to Study Publics." *PRism* 8 (2011): 1–14. Accessed January 6, 2011. http://www.prismjournal.org/homepage.html.

Strollerderby (blog). "Are Moms Drinking Too Much?" Accessed April 10, 2012. http://blogs.babble.com/strollerderby/2011/06/30/are-moms-drinking-too-much.

Thornberg, Molly. *Digital Mom* Blog (blog). Accessed April 10, 2012. http://www.digitalmomblog.com/about.

Veronica. "Anti-Abortion Mommy Blog Hoax Exposed." *Bitch Magazine*. Accessed January 24, 2012. http://bitchmagazine.org/post/anti-abortion-mommy-blog-hoax-exposed.

Wei, Lu. "Filter Blogs vs. Personal Journals: Understanding the Knowledge Production Gap on the Internet." *Journal of Computer-Mediated Communication* 14 (April 2009): 532–58.

West, Richard, and Lynn H. Turner. *Introducing Communication Theory: Analysis and Application*. Boston: McGraw-Hill, 2010.

Wood, Julia T. "Feminist Standpoint Theory and Muted Group Theory: Commonalities and Divergences." *Women & Language* 28 (Fall 2005): 61–64.

Chapter 16

Love Thy Mother? Traitorous Constructions of Motherhood in the "Outsmart Mother Nature with Tampax" Campaign

by Dacia Charlesworth

Menstruation affects brides, wives, and mothers throughout their lives. Given the stigma of menstruation, it makes sense that brides would want to avoid it on their wedding day when they are the center of attention.[1] Wives and husbands might also react to that same stigma and avoid sexual intercourse while a woman is menstruating. When a woman becomes menopausal, she is likely to be reminded that the loss of her menstrual cycle signals the loss of her youth.[2] As expectant mothers, women are granted a respite from menstruation; later, those mothers are expected to discuss the menstrual cycle with their children[3] and purchase fem-care products.[4]

Mothers now have an abundance of resources available to educate children about menstruation. In addition to books,[5] many websites provide advice for the all-important "talk." Most mothers would expect to find information on the Mayo Clinic's site as well as at KidsHealth (the most visited website for information relating to children's behavior, growth, and similar concerns). Fem-care websites also offer to prepare parents to speak with their daughters about menstruation. For example, the Always website has a section titled "For Moms," and Kotex has one called "My Daughter's Period." One could argue that these companies are more interested in persuading mothers that their products are ideal for their daughters as opposed to actually providing mothers with an objective overview of menstruation, yet the fact that these sites contain information meant for mothers points to the adaptive nature of the fem-care industry. In addition to selling their products, they are also selling their version of menstruation.

The fem-care industry maintains a powerful ideological influence that creates, shapes, and reifies the negative perception of menstruation via "educational" pamphlets[6] and films,[7] magazine advertising,[8] and even the medical community.[9] Thus, it should come as no surprise that fem-care companies are now using their websites to perpetuate the taboo of menstruation by stressing that the worst thing that could happen to a menstruator would be for her to have a "hygienic crisis"[10]—that is, others detecting a woman's menstruation because her "protection" failed.

The Tampax Pearl "Outsmart Mother Nature with Tampax" advertising campaign capitalizes on women's fear of hygienic crises. The campaign features an anthropomorphized Mother Nature whose sole task is to provide young women with their "monthly gift." The focus of this chapter, then, is on the rhetorical construction of the Mother Nature character and what it suggests about motherhood, femininity, and the female body.

The campaign casts Mother Nature as a discrepant role who serves as a traitor to menstruators due to her lack of dramaturgical loyalty, discipline, and circumspection.

In this chapter, I begin with an overview of menstrual ideology in the United States. Next, I describe the "Outsmart Mother Nature with Tampax" campaign and outline the theoretical approach used for analysis. Finally, I present the findings and discuss the implications of Tampax's Mother Nature character.

The Rhetorical Construction of Gender

As in most cultures, menstruation is a taboo topic in the United States. When researching the etymology of the word "taboo," Delaney, Lupton, and Toth discovered that it derives from the Polynesian word "tupua," which means "menstruation."[11] Menstrual taboos impact a woman regardless of where she is in her menstrual cycle. Her most important task is to never allow others to detect her identity as a menstruator. To determine how concealment became so paramount, I situate menstruation as a gendered performance and address the research on communication habits surrounding menstruation.

Feminist scholars argue that gender is a type of requisite everyday life performance, that it is "a norm that we struggle to embody,"[12] and that to "do" one's gender "involves a complex of socially guided perceptual, interactional, and micropolitical activities."[13] West and Zimmerman[14] offer three important categories for those examining the concept of gender: sex, sex category, and gender. Sex is "a determination made through the application of socially agreed upon biological criteria for classifying persons as females or males."[15] They note that placement in a "sex category" is "achieved through application of the sex criteria, but in everyday life, categorization is established and sustained by the socially required identificatory displays that proclaim one's membership in one or the other category."[16] West and Zimmerman define gender as "the activity of managing situated conduct in light of normative conceptions of attitudes and activities appropriate for one's sex category."[17] Gender is the required display that establishes one's membership in a particular category. That is, if one's gender falls into the category of "feminine" and one wishes to be considered "feminine," then one must embody culturally agreed upon norms that denote "femininity." Despite the fact that genitalia are usually hidden from public view, we continue to place individuals into sex categories. This placement punctuates the importance of socially required gender display because individuals are credited with membership in a sex category without their genitalia, organs that constitute *biological* sex, being directly observed.

What is most significant about the construction of gender, however, is that it not appear to be a struggle or a complex activity "but that it appear *natural*—that it appear to be quite a direct consequence of facts . . . beyond the scope of human manipulation."[18] While the culture at large should be unable to discern the structure of gender, French reminds us of the importance of ensuring the oppressed do not blame the oppressors: "To keep a group subordinate, an elite must persuade it that it deserves subordination because of *innate* inferiorities. A person of an inferior group cannot be the author of her or his own life but must center on the superior group. . . . And it is essential that a subordinated group not perceive its dominators as oppressors."[19]

The structure of gender is held in place through rhetoric, defined as "the use of words by human agents to form attitudes or induce actions in other human agents."[20] Kenneth Burke notes that rhetoric must be thought of "not in terms of some one particular address, but as a general *body of identifications* that owe their convincingness much more to trivial repetition and dull daily reënforcement than to exceptional rhetorical skill."[21] Burke's definition of ideology also demonstrates its relationship to rhetoric: though ideology once meant a study of ideas, today the term usually refers to "a system of political or social ideas, framed and propounded for an ulterior purpose."[22] Burke considers ideology as a type of rhetoric since "the ideas are so related that they have in them, either explicitly or implicitly, inducement to some social and political choices rather than others."[23] Gender is naturalized through rhetoric, ideology, and daily reinforcement.

Gender, then, is an all-encompassing, continuous process that one may never avoid. Butler notes that the sculpting of a gendered self is not simple: "Taking on a gender is not possible at a moment's notice, but is a subtle and strategic project, laborious and for the most part covert. Becoming a gender is an impulsive yet mindful process of interpreting a cultural reality laden with sanctions, taboos and prescriptions. . . . Less a radical act of creation, gender is a tacit project to renew a cultural history in one's own corporeal terms."[24] Thus, by analyzing rhetorical messages developed to assist us with becoming gendered selves (e.g., menstrual advertisements), critics may problematize the dichotomous roles of gender as well as how the body functions in a gender system.

Menstruation as Rhetorical Construct

Menstruation is significant for patriarchy to justify women's "one-down" status. Since only women menstruate, the constructions of the process can only directly affect them. Thus, the distinctions between sex, sex category, and gender become even more significant when considering the paradox of menstruation. Biologically, menstruation is a key indicator of the female reproductive system and serves as evidence that a woman's body is functioning as it should. Culturally, however, menstruation directly opposes the feminine ideal of purity. That is, when a woman's menstrual cycle is detected by others, the biological construction of "female" contradicts the cultural construction of "feminine."

As is usually the case with gender roles, the cultural view inflicts more sanctions on violators than the biological view. Carol Tavris has shown how medical science views women's bodies as not only abnormal, but also as the "other."[25] The designations of abnormal and "other" lead many to believe menstruation is a defect to be concealed. This biological/cultural paradox is borne out in scholarship that focuses on the language and situations various organizations (e.g., fem-care companies and the mass media) use to rhetorically construct menstruation. Havens and Swenson found fear and embarrassment were always mentioned in the thirty educational films about menstruation they analyzed, and the two were almost always discussed together.[26] Other studies found advertisements for menstrual products focus explicitly on the impending "hygienic crisis" menstruating women face[27] and the message that only sanitary products can reduce that threat.[28]

More recent advertisements send the same negative messages. Merskin duplicated Havens and Swenson's study by conducting a content analysis of menstrual product ads that appeared in *Seventeen* and *Teen* magazines from 1987 to 1997.[29] Merskin claims that the more recent advertisements contained messages dispelling the myths Havens and Swenson initially reported; however, she noted that most ads (94 percent) focus on a menstruator being "found out" in class, contain general concerns about signs of one's period being detected (60 percent), and stress the need for menstruation to be kept secret (38 percent).

Morse and Doan surveyed 113 junior high school girls (both pre- and post-menarcheal) and found 69 percent of the participants reported negative feelings toward menstruation, including feeling scared, sick, moody, rejected, embarrassed, strange, gross, and inconvenienced.[30] Brooks-Gunn and Ruble interviewed young women who just began menstruating and noted that most participants felt negatively about menstruation due to concerns about inconvenience.[31] Chrisler surveyed 158 young women and men and found young women view menstruation as bothersome, while young men perceive menstruation as debilitating.[32] Walker surveyed 109 college students and found these students believed premenstrual and menstrual phases were likely to negatively impact a woman's academic performance.[33]

Only one study found girls felt positively about menstruation; however, these initial positive feelings were later replaced with negativity.[34] A later study found feelings of secrecy, shame, embarrassment, greater self-consciousness, ambivalence, and confusion about expected behaviors developed later in junior high school students.[35]

While several studies have focused on mediated messages about menstruation, few studies specifically examine mother-daughter communication. Although scholars note the importance of mothers' role in menstrual education and advocate that they be well-educated about menstruation, emotionally supportive, and cognizant that menarche is a significant point in the mother-daughter relationship, McKever reveals that mothers found menstruation an uncomfortable topic and thus became secretive and uncommunicative about the event.[36] Kissling examined discussions between girls and their mothers about educational material directed at pre- and post-menarcheal girls and suggested using language free of euphemisms.[37] Fox and Inazu focused on mother-daughter communication about sexual topics in general, including menstruation.[38] Their findings indicate menstruation was the topic most frequently discussed, daughters usually initiated the discussion, mothers were comfortable discussing the topic, and daughters were not as comfortable discussing menstruation. Cooper and Koch interviewed seventeen African American women from a public housing project and discovered that, unlike Fox and Inazu, these women had few resources related to menstrual education and learned little to nothing about menstruation from school, their mothers, or other women.[39] In the most detailed study, Costos, Ackerman, and Paradis interviewed women about how they gained their education about menstruation.[40] Half the participants reported first learning about menstruation from their mother, 59 percent only told their mother about their first period, and 64 percent received negative messages from their mothers about menstruation.

Given the significant role mothers play in helping to form a menstruator's identity, it is useful to examine Tampax's conceptualization of the "stand-in" mother in their "Outsmart Mother Nature with Tampax" campaign to determine their ideological stance toward a mother's role in a menstruator's life.

"Outsmart Mother Nature with Tampax" Campaign

The "Outsmart Mother Nature with Tampax" campaign was introduced in July 2008 and was developed by the Leo Burnett advertising agency.[41] An actor portraying Mother Nature is tasked with delivering "Mother Nature's Monthly Gift" to each woman every month. In case the enthymematic and visual cues are not clear enough, the "monthly gift" is a woman's period. Of course, since this is a campaign for Tampax, the way for women to "outsmart" Mother Nature is by using Tampax Pearl tampons. According to Becky

Swanson, a creative director from the Leo Burnett agency, the campaign sought to "focus on the brand's 'fun and lighthearted nature'" as well as "avoid[ing] advertising clichés by allowing women to admit 'that they don't always welcome their periods.'"[42] Mother Nature was conceptualized as a "worthy opponent who is all-powerful and very much in control, more of a mother-in-law figure"[43] and was targeted to younger women because "the idea of having this worthy opponent really resonates with younger girls, because when someone tries to tell them how to lead their life or what they can or cannot do, they want to outsmart that person."[44]

The campaign, which received the 2010 Bronze Effie Award[45] features print advertisements published in young women's and women's magazines, television advertisements, seeded videos on YouTube, and accounts for Mother Nature on Facebook and Myspace. The premise is consistent: seemingly unsuspecting women are approached by Mother Nature and handed their "gift." The women in the print ads and videos on Facebook are startled by Mother Nature's appearance (some women in the unscripted video even run from her—a likely response to a stranger, regardless of whether they were aware of the campaign). To analyze how Tampax constructs the role of mother, it is first necessary to position the role of menstruator as not only a gendered everyday life performance but as one that is symbolically interactive. Viewed through the lens of symbolic interactionism, it becomes clear that Mother Nature betrays her insider status and, in so doing, reifies dominant patriarchal codes.

Symbolic Interactionism

Symbolic interactionism offers scholars an opportunity to analyze communicative experiences from the perspective of the participants in context. Meaning is constructed via one's interactions with others and one's interpretations of the interactive experiences.[46] It is useful to view gender as symbolic interaction since, as Butler notes, gender is "a subtle and strategic project, laborious and for the most part covert."[47] Menstruation may also be analyzed from this perspective as menstruators come to learn and adapt their identities based on interactions with mothers, teachers, friends, schools, and mass media.

Goffman's dramaturgical approach to symbolic interactionism will be especially helpful to this study since women performing the role of menstruator are given clear parameters for performing appropriately. As Goffman notes, "When the individual presents [her-] or himself before others, [her or] his performance will tend to incorporate and exemplify the officially accredited values of the society, more so, in fact, than does [her or] his behavior of the whole."[48] Central to Goffman's perspective are the performer(s), teams, audience, regions, secrets, and collusion. A "performance" refers to "all the activity of an individual which occurs during a period marked by his [or her] continuous presence before a particular set of observes and which has some influence on the observers."[49] Each performance contains a "front" that consists of settings, appearances, and manners. A "front" is "that part of the individual's performance which regularly functions in a general and fixed fashion to define the situation for those who observe the performance" and may be "intentionally or unwittingly employed by the individual during his [or her] performance."[50] The object of the performer is "to sustain a particular definition of the situation, this representing, as it were, [her or] his claim as to what reality is."[51] The "setting" includes "furniture, décor, physical layout, and other background items which supply the scenery and stage props for the spate of human action played out before, within, or upon it."[52] The "appearance" indicates an individual's social status and where the performer is in terms of his or her temporary ritual state and/or life-cycle, whereas the "manner" includes "those stimuli which function at the time to warn us of the interaction role the performer will expect to play in the oncoming situation."[53] Notably, "When an actor takes on an established social role, usually he [or she] finds that a particular front has already been established for it. Whether his [or her] acquisition of the role was primarily motivated by a desire to perform the given task or by a desire to maintain the corresponding front, the actor will find that he [or she] must do both."[54]

Performers may form "performance teams" wherein "participants co-operate together as a team or are in a position where they are dependent upon the co-operation in order to maintain a particular definition of the situation."[55] A team refers to "any set of individuals who co-operate in staging a single routine."[56] Goffman also notes that the team concept allows critics to consider performances delivered by more than one performer and also acknowledges that a performer may become his or her own audience; this is significant because "the individual may privately maintain standards of behavior which he [or she] does not personally believe in, maintaining these standards because of a lively belief that an unseen audience is present who will punish deviations from these standards."[57] Some teams often allow a member to function as director: "Sometimes the individual who dominates the show in this way and is, in a sense, the director of it, plays an actual part in the performance he [or she] directs."[58] The director primarily fulfills two tasks: The first is "the special duty of bringing back into line any member of the team whose performance becomes unsuitable," and the second is to allocate "the parts in the performance and the personal front that is employed in each part."[59] A team operates in front and back regions, and its members dictate the audience's (those watching the performance) access to those regions. A performance in the front region "may be seen as an effort to give the appearance that his [or her] activity in the region maintains and embodies certain standards" whereas the back region, or "back stage," is "a place, relative to a given performance, where the impression fostered by the performance is knowingly contradicted as a matter of course. . . . Here costumes and other parts of personal front may be adjusted and scrutinized for flaws."[60]

Since all performances depend on the team members' performance abilities, discrepant roles may arise. The source of the discrepancy often lies in the disclosing of secrets. While Goffman describes five types of secrets, only three are relevant to this study. The first, the "dark secret," consists "of facts about a team which it knows and conceals and which are incompatible with the image of self that the team attempts to maintain before its audience."[61] Next, "inside secrets" are "ones whose possession marks an individual as being a member of a group and helps the group feel separate and different from those individuals who are not 'in the know.'"[62] Finally, an "entrusted secret" is "the kind which the possessor is obliged to keep because of his [or her] relation to the team to which the secret refers."[63]

Essentially, "Performers are aware of the impression they foster and ordinarily also possess destructive information about the show. The audience know what they have been allowed to perceive, qualified by what they can glean unofficially by close observation. . . . performers appear in the front and back regions: the audience appears only in the front region."[64] Applying Goffman's dramaturgical approach provides insight into the rhetorical construction of motherhood within Tampax's campaign.

Analysis: Mother Nature and Symbolic Interactionism

Although there are many artifacts from this campaign suitable for analysis, the compilation "My Best Deliveries," posted on YouTube and Facebook, is representative of the entire campaign. This is an ideal artifact to examine the construction of Mother Nature's persona since the video depicts her trying to bestow her gift on no less than ten women. The setup for each woman is the same: Mother Nature approaches her in a public outdoor shopping center and tries to give her a "monthly gift." Each woman quickly determines the contents of Mother Nature's gift and refuses to accept it. Mother Nature approaches both women by themselves and those who appear to be with romantic partners; all gift recipients appear to be Caucasian women between the ages of sixteen and thirty.

Mother Nature's appearance is feminine, with a dressy skirt suit and pumps that connote a high-class status associated with wealth. The only accessory is a green flower she wears in her hair. She is also wearing makeup and styled hair. Mother Nature's appearance may be compensating for her manner, as she behaves in an unfeminine fashion, aggressively approaching most of the women and hounding them until they accept her gift. While the act of gift-giving may be stereotypically feminine, the way Mother Nature almost forces the women to accept the gifts is not.

This construction of Mother Nature exemplifies what Feder refers to as "overdetermined femininity."[65] Feder argues that when a woman becomes too powerful or adopts masculine characteristics, she has to convince others that, underneath it all, she is still a "lady." Presenting a powerful mythical figure such as Mother Nature doing something so menial (really, does she have to do this for every woman, each and every month?) undermines her powers.

Mother Nature's task is recognized by the participants as a violation to the front menstruators are encouraged to construct. The menstruators recognize the importance of keeping their identities concealed as some look visibly bothered and others surprised that Mother Nature would broach such a topic in public, much less present them with a visual representation of their period. Mother Nature's violation of the menstrual front also violates her allegiance to her team. Menstruators may be thought of as a team as "the performance serves mainly to express the characteristics of the task that is performed, not the characteristics of the performer."[66] Performances related to menstruation, or rather the lack of such a performance, are expressly intended to remind the performers (and the audience) that this identity must remain invisible. Women are encouraged to prevent any seepage (both figuratively and literally) of the menstrual role since women's performance of femininity and the process of menstruation are at odds. Through her discrepant actions, Mother Nature functions as a purveyor of patriarchy—she is a director for the team, but her actions violate the menstrual front.

As Goffman notes, the director has the duty of bringing any team members' unsuitable performances back into line and is permitted to allocate the parts of the performance.[67] On the surface, it appears that through her act of gifting, Mother Nature is able to bring menstruators into line who may be embarrassed by their periods; however, Mother Nature's violations of the front and back regions suggest that she is the one who is out of line. Goffman notes that directors correct improper appearances, allocate major and minor prerogatives, and may cause other team members to feel estranged.[68] The sense of estrangement is evident in this campaign. The team members in the video do not identify with Mother Nature; she is viewed as the "other," the rule violator. As such, while the women may finally take Mother Nature's gift, they do not accept her as one of their own; Mother Nature is, as Goffman predicts, "slowly edged into a marginal role between audience and performers."[69] It is not clear in this artifact whether Mother Nature herself menstruates any longer (on her Facebook page, she admits that she's 4.5 billion years old and no longer menstruates), which adds to her liminal status. Whatever the case, the team members' reactions to Mother Nature indicate she is not really delivering any "gifts." Rather, the women's reactions remind viewers that menstruation is to be unwelcome and kept hidden.

Emphasizing her femininity may also help Mother Nature as her manner and tactics clearly violate the norms traditionally associated with the front and back regions related to the performance of menstruation. Although she operates (and violates codes) within the public sphere, she reminds viewers through her inappropriate behavior that menstruation truly belongs in the private sphere. Most menstruators know the lavatory is the one constant back stage setting; there, they may scrutinize their clothing to make sure no seepage has occurred and ensure their identities remain concealed. The front regions, ideally any place except the lavatory, are areas where menstruators can still prove they are feminine by concealing evidence of menstruation. When Mother Nature begins "gifting" team members, she commits a serious breach by bringing backstage behavior to the front region.

Mother Nature also reveals team secrets. The act of menstruating represents a dark secret for most women. Women are taught to go to great lengths to conceal any signs of the menstrual cycle as those signs are incompatible with the feminine image women are encouraged to project. By "outing" menstruators in public, Mother Nature violates the trust of the team. Through her euphemistic use of the word "gift," Mother Nature also violates insider secrets. Menstruators have long used euphemisms to discuss the menstrual cycle in "appropriate" (i.e., "ladylike") terms, but viewers are not to believe that Mother Nature (or anyone else) really considers menstruation a gift. Her sardonic nature reaffirms the belief that menstruation should actually be referred to as "the curse."

Finally, Mother Nature's actions demonstrate how the males in the artifact enact "entrusted secrets." While Mother Nature discloses menstruators' secrets (e.g., "Isn't it terrible she always gets it on Saturday nights?"), the men remain silent or, as is the case with one man, respond with uncomfortable laughter. The men in the video demonstrate their ability to avoid mentioning menstruation because of their relation to the team of menstruators. Admittedly, this video was edited and some men may have responded by offering information about their partners' periods, but the campaign chose to show men not engaging in that behavior. Thus, for some viewers, Mother Nature becomes a traitor to other women, and by contrast men become trustworthy because they do not comment on the menstrual secret.

To prevent incidents and the resulting embarrassment, team members must exhibit dramaturgical loyalty, discipline, and circumspection. Mother Nature clearly does not exhibit any loyalty to menstruators in her discrepant role. She is more interested in completing her own tasks than protecting her "daughters." As Gibson and Heyse note, "Although there are many variations of symbolic motherhood, the maternal persona is consistently described as anchored by the values of interconnection and nurturance. . . . These central values follow from what scholars describe as the traditionally maternal practices of empathy and caregiving."[70] Mother Nature exhibits no traces of empathy: why would she keep pushing her gift on menstruators when they clearly do not want it? Mother Nature also exhibits an inability to function as a caregiver: she seems more concerned about her own appearance—making sure no hair is out of place and that she completes all of her occupational tasks—than the well-being of her "daughters." Mother Nature's "daughters" are physically healthy (otherwise, they would not be receiving their periods), but their emotional well-being is jeopardized by Mother Nature's actions.

While it may seem liberating that Mother Nature is bringing menstruation into public view, the women's reactions reveal she is only making these women *more* embarrassed about discussing menstruation in public. This action is illustrated by Glenn's description of the motherhood paradox: "Mothers are romanticized as life giving, self-sacrificing, and forgiving, and demonized as smothering, overly involved, and destructive."[71] Mother Nature, as an environmental force, is known for her destructive nature. In the Tampax campaign, viewers are allowed to witness firsthand Mother Nature's ability to smother, be overly involved, and expose a menstruator's identity. This mother may well believe she is bringing gifts (though this is highly unlikely); however, her complete disregard of the consequences marks her as self-centered at best and malicious at worst.

Mother Nature also lacks dramaturgical discipline. Goffman notes the importance of this concept: "A performer who is disciplined, dramaturgically speaking, is someone who remembers [her or] his part and does not commit unmeant gestures or faux pas in performing it."[72] While she may try to use humor to defuse the breach in her performance of the menstrual front, Mother Nature is unable to reduce the significance of her disruption. Even when the first woman in the video informs Mother Nature that she has no desire to accept her gift, Mother Nature relentlessly chases her down until the woman gives in.

Finally, Mother Nature lacks dramaturgical circumspection. Goffman notes that a disciplined performer should have the "presence of mind" to present a plausible reason for disruptions in a performance and cover up inappropriate team member behavior.[73] Mother Nature is antithetical to dramaturgical discipline: she behaves without caution, not seeming to care that audiences other than team members are around when she engages in back stage talk and behavior with menstruators. The song in the video also cues viewers that Mother Nature is behaving badly, is unavoidable, and can drive women mad.

Conclusion

With her aggressive and careless manner, Mother Nature demonstrates to viewers that the current menstrual front is in place for a reason and should remain so. Thus, while one goal of the campaign may have been to reduce the stigma of menstruation, Mother Nature's actions only serve to reify the belief that menstruation should not be discussed in front regions and that aggressive women, such as Mother Nature, rely on tactics that are less than feminine. As Gibson and Heyse note, "The significant advantage of maternal rhetoric is its potential to introduce feminine values into public life that have previously been disqualified by the scripts of hegemonic masculinity."[74] Rather than provide menstruators with a feasible way to reduce the stigma of menstruation, Mother Nature presents a ludicrous notion of how menstrual taboos can be broken: a mythical figure will appear and give women their periods, pointing out the differences between men and women's bodies (something patriarchal ideology uses to subjugate women).

While this campaign may have attempted to empower women, all Mother Nature manages to do is encourage viewers to dislike (or even hate) her, which, in turn, encourages women to dislike their own bodies. By bracketing off the menstrual experience from their own bodies and transferring their disdain for their menstrual cycle to Mother Nature, women are encouraged to disassociate themselves from their bodies, making it more likely that women will continue to view their menstruating bodies in a "one-down" position.

In trying to present younger viewers with a worthy adversary, the "Outsmart Mother Nature with Tampax" campaign seems to have outsmarted itself. Mother Nature is constructed as a shrill, unlikable woman. This is good, Tampax may argue, because now menstruators may turn their disdain for menstruation toward Mother Nature. What Mother Nature ultimately serves to do, however, is present negative messages about menstruation, just as the mothers in Costos, Ackerman, and Paradis's study did.[75] Mother Nature becomes someone to be feared, and by extension, so does the arrival of one's menstrual cycle.

This analysis demonstrates that Mother Nature is a bad mother; that is, one who does not care about her daughters and only has her own goals in mind. When discussing the dangers of the faux maternal performance, Gibson and Heyse note, "Although we recognize and appreciate that motherhood is complex and that it is experienced and expressed in a variety of legitimate ways, the rhetorical person of motherhood has repeatedly been authenticated through its connection to nurturance, empathy, and community. Divorced from these traditionally maternal values, maternal appeals may simply be a guise for masculinist politics."[76] The Tampax version of motherhood is one example of such masculinist politics. Mother Nature functions as any other artifact developed by the fem-care companies, serving to remind viewers of the dangers of the hygienic crises they face as menstruators and perpetuating a negative view of menstruation and, consequently, women's bodies.

Notes

1. A Google search using the following string yielded 10,400,000 results in .29 seconds: "how to delay having my period on my wedding day." Results included information from more general websites (e.g., Yahoo and eHow), wedding websites (e.g., weddingwire.com and weddingbee.com), and even medical websites (e.g., the Mayo Clinic and NetDoctor).

2. For further explanation, see Germaine Greer, *The Change: Women, Aging, and the Menopause* (New York: Fawcett Columbine, 1991) and Gail Sheehy, *The Silent Passage: Menopause* (New York: Simon and Schuster, 1998).

3. Megan K. Beckett, Marc N. Elliot, Steven Martino, David E. Kanouse, Rosalie Corona, David J. Klein, and Mark A. Schuster, "Timing of Parent and Child Communication About Sexuality Relative to Children's Sexual Behavior" *Pediatrics* 125 (2010): 34–43. Beckett, et al. found 34.2 percent of their sample, which consisted of 73 percent mothers, discussed menstruation with daughters before it occurred and that 13.1 percent of the sample discussed menstruation with their daughters after it occurred, whereas 9.7 percent of the sample discussed menstruation with their sons prior to menstruators' average age, and 55.5 percent discussed menstruation with their sons after it was likely their peers had begun menstruating.

4. Since this project focuses on an advertising campaign created by Tampax, I grudgingly adopt the industry terminology of "fem-care" but would also like to point to the problematic nature of other terms associated with these products (i.e., when one uses the term "feminine hygiene" or "feminine protection," the implicit logic suggests that women are unclean and must be protected from themselves).

5. See, for example, Jessica B. Gillooly, *Before She Gets Her Period: Talking with Your Daughter About Menstruation* (Glendale, CA: Perspective Publishing, 1998) and Lynda Madaras with Area Madaras, *The "What's Happening to My Body" Book for Girls* (New York, New Market Press, 2007).

6. Dacia Charlesworth, "Paradoxical Constructions of Self: Educating Young Women About Menstruation," *Women and Language* 24 (2001): 13–20; Mindy J. Erchull, Joan C. Chrisler, Jennifer A. Gorman, and Ingrid Johnston-Robledo, "Education and Advertising: A Content Analysis of Commercially Produced Booklets About Menstruation," *Journal of Early Adolescence* 22 (2002): 455–74.

7. Beverly Havens and Ingrid Swenson, "A Content Analysis of Educational Media About Menstruation," *Adolescence* 24 (1989): 901–7.

8. Beverly Havens and Ingrid Swenson, "Imagery Associated with Menstruation in Advertising Targeted to Adolescent Women," *Adolescence* 23 (1988): 89–97; Debra Merskin, "Adolescence, Advertising, and the Ideology of Menstruation," *Sex Roles* 40 (1999): 941–57; M. R. Simes and D. H. Berg, "Surreptitious Learning: Menarche and Menstrual Product Advertisements," *Health Care for Women International* 22 (2001): 455–69; Ann Treneman, "Cashing in on the Curse: Advertising and the Menstrual Taboo," in *The Female Gaze: Women as Viewers of Popular Culture*, eds. Lorraine Gamman and Margaret Marshment (Seattle: The Real Comet Press, 1989), 153–65.

9. Joan C. Chrisler and Paula Caplan, "The Strange Case of Dr. Jekyll and Ms. Hyde: How PMS Became a Cultural Phenomenon and a Psychiatric Disorder," *Annual Review of Sex Research* 13 (2002): 274–306.

10. Lynn E. Whisnant, Elizabeth Brett, and Leonard Zegans, "Implicit Messages Concerning Menstruation in Commercial Education Material Prepared for Young Adolescent Girls," *American Journal of Psychiatry* 132 (1975): 815–20.

11. Janice Delaney, Mary Jane Lupton, and Emily Toth, *The Curse: A Cultural History of Menstruation* (Toronto: Clarke, Irwin and Co., 1976).

12. Judith Butler, "Variations on Sex and Gender: Beauvoir, Wittig, Foucault," in *Feminism as Critique*, eds. Seyla Benhabib and Drucilla Cornell (Minneapolis, MN: University of Minnesota Press, 1987), 135.

13. Candace West and Don H. Zimmerman, "Doing Gender," *Gender and Society* 1 (1987): 126.

14. West and Zimmerman, "Doing Gender," 125–51.

15. West and Zimmerman, "Doing Gender," 127.

16. West and Zimmerman, "Doing Gender," 127.

17. West and Zimmerman, "Doing Gender," 127.

18. Marilyn Frye, *The Politics of Reality: Essays in Feminist Theory* (Trumansburg, New York: The Crossing Press, 1983), 34.

19. Marilyn French, *The War Against Women* (New York: Summit Books, 1992), 172–73, emphasis in original.

20. Kenneth Burke, *A Rhetoric of Motives* (Berkeley: University of California Press, 1969), 41.

21. Burke, *A Rhetoric of Motives* 26, emphasis in original.

22. Burke, *A Rhetoric of Motives*, 88.

23. Burke, *A Rhetoric of Motives*, 88.

24. Butler, "Variations," 131.

25. Carol Tavris, *The Mismeasure of Woman* (New York: Simon and Schuster, 1992).

26. Havens and Swenson, "Content Analysis," 901–7.

27. Janice M. Morse and Helen McKinnon Doan, "Adolescents' Response to Menarche," *Journal of School Health* 57 (1987): 385–89; Whisnant, Brett, and Zegans, "Implicit Messages," 815–20.

28. Havens and Swenson, "Imagery Associated with Menstruation," 89–97.

29. Merskin, "Adolescence," 941–57.

30. Morse and Doan, "Adolescents' Response to Menarche," 385–89.

31. Jeanne Brooks-Gunn and Diane N. Ruble, "The Development of Menstrual-Related Beliefs and Behaviors During Early Adolescence," *Child Development* 53 (1982): 1567–77.

32. Joan C. Chrisler, "Age, Gender-Role Orientation, and Attitudes Toward Menstruation," *Psychology Reports* 63 (1988): 827–34.

33. Anne Walker, "Men's and Women's Beliefs About the Influence of the Menstrual Cycle on Academic Performance: A Preliminary Study," *Journal of Applied Social Psychology* 22 (1992): 896–909.

34. Havens and Swenson, "Imagery Associated with Menstruation," 89–97.

35. Havens and Swenson, "Content Analysis," 901–7.

36. As cited in Daryl Costos, Ruthie Ackerman, and Lisa Paradis, "Recollections of Menarche: Communication Between Mothers and Daughters Regarding Menstruation," *Sex Roles* 46 (2002): 49–59.

37. Elizabeth A. Kissling, "Bleeding out Loud: Communication About Menstruation," *Feminism and Psychology* 6 (1996): 481–504.

38. Greer Litton Fox and Judith K. Inazu, "Mother-Daughter Communication About Sex," *Family Relations* 29 (1980): 347–52.

39. Spring C. Cooper and Patricia B. Koch, "'Nobody Told Me Nothin': Communication About Menstruation Among Low-Income African-American Women," *Women and Health* 46 (2007): 57–78.

40. Cooper and Patricia B. Koch, "'Nobody Told Me Nothin.'"

41. Andrew Adam Newman, "A Campaign That Erases a Layer of Euphemisms," *New York Times*, March 19, 2009, accessed January 3, 2012, http://www.nytimes.com/2009/03/20/business/media/20adco.html?pagewanted=all.

42. Amy Golding, "Tampax to Launch 'Nature' Activity," *Marketing*, April 29, 2009, 8.

43. Newman, "Campaign."

44. Newman, "Campaign."

45. Effie Worldwide "exists to provide information regarding effectiveness and results in marketing communications. Its main priority is to educate and share with the industry (and all interested parties) its wisdom and definition of effectiveness by spotlighting great ideas that work and encouraging thoughtful dialogue about the ever-changing world of marketing communications." See "About Effie Worldwide," Effie Worldwide, accessed January 3, 2012, http://www.effie.org/about.

46. Herbert Blummer, *Symbolic Interactionism: Perspective and Method* (Berkeley: University of California Press, 1986), 2.

47. West and Zimmerman, "Doing Gender."

48. Erving Goffman, *The Presentation of Self in Everyday Life* (New York: Doubleday, 1959), 35.

49. Goffman, *Presentation of Self*, 22.

50. Goffman, *Presentation of Self*, 22.

51. Goffman, *Presentation of Self*, 85.

52. Goffman, *Presentation of Self*, 85.

53. Goffman, *Presentation of Self*, 85.

54. Goffman, *Presentation of Self*, 27.

55. Goffman, *Presentation of Self*, 91.

56. Goffman, *Presentation of Self*, 79.

57. Goffman, *Presentation of Self*, 81.

58. Goffman, *Presentation of Self*, 97.

59. Goffman, *Presentation of Self*, 98–99.

60. Goffman, *Presentation of Self*, 107, 112.

61. Goffman, *Presentation of Self*, 141.

62. Goffman, *Presentation of Self*, 142.

63. Goffman, *Presentation of Self*, 143.

64. Goffman, *Presentation of Self*, 144–45.

65. Abigail M. Feeder, "A Radiant Smile from the Lovely Lady: Overdetermined Femininity in 'Ladies' Figure Skating," *Drama Review* 38 (1994): 62–78.

66. Goffman, *Presentation of Self*, 77.

67. Goffman, *Presentation of Self*, 98–99.

68. Goffman, *Presentation of Self*, 99.

69. Goffman, *Presentation of Self*, 99.

70. Katie L. Gibson and Amy L. Heyse, "'The Difference Between a Hockey Mom and a Pit Bull': Sarah Palin's Faux Maternal Persona and Performance of Hegemonic Masculinity at the 2008 Republican National Convention," *Communication Quarterly* 58 (2010), 238.

71. Evelyn N. Glenn, "Social Constructions of Mothering: A Thematic Overview," in *Mothering, Ideology, Experience, and Agency*, eds. Evelyn N. Glenn, Grace Chang, and Linda N. Forcey (New York: Routledge, 1994), 11.

72. Goffman, *Presentation of Self*, 216.

73. Goffman, *Presentation of Self*, 216.

74. Gibson and Heyse, "Social Constructions of Mothering," 239.

75. Cooper and Patricia B. Koch, "'Nobody Told Me Nothin'."

76. Gibson and Heyse, "Social Constructions of Mothering," 253.

Bibliography

Beckett, Megan K., Marc N. Elliot, Steven Martino, David E. Kanouse, Rosalie Corona, David J. Klein, and Mark A. Schuster. "Timing of Parent and Child Communication About Sexuality Relative to Children's Sexual Behavior." *Pediatrics* 125 (2010): 34–43.

Blummer, Herbert. *Symbolic Interactionism: Perspective and Method*. Berkeley: University of California Press, 1986.

Brooks-Gunn, Jeanne, and Diane N. Ruble. "The Development of Menstrual-Related Beliefs and Behaviors During Early Adolescence." *Child Development* 53 (1982): 1567–77.

Burke, Kenneth. *A Rhetoric of Motives*. Berkeley: University of California Press, 1969.

Butler, Judith. "Variations on Sex and Gender: Beauvoir, Wittig, Foucault." In *Feminism as Critique*, edited by Seyla Benhabib and Drucilla Cornell. Minneapolis: University of Minnesota Press, 1987.

Charlesworth, Dacia. "Paradoxical Constructions of Self: Educating Young Women About Menstruation." *Women and Language* 24 (2001): 13–20.

Chrisler, Joan C. "Age, Gender-Role Orientation, and Attitudes Toward Menstruation." *Psychology Reports* 63 (1988): 827–34.

Chrisler, Joan C., and Paula Caplan. "The Strange Case of Dr. Jekyll and Ms. Hyde: How PMS Became a Cultural Phenomenon and a Psychiatric Disorder." *Annual Review of Sex Research* 13 (2002): 274–306.

Cooper, Spring C., and Patricia B. Koch. "'Nobody Told Me Nothin': Communication About Menstruation Among Low-Income African-American Women." *Women and Health* 46 (2007): 57–78.

Costos, Daryl, Ruthie Ackerman, and Lisa Paradis. "Recollections of Menarche: Communication Between Mothers and Daughters Regarding Menstruation." *Sex Roles* 46 (2002): 49–59.

Delaney, Janice, Mary Jane Lupton, and Emily Toth. *The Curse: A Cultural History of Menstruation*. Toronto: Clarke, Irwin, and Co., 1976.

Effie Worldwide. "About Effie Worldwide." Accessed January 3, 2012. http://www.effie.org/about.

Erchull, Mindy J., Joan C. Chrisler, Jennifer A. Gorman, and Ingrid Johnston-Robledo. "Education and Advertising: A Content Analysis of Commercially Produced Booklets About Menstruation." *Journal of Early Adolescence* 22 (2002): 455–74.

Feder, Abigail M. "A Radiant Smile from the Lovely Lady: Overdetermined Femininity in 'Ladies' Figure Skating." *Drama Review* 38 (1994): 62–78.

Fox, Greer Litton, and Judith K. Inazu. "Mother-Daughter Communication About Sex." *Family Relations* 29 (1980): 347–52.

French, Marilyn. *The War Against Women*. New York: Summit Books, 1992.

Frye, Marilyn. *The Politics of Reality: Essays in Feminist Theory*. Trumansburg, New York: The Crossing Press, 1983.

Gibson, Katie L., and Amy L. Heyse. "'The Difference Between a Hockey Mom and a Pit Bull': Sarah Palin's Faux Maternal Persona and Performance of Hegemonic Masculinity at the 2008 Republican National Convention." *Communication Quarterly* 58 (2010): 235–56.

Gillooly, Jessica B. *Before She Gets Her Period: Talking with Your Daughter About Menstruation*. Glendale, CA: Perspective Publishing, 1998.

Glenn, Evelyn N. "Social Constructions of Mothering: A Thematic Overview." In *Mothering, Ideology, Experience, and Agency*, edited by Evelyn N. Glenn, Grace Chang, and Linda N. Forcey. New York: Routledge, 1994.

Goffman, Erving. *The Presentation of Self in Everyday Life*. New York: Doubleday, 1959.

Golding, Amy. "Tampax to Launch 'Nature' Activity." *Marketing*, April 29, 2009.

Greer, Germaine. *The Change: Women, Aging, and the Menopause*. New York: Fawcett Columbine, 1991.

Havens, Beverly, and Ingrid Swenson. "A Content Analysis of Educational Media About Menstruation." *Adolescence* 24 (1989): 901–907.

———. "Imagery Associated with Menstruation in Advertising Targeted to Adolescent Women." *Adolescence* 23 (1988): 89–97.

Kissling, Elizabeth A. "Bleeding out Loud: Communication About Menstruation." *Feminism and Psychology* 6 (1996): 481–504.

Madaras, Lynda, with Area Madaras. *The "What's Happening to My Body" Book for Girls*. New York, New Market Press, 2007.

Merskin, Debra. "Adolescence, Advertising, and the Ideology of Menstruation." *Sex Roles* 40 (1999): 941–57.

Morse, Janice M., and Helen McKinnon Doan. "Adolescents' Response to Menarche." *Journal of School Health* 57 (1987): 385–89.

Newman, Andrew Adam. "A Campaign That Erases a Layer of Euphemisms." *New York Times*, March 19, 2009. Accessed January 3, 2012. http://www.nytimes.com/2009/03/20/business/media/20adco.html?pagewanted=all.

Sheehy, Gail. *The Silent Passage: Menopause*. New York: Simon and Schuster, 1998.

Simes, M. R., and D. H. Berg. "Surreptitious Learning: Menarche and Menstrual Product Advertisements." *Health Care for Women International* 22 (2001): 455–69.

Tavris, Carol. *The Mismeasure of Woman*. New York: Simon and Schuster, 1992.

Treneman, Ann. "Cashing in on the Curse: Advertising and the Menstrual Taboo." In *The Female Gaze: Women as Viewers of Popular Culture*, edited by Lorraine Gamman and Margaret Marshment, 153–65. Seattle: The Real Comet Press, 1989.

Walker, Anne. "Men's and Women's Beliefs About the Influence of the Menstrual Cycle on Academic Performance: A Preliminary Study." *Journal of Applied Social Psychology* 22 (1992): 896–909.

West, Candace, and Don H. Zimmerman. "Doing Gender." *Gender and Society* 1 (1987): 125–51.

Whisnant, Lynn E., Elizabeth Brett, and Leonard Zegans. "Implicit Messages Concerning Menstruation in Commercial Education Material Prepared for Young Adolescent Girls." *American Journal of Psychiatry* 132 (1975): 815–20.

Chapter 17

Taking the Audience Perspective: Online Fan Commentary about the Brides of *Mad Men* and Their Weddings

by Lynne M. Webb, Marceline Thompson Hayes, Hao-Chieh Chang, and Marcia M. Smith

Are brides and their weddings hot topics of conversation on *Mad Men* fan websites? Would *Mad Men*'s portrayal of two 1960s weddings (one elaborate, one modest) prompt fans to contrast the two events? Would the conscripted roles of engaged and married women in the 1960s prompt fans to compare brides then to brides now? Do fans engage in feminist deconstructions of *Mad Men*'s portrayals of brides and their weddings? Given the critical acclaim and popularity of *Mad Men*, we wondered what fans of the television show talk about on their fan websites when discussing *Mad Men*'s brides and their weddings. Using Audience Reception Theory as our guide, we content-analyzed comments from eleven popular fan websites to discover fans' interpretations of the show's portrayal of brides and their weddings. For purposes of this study, we defined a fan website, hereafter called a fansite, as any online location devoted primarily to fan discussion of a cultural text.

Literature Review

Mad Men, the television drama created and produced by Matthew Weiner and broadcast on AMC, debuted to great critical acclaim on July 19, 2007. Set in 1960s New York, the series centers on Dan Draper, a highly successful ad man with a shadowy past who serves as creative director at the prestigious Madison Avenue advertising agency Sterling Cooper (later renamed Sterling Cooper Draper Pryce). The series follows Draper and his colleagues in the conflicted 1960s, a cultural background of casual sexism bumping up against burgeoning feminism, ruthless competition played out during the three-martini lunches, rampant gender and racial biases, unapologetic homophobia, and ubiquitous smoking and drinking. Such portrayals hold huge promise for audience appeal, as Stanley noted in her *New York Times* review that followed the premier episode: "There were seven deadly sins practiced at the dawn of the 1960s: smoking, drinking, adultery, sexism, homophobia, anti-Semitism, and racism. In its first few minutes *Mad Men* taps into all of them."[1]

Mad Men has lived up to its early acclaim, garnering numerous nominations and awards, including the Writers Guild of America Award for Best New Series of 2007. The American Film Institute selected *Mad Men* as one of the ten best television series of 2007, 2008, and 2009. *Mad Men* won the Golden Globe for Best Television Series: Drama in

2008, 2009, and 2010 as well as the Screen Actors Guild Award for Outstanding Performance by an Ensemble in a Drama Series in 2008, 2009, and 2010. Finally, *Mad Men* has won fifteen Emmys to date, including the Primetime Emmy Award for Outstanding Drama Series every year in its first four seasons—tying the record for a serial drama.[2] We were curious how fans of this award-winning drama series reacted to the depiction of 1960s brides and their weddings.

Previous Research on Mad Men

Despite its critical acclaim, *Mad Men* has received limited attention from scholars. The few published articles focus primarily on social values and social roles depicted on the show[3] or on contemporary advertising partnerships with *Mad Men* such as Banana Republic's "Mad About Style" guide and contest.[4] No previously published scholarship on *Mad Men* has analyzed fansites or identified fans' interpretations of the show's content. Despite its limited previous analysis, we believe *Mad Men* provides a cultural text ripe for analysis. Guided by Audience Reception Theory, we investigated which aspects of the show's portrayals of brides and their weddings are subjected to analysis and discussion, not in the scholarly literature but rather on fansites.

Audience Reception Theory

Audience Reception Theory, one of the main strands of the culturalist approach, views media use as a significant element in everyday life. Media use is framed as a reflection of a particular social-cultural context and as a process of assigning meaning to cultural products and experiences in our lives.[5] Rejecting both the stimulus-response model of effects and the notion of dominant messages or directive texts, this theory focuses on the media users' *active interpretation and meaning negotiation of media contents*. In other words, the media text must be "read" through the perceptions of its audience members, who construct meanings from the media texts. "As the reader passes through the various perspectives offered by the text, and relates the different views and patterns to one another, [he or she sets] the work in motion, and so [sets his or her] self in motion too."[6] Thus, meanings are activated on reading the cultural text and depend on the interaction between text and reader.

The interaction between text and reader occurs within a framework that controls and limits the interaction through genre, tone, and structure as well as the sociocultural background and life experiences of the reader and the author. In essence, texts are dynamic, meanings are context-dependent, and readings may be divergent across various "interpretive communities."[7] The intended meanings and the meanings interpreted by the readers may vary not only because readers may focus on differing program segments and because texts may target different audiences but also because the same text may evoke varied meanings in various audiences.[8] Therefore, reception research studies the activities of actual audiences to decipher how they interpret texts within contexts. If Audience Reception Theory provides a viable explanation of media processing, then an understanding of *Mad Men*'s portrayals of brides and their weddings is simply not possible without knowing how fans decode the show within interpretive communities such as the virtual communities on fansites.

Audience Reception Theory has been widely applied in empirical research to examine the interpretative relationships between viewers and television programs ranging from primetime dramas to soap operas. For example, Katz and Liebes conducted focus groups to explore viewers' perceptions of cultural imperialism on popular primetime drama *Dallas* across diverse cultural populations.[9] They found each cultural group's reading was based on and constrained by the text, but the interaction between cultural resources and textual openness allowed the negotiation of quite different readings of a given episode. Livingstone asked regular viewers of the British soap opera *Coronation Street* to recall a key incident involving several characters over a year after the episode was aired. Viewers' interpretive stances (e.g., their romantic versus cynical readings of such an incident) corresponded with their identification with, liking of, and sympathy for key characters in their narratives.[10] By examining the discussion on *Mad Men*'s fansites, we seek to identify the elements of the show's portrayals of brides and their weddings that prompted postings, discussion, and analysis.

Research on Fansites

Two behaviors distinguish fans from audience members: 1) fans actively attempt to decode, understand, make sense of, or interpret messages rather than simply accepting the messages as passive observers, and 2) fans faithfully participate in fan communities associated with the object of fandom, in this case the *Mad Men*, rather than observing and processing messages simply as individuals. Kirby-Diaz contends that fans watch and dissect each episode of a television series, become immersed in characters, long for character development, and live vicariously through characters' experiences.[11] Fans typically commit to a fandom—a fan culture that develops around a specific entertainment phenomenon and often engages in the ongoing interpretation of currently serialized television programs. Despite the existence of numerous fansites and increasing academic interest in fansites, few studies directly inquire how fans interpret television shows.

Despite a long and continuing tradition of content analysis of media-related texts,[12] researchers have published few content analyses of fansite commentary. Instead, research on fans' online activities examines fans' general behaviors in the virtual community,[13] how fans develop a sense of community,[14] practices and characteristics of fans' virtual communities,[15] fans' degree of media literacy in making sense of a show's special features,[16] participatory culture,[17] and implications for TV programs' marketing and managerial strategies.[18]

Only three studies analyze the content of fansites.[19] Bury compares fans' interpretative strategies on two fansites dedicated to the American drama series *Six Feet Under*, originally aired on HBO. She found fans posting on the non-elite fansite (e.g., HBO official site) and those posting on the elite fansite (e.g., Television Without Pity) use similar interpretative strategies to negotiate meanings with fellow fans when attempting to make sense of a relatively open text involving an ambiguous pregnancy narrative of a minor character. Bury reports that fans from both fansites are equally critical of the text and respectful of the authorial meaning.[20] Walters demonstrates that fans discuss the intersection of gender and race concerns as portrayed by differing funeral practices, and she advocates the use of fansites as a vehicle for activism.[21]

Kirby-Diaz examines favorite topics on four fansites of *Buffy the Vampire Slayer* and its spin-off *Angel* in relation to Spike—the most popular character in the Buffyverse, according to the syndication's demographic research. Topics discussed by fans included the main cast, possible storylines, plot arcs, and relationships that might occur.[22]

The findings of these three studies illustrate fans' participation in virtual communities and their active role in negotiating meanings of media texts. These findings illustrate the viability of studying the content of fansites to gain a better understanding of how the fans decode and interpret portrayals on TV shows. Bury's and Kirby-Diaz's research provide germinal steps in this direction, but their findings are constrained by methodological limitations.[23] The scholars subjectively selected limited fansites for comparison and analysis. Thus, findings from these studies may not be representative of the content on all fansites. Our study, based on selecting the longest threads on all eleven *Mad Men* fansites, definitively identifies the topics of conversation about *Mad Men* brides and their weddings.

Previous Research on Brides

Communication scholars' previous research on brides and weddings has been simultaneously diverse and limited. Topics vary widely from trafficking Internet brides[24] to wedding planning[25] and from Hindu wedding rituals[26] to wedding anniversaries as a public component of private relationships.[27] In addition, lines of research examine cultural wedding practices[28] as well as feminist critiques of weddings.[29] We could locate no previously published research examining fictional televised portrayals of brides or weddings, however. Instead, scholars explain reality television portrayals of weddings[30] and news coverage of actual weddings such as the royal wedding of Kate Middleton to Prince William.[31] Such examinations ignore how fans decode messages.

Purpose and Research Question

Our study follows in the tradition of four previous lines of research: (a) research on Audience Reception Theory, (b) scholarship examining *Mad Men*, (c) studies of fansites, and (d) research on televised brides and weddings. Our research is unique in featuring the first content analysis of representative posts from the fansites devoted to one TV show following its first three seasons. It also offers the first systematic and detailed examination of fan feedback on the cultural text *Mad Men*. Further, our research provides a first application of Audience Reception Theory to an array of fansites simultaneously. Finally, we present the first analysis of fictional, televised portrayals of brides and their weddings. Thus, our purpose was to discover fans' conversational topics concerning brides and their weddings on the fansites devoted to *Mad Men* during its first three broadcast seasons.

Method

Sampling and Procedures

We gathered data just weeks before the beginning of *Mad Men*'s fourth season. The third season features the first detailed scenes of a bride, Margaret Sterling, as well as an extensive portrayal of her wedding. This season also contains references to (although no footage of) the Draper wedding, a much discussed phenomenon on fansites. Previous and subsequent seasons do not feature brides or weddings in a prominent way.

To identify fansites, we searched for the phrase "Mad Men" on seven popular websites users might rationally employ searching for fansites (Bing, Facebook, Google, Google Blogs, MySpace, Yahoo, and YouTube). We looked at the first three pages of results from each website, clicking on links to discover websites where fans posted comments. This screening process yielded thirty websites. Next, we closely examined each of the thirty websites to exclude (a) duplicate web addresses, (b) websites where *Mad Men* was not discussed, (c) websites where fans commented on mass media stories about *Mad Men* rather than about the show itself, and (d) web addresses to blogs focused on matters other than *Mad Men* and garnering fewer than ten posters in response to the occasional blog entry on *Mad Men*. The remaining eleven fansites constituted our sampling frame, which included websites devoted exclusively to *Mad Men* fan commentary, discussion boards devoted to *Mad Men* on larger websites, and blogs focused primarily on *Mad Men* that attracted more than ten posters.

Next, working in reverse chronological order, we downloaded the five longest strings of conversation (those with the most comments) appearing on each of the eleven fansites. We cut and pasted the fifty-five strings into text files, creating a permanent copy of the fan discussions. Next, we searched the files using the keyword "bride," which appeared in seven of the fifty-five strings. Then, we searched the same seven files for the keyword "wedding," identifying 128 pages of text containing one or both keywords. The 128 pages comprised the text we analyzed in this study; they contained 10 incidences of the word "bride" and 175 incidences of the word "wedding."

Coding and Analysis

We employed a grounded theory approach to coding.[32] The unit of analysis was the individual post or, for long posts, the individual idea expressed within the post. All themes emerged from the data; we imposed no a priori categories on the data. Any idea stated by three or more posters across one or more fansites was considered a theme. To locate themes, two coders read the sampled portions of the files, discovering themes as they emerged. Data examined later led to the revision of earlier categories via a constant comparison process. After coding independently, the coders conferred via telephone to compare findings. They independently coded the majority of themes identically. One coder suggested four unique themes, which the other coder agreed were present in the data. Together the coders identified three supra-themes: feminist concerns, cultural framing, and weddings as social occasions. We also noted ideas absent from discussion that the reader might reasonably expect to be present. Each of these four overarching categories is discussed in detail below.

Results and Discussion

Fans' conversations about brides and their weddings focus primarily on two weddings featured prominently in Season Three: Margaret Sterling's wedding on the day after John F. Kennedy's assassination and the Draper wedding attended by family only from bride Betty's side. Also present are rare references to the engaged Joan's impending wedding and to Jane, Roger's former secretary and second wife, his "child bride."

Feminist Concerns

The first supra-theme, feminist concerns, contains the two ideas widely critiqued by feminists but discussed naively by fans: attire ("That brocade suit with the fur collar that Betty wore to the wedding—how do you spell M-A-T-R-O-N-L-Y?" "Trudy's blue dress was to die for.") and brides' weight ("I think her [Joan's] initial weight 'gain' may have been due to the (VERY) temporary 'happiness' she had (or thought she had) at the beginning of her marriage, where calories are ignored after the wedding."). In contrast, the fans provide feminist critique on the topics of child brides and symbolic use of color.

The fans widely discuss wedding attire but mention only female characters' attire. Such a finding is consistent with Filak's claim that images of ideal female beauty comprise the majority of bridal magazines' content, thus pointing the focus of real-world observers to wedding attire and bridal weight, the foundation of female image.[33] Moreover, images of brides offer the ideal standard of the perfect bride as being White, thin, and pretty[34] and rarely African American.[35] In contemporary "Bridezilla" wedding culture, where brides control every aspect of weddings, brides must appear feminine[36] as the identification with brides and femininity is assumed in our culture. Thus, the emergence of the theme of women's wedding attire in our analysis is consistent with cultural notions of weddings and brides.

In contrast, fans offer feminist interpretations of *Mad Men*'s portrayals of child-brides ("Roger's mid-life crisis child bride is so pathetic; 'you look foolish' as Don aptly put it"). Roger Sterling's relationship with his young, beautiful wife is the subject of ridicule on both the show and fansites. The very act of taking a young wife to replace the "old" wife during the husband's midlife crisis reinforces the equating of female worth with youth and beauty.[37]

We also placed the symbolic use of color in the supra-theme of feminist concerns. Fans note, "Margaret is wearing a blue dress in this scene. She feels trapped by the impending wedding and only reluctantly commits after Roger's threats. Again, this corresponds to the idea of blue representing confining institutions, not new ones (the institution of marriage being the ultimate confining institution in *Mad Men*)." Fans discuss *Mad Men*'s use of the color blue as representing women's confinement within conservative institutions such as marriage. Consistent with feminist critiques of weddings,[38] the fans only discuss color in relation to women's attire.

Cultural Framing

The second supra-theme, cultural framing, contains the themes of "big" wedding ("Margaret wanted to get married; she emphatically didn't want a big wedding. She's been bullied by her parents to have it."), disaster wedding ("a note of comedy in the disastrous wedding; probably harbinger of that marriage as well."), and references to popular media ("Betty's robe looks just like Gwyneth Paltrow and Colin Firth's wedding outfits in *Shakespeare in Love*. It was terribly distracting."). The fans' descriptions of "big" weddings are consistent with Engstrom and Semic's description of the American cultural tradition of the "white wedding" (a wedding with many standard traditions such as a white gown and large reception).[39] The theme of disaster wedding references the failure of a planned "big" wedding. For example, multiple fans use the label "disaster" to describe Margaret's planned wedding reception in a spacious, beautifully decorated room with mounds of food and few guests. In sum, fans interpret the text of *Mad Men*'s weddings in terms consistent with previous research identifying cultural wedding practices.[40]

Finally, fans often reference popular culture media texts beyond *Mad Men* when explaining their takes on *Mad Men*. Such references include novels (Mary McCarthy's 1963 *The Group* and Dorothy West's 1996 *The Wedding*), other television shows (*Bridezillas* and *The Wedding* miniseries), and films (the 1946 Bette Davis film *A Stolen Life*, *Four Weddings and a Funeral*, and *Shakespeare in Love*). Audience Reception Theory frames media use as a process of giving meaning to cultural products and experiences in our lives.[41] It appears *Mad Men* fans use additional popular media texts to give meaning to Man Men's brides and weddings.

Weddings as Social Occasions

The third and final supra-theme, weddings as social occasions, contain the themes of attendance (see below), appropriate wedding behavior ("You are at your stepdaughter's wedding. Grow up and realize that there are other things going on and other obligations than sitting in front of the television"; "If Jane was going to weep and carry on at the wedding, she should have stayed home."), and weddings as time markers ("Several weeks have elapsed since the wedding. During that time . . ."). Fans widely discuss who attends both Margaret's and the Draper wedding ("Roger would wonder about HF showing up at the wedding escorted by his daughter."), who does not attend ("Somebody doesn't have relatives at their wedding, they must be slimy."), why guests attend/do not attend ("When they both stayed home from the wedding, their bond was solidified."), and the consequences of attendance versus nonattendance. Because President Kennedy is assassinated the day before Margaret's wedding, some fans laud characters for deciding to remain at home and watch the television coverage rather than attending the wedding: "My respect for Pete shot up 100% when he decided not to attend the 'spoiled brat's' wedding." Other fans complain about characters' rudeness when failing to attend the wedding: "I know people were shocked/saddened, but that just seemed incredibly rude [to not attend the wedding reception]." Fans' disagreement about the appropriateness of attendance versus nonattendance is consistent with Audience Reception Theory's notion that meanings of media texts may be divergent.[42] Indeed, while fans across multiple websites engage in earnest debate about what, if anything, can justify absence from a wedding after committing to attend, for all these posters, wedding attendance clearly represents an important part of the protocol for important social occasions.

In addition to attendance, fans widely discuss appropriate social behavior at weddings, praising characters for certain behaviors ("For the first time in ages, I started liking Roger again when he made that poignant toast.") but primarily chiding characters for their inappropriate behaviors ("If she wanted to be there [at the wedding], the least she could do was get her butt out from the kitchen."). The fans dissect and evaluate the behavior of virtually every character in the wedding scenes. Such discussion presents weddings as important social occasions that require compliance with a set of expected, "best" behaviors—a widely accepted cultural notion in contemporary U.S. culture. The fans' frequent mention of and allusions to contemporary cultural notions described here as well as in the supra-themes discussed above are consistent with Audience Reception Theory's notion that media use is framed as a reflection of a particular social-cultural context,[43] including contemporary U.S. society.

Finally, fans use Margaret's wedding as a social marker of time. Rather than saying "three weeks ago," they reference the past in terms of "after the wedding" or "before the wedding." One fan uses elements of the wedding to mark time *at the wedding* by describing one social encounter as "long enough for some bridesmaids to come walking by them."

Absent Ideas

We were struck by fans' lone comments that garnered no response, did not become topics of conversation, or only occurred twice across the 128 pages of conversation we analyzed. Many of the lone ideas are commonplace notions about brides and their weddings, including love ("About Margaret's upcoming wedding, he [Roger] couldn't identify with the love they felt.") and wedding details such as kissing, food, and the typical day for weddings (Saturday). Further, only one fan references brides of the 1960s ("In those times . . . brides-to-be were coached on how they should look and behave for their husbands."), and only two fans relate their comments to real-world weddings ("My mother got her wedding gown from the Newark S. Klein. In 1955, $75 was a huge chuck [sic] of change for a garment."). We were particularly surprised by the latter comments garnering little response as many popular press media critics identify *Mad Men* portrayals as 1960s notions but then proceed to use these same ideas to explain contemporary events.[44] In contrast, these fans appear totally engaged in the world of *Mad Men* to the point where the notion of the cultural timeframe of the 1960s as "the past" disappears and *Mad Men* occurs in the twenty-first century. Indeed, the fans offer a critique of *Mad Men*'s 1960s behavior via contemporary norms and values. Concurrently, fans talk infrequently about their off-line lives. Perhaps fans writing on fansites do so to escape the reality of their lives and thus avoid discussion of their "real" lives.

Summary of Findings

Audience Reception Theory argues that a media text must be "read" through the perceptions of its audience, who construct meanings from media texts. Taking this notion as a guide, our analysis indicates that the fans discussing brides and their weddings on *Mad Men*'s fansites did *not* perceive the *Mad Men* text as linking marriage to love or subjugating women in terms of weight or attire. Rather, the fans "read" the text as discussing attendance and appropriate behavior at "big," disaster weddings. Further, the fans "read" child-brides as a negative phenomenon. Finally, the fans "read" these texts using the symbolic use of color, references to popular media, and weddings as social markers of time.

We limited our analysis to *Mad Men* fansites. Given that there are only three previous content analyses of fansites, it is difficult to ascertain whether our observations of common topics of conversation about brides and their weddings are typical of all fansites or unique to *Mad Men* fansites. Further, while we believe our sampling procedures yielded representative comments from *Mad Men* fansites, generalizing the findings to all *Mad Men* fans may be inappropriate since not all fans post on fansites. Finally, while we analyzed our data appropriately in light of our purpose, much information remains in the files for further study. For example, future analyses could examine fan comments about women in the workplace as well as in private life (women as dating partners, wives, mothers, daughters, and friends).

Conclusion

Despite these limitations, our study contributes to an understanding of televised portrayals of brides and their weddings in multiple ways. First, we provide evidence that dialogue on fansites can reveal insights into interpretations of cultural texts such as *Mad Men*'s portrayals of brides. Secondly, our results offer support for Audience Reception Theory by demonstrating that cultural texts such as *Mad Men* can mean different things to different audience members. Thirdly, we studied posts on *Mad Men* fansites to discover how they interpret the "text" of brides and their weddings on the show. Our analyses show that fans engage in multifaceted analyses and interpretations commenting on three supra-themes: feminist concerns (attire, brides' weight, child brides, and the symbolic use of color), cultural framing (references to a "big" wedding, disaster weddings, and popular media), and weddings as social occasions (concerns about attendance, appropriate wedding behavior, and the use of wedding as a time marker). Further, the study identifies absent ideas the fans *elected* not to discuss—ideas that are conspicuous by their absence (explanations of the 1960s, references to real-world weddings, love and marriage). Finally, the discovery of detailed commentary on brides and their weddings proves audiences interpret such texts. In sum, our study demonstrates viewers' active and interpretive role in making sense of *Mad Men*'s brides and their weddings. Our study identified the topics of fan conversations about *Mad Men*'s brides and their weddings that garnered sufficient interest to prompt postings and conversation on fansites.

Notes

1. Alessandra Stanley, "Smoking, Drinking, Cheating, and Selling," *New York Times*, July 19, 2010, Arts Section, E1, New York Edition.

2. "Awards for *Mad Men*," IMDB: Internet Movie Database, accessed April 27, 2012, http://www.imdb.com/title/tt0804503/awards.

3. Rand Richards Cooper, "Fear and Self-Loathing," *Commonweal*, February 27, 2009; Boris Irbic, "Social Values in *Mad Men* and *Revolutionary Road*: Conformity and Loss of the Dream in the Golden Age of Ascendency," *Screen Education* 54 (2009): 78–84; J. M. Tyree, "No Fun: Debunking the 1960's in *Mad Men* and *A Serious Man*," *Film Quarterly* 63 (2010): 33–39; Amanda Vickery, "Mad for It," *History Today* 59 (2009): 51–54.

4. Barbara Lippert, "It's a Mad, Mad World," *Media Week* 19 (2009): 6–9; Barbara Lippert, "*Mad Men* Unvarnished," *Media Week* 20 (2010): 16–17.

5. Denis McQuail, *McQuail's Mass Communication Theory* (Thousand Oaks, CA: Sage, 2000).

6. Wolfgang Iser, "The Reading Process: A Phenomenological Approach," in *Reader-Response Criticism: From Formalism to Post-Structuralism*, ed. Jane P. Tompkins (Baltimore: Johns Hopkins University Press, 1980), 106.

7. Sonia M. Livingstone, "Audience Reception: The Role of the Viewer in Retelling Romantic Drama," London: LSE Research Online, accessed February 6, 2012, http://eprints.lse.ac.uk/999. Originally published in *Mass Media and Society*, ed. James Curran and Michael Gurevitch (London: Arnold Publishing, 1991); McQuail, *McQuail's Mass Communication*.

8. Livingstone, "Audience Reception."

9. Elihu Katz and Tamar Liebes, "Interacting with *Dallas*: Cross Cultural Readings of American TV," *Canadian Journal of Communication* 15 (1990), accessed February 6, 2012, http://www.cjc-online.ca/index.php/journal/article/view/538/444.

10. Sonia M. Livingstone, "Divergent Interpretations of a Television Narrative." *Journal of Communication* 16 (1990): 25–57.

11. Mary Kirby-Diaz, "Buffy, Angel, and the Creation of Virtual Communities," in *Buffy and Angel Conquer the Internet: Essays on Online Fandom*, ed. Mary Kirby-Diaz (Jefferson, NC: McFarland and Company, 2009), 18–41.

12. Charles U. Larson, "A Content Analysis of Media Reporting of the Watergate Hearings," *Communication Reports* 1 (1974): 440–48; Jorg Matthes and Matthias Kohring, "The Content Analysis of Media Frames: Toward Improving Reliability and Validity," *Journal of Communication* 58 (2008): 258–79.

13. Nancy K. Baym, *Tune in, Log on: Soaps, Fandom, and Online Community* (Thousand Oaks, CA: Sage, 2008); Christine A. Wooley, "Visible Fandom: Reading the X-Files through X-Philes," *Journal of Film and Video* 53 (2002): 29–53.

14. Elizabeth S. Bird, "Chatting on Cynthia's Porch: Creating Community in an Email Fan Group," *Southern Communication Journal* 65 (1999): 49–65; Siddhartha Menon, "A Participation Observation Analysis of the Once and Again Internet Message Bulletin Boards," *Television and New Media* 8 (2007): 341–74.

15. Kaarina Nikunen, "The Intermedial Practices of Fandom," *Nordicom Review* 28 (2007): 111–28; Christine Scodari and Jenna L. Felder, "Creating a Pocket Universe: 'Shippers,' Fan Fiction, and the *X-Files* Online," *Communication Studies* 51 (2000): 238–57.

16. Janet M. Jones, "Show Your Real Face/A Fan Study of the UK *Big Brother* Transmissions (2000, 2001, 2002): Investigating the Boundaries Between the Notions of Consumers and Producers of Factual Television," *New Media & Society* 5 (2003): 400–21; Madeleine Shufeldt and Kendra Gale, "Under the (Glue) Gun: Containing and Constructing Reality in Home Makeover TV," *Popular Communication* 5 (2007): 263–82; Ruth Woods, "I Like to See My Worst People Get Voted Off," *Journal of Children and Media* 2 (2008): 129–46.

17. Gunn S. Enli, "Mass Communication Tapping into Participatory Culture: Exploring Strictly Come Dancing and Britain's Got Talent," *European Journal of Communication* 24 (2009): 481–93; Ling Yang, "All for Love: The Corn Fandom, Prosumers, and the Chinese Way of Creating a Superstar," *International Journal of Cultural Studies* 12 (2009): 527–43.

18. Mark Andrejevic, "Watching Television Without Pity: The Productivity of Online Fans," *Television and New Media* 9 (2008): 24–46; Louisa Ha and Sylvia M. Chan-Olmsted, "Enhanced TV as Brand Extension: TV Viewers' Perception of Enhanced TV Features and TV Commerce on Broadcast Networks' Websites," *JMM: The International Journal of Media Management* 3 (2001): 202–13.

19. Rhiannon Bury, "Textual Poaching or Gamekeeping? A Comparative Study of Two *Six Feet Under* Internet Fan Forums," in *New Directions in American Reception Study*, ed. Philip Goldstein and James L. Machor (New York: Oxford University Press, 2009), 289–305; Kirby-Diaz, "Buffy, Angel"; Shannon Walters, "Everyday Life, Everyday Death," *Feminist Media Studies* 11 (2011): 363–78.

20. Bury, "Textual Poaching."

21. Walters, "Everyday Life."

22. Kirby-Diaz, "Buffy, Angel."

23. Bury, "Textual Poaching"; Kirby-Diaz, "Buffy, Angel."

24. Jackie Jones, "Trafficking Internet Brides," *Information and Communications Technology Law* 20 (2011): 19–33.

25. Diana Mathis, "Here Comes the Bride: A Look at Wedding Planning from a Relational Dialectics Perspective," paper presented at the annual meeting of the National Communication Association, Chicago, November 2009.

26. Karen V. Fernandez, Ekant Veer, and John L. Lastovicka, "The Golden Ties That Bind: Boundary Crossing in Diasporic Hindu Wedding Ritual," *Consumption, Markets, and Culture* 14 (2001): 245–65.

27. Wendy Leeds-Hurwitz, "Making Marriage Visible: Wedding Anniversaries as the Public Component of Private Relationships," *Text* 25 (2005): 595–631.

28. Jyotsna Kapur, "An 'Arranged Love' Marriage: India's Neoliberal Turn and the Bollywood Wedding Culture Industry," *Communication, Culture, and Critique* 2 (2009): 221–33; Rosaleen

Oabona, and Brankie Nhlekisana, "The Dual Nature of Setswana Wedding Songs: Expressions of Peace and Conflict within Families," *NAWA Journal of Language and Communications* 1(2007): 74–84.

29. Maria Mastronardi, "Feminist and Feminine: Becoming the Bride," paper presented at the annual meeting of the International Communication Association, Chicago, May 2009; Laura Sloan Patterson, "Why Are All the Fat Brides Smiling?: Body Image and the American Bridal Industry," *Feminist Media Studies* 5 (2005): 243–46; Renee M. Sgroi, "*Joe Millionaire* and Women's Positions: A Question of Class," *Feminist Media Studies* 6 (2006): 281–94.

30. Sgroi, "Joe Millionaire"; Erika Engstrom, "Creation of a New 'Empowered' Female Identity in WE-TV's *Bridezillas*," *Media Report to Women* 37 (2009): 6–12; Erika Engstrom and Beth Semic, "Portrayal of Religion in Reality TV Programming: Hegemony and the Contemporary American Wedding," *Journal of Media and Religion* 2 (2003): 145–64.

31. Ben Grossman, "Have You Made a Royal Investment? (In a Flyover State)," *Broadcasting and Cable* 141 (March 14, 2011): 26; R. Thomas Umstead, "Cable Networks Roll out Red Carpet for Royals," *Broadcasting and Cable* 141 (2011): 22.

32. Juliet Corbin and Anselm Strauss, *Basics of Qualitative Research: Grounded Theory Procedure and Techniques*, 3rd ed. (Newbury Park, CA: Sage, 2008).

33. Vincent F. Filak, "Marriage, Magazines, and Makeup Tips: A Comparative Analysis of *Brides* Magazine and *Glamour* Magazine," paper presented at the annual meeting of the Association for Education in Journalism and Mass Communication, Miami, August 2002.

34. Filak, "Marriage, Magazines."

35. Cynthia M. Frisby and Erika Engstrom, "Always a Bridesmaid, Never a Bride: Portrayals of Women of Color in Bridal Magazines," *Media Report to Women* 34 (2006): 10–14.

36. Engstrom, "Female Identity."

37. Donald Symons, "Beauty Is in the Adaptation of the Beholder: The Evolutionary Psychology of Human Female Sexual Attractiveness," in *Sexual Nature and Sexual Culture*, ed. Paul R. Abramson and Steven D. Pinkerton (Chicago: The University of Chicago, 1995), 80–118.

38. Mastronardi, "Feminist and Feminine"; Patterson, "Fat Brides"; Sgroi, "Joe Millionaire."

39. Engstrom and Semic, "Portrayal of Religion."

40. Kapur, "Arranged Love"; Oabona and Nhlekisana, "The Dual Nature."

41. McQuail, *McQuail's Mass Communication*.

42. Livingstone, "Audience Reception"; McQuail, *McQuail's Mass Communication*.

43. McQuail, *McQuail's Mass Communication*.

44. For example, see Steven Aoun, "2008 Idiot's Box Awards," *Metro Magazine* 159 (2008): 142–50.

Bibliography

Andrejevic, Mark. "Watching Television Without Pity: The Productivity of Online Fans." *Television and New Media* 9 (2008): 24–46.

Aoun, Steven. "2008 Idiot's Box Awards." *Metro Magazine* 159 (2008): 142–50.

"Awards for *Mad Men*." IMDB: Internet Movie Database. Accessed April 27, 2012. http://www.imdb.com/title/tt0804503/awards.

Baym, Nancy K. *Tune in, Log on: Soaps, Fandom, and Online Community*. Thousand Oaks, CA: Sage, 2008.

Bird, Elizabeth S. "Chatting on Cynthia's Porch: Creating Community in an Email Fan Group." *Southern Communication Journal* 65 (1999): 49–65.

Bury, Rhiannon. "Textual Poaching or Gamekeeping? A Comparative Study of Two *Six Feet Under* Internet Fan Forums." In *New Directions in American Reception Study*, edited by Philip Goldstein and James L. Machor, 289–305. New York: Oxford University Press, 2009.

Cooper, Rand Richards. "Fear and Self-Loathing." *Commonweal*, February 27, 2009.

Corbin, Juliet, and Anselm Strauss. *Basics of Qualitative Research: Grounded Theory Procedure and Techniques*, 3rd edition. Newbury Park, CA: Sage, 2008.

Engstrom, Erika. "Creation of a New 'Empowered' Female Identity in WE-TV's *Bridezillas*." *Media Report to Women* 37 (2009): 6–12.

Engstrom, Erika and Beth Semic. "Portrayal of Religion in Reality TV Programming: Hegemony and the Contemporary American Wedding." *Journal of Media and Religion* 2 (2003): 145–64.

Enli, Gunn S. "Mass Communication Tapping into Participatory Culture: Exploring Strictly Come Dancing and Britain's Got Talent." *European Journal of Communication* 24 (2009): 481–93.

Fernandez, Karen V., Ekant Veer, and John L. Lastovicka. "The Golden Ties That Bind: Boundary Crossing in Diasporic Hindu Wedding Ritual." *Consumption, Markets, and Culture* 14 (2001): 245–65.

Filak, Vincent F. "Marriage, Magazines, and Makeup Tips: A Comparative Analysis of *Brides* Magazine and *Glamour* Magazine." Paper presented at the annual meeting of the Association for Education in Journalism and Mass Communication, Miami, August 2002.

Frisby, Cynthia M. and Erika Engstrom. "Always a Bridesmaid, Never a Bride: Portrayals of Women of Color in Bridal Magazines." *Media Report to Women* 34 (2006): 10–14.

Grossman, Ben. "Have You Made a Royal Investment? (In a Flyover State)." *Broadcasting and Cable* 141 (March 14, 2011): 26.

Ha, Louisa, and Sylvia M. Chan-Olmsted. "Enhanced TV as Brand Extension: TV Viewers' Perception of Enhanced TV Features and TV Commerce on Broadcast Networks' Websites." *JMM: The International Journal of Media Management* 3 (2001): 202–13.

Irbic, Boris. "Social Values in *Mad Men* and *Revolutionary Road*: Conformity and Loss of the Dream in the Golden Age of Ascendency." *Screen Education* 54 (2009): 78–84.

Iser, Wolfgang. "The Reading Process: A Phenomenological Approach." In *Reader-Response Criticism: From Formalism to Post-Structuralism*, edited by Jane P. Tompkins, 50–69. Baltimore: Johns Hopkins University Press, 1980.

Jones, Jackie. "Trafficking Internet Brides." *Information and Communications Technology Law* 20 (2011): 19–33.

Jones, Janet M. "Show Your Real Face/A Fan Study of the UK Big Brother Transmissions (2000, 2001, 2002): Investigating the Boundaries Between the Notions of Consumers and Producers of Factual Television." *New Media & Society* 5 (2003): 400–21.

Kapur, Jyotsna. "An 'Arranged Love' Marriage: India's Neoliberal Turn and the Bollywood Wedding Culture Industry." *Communication, Culture, and Critique* 2 (2009): 221–33.

Katz, Elihu, and Tamar Liebes. "Interacting with *Dallas*: Cross Cultural Readings of American TV." Canadian *Journal of Communication* 15 (1990). Accessed February 6, 2012. http://www.cjc-online.ca/index.php/journal/article/view/538/444.

Kirby-Diaz, Mary. "Buffy, Angel, and the Creation of Virtual Communities." In *Buffy and Angel Conquer the Internet: Essays on Online Fandom*, edited by Mary Kirby-Diaz, 18–41. Jefferson, NC: McFarland and Company, 2009.

Larson, Charles U. "A Content Analysis of Media Reporting of the Watergate Hearings." *Communication Reports* 1 (1974): 440–48.

Leeds-Hurwitz, Wendy. "Making Marriage Visible: Wedding Anniversaries as the Public Component of Private Relationships." *Text* 25 (2005): 595–631.

Lippert, Barbara. "It's a Mad, Mad World." *Media Week* 19 (2009): 6–9.

———. "*Mad Men* Unvarnished." *Media Week* 20 (2010): 16–17.

Livingstone, Sonia M. "Audience Reception: The Role of the Viewer in Retelling Romantic Drama." London: LSE Research Online. Accessed February 6, 2012. http://eprints.lse.ac.uk/999. Originally published in *Mass Media and Society*, edited by James Curran and Michael Gurevitch. London: Arnold Publishing, 1991.

———. "Divergent Interpretations of a Television Narrative." *Journal of Communication* 16 (1990): 25–57.

Mastronardi, Maria. "Feminist and Feminine: Becoming the Bride." Paper presented at the annual meeting of the International Communication Association, Chicago, May 2009.

Mathis, Diana. "Here Comes the Bride: A Look at Wedding Planning from a Relational Dialectics Perspective." Paper presented at the annual meeting of the National Communication Association, Chicago, November 2009.
Matthes, Jorg, and Matthias Kohring. "The Content Analysis of Media Frames: Toward Improving Reliability and Validity." *Journal of Communication* 58 (2008): 258–79.
McQuail, Denis. *McQuail's Mass Communication Theory*. Thousand Oaks, CA: Sage, 2000.
Menon, Siddhartha. "A Participation Observation Analysis of the Once and Again Internet Message Bulletin Boards." *Television and New Media* 8 (2007): 341–74.
Nikunen, Kaarina. "The Intermedial Practices of Fandom." *Nordicom Review* 28 (2007): 111–28.
Oabona, Rosaleen, and Brankie Nhlekisana. "The Dual Nature of Setswana Wedding Songs: Expressions of Peace and Conflict within Families." *NAWA Journal of Language and Communications* 1 (2007): 74–84.
Patterson, Laura Sloan. "Why Are All the Fat Brides Smiling?: Body Image and the American Bridal Industry." *Feminist Media Studies* 5 (2005): 243–46.
Scodari, Christine, and Jenna L. Felder. "Creating a Pocket Universe: 'Shippers,' Fan Fiction, and the X-Files Online." *Communication Studies* 51 (2000): 238–57.
Sgroi, Renee M. "*Joe Millionaire* and Women's Positions: A Question of Class." *Feminist Media Studies* 6 (2006): 281–94.
Shufeldt, Madeleine, and Kendra Gale. "Under the (Glue) Gun: Containing and Constructing Reality in Home Makeover TV." *Popular Communication* 5 (2007): 263–82.
Stanley, Alessandra. "Smoking, Drinking, Cheating, and Selling." *New York Times*, July 19, 2010, Arts Section, E1, New York Edition.
Symons, Donald. "Beauty Is in the Adaptation of the Beholder: The Evolutionary Psychology of Human Female Sexual Attractiveness." In *Sexual Nature and Sexual Culture*, edited by Paul R. Abramson and Steven D. Pinkerton, 80–118. Chicago: The University of Chicago, 1995.
Tyree, J. M. "No Fun: Debunking the 1960's in *Mad Men* and *A Serious Man*." *Film Quarterly* 63 (2010): 33–39.
Umstead, R. Thomas. "Cable Networks Roll out Red Carpet for Royals." *Broadcasting and Cable* 141 (2011): 22.
Vickery, Amanda. "Mad for It." *History Today* 59 (2009): 51–54.
Walters, Shannon. "Everyday Life, Everyday Death." *Feminist Media Studies* 11 (2011): 363–78.
Woods, Ruth. "I Like to See My Worst People Get Voted Off." *Journal of Children and Media* 2 (2008): 129–46.
Wooley, Christine A. "Visible Fandom: Reading the X-Files through X-Philes." *Journal of Film and Video* 53 (2002): 29–53.
Yang, Ling. "All for Love: The Corn Fandom, Prosumers, and the Chinese Way of Creating a Superstar." *International Journal of Cultural Studies* 12 (2009): 527–43.

Index

14 Children and Pregnant Again!, 64
19 Kids and Counting, 5, 30, 63–74
ABC, 4, 39–47, 160
abortion, 81, 161, 186, 202, 203
According to Jim, 49
The Addams Family, 91
adultery. *See* affair
affair, 30, 33, 39, 42, 80–84, 143, 146–50, 223
Alexander, Erika, 53
Aliens, 78
All in the Family, 49
Always, 209
AMC, 6, 223–35
the American Dream, 13, 78
American Football Coaches' Wives Association, 170, 171, 173–77
Angel, 226
Angelov, Jimmy, 96, 97
antifeminism. *See* postfeminism
anti-mom blogs, 2, 5, 197–205
Aphrodite, 51
Arthur, Bea, 52
Audience Reception Theory, 2, 223, 224–26, 229, 230, 231

Baby Boom, 78
A Baby Story, 13, 29, 68, 69
The Bachelor, 12
The Bachelorette, 12
Bachmann, Michele, 5, 181–89; Lucas, 183; Marcus, 183
BagNews, 159
Bailey, Sarah, 94–95
Basic Instinct, 79
Being Human, 92
Bewitched, 91
The Biggest Loser, 12
big wedding, 6, 228, 231
bitch, 17–18, 29, 49, 56; song, 51
Blaik, Earl and Merle, 174
Bradshaw, Carrie, 54–56, 58–59
bridal industry. *See* wedding industry
Bridalplasty, 12
bridesmaids, 1, 17
Bridezillas, 1, 4, 11–25, 228, 229
Bridget Jones's Diary, 79
Bucking the Wedding Industry, 20
Buffy the Vampire Slayer, 91, 95–97, 98, 226
Burke, Kenneth, 2–4, 130, 170, 172, 210–11
Burnette, Anne E., 5, 181–93
Bush, George W., 5, 115, 118, 119, 120, 121, 123, 157, 158, 159

Cake Boss, 30
Campbell, Karlyn Kohrs, 115, 116, 156
Campbell, Pete, 229
Casper, Mary Frances, 4, 27–38
Cattrall, Kim, 54
Chang, Hao-Chieh, 5, 223–35
Charlesworth, Dacia, 5, 209–22
Charmed, 91–97
child archetype, 5, 49, 51–56, 58, 59, 129, 182
child brides, 6, 103–11, 227, 228, 231
childless/childfree women, 6, 81, 163, 188
Christianity, 5, 44, 63–70, 95, 96, 98, 181, 186
Chuyia, 104–5, 107–11
Clark, Paige, 57
Clinton, Hillary, 129, 133, 181, 189
cluster criticism, 131, 134, 172–74
Coles, Kim, 53
Collins, Patricia Hill, 202
compulsory heterosexuality. *See* heteronormativity
Congress. *See* House of Representatives, U.S.

consumption, 4, 11, 13–14, 16–19, 78
Coronation Street, 225
Corrigan, Kat, 96
cosmetic surgery, 12, 33
CouponCabin.com, 33
courtship, 65–66
The Craft, 5, 91–95, 98
Craig, Larry, 143, 145; Suzanne, 151
Cunningham, Sheryl L., 5, 155–67

Dallas, 225
A Dating Story, 13
Davis, Kristin, 54
DC Cupcakes, 30
DeCarvalho, Lauren J., 5, 103–12
DeGeneres, Ellen, 57
Democratic Party, 5, 132, 157–63, 181
Designing Women, 40, 51
Desperate Housewives, 4, 39–47
Devereaux, Blanche, 52–53, 57
The Devil Wears Prada, 5, 77, 80, 84–87
Diana (goddess), 95–96
Digital Natives, 2
dilemma of difference, 155–56
disaster wedding, 228, 230, 231
Discovery Health Channel, 30, 33
Disneyworld, 13
Doherty, Shannen, 92
Downs, Nancy, 94–95
Draper, Don, 223, 226, 227, 228, 229; Betty, 226, 227, 228, 229
Duggar, Jim Bob and Michelle, 5, 63–70; Josh and Anna Keller, 65–67; Josie, 69; Jubilee Shalom, 64, 69–70

Earth, 103, 104
Ellen, 57
embedded feminism, 14
enlightened sexism. *See* postfeminism
Ensign, John, 143, 145; Darlene, 146–47, 148, 150, 151
Eshoo, Anna G., 161
Everybody Loves Raymond, 49
The Exhausted Mom, 201
Extreme Couponing, 30

Facebook, 200, 202, 213, 215, 216, 227
face-ism, 144–45
fairytale wedding, 13
fansites, 6, 223, 224, 225–28, 230–31
Fatal Attraction, 5, 77, 78, 79, 80–84
fem-care, 209, 211, 218
feminine rhetorical style, 115–21, 123–124, 157, 176, 188
Feminist Standpoint Theory, 199, 201–5
feminist televisual narrative analysis, 64, 68
fertility. *See* pregnancy
Fickell, Luke, 170; Amy, 170, 173–77
Fields, Kim, 53
Fire, 103, 104
Firth, Colin, 228
Fisher, Carrie, 1
Fisher, Joley, 57
The Flintstones, 49
Focus on the Family, 63, 68
Forest, Alex, 80–84
foster mother, 183–87
Four Weddings, 29
Four Weddings and a Funeral, 229
Fox Broadcasting Company, 51, 53–54
Fox News, 157, 161–62
Freaky Eaters, 30
Freud, Sigmund, 15
functional capabilities, 105–11

Gallagher, Dan and Beth, 80–84; Ellen, 80, 83
Gandhi, Mahatma, 104, 109–11
Gere, Richard, 84
Getty, Estelle, 52
Gibbons, Maisy, 43
Gilmour, Deneen, 4, 27–38
Glanville, Jerry, 173
Godwin, Victoria L., 5, 91–101
Godzilla, 15
Goffman, Erving, 213–17
Gold Star Families for Peace, 118
The Golden Girls, 5, 49, 51–53, 56–59
Goldman, Duff, 31
Good Housekeeping, 31
goodwife or good wife, 29, 31–32, 34, 80, 82, 84, 147, 171

Gosselin, Jon, 30–33; Kate. *See Kate Plus 8*
Gothic literature, 11–12, 15–20
grandmothers, 6, 34, 160–61
grooms, 1, 6, 11, 16, 17–20

Halliwell, Prue, 93; Phoebe, 97
Hamilton, Heidi E., 5, 115–27
Hamm, Jon, 201
The Hand That Rocks the Cradle, 79
Harris, Joan, 227
Harry Potter, 92
Hartsock, Nancy, 199
Hayes, Marceline Thompson, 5, 223–35
HBO, 51, 54–56, 225
Hecate, 95–96
Hegel, Georg, 199
Helen of Troy, 145
Hess, Rick and Jan, 64
heteronormativity, 11, 13, 15, 16, 19, 20, 30, 68–69, 131, 133
Hinduism, 5, 103–7, 110–11, 226
Hoarding: Buried Alive, 30
Hobbes, Miranda, 54–57
Hocus Pocus, 91, 97
Home Made Simple, 30
homemaking, 28, 30–31, 65, 68, 197, 198
homeschooling, 42, 65, 184, 185
homophobia, 3, 49, 79, 131, 223
The Honeymooners, 49
Hooker, Chris, 94–95
Hopeck, Paula, 4, 39–47
horror films, 15, 82
House of Representatives, U.S., 117, 143, 155, 157, 159–60, 181, 185, 187
Huguenots, 6
Hunter, Regine, 53–54, 57–58
Hyper, Bonnie, 94–95

identification, 3–4, 29, 78, 82, 116, 119–20, 124, 155, 158, 176, 186, 202, 211, 216, 225, 228, 230
I Didn't Know I Was Pregnant, 30
I Dream of Jeannie, 91
incognizant racism, 148–49
India, 5, 103–12
infidelity. *See* affair
iron maiden archetype, 5, 49, 51–57, 59, 182
Ivic, Rebecca K., 4, 39–47

James, Khadijah, 53–54, 56, 58–59
James-Jones, Synclaire, 53–54, 58, 59
Jon & Kate Plus 8. *See Kate Plus 8*
Jones, Samantha, 54–55, 57
Judaism, 96
Jung, Carl, 50–51

Kali (goddess), 95
Kalyani, 104, 107–9
Kanter, Rosabeth Moss, 40, 44, 129, 182
Kate Plus 8, 2, 4, 27–35, 64
Keller, Mike and Suzette, 66
Kennedy, John F., 227, 229
King of Queens, 49
Kitchen Boss, 30
Knox, Chuck, 173
Kotex, 209
Kramarae, Cheris, 198–99, 201, 204

LA Ink, 30
Lagasse, Emeril, 31
Lee, Barbara, 162
Leo Burnett advertising agency, 212–13
lesbianism, 6, 20, 57, 104
Lewis, Clea, 57
Lifetime Television, 12
The Little Couple, 29
Little People, Big World, 30
Little Women, 51
Living Single, 5, 49, 51, 53–54, 56–59
Lost Girl, 92
lovelywives, 5, 171
Lyne, Adrian, 79, 80, 82, 84

Macey, Deborah A., 5, 49–62
Madhumati, 104, 107–10
Madison, Amy, 95–96; Catherine, 96, 97
Mad Men, 6, 223–31
madonna/whore dichotomy, 27, 34–35, 58

Mahoney, Tim, 143, 145, 147; Terry, 147, 151
male headship, 65, 67, 68
Mandell, Hinda, 5, 143–54
Martel, Paul, 82–84
maternal militancy, 5, 115, 117–18, 120–21, 123–24, 157
Mayer, Karl, 39; Susan, 39, 43–44
McCain, John, 130, 135
McClanahan, Rue, 52
McGreevey, James, 143, 145; Dina Matos, 151
media framing, 146, 181–82, 184–89
Mehta, Deepa, 5, 103–11
menstruation, 209–18
Mesaros-Winckles, Christy Ellen, 5, 63–74
metaphor, 2, 3, 5, 15, 121, 129–35, 144, 145, 171
Meyer, Urban, 169, 170, 175, 176; Shelley, 169, 170, 174–77
Middleton, Kate, 226
Milano, Alyssa, 92
militant motherhood. *See* maternal militancy
Miller, Louise, 93, 96–98
Million Mom March, 116, 117, 122, 157
Miranda, 96, 97
Mom365, 202
mommy blogs, 5, 197–98, 200–201, 202
momtini blogs, 2, 5, 197–205
The Momtini Lounge, 201
Mona Lisa Smile, 51
monstrosity, 1, 4, 11–13, 15–20, 80, 81, 82, 83, 91, 92
moral motherhood, 27, 34–35, 116, 119–22, 124
Moran, Terry, 160
Morgan, Ellen, 57
Mormonism, 200
mother archetype, 5, 49, 51–56, 58–59, 129, 182
motherhood as rhetorical appeal, 116–17, 119–21, 122–23, 155, 157–60, 162–63, 181, 184–89
Mother Jones (Mary Harris), 117, 157
Mother Nature. *See* Tampax
Mrs. Coach, 170
Murphy Brown, 40, 56
Murray, Patty, 159, 186
Muted Group Theory, 198–201, 204–5
My Big Fat Gypsy Wedding, 29
My Fair Wedding, 12
My Future Babies Scare Me, 201
My Strange Addiction, 30

Narayan, 104, 108, 109, 111
National Review, 157, 161–62
NBC, 12, 51, 52–53
Next Great Baker, 30
Nixon, Cynthia, 54
No Child Left Behind, 158–59
The Now I Lay Me Down to Sleep Foundation, 69
Nussbaum, Martha, 5, 103, 105–11
Nylund, Rose, 52–53, 58

Obama, Barack, 134, 135, 181
Offbeat Bride, 20
The Ohio State University Buckeyes, 5, 169–70, 174, 176, 177
Once upon a Time, 92
Orange County Choppers, 31
O'Reilly, Bill, 161
the outsider within, 199, 202
overdetermined femininity, 215
Owens, Sally, 93, 96, 97, 98; Gillian, 96, 97

Palin, Sarah, 5, 129–35, 163, 181, 186, 189
Paltrow, Gwyneth, 228
Parker, Sarah Jessica, 54
Paterno, Joe, 169, 173; Sue, 169
Pelosi, Nancy, 5, 122, 155–63
Penney, Audrey, 57
perfection, 1, 11–20, 31, 39, 68, 93, 170, 174, 175, 177, 228
Perry, Rick, 184–85, 186, 188
Petrillo, Sophia, 52–53, 58–59
Platinum Weddings, 12
Police Women of Broward County, 30
Poltergeist: The Legacy, 92, 96, 97, 98
polyamory, 6
postfeminism, 11, 14–16, 19–20, 77–80, 84–87, 92

Practical Magic, 5, 91, 93, 95, 96, 97, 98–99
pregnancy, 30, 32, 63, 67, 69–70, 81, 129, 133, 200–204
Pregnant Chicken, 201
Presumed Innocent, 79
Pride, Mary, 64
Priestly, Miranda, 84–87; Stephen, 85–86
Princess Leia Organa, 1–2, 6
Prince William, 226
prostitution, 52, 104, 107–11, 150

Queen Latifah (Dana Owens), 53
Quiverfull, 5, 63–70

Rahoi-Gilchrest, Rita L., 5, 197–208
recombinant television, 49–50, 52
Reid, Bill, 173
Republican Party, 5, 130, 131–32, 134–35, 160, 161, 162, 163, 181–87
Reynolds, Ryan, 201
Rich Bride Poor Bride, 12
Romney, Mitt, 188
Roseanne, 40
Rosenberg, Willow, 96
Ruggerio, Alena Amato, 1–7, 129–41

Saban, Nick and Terry, 169
Sabrina the Teenage Witch, 91, 93, 96–97, 98
Sachs, Andy, 84–87
Samek, Alyssa Ann, 4, 11–25
Sanderson, Winifred, 97
Sanford, Mark, 143, 145, 149; Jenny, 147, 148, 150, 151
Santorum, Rick, 68, 184
Sarah Palin's Alaska, 134
Say Yes to the Dress, 12, 29
scandal, 5, 39, 41–44, 143, 145–51
scapegoating, 3, 170, 174–75
Scavo, Lynette, 39, 41–44; Tom, 42–44
The Secret Circle, 92
Senate, U.S., 157, 159, 186
Seriously So Blessed, 198
Sex and the City, 5, 49, 51–52, 54–59
sex object archetype, 5, 49, 51–59, 129, 182
Shakespeare in Love, 228, 229
Shakuntala, 104, 107–11
Shaw, Maxine "Max," 53–54, 56, 59
Shedding for the Wedding, 12
Sheehan, Cindy, 5, 115–25; Casey, 118, 119, 122, 123
Shuler, Heath, 162
The Simpsons, 49
Single White Female, 79
single women, 31, 34, 39, 49–59, 77, 78, 80–82
Sister Wives, 30
The Sisterhood of the Traveling Pants, 51
Six Feet Under, 225
Skywalker, Luke, 6
Smith, Marcia M., 5, 223–35
Snarky Mommy, 199–200
Solis, Carlos, 42, 44; Gabrielle, 39, 42–44
Solo, Han, 6
Speaker of the House. *See* Nancy Pelosi
Spellman, Sabrina, 93, 96–97
Spitzer, Eliot, 143, 145, 149, 150; Silda, 145, 147, 151
standing by your man, 5, 143, 145–49, 151
Star Wars. *See* Princess Leia Organa
stereotypes, 6, 13, 14, 44, 50, 51, 58, 86, 122, 144–45, 149, 182, 188
Sterling, Roger, 227, 228, 229, 230; Margaret, 226, 227, 228, 229, 230, 230; Jane, 227, 228, 229
A Stolen Life, 229
Strange Sex, 30
Strollerderby, 202
Suburban Bliss, 201
Summers, Buffy, 96, 97
Sumner, Edward and Connie, 82–84; Charlie, 82
Swift, Jane, 133
symbolic interactionism, 213–17

Tampax, 5, 209–18
Teen Witch, 92, 96–97, 98
Television Without Pity, 225
Terminator 2, 78
thematic analysis, 41
third-wave feminism, 14, 58, 77
Thomas, Erika M., 5, 77–89

TLC, 4, 5, 12–13, 27–38, 63–74
Toddlers & Tiaras, 30
Tressel, Jim, 169–70, 172, 175, 176; Ellen, 169, 170, 172–77
True Womanhood, 29, 156, 171, 175
Tucker, Diana L., 5, 169–80
Twist of Kate, 33–34

Unfaithful, 5, 77, 80, 82–84

The Vampire Diaries, 92
van de Kamp, Bree, 39, 43–44; Rex, 43
Van Horne, Daryl, 93
Vision Forum, 63
Vitter, David, 143, 145; Wendy, 151

Water, 5, 103–12
WE tv, 4, 11–15
Webb, Lynne M., 5, 223–35
The Wedding, 229
wedding cake, 18
wedding dress, 1, 12, 17, 228, 230
wedding industry, 4, 11, 13–15, 18, 20
A Wedding Story, 12, 13, 68, 69
weight, 1, 33, 228, 230–31
Weiner, Matthew, 223
What Not to Wear, 30
White, Betty, 52
White, Daniel, 1
white wedding, 2, 11, 17, 19, 228
Wicca. *See* witches
widows, 5, 103–11
Williams, George, 43
witches, 5, 15, 91–101
The Witches of Eastwick, 91, 93
The Wizards of Waverly Place, 92

Yates, Andrea, 70
York, Charlotte, 54–55, 58
Young, Mary Alice, 39, 41, 42

Zbornak, Dorothy, 52–53, 56
Zimmerman, Rochelle, 94–95

Contributors

Ann E. Burnette holds a PhD from Northwestern University. She is an associate professor of communication studies at Texas State University–San Marcos. Her work has appeared in *Communicating Politics: Engaging the Public in Democratic Life* (Peter Lang) and *Inventing a Voice: The Rhetoric of American First Ladies in the Twentieth Century* (Rowman & Littlefield).

Mary Frances Casper holds a PhD from North Dakota State University. She is an associate professor of communication at Boise State University. Her work has appeared in the *Journal of Intercultural Communication Research, Health Communication*, and *Feminist Media Studies.*

Hao-Chieh Chang holds a PhD from Syracuse University. He is an assistant professor of communication at Hong Kong Baptist University. His work has appeared in the *Journal of Broadcasting & Electronic Media* and *Media Asia.*

Dacia Charlesworth holds a PhD from Southern Illinois University Carbondale. She is an associate professor of communication at Indiana University–Purdue University Fort Wayne. Her work has appeared in *Women and the Media: National and International Perspectives* (University Press of America) and the journal *Women's Studies in Communication.*

Sheryl L. Cunningham holds a PhD from the University of Washington. She is an assistant professor of communication at Wittenberg University. Her work has appeared in the *Journal of Women, Politics, and Policy* and *Feminist Interventions in International Communication: Minding the Gap* (Rowman & Littlefield).

Lauren J. DeCarvalho is an ABD doctoral candidate at Penn State University. This is her debut publication.

Deneen Gilmour holds a PhD from North Dakota State University. She is an assistant professor of multimedia journalism at Minnesota State University Moorhead. Her work has appeared in the *Review of Communication* and *American Communication Journal.*

Victoria L. Godwin holds a PhD from Indiana University. She is an assistant professor of languages and communications at Prairie View A&M University. Her work will appear in a forthcoming issue of *Interactions: Studies in Communication & Culture.*

Heidi E. Hamilton holds a PhD from the University of Iowa. She is an associate professor of communication and theatre at Emporia State University. Her work has appeared in *Gender and Political Communication in America: Rhetoric, Representation, and Display* (Lexington); *The Functions of Argument*; and *Controversia: An International Journal of Debate and Democratic Renewal.*

Marceline Thompson Hayes holds a PhD from The University of Memphis. She is an associate professor and interim department chair of communication studies at Arkansas State University. Her work has appeared in the *Journal of Family Communication* and *Motherhood Online*.

Paula Hopeck is a doctoral student at Purdue University. Her work has appeared in the *International Journal of Conflict Management* and *Health Communication*.

Rebecca K. Ivic holds a PhD from Purdue University. She is an assistant professor of communication at the University of Akron. Her work has appeared in *Critical Studies in Media Communication*, *Journal of Communication*, *Health Communication*, *Media Psychology*, and *Communication Teacher*.

Deborah A. Macey holds a PhD from the University of Oregon. She is a visiting assistant professor at Saint Louis University. She frequently participates in conferences, including the Organization for the Study of Communication, Language, and Gender; Women and Society; National Communication Association; and International Communication Association. Her work has appeared in the *International Encyclopedia of Communication* (Blackwell) and *Human Studies: A Journal for Philosophy and the Social Sciences*.

Hinda Mandell holds a PhD from Syracuse University. She is an assistant professor in the Department of Communication at Rochester Institute of Technology. Her work has appeared in *Popularizing Research* (Peter Lang) and the *Boston Globe*.

Christy Ellen Mesaros-Winckles holds a PhD from Bowling Green State University. She is an assistant professor of English-communication at Siena Heights University. Her work has appeared in *The Journal of Religion and Popular Culture* and *Westminster Papers in Communication and Culture*.

Rita L. Rahoi-Gilchrest holds a PhD from Ohio University. She is a professor of communication studies and director of general education at Winona State University. Her work has appeared in the *International Journal of Communication*, the *Howard Journal of Communication*, and *Communication Quarterly*.

Alena Amato Ruggerio holds a PhD from Indiana University. She is an associate professor of communication at Southern Oregon University. Her work has appeared in the journal *Feminist Media Studies* and the *Encyclopedia of Christianity* (Eerdmans). She is also the author of *You Get a Lifetime: The Chronicle of a Semester in Greece* (Blurb).

Alyssa Ann Samek is an ABD doctoral candidate at the University of Maryland. Her work has appeared in the journals *Communication Quarterly* and *Feminist Media Studies*.

Marcia M. Smith holds a PhD from the University of Memphis. She teaches rhetoric and writing at the University of Arkansas at Little Rock. Her work has appeared in *Critical Perspectives on* Mad Men and the *Kentucky Journal of Communication*.

Erika M. Thomas holds a PhD from Wayne State University. She is an assistant professor of human communication studies and Director of Forensics at California State University, Fullerton. Her work has appeared in the journal *Contemporary Argumentation and Debate*.

Diana L. Tucker holds a PhD from Southern Illinois University Carbondale. She is core faculty and academic coordinator in communication at Walden University. Her work has appeared in *Sports, Rhetoric, and Gender: Historical Perspectives and Media Representations* (Palgrave Macmillan).

Lynne M. Webb holds a PhD from the University of Oregon. She is a professor of communication at the University of Arkansas. Her work has appeared in the *Journal of Applied Communication Research* and *Computers in Human Behavior*.

About the Editor

Alena Amato Ruggerio holds a PhD from Indiana University. She is an associate professor of communication at Southern Oregon University in Ashland, Oregon, where she also served as the interim coordinator of Gender, Sexuality, and Women's Studies. A life member of the National Communication Association, Alena is an officer in the Feminism and Women's Studies Division. Her work has appeared in *Feminist Media Studies, Kenneth Burke Journal, Oregon Humanities, Christian Century,* and the *Encyclopedia of Christianity* (Eerdmans). Alena is the author of *You Get a Lifetime: The Chronicle of a Semester in Greece* (Blurb) and a contributor to the *I Speak for Myself* series (White Cloud Press). Her teaching specializations include feminist rhetorical theory, rhetorical criticism, persuasion, argumentation, and advanced public speaking. The recipient of the AHA International Outstanding Visiting Faculty of the Year Award, Alena was voted Most Warm and Welcoming Professor by the Associated Students of Southern Oregon University. She is an active member of the inclusive Christian feminist organization EEWC, for which she served as a plenary speaker, council member, and guest editor of the magazine *Christian Feminism Today*. She resides in Medford, Oregon, with her husband, Bradley; their three astonishingly adorable cats; and her collection of rhinestone tiaras.

Visit Alena's website at **www.alenaruggerio.com** *to view photos, clips, and links referenced in* Media Depictions of Brides, Wives, and Mothers.